This volume contains nine substantial essays by some of the world's leading Berlioz scholars. They cover various aspects of Berlioz's life and works, and represent an important contribution to Berlioz research. The book includes essays based on newly discovered documents, both biographical and musical, that give us, among other things, a new portrait of the artist as a young man and a revealing view of an important but little-studied work of his maturity. There are readings of *Roméo et Juliette* and *La Damnation de Faust* that wrestle anew with the problems of the relationships between literature and music and – as Berlioz's music nearly always requires – with the problems of genre. Two views of Berlioz's *Les Nuits d'été* are presented showing when and why the work was conceived, and how it coheres. The practical question of Berlioz's metronome marks is here thoroughly studied for the first time.

The volume closes with a novel piece, in dialogue form, by the elder statesman of Berlioz scholars, Jacques Barzun, who treats with exceptional grace the profound issues raised by Berlioz the man and musician.

Berlioz Studies

Berlioz Studies

Edited by

PETER BLOOM

Professor of Music, Smith College,
Northampton, Massachusetts

CAMBRIDGE
UNIVERSITY PRESS

Published by the Press Syndicate of the University of Cambridge
The Pitt Building, Trumpington Street, Cambridge CB2 1RP
40 West 20th Street, New York, NY 10011-4211, USA
10 Stamford Road, Oakleigh, Victoria 3166, Australia

First published 1992

Printed in Great Britain at the University Press, Cambridge

A catalogue record for this book is available from the British Library

Library of Congress cataloguing in publication data

Berlioz studies/edited by Peter Bloom.
    p.   cm.
English and French.
Includes bibliographical references and index.
ISBN 0 521 41286 2
1. Berlioz, Hector, 1803-1869 – Criticism and interpretation.   I. Bloom, Peter.
ML410.B5B363   1992
780′.92 – dc20   91-26055   CIP   MN

ISBN 0521 41286 2 hardback

Contents

Preface

Closure – poetic and musical – occupied much of Berlioz's creative energy. The *Memoirs*, with Postscript and Postface appended to the main text, with Travels in Dauphiné returning us to the scene of the beginning, and with lines from *Macbeth* recapitulating at the close the epigraph of the opening, bear witness to the man's compelling sense of order and design. The current proliferation of Berlioz scholarship would suggest – now that the *œuvres littéraires*, the complete works, the complete correspondence, the complete *feuilletons* and those who are responsible for seeing these monumental editions into print have brought modern Berlioz studies into adulthood; now that Hugh Macdonald, David Cairns and D. Kern Holoman have written biographies in English, the first of significance since the appearance over forty years ago of Jacques Barzun's *Berlioz and the Romantic Century* – that the moment is ripe for an international gathering of *Berlioz Studies*, not of course to close them out, but to attempt to lend them a sense of order and design.

Future collections may prefer to use the title figure as the hub of a wheel, and offer as fare to the reader items about music critics in Paris, orchestras in Riga, baritones in Vienna, cellists in Brunswick, duchesses in Weimar and railroads in Central Europe. Such is the hope expressed to me in correspondence by the senior-most contributor to this volume, Jacques Barzun, and it is a hope shared by all who have become aware, as that excellent collector Sarah Fenderson used to put it, that 'Berlioz leads everywhere'. Yet the present collection keeps fairly close to home, largely focused on our man and his work, for there is still, in the hallowed old phrase, much to be done. Indeed, there will always be much to be done: conclusions *ripen*, as the wise and wizened critic J. B. Stead will tell us in Jacques Barzun's 'Famous last words'; it follows not that they wither, and rot, but that they require rejuvenation, and replacement. We hope that these *Berlioz Studies* will signify and perhaps inspire during their 'hour upon the stage'; we hope that they will sound and illumine, at least provisionally, before they are 'heard no more'.

The articles here are by scholars many of whose names are familiar to students of Berlioz. They are organised in a way that is roughly chronological by subject matter, but intersections and overlappings are legion: the reader may proceed in any order without damage to 'plot'. David Cairns, translator of the *Mémoires* and author of *Berlioz: the Making of an Artist*, introduces us to the fascinating collection of letters and documents formerly in the possession of Madame Yvonne Reboul-Berlioz (whose husband was the great-grandson of Berlioz's sister Nanci Pal) – a collection that sheds new light on our portrait of the artist as a young man. From youth to old age Berlioz put metronome marks on his music, and for the first time these are systematically surveyed and studied in the timely article by Hugh Macdonald, general editor of the *New Berlioz Edition*. Ian Kemp, editor of *NBE* 13 and of Cambridge's Opera Handbook on *Les Troyens*, gives us a reading of Berlioz's dramatic symphony, *Roméo et Juliette*, showing by close analysis precisely how Berlioz knew the play and how he transmogrified it into music. In two separate and, we hope, complementary studies of *Les Nuits d'été*, Julian Rushton, editor of *NBE* 5, 8a/b, 12a and author of *The Musical Language of Berlioz*, and I, editor of *NBE* 7 and of a collection of essays entitled *Music in Paris in the Eighteen-Thirties*, discuss the genesis, *raisons d'être*, and musical structure of this work by a composer 'au milieu du chemin'. What might be said to be the decisive element of the picture of Berlioz at mid-career, his 'Vagabondage' (as D. Kern Holoman has put it), is the setting of the article by David Levy (whose earlier work has been on Beethoven) – an essay on early Berlioz reception in Germany that centres on what Berlioz called an 'erudite pamphlet', Robert Griepenkerl's *Ritter Berlioz in Braunschweig*. Though received rather more positively there than in his homeland, it was not long before Berlioz was accused, in Germany, with *La Damnation de Faust*, of 'mutilating a monument'. Katherine Reeve, author of the chapter on Berlioz that appeared in Scribners' *European Writers: the Romantic Century* and of a forthcoming book entitled *The Poetics of Berlioz*, wrestles with the character of Berlioz's (and Goethe's) Faust and the ambiguous notion of the hero – its feminine and masculine aspects, its alteration by musical setting – in a textual analysis and interpretation of Berlioz's 'dramatic legend'. Working with documents never before closely scrutinised, Joël-Marie

Fauquet, author of *Les Sociétés de Musique de Chambre à Paris de la Restauration à 1870* and most recently editor of the correspondence of Edouard Lalo, demonstrates for us precisely how Berlioz went about arranging a new version of Gluck's celebrated *Orphée*. And to conclude the volume, Jacques Barzun, recently the author of *An Essay on French Verse for Readers of English Poetry*, gives us an entertaining and instructive piece in dialogue form that offers 'from Parnassus' an overview of aspects of Berlioz's work, mind and character.

If the various contributors to this volume are in any way united, it is, it seems to me, by an avoidance of what has been called the 'politics of knowledge' and by an unspoken respect for a traditional kind of music history writing that may be said to draw 'upon a variety of techniques, disciplines, and sources' (I quote from Gertrude Himmelfarb's *The New History and the Old*),[1] a kind of history that 'counts, psychologizes, analyzes, compares, reflects, and judges'. Far from envisioning what has been facetiously called a history without people, most of us here study the past with a view towards comprehending the manifold relations that we, like our Romantic forebears, take to exist between the work of art and the artist who produced it. This compelling aspect of Romantic criticism has left a powerful legacy which most of us have chosen to pursue. Following Jacques Barzun – whose refusal in his own historical studies to rob events of their complexity and people of their individuality is the subject of Himmelfarb's praise in the passage cited above – most contributors to this volume seem inconspicuously to wear their methodological mantles; most seem ineluctably to deal with notes and words and documents, to seek truths, 'provisional' though they may be, to seek conclusions which, with luck, will ripen.

It seems appropriate, then, to offer as an *hors d'œuvre* to these studies a document – brief, removed from view since the day of its publication – which tells us something of how Berlioz (himself still a bit raw) appeared to his contemporaries in the fateful year of 1830, when he captured the Prix de Rome and composed the work by which he was then and remains to this day most closely identified, the *Symphonie fantastique*. Of the rare reviews of the symphony that appeared in the daily press – the restrained number of critics in the crowd provided 'a foretaste', David Cairns tells us, 'of the difficulties Berlioz would experience in his struggle to impose his music on the Paris of Louis-Philippe' – this one, on a page apparently

1 Cambridge, Mass., 1987.

xi

missing from certain copies of the newspaper, paints the liveliest picture of the concert of 5 December 1830, that singular episode in the life of our artist. (A translation begins on p. xiv.)

LE TEMPS, Dimanche 26 décembre 1830, col. 5,637

Revue Musicale. Concert de M. Berlioz

C'est un homme jeune, grêle, faible avec une longue chevelure blonde dont le désordre a quelque chose qui sent le génie; tous les traits de sa figure osseuse se dessinent avec force, et ses grands yeux creusés, sous un large front, lancent des jets de lumière. Le nœud de sa cravate est serré comme avec colère; son habit est élégant parce que le tailleur l'a fait élégant, et ses bottes sont crottées parce que l'impétuosité de son caractère ne lui laisse pas supporter l'inaction de l'homme traîné dans une voiture, parce qu'il faut que l'activité de son corps satisfasse à l'activité de sa tête. Il court à travers les cent musiciens qui remplissent la scène du Conservatoire, et quoique tous ces habiles de la société des concerts forment peut-être l'orchestre le plus admirable que l'on ait jamais entendu, il prie, il gronde, il supplie, il excite chacun d'eux. Cet homme, c'est Berlioz, c'est le jeune compositeur qui, malgré son talent, vient de remporter un prix à l'Institut; et quand le public lui bat les mains, il ne s'avance point avec symétrie pour courber l'épine dorsale et laisser servilement tomber ses bras devant le parterre; il s'arrête seulement au point où il se trouve; il hoche de la tête pour saluer les applaudissements dont la salle retentit, et il continue l'observation qu'il faisait à Launer ou à Tulou. C'est là ce que nous avons vu au concert que donnait le jeune compositeur au profit des blessés de juillet.

A deux heures précises, Habeneck, le chef de cette troupe merveilleuse, dont il n'est pas un soldat qui n'ait commandé quelque part ou qui ne soit digne de commander, Habeneck frappait son pupitre de la pointe de l'archet, et le plus profond silence régnait aussitôt dans la salle, où un essaim de jeunes femmes brillantes de goût écoutaient bruyamment tout à l'heure.

L'ouverture des *Francs-Juges*, par laquelle commençait le concert, est une grande symphonie, plus remarquable encore par la bizarrerie et la force de la pensée que par le bonheur de l'expression. Ses formes sont gigantesques, et je ne crois pas que les trompettes du jugement dernier produisent un effet plus incisif que les foudroyants trombones qui accompagnent; mais cette instrumentation, si belle et si frappante, a peut-être un caractère trop mélodramatique. Après l'ouverture, qui a été exécutée avec une verve et une perfection dont on n'a d'exemple qu'à la société des concerts, sont venues les scènes de *Sardanapale*, et si on a été peu satisfait du chant qui précède le final, si on le a droit de lui reprocher de la faiblesse, sans doute parce que l'on attend bien mieux de l'auteur, du moins des applaudissements d'enthousiasme ont accueilli l'incendie du palais du roi voluptueux; on voyait la flamme courir, embraser les poutres, rugir sous les longues voûtes, et on entendit en réalité tout s'écrouler avec un fracas épouvantable. Cette dernière partie a produit le plus grand effet, et les amateurs ne se rappelaient que l'admirable ouverture du *Jeune Henri* qui pût rivaliser avec ce morceau, comme musique imitative.

Mais il faut parler de la symphonie fantastique intitulée *Episode de la vie d'un artiste.*

L'auteur avait développé dans un programme le sujet de cette étrange composition ; il suppose d'abord qu'un jeune musicien, affecté de la maladie *du vague des passions* (style de 1830), devient éperdument amoureux d'une femme, et que, par une singularité bizarre, l'image de cette femme chérie ne se présente jamais à son esprit que liée à une pensée musicale, rappelée sans cesse au milieu de toutes les situations où il se trouve. Dans la seconde partie, il l'admire au milieu d'un bal, du tumulte d'une fête, et les sentiments de l'amour et de la jalousie l'agitent alternativement. Dans la troisième, une scène champêtre donne à ses idées un calme inaccoutumé, une couleur plus riante ; et la pensée musicale, si spirituellement jetée dans cette conception pour l'intelligence de l'auditeur, revient plus douce et plus tendre que jamais. Dans la quatrième, il acquiert la certitude que celle qu'il aime est indigne de son amour, et il s'empoisonne avec de l'opium : mais la dose, trop faible, ne lui procure qu'un sommeil accompagné des plus horribles visions. Il rêve qu'il assassine sa maîtresse, que l'on le condamne à mort, et qu'il assiste à sa propre exécution. Dans la cinquième, le songe durant toujours, il est transporté au sabbat, au milieu d'une troupe affreuse d'ombres, de sorciers et de monstres. On crie, on chante, on rit, on grince les dents, et l'idée musicale reparaît encore, mais dégradée, avilie, changée en un air de danse grotesque, trivial, ignoble. (C'est là une pensée sublime.) Enfin cette horrible scène est terminée par une ronde de sabbat où tous les monstres dansent en parodiant le *Dies irae.*

Une telle invention est certainement bien folle, mais elle est dramatique et remplie de poésie. On voit que l'audacieux compositeur n'a pas reculé devant les plus immenses difficultés d'exécution.

Le talent de M. Berlioz est éminemment sombre et fantastique ; il semble qu'il vise à la férocité : sa pensée est toujours en quelque sorte pleine de colère, et il n'excelle à peindre que les mouvements violents, les déchiremens de l'âme et de la nature. Les rêveries, les passions douces des trois premières parties, il ne les a pas rendues heureusement. Son orchestre, quoique toujours instrumenté avec une rare facilité, est généralement confus, vide, et manque de pensée ; mais avec quel éclat terrible il se relève dans les deux dernières parties ! comme chacun se resserre sous les impressions de cette marche solennelle, funèbre, à travers laquelle s'entend encore de loin, avec un bonheur inouï, l'idée musicale affaiblie ! comme on a frissonné d'horreur devant le supplice, rendu par des images si belles et d'une si effrayante vérité, qu'elles ont soulevé au milieu même de l'exécution un tonnerre d'applaudissements que rien n'a pu comprimer ; et comme chacun riait au sabbat du rire des monstres, et comme on se regardait les uns et les autres frappés de surprise en écoutant cette musique réellement infernale, ces cris, ces gémissements, ces éclats de rire et ces efforts de rage ! Il y a du désespoir dans ce singulier talent. C'est du Salvator Rosa, de l'Hoffmann, c'est plus noir encore. Je conviens que cette symphonie est d'une étrangeté inconcevable, et les maîtres de l'école auront sans doute à frapper d'anathème ces profanations du *vrai beau* ;

mais, je l'avoue, pour qui se soucie peu de règles, M. Berlioz, s'il répond à ce début, sera un jour digne de prendre place auprès de Beethowen [*sic*].

He is a frail and slender young man with a wild head of long blond hair that is somehow suggestive of genius. The lines of his face are strong and inflexible, and his large, cavernous eyes, set beneath a wide brow, seem to cast brilliant rays of light. His cravat is tightly knotted as though tied in anger. His clothes are elegant only because his tailor made them so; and his boots are muddy because such an impetuous man could never allow himself passively to be transported about in a carriage – because, that is, he has to move about vigorously in order to satisfy the needs of his vigorously active mind. He runs around among the one hundred musicians who fill the stage at the Conservatoire; and even though these excellent artists from the Société des Concerts comprise what may well be the most admirable orchestra anyone has ever heard, he begs, he growls, he supplicates and stirs up every one of them. Who is he? He's Berlioz! He's the young composer who despite his talent just won a prize at the Institute. And when the public applauds, he does not come gracefully forward to bend his spinal column and allow his arms to fall humbly before those standing below; he rather stops wherever he is, nods his head to acknowledge the applause resonating from the auditorium and continues on with the observations he was making to [the violinist] Launer or to [the flautist] Tulou. This is what we saw at the concert this young composer gave for the benefit of those who were wounded [during the three-day revolution] in July.

At precisely two o'clock, Habeneck, the leader of these marvellous troops whose soldiers have all of them at one time or another been themselves commanders or who have certainly been worthy of taking command – Habeneck tapped his music rack with the point of his bow and caused a profound silence to spread over the concert hall, where swarms of brilliantly and tastefully garbed young ladies had been babbling boisterously only moments before.

The Overture to *Les Francs-Juges*, which opened the concert, is a grand symphony more remarkable for the strength and singularity of its conception than for the elegance of its style. Its structures are gigantic, and I doubt whether the trumpets of the Last Judgement could produce an effect more incisive than the terrifying one created here by the trombones. But the character of this instrumentation, so beautiful and so striking, is perhaps rather overly melodramatic. After the Overture, which was performed with the kind of verve and perfection found only at the Société des Concerts, came the cantata *Sardanapale*. And if the audience was little satisfied by the singing that preceded the Finale, if the public justly found it ineffective (no doubt because the audience expected more from the composer), we can at least report the enthusiastic applause that greeted the final conflagration of the palace and the immolation of the voluptuous king: we saw the flames rise up, illuminate the beams of the ceiling and howl under its lengthy vaults; and we literally heard everything come tumbling down in uproarious pandemonium. These final moments produced a most impressive effect; the only example of 'musique imitative'[2] that some listeners were able to think of as a match for this piece is [Méhul's] admirable Overture to *Jeune Henri*.

But now we must speak of the *Symphonie fantastique* entitled *Episode de la vie d'un artiste*. The author had explained the subject of this curious composition in a programme. First, he supposes that a young musician, afflicted by a kind of indefinable longing (1830s'-style), falls hopelessly in love with a woman; by some wondrous oddity, the image of the beloved woman always appears in the young man's imagination accompanied by a musical idea – an *idée fixe* – that he recalls incessantly in the thick of whatever circumstances he finds himself. In Part Two he admires her in the midst of a ball, in the fracas of a celebration, and he is assailed alternately by feelings of jealously and love. In Part Three a rustic scene renders his feelings unexpectedly more serene and cheerful, and the *idée fixe*, which has been so cleverly introduced into the proceedings for the edification of the listener, recurs here more softly and tenderly than ever. In Part Four he becomes convinced that she whom he adores is in fact unworthy of his love, and he poisons himself with opium. But the dose, too weak to kill him, leads only to a deep sleep accompanied by the most horrible visions. He dreams that he assassinates his mistress, that he is condemned to death and that he witnesses his own execution. In Part Five, as the dream continues, he is carried off to a midnight revel and finds himself in the midst of a hideous troupe of ghosts, sorcerers and monsters. They scream, they sing, they gnash their teeth, and the *idée fixe* reappears yet again, this time besotted, debased and transformed into a dance tune at once trivial, grotesque and vile. (This is really a sublime idea.) This terrifying scene is finally brought to a close by a witches' round-dance in which all the monsters dance to a parody of the *Dies irae*.

Such a conception is certainly most bizarre, but it is dramatic and full of poetry. It is obvious that the composer did not retreat even in the face of the tremendous problems of performance [presented by this work].

Monsieur Berlioz's talents are pre-eminently dark and fantastical. He seems naturally inclined to ferociousness; his thoughts are always full of anger, as it were, and he excels only when he portrays violent actions – the torments of the soul, the convulsions of nature. The gentle reveries and passions of the first three parts are not suitably rendered; and though the instrumentation is carried out with rare facility, the orchestra is generally confused, vapid and lacking in significance. But how brilliantly the composer reveals himself in the two final parts! How everyone quivered under the impact of that solemn funeral march over which one heard yet again, ever so fittingly, and from afar, the now enfeebled *idée fixe*! How everyone shook with horror before the scaffold, painted with such magnificent and terrifying accuracy that it roused thunderous and unabated applause, right in the middle of the performance. How everyone rejoiced at the laughing monsters of the witches' round-dance, and how everyone in the audience looked at each other, shocked and surprised by this truly infernal music with its shrieks, its moans, its bursts of laughter and its cries of rage. There is something despairing about Berlioz's talent: it is like Salvator Rosa, it is like

2 'Musique imitative', for many English speakers – if I may use the expression without opening Pandora's box – is 'programme music'.

Hoffmann, but it is even more sinister. I confess that this symphony is inconceivably strange; the schoolmasters will surely issue a total condemnation of such a profanation of the 'truly beautiful'. But for those who worry little about the 'rules', I believe that Monsieur Berlioz, if he perseveres beyond these beginnings, will one day be considered worthy of taking a place next to Beethoven.

To assign a 'place' to a composer is a game many of us still enjoy, but it is a game we wish not to play here. Assigning a place, as an important strain of modern scholarship has been at pains to demonstrate, may say as much about the assigner as about the assignee. I should like to believe that it is in all ways reasonable to say that Berlioz long resisted traditional categorisation and analysis because of his 'conspicuous uniqueness and multiple gifts' (the phrase is Barzun's). The epithets of strange or 'bizarre' sometimes occur to observers today as they did to our reviewer – who was an enthusiastic and cultured and careful listener, but who remains anonymous. Who might he have been? Was he Ernest Legouvé, who tells us, in *Soixante ans de souvenirs*, that he wrote an article about Berlioz and the *Symphonie fantastique* when the work had been heard only once – an article 'full of hopeful enthusiasm'?[3] Could he possibly have been F. J. Fétis, the principal music critic for Jacques Coste's youthful newspaper? Was he Musset, or Nodier, or Mérimée, or Stendhal – all then associated with this important journal? The descriptions are so graphic as to seem Balzacian – and Balzac, too, was associated with *Le Temps* in the autumn of 1830.[4] Was the author a member of the composer's circle, or clique, prepared, as were many at the time, to offer favours for friendship and fidelity? He was clever enough to associate Berlioz's brand of Romanticism with that of Rosa and Hoffmann (thus anticipating by just over a century Barzun's like observation),[5] and to lampoon the academicians and the schoolmasters for awarding the Rome Prize to Berlioz *despite* his talent (which sounds like Berlioz himself), for adhering to the 'rules' and for believing in something called the 'vrai beau' (which may be a specific allusion to Victor Cousin's popular lectures of the late 1820s that led, eventually, to the publication of his *Du Vrai, du beau et du bien*). And he

3 12e éd., 4 vols. (Paris: J. Hetzel, s.d.) II, 141–2. 'Elle n'avait été exécutée qu'une fois encore en public et j'avais écrit sur l'œuvre et sur l'auteur un article plein d'espérance enthousiaste.'
4 See Roland Chollet, *Balzac Journaliste* (Paris: Klincksieck, 1983), chapter 7.
5 The genre of 'the Terrible', after Michelangelo, 'was not cultivated again until Salvator Rosa, whom Hoffmann and Berlioz felt kinship with'. Barzun, *Berlioz and the Romantic Century* (New York, 1969) II, 165, note 33.

was clever enough to provide us with crucial information about Berlioz's behaviour before and during the performance itself: the composer appears to have been much in evidence, on the orchestral platform, supplementing the conductor with comment and advice. What are advocates of historical performance practice to make of *this*? (When the elderly Igor Stravinsky conducted a new work in Philadelphia, in the 1960s, his lieutenants, on the concert platform – but only at rehearsal – offered the players supplemental comment and advice. The players, I recall, were not amused.)

Does it matter that Berlioz, in the eyes of this journalist, was 'young, slender and frail', with a wild head of hair? 'Physiognomy' – the practice of assessing the character from the countenance – was common enough at the time (the practice is not dead); let us thus appreciate our observer's method as we savour the marrow and meaning of his words.

Before turning to the words of our contributors, I should like to acknowledge with gratitude support received from the National Endowment for the Humanities (USA), which provided a Summer Stipend in 1989 in part for work on this volume. I should like to thank Penny Souster of Cambridge University Press for her unfailing enthusiasm for *Berlioz Studies*. And, finally, for her assistance and her Berliozian scepticism ('tu consacres plus de temps aux morts qu'aux vivants'), I should like to thank my wife, Catherine Marchiset Bloom, who has been my excellent 'editor' for many matters relating to the French language.

PETER BLOOM

Abbreviations

CG	Hector Berlioz, *Correspondance générale*
	Pierre Citron, General Editor (Paris: Flammarion, 1972–)
CG I	1803–1832, ed. Pierre Citron (1972)
CG II	1832–1842, ed. Frédéric Robert (1975)
CG III	1842–1850, ed. Citron (1978)
CG IV	1851–1855, ed. Citron, Yves Gérard and Hugh Macdonald (1983)
CG V	1855–1859, ed. Hugh Macdonald and François Lesure (1988)
CG VI	1859–1863, ed. Hugh Macdonald (in preparation)
CG VII	1863–1869
CG VIII	Supplement
Mémoires	Hector Berlioz, *Mémoires*, ed. Pierre Citron
	(Paris: Flammarion, 1991)
Cairns	*The Memoirs of Hector Berlioz*, trans. and ed. David Cairns
	(London: Cardinal, 1990)
	All references to Cairns in *Berlioz Studies* are to the Cardinal edition.

Les Soirées de l'orchestre (1968),	Hector Berlioz, *Œuvres Littéraires*
Les Grotesques de la musique (1969)	Edition du Centenaire, ed. Léon Guichard
A Travers chants (1971)	(Paris: Grund, 1968–71)

The Reboul-Berlioz Collection

DAVID CAIRNS

Traditions preserved in families, whether about the individual members or about family matters, can sometimes be of great importance. Our curiosity naturally loves to feed on information concerning our forebears. We take pride in knowing where they came from and what they did; most men feel respect for the past. The young can be checked in their follies and excesses when they see how much it cost their ancestors to assure the affluence their descendants enjoy. They will hesitate more than once before deciding to sell property which bears on all sides the identifiable imprint of their kith and kin. On reading the record of merit and repute they will strive to emulate it; the spirit of a virtuous father, revealed to his children, must keep them in the way of duty. Sustained by these hopes, I am resolved to set down the history of my family, and I counsel my posterity to carry it on likewise.[1]

Dr Berlioz's hopes, embodied in the introductory paragraph of his Livre de Raison, were to be disappointed. His eldest child and heir, though attached all his life by strong family ties, pursued his career elsewhere, and had his fair share of follies; his younger son, Prosper, died at the age of eighteen. After the old man's death the property was split up. Within a few years, most of the accumulated labours of Louis Berlioz and his ancestors were dispersed to the winds.

---

1 'Les traditions, conservées dans les familles, tant sur les individus dont elles sont composées que sur les affaires domestiques, sont d'une assez grande importance quelque fois. Notre curiosité, d'ailleurs, aime à se repaître des détails concernant nos ancêtres. Nous mettons de l'amour propre à connaître et leur origine et leurs actions; l'antiquité paraît respectable à la plupart des hommes. Quelques jeunes gens peuvent être arrêtés dans leurs débordements et leurs folies, en voyant combien il a coûté à leurs aïeux pour assurer l'aisance de leurs descendants. Ils hésiteront plus d'une fois avant de se décider à vendre des propriétés sur lesquelles ils reconnaîtront partout les traces de leurs parents. En voyant retracés d'honorables souvenirs, ils s'efforceront de les imiter; l'ombre d'un père vertueux, lorsqu'elle apparaît à ses enfants, doit les retenir dans le devoir. Fondé sur de pareilles espérances, j'entreprends d'écrire la chronique de ma famille; et j'engage ma postérité à la continuer de la même manière.' (Louis Berlioz, Livre de Raison.)

In one respect, however, his offspring were faithful to the spirit of his admonitions: in the preservation of documents. It is to the family piety of his daughter Nancy and of her descendants that we owe the rich archive, hereinafter called the Reboul-Berlioz Collection, which is the subject of this article.

The documents that make up the Reboul-Berlioz Collection were preserved, for the best part of a hundred years, at the country retreat of St Vincent which Camille Pal, who married Nancy Berlioz, inherited from his father in 1830. This property, situated a few miles north of Grenoble off the main road to Lyons (the house standing against the wooded lower slopes of the Grande Chartreuse massif), remained in the family till the middle of this century, when, after the death of Admiral Reboul-Berlioz, it was sold.[2] At the time of writing, the collection is housed in the Paris apartment of his widow the late Yvonne Reboul-Berlioz (herself a direct descendant of Camille Pal's brother Henry), who generously gave me access to it.

Parts of the collection had been seen by scholars active in the last decades of the nineteenth century and the first decades of the twentieth. Edmond Hippeau refers to Dr Berlioz's Livre de Raison; Julien Tiersot quotes from it at some length. Tiersot's three volumes of Berlioz's correspondence published between 1904 and 1930 include a number of letters 'communicated by Madame Reboul'. But it is only since the 1960s, when it became more generally accessible, that the collection has had a decisive impact on Berlioz biography, most obviously by making available many hitherto unknown Berlioz letters. The first volume of the *Correspondance générale*, which came out in 1972 under the editorship of Pierre Citron, contained no fewer than twenty-eight (from the collection) whose existence had not been suspected until a few years before;[3] and the collection's contribution to subsequent volumes of the *Correspondance* has been hardly less significant.

Though its Berlioz letters are the crown of the collection, they are far from being the only thing in it to excite the student of his life. In any case, whereas their contents are now common property, or will be when the *Correspondance générale* is complete (the final volumes are expected to be

---

2 Admiral Georges Reboul, son of Marie Reboul née Masclet and grandson of Nancy Berlioz's daughter Mathilde Pal, took the name Reboul-Berlioz in the 1930s.
3 While the volume was being edited, nine of these were published by François Lesure in the *Figaro littéraire* and the *Nuova Rivista Italiana* during the centenary year, 1969, together with three from the Chapot Collection.

out before the end of the century), most of the other letters in the collection are unpublished. There are a very large number of them. Both Berlioz's surviving sisters, Nancy and Adèle, were prolific letter-writers. In a collection that originated with Nancy herself, her letters are naturally less numerous than Adèle's. However, many were subsequently retrieved, including some written to her friend and contemporary Rosanne Goletty née Rocher, and there are a few written to her mother Joséphine Berlioz, or to Adèle, while Nancy was away from home, staying with Rosanne or with Rosanne's Rocher cousin Elise Julhiet. In addition, Nancy regularly drafted her letters, wholly or in part, before writing the finished version, and a few of these drafts survive. (Some of Nancy's drafts and letters are quoted in the *Correspondance générale*, but often in abridged form.) And after her marriage to Camille Pal and her move to Grenoble in 1832 she had much more occasion to write letters to her family in La Côte St André.

Dr Berlioz too was a diligent correspondent, if a more laconic one than his daughters or his wife Joséphine. His surviving letters are most frequent for the years following Nancy's marriage (and later Adèle's), but there are one or two very revealing examples from 1803 and 1804 (the first two years of his marriage), written to his wife while she was staying with friends or relatives in Grenoble. Add the handful of Joséphine's that survive, a couple of dozen from Joséphine's brother Félix Marmion, several notebooks of verse-letters written by their father Nicolas Marmion (an inveterate rhymester) between the last years of the eighteenth century and the mid-1830s, and a long series of gossipy missives from Joséphine's close friend and Nancy's godmother Nancy Clappier, and you have a very useful source for the biography of Berlioz, especially for the years least well covered by his letters, those of his youth and early manhood.[4]

Its importance is twofold. First, it fills gaps in the known record of Berlioz's life, and corrects or corroborates and consolidates details derived from other sources. Second, it enables us to reconstruct something of the environment of his boyhood, both the background society and culture in which he was raised and the foreground, the place he lived in, the people he grew up with – many of whom, before merely names, begin

---

4 From Nancy Clappier, writing to Nancy Berlioz on 22 July [1828], we learn of the unexpected marriage of Berlioz's childhood flame Estelle Dubœuf (she was over thirty) to a rich judge. There are quite a number of letters from other family friends, generally less directly informative – though one, an unsigned letter of March 1816 from a friend of Joséphine Berlioz who had just seen Dr Berlioz in Genoble, is notable for the prophetic remark: ' J'embrasse Hector le musicien'. This is exactly the period when Berlioz, at age twelve, had begun to play the flageolet. See my *Berlioz, 1803–1832: the Making of an Artist* (London, 1989) 82–3.

to take on the lineaments of recognisable men and women. Some of them, already familiar from secondary accounts, become more rounded, detailed portraits in the light of their letters.

With others, the picture changes. This is true of both Berlioz's parents. The traditional view of Dr Berlioz – that of a personality as balanced, rational and judicious as Mme Berlioz was emotional and 'mal equilibrée' – must be modified. He emerges as a surprisingly volatile and contradictory character, and despite his liberal opinions more deeply hostile to Berlioz's musical vocation than is his wife. She, with all her conventional religious horror of a career in the arts (which at one point drives her to disown her son for refusing to give it up), is in practice less implacable; she cannot prevent herself feeling pleased at the success of Hector's Mass in 1825 – whereas Dr Berlioz 'will not suffer anyone to congratulate him on it' and 'has never been less favourably disposed towards his art'.[5] The scenario which Adolphe Boschot liked to imagine, in which the well-meaning but timid father was goaded on by his hysterical wife, does not survive a study of the documents in the Reboul-Berlioz Collection.

This shift in emphasis, combined with her own letters – rambling, unpunctuated, prone to look on the dark side, but full of life – and with the testimony of friends to her fundamentally kindly and hospitable nature, alters the received idea of Joséphine Berlioz. You can understand why Berlioz, in his *Memoirs*, cast her as representative of provincial French prejudice against the arts, and why his close affinity with his father led him, consciously or not, to soften the harshness and bitterness of Dr Berlioz's resistance to his career (in contrast to his mother, his father is 'totally without prejudice');[6] but, as the documents show, it is a misleading account.

Our portrait of Berlioz's uncle the debonair cavalry officer Félix Marmion – a key figure in his formative years, whose visits on leave from the Grande Armée made such a vivid impression on his nephew and implanted in his imagination a lasting vision of Napoleonic grandeur and daring – does not have to be similarly modified; but it is rounded out and added to. The late 1800s and early 1810s, when he was 'following the glittering trail of the great Emperor',[7] was the most memorable time in Félix Marmion's life. Several letters in the collection, written by him in

---

5 Drafts of letters from Nancy, respectively to Berlioz (24 July [1825]) and to an unnamed female correspondent, possibly Nancy Clappier (undated, but referring to the same performance of the Mass).   6 *Mémoires*, 41.   7 *Mémoires*, 45.

1839 and 1840 to the former commander of his regiment in an attempt to restore two missing *actions d'éclat* to his war record, confirm it: nothing subsequently came up to the excitements of the war in Spain.

The papers relating to his service in the French army (which duplicate and supplement those in the Archives de Guerre at the Château de Vincennes) show that the *Memoirs'* statement that he was in the Lancers during the Napoleonic Wars is wrong – the First Dragoons became the First Lancers only at the Bourbon Restoration of 1814 – but they also show that Berlioz remembered his uncle's wounds correctly: a sabre cut across nose and lips outside Cadiz (commemorated by his father Nicolas Marmion in a verse-letter as 'Il montrera les cicatrices / Qui sont empreintes sur son front'), and a round of canister in the foot at the Battle of Borodino. That the latter wound did not get him invalided back to France but that he took part in the Retreat from Moscow is confirmed by a letter of Nancy Clappier's. Even those terrible months could not quench his congenital cheerfulness. But we can imagine Berlioz drinking in his uncle's descriptions of that disastrous retreat, which recurs in many a later allusion.[8]

We catch the flavour of his carefree disposition in a letter to his father Nicolas Marmion, written three months after Waterloo, describing a journey made with his cousin Raymond de Roger and Raymond's two small children from Moisson to Martel:

MY DEAR PAPA

Can you imagine my delight? I've been here two days. As I think you'll find all the circumstances of this journey not without interest, I shall go back to the beginning. I left Agen, where my regiment is, on the 12th [of September], to pick up Raymond at Moisson, as we had agreed. For some time he had been looking forward to showing his son and daughter (two charming children) to his family, especially to his father. His wife at first had great difficulty in making up her mind. Her grief at being separated and her fears about the journey were very natural. As she was nursing a third child, to her great regret she could not come with us. However, we parted, in tears. The journey was perfect; the children were quite untroubled, and were no trouble themselves. Not being able to bring our carriage all the way to Martel, we took horses at Souillac (last town on the main road), and set off in the following formation: at the head, Raymond, carrying his daughter [aged three], and with a countenance you will have no difficulty in imagining, the joys of anticipation written all over it. Next, your highly respected son, in full uniform, helmet on head, mounted on one of the choicest Rosinantes of the

---

8 See, for example, *Mémoires*, 150 and 497; *Le Rénovateur* (15 December 1833), etc.

region and bearing, in front of his saddle, Ferdinand [aged four], eldest son of Raymond and object of all the hopes and prayers of the Rogers. After me marched Delphine, my cousin Philippine's daughter, whom we had picked up on the way through Montauban and whom we were taking to her mother. Behind Delphine, Jeanneton (the children's maid), looking with all a mother's anxious concern at the two little persons, perched on our horses and calling out to her incessantly. A mule carried our baggage, and two servants on foot completed the column.

In the same marching order and without mishap we reached Martel at two o'clock on the 17th, surrounded by all the curious who had been attracted by our bizarre caravan. My aunt, with part of her family, was waiting for me on the front doorstep. Here I feel inclined to leave it to your imagination to portray the touching family group presented by this reunion. Picture all the actors in that moving scene as you know them, more or less. Behold me leaping from my steed and throwing myself into the arms of that good aunt, whom I recognised at once from the description I had been given of her. She had been a little ill for the past two days but claimed that the sight of me effected a three-quarters cure. Behold me embracing next the good M. de Roger, who greeted me with that frank and soldierly cordiality of which as you may suppose I am something of a judge. His joy seemed heightened by all that my aunt was experiencing. Watch me embracing right and left male and female cousins whom I had not seen before but whom I love already with all my heart and never want to leave. Next see Raymond's children handed from one pair of arms to another, and smothered with caresses on every side. [...] As I have undertaken to show them my letter, I cannot give you a portrait of my female cousins here and now, as I saw them. I should go too far and embarrass their modesty; it must be the subject of another letter which I shall write when I am no longer here.

My cousin Emilie, whom I see the most often, as she lives with her mother, sings and speaks Spanish. There is a guitar. I need say no more. [...][9]

9 Mon cher père,
Concevez vous toute ma joie? Je suis ici depuis deux jours, et comme je pense que toutes les circonstances de ce voyage ne vous seront pas indifférentes, je les prendrai de plus loin. Je partis le 12 d'Agen, où est mon régiment, pour venir prendre Raymond à Moisson, ainsi que nous en étions convenus. Il se faisait depuis longtemps une fête de faire voir à sa famille, et surtout à son pere, son fils et sa fille (deux enfants charmants). Sa femme eût d'abord beaucoup de peine à s'y décider. Sa douleur de s'en séparer et ses craintes pour le voyage étaient bien naturelles. Nourrissant un troisième enfant, elle ne pouvait être du voyage, à son grand regret. Nous partîmes pourtant en sanglotant. Le voyage a été fort heureux; les enfants n'ont été ni incommodés ni incommodants. Ne pouvant amener notre voiture jusqu'à Martel, nous avons pris des chevaux à Souillac (dernier bourg sur la grande route) et nous nous sommes mis en marche dans l'ordre suivant: en tête Raymond portant sa fille, une figure que vous concevez sans peine et où peignait la joie dont il jouissait par avance. Venait ensuite votre tres honoré fils en grande tenue, le casque en tête, monté sur un des plus beaux Rocinantes du pays et portant sur le devant de sa selle Ferdinand, fils ainé de Raymond et l'objet de tous les voeux et de toutes les espérances des Rogers. Apres moi marchait Delphine, fille de ma cousine Philippine, que nous avions pris à Montauban en passant et que nous ammenions a sa mère. Derrière Delphine marchait Jeanneton (la bonne des enfants) regardant, avec toute la sollicitude d'une mère, perchés sur nos chevaux les deux bambins qui l'appelaient continuellement. Une mule portant nos bagages et deux domestiques à pied fermaient la marche.
Dans le même ordre et sans accident nous arrivons à Martel le 17 à deux heures, entourés de

Félix Marmion's love of singing – *opéra comique* especially – is attested not only by the *Memoirs*[10] but by several documents in the Reboul-Berlioz Collection, where we read of his voice being in demand in the drawing-rooms of Grenoble. He himself, in a letter of 18 December [1821] to Nancy Berlioz, expresses his surprise that Hector should put the Opéra so high, when the Opéra-Comique is the mecca of all true 'children of Apollo'. A series of letters from a Mme Husson, with whom he appears to have had an affair when garrisoned with the Chasseurs des Ardennes at Toul in the late 1810s, refer quite often to music. A Cherubini Mass that she alludes to his having heard at Valenciennes evidently made a deep impression. From Mme Husson we may also infer that the teenage Berlioz confided his musical ambitions to his uncle, if not to his parents; she writes in February 1821, when Félix Marmion is in Dauphiné on leave: 'You must be finding it difficult not to sympathise with your nephew in his enthusiasm for music. Indeed, though I say it to you alone, I would rather be Mozard [*sic*] or Grétry or Baillot, etc. (and others too whom I do not know and who are perhaps greater) than an inspector of domains or forests'.

These letters and others in the collection tell us something else: that Félix Marmion was a serious gambler, who ran up quite hefty debts to his fellow officers at the gaming tables and often had to take drastic steps to extricate himself. His father Nicolas Marmion seems to have paid up at first; but by 1822 he had had enough: a letter to Joséphine Berlioz (undated but attributable to that year) instructs her to stop interceding on behalf of her brother, who, a mutual acquaintance has informed him, is 'the most notorious officer in the garrison [...] and lives beyond his means'.

tous les curieux que notre pittoresque caravanne avait attirés. Ma tante avec une partie de la famille m'attendait sur sa porte. Ici je serais tenté de laisser faire votre imagination pour vous peindre le tableau touchant de famille que cette réunion a présenté. Figurez-vous tous les acteurs de cette scène attendrissante tels que vous les connaissez à peu près. Voyez-moi sauter de cheval et courir dans les bras de cette bonne tante que j'ai d'abord reconnue au portrait qu'on m'en avait fait. Elle était un peu malade depuis deux jours et a prétendu que ma vue l'avait guérie aux trois quarts. Voyez-moi ensuite embrasser ce bon M. de Roger qui m'a témoigné cette amitié franche et militaire à la quelle vous pensez bien que je me connais un peu. Sa joie paraissait augmentée de toute celle que ma tante ressentait. Regardez-moi embrassant à droite et à gauche des cousins et des cousines que je n'ai jamais vus, mais que j'aime déjà de tout mon cœur et que je ne voudrais plus quitter. Voyez ensuite les enfants de Raymond passant des bras de l'un dans les bras de l'autre et étouffés de caresses partout. [...] Comme je me suis engagé à faire voir ma lettre, je ne puis ici vous faire un portrait de mes cousines, tel que je les ai vues. J'irais trop loin et j'embarrasserais leur modestie; ce sera le sujet d'une autre lettre que j'écrirai quand je ne serai plus ici.

Ma cousine Emilie que je vois le plus souvent, puisqu'elle habite avec sa mère, chante et parle l'espagnol; il y a une guittare; je n'en dis pas davantage. [...]

10 *Mémoires*, 45.

To discover what Félix Marmion did next, we have to turn to Dr Berlioz's Livre de Raison. There we read that in the spring of 1826 Louis Berlioz, having previously lent him, 'without IOUs, various sums amounting to 1,500 francs', withdrew 3,400 francs from the bank in Grenoble 'to settle my brother-in-law's debts' in Paris. He also had 700 francs sent to the colonel of Félix's regiment in Lille, followed a few days later by a much larger sum, 4,670 francs, to the same person and 3,600 to a captain in the Dragoon Guards. By 1 April 1833 – the last mention of the subject in the Livre de Raison – the sum 'for which my brother-in-law acknowledges himself indebted' has risen, with further loans and interest, to more than 15,000 francs.

Félix Marmion seems to have carried off this tricky situation with characteristic insouciance and urbanity. At any rate his letters convey no hint that he suffered any embarrassment in his relations with the family at La Côte St André. Perhaps a tacit acknowledgment of obligation made him particularly assiduous in the role of go-between in the conflict over his nephew's career and, later, over his entanglement with an actress.[11] But I am more inclined to think that he undertook the role because he liked it; it appealed to his temperament. He enjoyed playing the diplomat, sympathising with the distress of his sister and brother-in-law, sharing their sense of outrage and agreeing that their son is 'sick', but reassuring them that all may yet be well, and eventually advising them that they must let him work out his own salvation.

The three letters sent from Valenciennes in March and April 1823 (to Nancy) and in June (to Dr Berlioz) show him trimming with the wind.[12] These letters are our sole source of information about a major crisis in the struggle over Berlioz's choice of career, when the erring ex-medical student was summoned hot-foot to La Côte. It may well have been on this occasion that Dr Berlioz's decision to allow him to return to Paris precipitated the traumatic scenes with his mother described in chapter 10 of the Memoirs.

The Memoirs place the incident later in the saga of the conflict; but we now know that the chapter, though ostensibly about a single visit, is a conflation of several. Until the Reboul-Berlioz Collection became accessible, biographers followed the Memoirs in speaking of only one such visit in the years from 1822 to 1826. In fact Berlioz came home four years

---

11 See the interesting series of letters quoted in CG II, 70–71, 74–6, 82–3 (notes).
12 The letters are quoted in abridged form in CG I, 47–8 (notes), more fully in Cairns, Berlioz, 123–5.

running, from 1822 to 1825, but not in 1826, the year given by Boschot and still repeated from time to time. Thanks to the Livre de Raison (which records the date of Hector's departures for Paris, together with the amount of money given to him), and also to Nancy Berlioz's diaries and the draft of a letter of August 1825 from her to Elise Julhiet, we can assign fairly precise dates to all four:

1822 ?early/mid-September[13] to 22 October
1823 ?early/mid-March[14] to 11 May
1824 6 June to 25 July[15]
1825 16 August to 7 November.

The 'Livre de Raison of Louis Joseph Berlioz, doctor of medicine residing at La Côte St André' – a large folio volume, half family chronicle half estate register, begun on 1 January 1815 and continued till 1838 – is the single most important documentary source of information for the first part of Berlioz's life. Its uses are many. In addition to the above-mentioned dating, it gives the date of the purchase of the new flute which Berlioz says his father promised to buy for him in Lyons – 'garnie de toutes les nouvelles clefs' – in return for an undertaking to begin studying medicine:[16] 26 January 1819, from 'Simiot the younger, instrument maker, place du Plâtre, Lyon, made of red ebony, with 8 keys and a slide, both silver, and a foot joint in C'. Seven weeks later, on 16 March, the book records the purchase, in Grenoble, of a guitar. As I have argued,[17] given that under his contract the music master Dorant was paid ten francs a month for lessons,[18] the 220 francs which the Livre de Raison records for 'Maître de Musique' under 'Dépenses faites en 1819' could be made up of 120 francs for twelve months of Nancy's guitar lessons and 100 for ten months of Hector's. According to the *Memoirs* Nancy was the first to be given guitar lessons (her diaries contain frequent references to playing the instrument), whereupon Berlioz sat in on them and was then allowed to have some himself.[19] On this reckoning, his lessons began in the third month, March – the month when Dr Berlioz, the Livre de Raison records, bought a new guitar.

13 If the reasoning in my *Berlioz*, 117, is correct, the letter from Berlioz to his father which precipitated his recall was written immediately after the performance of Gluck's *Iphigénie en Tauride* at the Opéra on 21 August 1822.
14 I.e. some time between the beginning of March, when Berlioz deposited copies of some recently published songs at the Bibliothèque Royale, and 20 March, when Dr Berlioz sent Alphonse Robert money to settle 'debts left by Hector in Paris' (Livre de Raison).
15 Date as in Nancy's diary; the Livre de Raison gives the 26th.   16 *Mémoires*, 53.
17 *Berlioz*, 85–6.   18 The contract is in the Musée Berlioz at La Côte.
19 *Mémoires*, 50.

The author of the Livre de Raison is not the most consistent of account-keepers. After itemising his expenses for several years he fails to do so for 1820; there is nothing to tell us whether or not a music master was employed that year, as he had been in 1819. (When expenses are itemised again, in 1821, there is no mention of one.) The book also lets us down over the not unimportant matter of the date of Berlioz's first journey to Paris, towards the end of 1821. Unlike the later entries discussed above, this one merely records that the sum of 540 francs was given to him 'lorsqu'il est parti pour Paris'.

Nor is he always accurate. He gives the year of his marriage not as 1803 (the year attested by the marriage contract, a copy of which is in the collection, as well as by letters from his wife's friends) but as 1802. This was possibly due to a mistake, easily made, in converting 'l'an onze' into the Gregorian 1803 (Dr Berlioz, like Stendhal but apparently unlike his fellow inhabitants of La Côte St André, was punctilious about using the Republican Calendar). But the month of his son's marriage, 'malgré les Parents', is also entered incorrectly: he gives it as July instead of October.[20]

The book is none the less a mine of information for the student of Berlioz. Even the most mundane tallies of bricks and mortar can have a Berliozian significance: for example, the construction of the turreted two-storey pavilion at the western corner of the garden at Le Chuzeau, known in local legend as 'Le Pavillon de la Malédiction' from its being supposedly the site where Joséphine Berlioz cursed her son. But the Livre de Raison tells us that it was built in 1827 – too late for that event to have taken place there.

The Livre de Raison would repay study by an agricultural historian, as the record of the economy of a gentleman-farmer's property in the early decades of the nineteenth century: cultivation of grapes, various kinds of corn, vegetables and fruit; the wine harvest; tree-planting; hedging and ditching; renovation of mills and haylofts; construction of carts and wine-vats; employment of farm-labourers and building workers, leasing of land, houses and barns to a numerous tenantry. Or by a specialist in the Napoleonic Wars: Dr Berlioz gives an almost day-by-day account of the second occupation of La Côte St André by foreign troops, together with

20 Berlioz himself makes a similar mistake in *Mémoires*, 260, when he says he married Harriet 'in the summer' of 1833. Perhaps he was misled by reading the Livre de Raison shortly before writing this passage, on his return to La Côte in 1848 after his father's death, or perhaps he was remembering the beautiful Indian summer of 1833.

the commentary of a one-time republican turned liberal monarchist on the rise and fall of 'Buonaparte', the restoration of the Bourbons and the state of the nation in 1815. A historian of medicine, too, might find interesting material in the inventory of Dr Berlioz's surgical instruments and in the clinical details of family illnesses and deaths.

For the Berliozian the Livre de Raison, apart from its factual contribution to knowledge, is invaluable for the light it sheds on the physical, social and cultural environment of the composer's first years and on the great issue that set him at odds with his nearest and dearest.

Dr Berlioz's library, listed immediately after the inventory of his property, is that of a highly educated man with a wide-ranging mind utterly unlike that of the average Dauphinois property-owner (who, as Stendhal remarked, would never dream of investing so much money in things as unproductive as books). In it, along with nearly three hundred medical works, among them Monroe's *Osteology* and several by Bichat, and a selection of English classics (including *A Sentimental Journey* and *The Vicar of Wakefield*), we find many of the books and authors referred to in Berlioz's autobiographical writings or quoted in his articles and letters: Virgil,[21] Horace, Plutarch, Boileau, Racine, Molière, Locke, Voltaire, Bernardin de St Pierre, Rousseau's *La Nouvelle Héloïse*, Florian's *Estelle et Némorin* and *Galatée*, Volnay's *Voyage en Syrie et en Egypte* and *Considérations sur les ruines*, Humboldt's *Tableaux de la nature*, D'Alembert's *Eléments de musique théorique*. Even so the inventory, drawn up in 1815, is certainly not complete. Additions made subsequently were not always entered, to judge by the catalogue of the sale of the library after Dr Berlioz's death, referred to by Hippeau in his *Berlioz intime*,[22] which mentions several authors of Berlioz's childhood, including Cervantes and Montjoie, who do not figure in the Livre de Raison's 'Catalogue de ma Bibliothèque'. Michaud's *Biographie universelle*, whose entry on Gluck (volume 17, published in 1816) made a crucial and lasting impression on the imagination of the young Berlioz, appears neither in the 'Catalogue' nor in Hippeau's list. Yet we know, from an unpublished letter of 6 March 1846 enquiring about the supplementary volume, that Dr Berlioz subscribed to it.

---

21 There is a nice poetic aptness in the examiners' choice of one of the passages from the *Aeneid* given to Berlioz to construe for his baccalauréat (the diploma for which is in the Reboul-Berlioz Collection). It is the scene during the capture of Troy when Cassandra is dragged from Minerva's sanctuary, 'her burning eyes raised to heaven – her eyes only, for chains bound her hands', and Corebus attempts to rescue her.   22 (Paris, 1883) 161.

11

Above all, the Livre de Raison explains why Dr Berlioz was so opposed to his son's vocation and why he fought the unequal battle against it so long. The book is the record, the loving record, of a family and its history and possessions, kept by a man who is deeply conscious of his links with his forebears and of his duty to consolidate what they achieved and hand it on intact and flourishing to his descendants – a father who dreams of his eldest son becoming his successor both as doctor and benefactor of the poor and as custodian of the estate. 'It was not his son's artistic career as such that shattered him but what it involved: the abandonment of the cherished heritage, the breach in the continuity of the race.'[23]

The Livre de Raison does not seem to have been consulted other than very cursorily by any writer before Tiersot – who himself appears not to have grasped its full importance – nor indeed by any after him until Citron, editor of the *Correspondance générale*. The fact that Boschot cites only one brief passage from it[24] – Claude Berlioz (seventeenth-century merchant-tanner of La Côte) leaving instructions in his will that he be buried 'dans le tombeau de ses ancêtres' – suggests that he had no direct access to it. Had he seen it he would hardly have described the liberal conservative Dr Berlioz as an 'ultra' – a political reactionary.

Tiersot transcribes large parts of the introduction to the Livre de Raison in *Les Années romantiques*:[25] genealogy, family history, homilies to Dr Berlioz's children (omitting the paragraph quoted at the head of this article), but often in the wrong order and – a curiosity – with anti-republican references systematically expunged. Thus the following italicised passages are removed: '[...] depuis la Révolution il [Dr Berlioz's father] n'a exercé aucune fonction publique. *Il détestait les maximes révolutionnaires qui avaient amené la chute de la Monarchie.*' '*Il ne fut jamais partisan des révolutionnaires et* il se tint constamment eloigné des fonctions publiques.' '*Pendant les discussions politiques, on doit se méfier des novateurs; et de ressouvenir qu'en général, le meilleur gouvernement est celui que l'on a; qu'il est bien rare que les peuples gagnent à le changer.*' 'En tous les temps de la vie, ne recherchez jamais les emplois. [...] Cependant acceptez-les avec dévouement, lorsque vous croirez les pouvoir remplir d'une manière utile pour la patrie *et pour le souverain.*'

A reference to the aforementioned Claude Berlioz being unable to sign his will, 'étant illitéré', is also removed. So is the phrase 'malgré les

23 Cairns, *Berlioz*, 24.
24 *La Jeunesse d'un romantique: Hector Berlioz, 1803–1831* (Paris, 1906) 15.
25 (Paris, 1904) [xxxi]–xl.

Parents' from the entry of Berlioz's marriage. This prompts the thought: did Tiersot actually see the Livre de Raison, or were selected paragraphs transcribed (and doctored) for him by the possessor, Marie Masclet-Reboul? The offended republicanism sorts better with him, one imagines, than with Mme Reboul. But both propositions could be true. There could have been a double process of bowdlerisation, whereby Tiersot struck out the anti-republican sentiments after Mme Reboul had struck out those that offended bourgeois respectability. (Remember Berlioz's Aunt Laure and her 'a good name matters more than anything'.) If Tiersot did personally consult the book, he did not have unlimited time for doing so. He describes it simply as 'un document digne d'être conservé sur les origines, l'histoire et la personnalité des différents membres de la famille[...] un *livre de raison* où il écrivait au jour le jour les dépenses, recettes etc. de sa maison, pêle-mêle avec d'autres indications'.[26] Clearly, he did not read far enough to find the entries that illuminate the chronology of Berlioz's student years.

Another suggestive detail that he omits (or that Mme Reboul removed) is in the section of the genealogy which lists Dr Berlioz's children ('De ce mariage sont nés à la Côte' etc.). Tiersot gives the entry for the eldest son as 'LOUIS-HECTOR le 11 decembre 1803'.[27] This is how it appears in the Livre de Raison: 'LOUIS NICOLAS [*sic*] HECTOR' etc. Berlioz was baptised Louis Hector. Nicolas must be the extra name given him at his confirmation, chosen because it was the name of his godfather (and grandfather) Nicolas Marmion. But why the subsequent crossing out? What family drama lies behind it? It is tempting to link it to two passages in Nicolas Marmion's verse-letters from the 1830s, the period of his grandson's scandalous marriage to a penniless foreign actress. In one of them he says he does not intend to see Hector again; in another he describes the young Prosper as having replaced his brother as the true heir. Did Grand-père Marmion temporarily disown his grandson, and Dr Berlioz reflect his action by scoring through his name?[28]

The Reboul-Berlioz Collection has echoes of other family dramas. One of the most compelling, revealed in a rapid sequence of nearly thirty letters covering a period of a few weeks, concerns an episode in the life of the thirteen-year-old Adèle Berlioz, who in March 1828 was sent to a girl's boarding school in Grenoble but, with a tenacity worthy of her brother,

---

26 *Les Années romantiques*, xxx.   27 *Ibid.*, xxxiv.
28 The validity of 'Louis Nicolas Hector' is confirmed by a passage later in the book, where Dr Berlioz gives a summary of his will: 'Je donne à mon fils Louis Nicolas Hector [...]'.

forced her parents to take her away by crying night and day, bombarding everyone with heart-rending letters and making herself ill, until the headmistress had to admit defeat.

The collection contains letters from many more relatives and friends than it is possible to name within the scope of this article.[29] Reading their correspondence, feeling the renewed heartbeat of lives long vanished, one begins to know them personally and to re-create a network of social relations and, through it, a community and its world. If we except Berlioz's own letters (all of them now published or about to be) and the large number – nearly a hundred – from his son Louis, the bulk of the correspondence in the collection is from women. Extending over more than a century, it provides a useful index of the advance in female education. The older generation have a very limited range of expression and, if no longer illiterate like the seventeenth-century Claude Berlioz, spell execrably. Marie-Antoinette de Roger de la Londe (the aunt who welcomed Félix Marmion from the steps of her house in Martel) writes to her niece Joséphine Berlioz to sympathise with 'la painne que vous aviez du gout dessider cas [i.e. qu'a] votre fils ectors [*sic*] pour la cariere qu'il veut suivre'. Antoinette Rocher writes to Nancy Berlioz: 'J'ai recu dan son tempts vottre trotp aimable lettre [...] vous ecriver et vous vous exprimer si bien que pour vous repondre il faut mettre lamour propre de cotte et cet [c'est] ce que je fait'. Joséphine Berlioz, of the next generation, already writes with far greater flow and flexibility, and her daughters, Nancy especially, improve on her by an even greater margin.

What do not change are the mores of the bourgeoisie and women's role as their guardians and spokesmen. The appearance of the *Memoirs*, soon after Berlioz's death, decidedly does not amuse the starchier members of the family; even his niece Nancy Suat – his beloved Adèle's daughter – writes to her cousin Mathilde Masclet (née Pal): 'I say nothing to you of the Memoirs, despite the enormous vexation I feel about them'.

Berlioz clearly considered that his sister Nancy, to whom he had been so close, succumbed to bourgeois values on her marriage into the self-important, philistine world of the Grenoble legal profession. But it is impossible not to feel sympathy for the adolescent and the young woman whom her diaries lay bare – so like her brother in many respects, stirred by similar longings and idealisms, prey to similar despairs but, unlike him, without the means of escape. I have left Nancy Berlioz's diaries till last; but they are as fascinating as anything in the collection. Even if she had no

29 One set of friends, the Malleins, provide a link between the Berlioz family and Stendhal.

connection with a famous artist and historical figure, they would hold our interest for their record of the intimate thoughts of a sensitive, acutely intelligent girl gifted with a sharp and fluent pen but trapped in a society that denies her the freedoms her spirit yearns for.

As it is, the diaries are full of precious information and insight for the Berlioz biographer. Pierre Citron was the first to make proper use of them, in volume I of the *Correspondance générale*, which includes the years covered by the diaries (1822–32). (Boschot refers to them, but with such a garbling of the text and such a confusion of chronology that he might as well have passed them by altogether.) Frustratingly, they have a habit of breaking off – owing to the self-dissatisfaction of the diarist – just when one most needs them to continue. Nancy's first 'Tableau journalier', begun on 1 February 1822 when she was about to be sixteen, stops on 12 June; the next does not begin till May 1824.[30] They therefore miss Berlioz's first two return visits – the first in the autumn of 1822, the second in the spring of 1823 (when, as I have argued, the famous confrontation with his mother probably took place). Luckily the second tableau journalier is still going strong during the third visit, in June–July 1824, and gives a vivid picture of the family in turmoil over its prodigal son.[31]

The fourth visit, in August 1825, is again not covered, the diary having stopped on 15 March 'until such time as I can paint a less gloomy picture' (Prosper had been dangerously ill since January). By the time Berlioz reappears in La Côte St André, at the beginning of September 1828, the tableaux journaliers have given way to more sporadic 'Cahiers de souvenirs', but her brother's return stimulates Nancy to take up her pen; the diarist is on hand for the visit of Humbert Ferrand. Thanks to it we have a description – at first quizzical, later admiring – of the man who was one of Berlioz's closest friends.[32]

The fourth and fifth cahiers de souvenirs, which cover the years 1829 to 1831, provide a running commentary on Berlioz's love affair with Camille Moke, of which Nancy was kept informed by frequent letters from her brother and then by Berlioz himself during his five-week stay in La Côte, *en route* for Rome, in January–February 1831. Nancy copied into her diary the friendly letter she wrote to Camille on 31 January 1831 and also Camille's significantly formal and distant reply,[33] in which Nancy finds

---

30 That no other diary, since lost, intervened between them is shown by the opening sentence of the second diary, in which Nancy announces her 'project of resuming the daily journal which she had started for a few months and then dropped because it was too depressing'.
31 See Cairns, *Berlioz*, 151–55.   32 See Cairns, *Berlioz*, 270–71.   33 See CG I, 410 n.

that 'nothing seems felt [...] nothing is addressed to the heart or comes from it'. When the blow falls the diary does it justice. No other source tells us that Camille called Berlioz 'le fiancé de mon cœur'. 'Camille qui l'aima la première! Qui lui prodigua tant de serments! Qui l'appelait *le fiancée* [*sic*] de son cœur.[34] Echanger avec lui l'anneau nuptial, tresser une couronne de ses cheveux, la lui donner, s'emparer en échange de toutes ses affections, de tout son avenir, et l'oublier, s'unir à un autre!'

What will happen to the collection now that its longtime owner is no more? (Mme Reboul-Berlioz died in 1990). One need not be so greatly concerned about its many Berlioz letters, should her children decide to dispose of any of them, as they may naturally wish to do; most have already been published, the rest will be before long, and all have been photocopied by the Association Nationale Hector Berlioz (as have the letters of Berlioz's son Louis, which still await study). In fact, quite a number which the *Correspondance générale* designates 'Coll. Reboul' are no longer there. Some may have been sold, but some were stolen by a one-time friend of the family who for obvious reasons cannot be named here but whose activities, including wholesale forging of Berlioz autographs, will have to be put on record one day.[35]

What must be of concern is the rest of the collection: the Livre de Raison, Nancy's diaries, and the large mass of correspondence, as yet uncatalogued, of which this article gives a sample. It is to be hoped they will be kept intact, not scattered. Individually most of them may be of small account and have little if any monetary value. Collectively they constitute a social history of a small corner of France made all the more interesting by its links – links often strained but never broken – with the great artist it engendered.

34 Nancy is often careless about genders. *CG* I, 433 n, interprets the phrase wrongly, transcribing it as 'qu'il appelait la *fiancée* de son cœur'.
35 There had been Berlioz forgeries before. Tiersot, in *Le Musicien errant* (Paris, 1919) 164, quotes one in which Berlioz is made to describe *La Damnation de Faust* as an opera, which because of lack of interest on the part of theatre directors he will have to perform in concert in order to get it heard (this 'autograph' was used to justify Raoul Gunsbourg's staging of the work at the Théâtre Sarah Bernhardt in 1893). The letter of 14 August 1819 to a music publisher printed in *CG* I, 32–3, and belonging to the Collection François Lang at Royaumont, is a fake, dating from the 1930s. The forgeries of the 1960s, however, were extensive, and the best of them of high quality; and they were produced over a long period. It is quite possible that some Berlioz letters that are accepted unquestioningly as genuine are not. A letter of 30 March [1843] to Félix Marmion, bought by the late Sarah Fenderson, was rejected by Professor Citron and not included in the *Correspondance générale*. If it is a forgery, it is a good one. Mrs Fenderson acquired the letter in 1963 – six years before the forger was unmasked and his activities apparently ceased. The disturbing implications of this chronology have yet to be faced.

2

Berlioz and the metronome

HUGH MACDONALD

In his *Memoirs* Berlioz recounts an exchange with Mendelssohn that took place in Rome in 1831. 'What on earth is the point of a metronome?' Mendelssohn had asked; 'Any musician who cannot guess the tempo of a piece just by looking at it is a duffer.' Berlioz said nothing, but later enjoyed Mendelssohn's annoyance when, looking at the newly completed manuscript of the *Roi Lear* Overture, Mendelssohn turned to Berlioz and said 'Give me the right tempo'. 'What on earth for?' replied Berlioz, 'I thought you said that any musician who couldn't guess the tempo was a duffer?'[1]

Unlike Mendelssohn and Brahms, who also scorned the metronome, Berlioz approved of it and used it all his life. A passage in *Le Chef d'orchestre* confirms his faith and offers a judicious note of caution:

If a conductor is not in a position to have received instruction directly from the composer or if the tempos have not been handed down by tradition, he must look to the metronome marks and study them carefully, since most composers today take the trouble to write them in at the beginning and in the course of their pieces.

I do not mean to imply that he must copy the metronome's mathematical regularity; any music done that way would be stiff and cold, and I doubt that one could maintain such level uniformity for many bars. But the metronome is, all the same, excellent to consult to establish the opening tempo and its main changes.[2]

Although Maelzel, the inventor of the metronome, is best known for his stormy dealings with Beethoven, he had been marketing his invention in Paris in 1816 before it was introduced in Vienna, and Parisian composers such as Spontini were quick to take it up. If the *Resurrexit* is a reliable guide, Berlioz was applying metronome marks (hereafter MMs) to his orchestral music from the very beginning. He supplied them for all but one

1 Cairns, 237, 'Travels in Germany, Fourth Letter'.
2 Berlioz, *Grand Traité d'instrumentation et d'orchestration modernes*, 2nd edn (Paris, 1855) 300.

of his major works. As we pass from an age which has permitted interpreters a good deal of licence towards a different, more rigorous obedience to the composer's instructions, it may be wise to examine Berlioz's MMs to discover, if we may, what store may be set by them and what pitfalls they dig in the performer's path.

There are MMs throughout the three operas, the symphonies (with the curious exception of the *Symphonie funèbre et triomphale*), and all the choral works. In *Benvenuto Cellini* and *La Damnation de Faust*, for example, figures are abundantly supplied for passages of recitative and elsewhere where the tempo fluctuates. The density of MMs is sometimes very striking, giving a detailed map of whole movements where the tempo moves constantly forward and back. The *Tempête* Fantasy in *Lélio*, the first movement of *Harold en Italie*, and the *Scène d'amour* in *Roméo et Juliette* are good examples, where the instructions and the numbers go hand in hand. Such movements are elaborately structured with changing tempos, all supported by verbal instructions and MMs. Directions such as 'Le mouvement a dû s'animer peu à peu jusqu'au Nº 132 = ♩ du metronome' are commonly found. Berlioz would often give an MM for a mere half bar of recitative. An example of the precision with which Berlioz sought to use the metronome is found in Dido's farewell scene at the end of *Les Troyens*, where alternate bars have pulses of 100 and 72, a remarkable effect very difficult to capture in performance. In the single bar of syncopated C's that leads into the Trio for Teresa, Cellini and Fieramosca in the opening tableau of *Benvenuto Cellini*, the slowing down is effected not with a word such as 'ritenuto' but with the MM ♩ = 69 before establishing the main tempo of ♩ = 50, again quite difficult to execute precisely.

The works which lack MMs are arrangements of other composers' music (where it would be impertinent to determine the speed), most of the songs with piano accompaniment, the harmonium pieces, *Rob Roy*, *La Mort d'Orphée* (with one exception), most of the *Francs-Juges* fragments, *Cléopâtre*, the *Symphonie funèbre et triomphale* (with one exception) and the *Chant des chemins de fer*. Furthermore, MMs are scarcely ever found in Berlioz's autographs. From this we might conclude that he did not enter them at the time of composition but added them for publication, sometimes many years later. This was certainly the case with the *Symphonie fantastique*, *Benvenuto Cellini*, *Les Troyens*, in fact all the major works. The scarcity of metronome entries in Berlioz's hand might even suggest that they are not his own. But they were subject to his usual proof-reading and correction, and a telling footnote to Brander's *Histoire d'un rat* in the *Huit Scènes de Faust* insists: 'Pour avoir le véritable mouvement il est indispensable de le prendre au métronome', an instruction which we may assume Berlioz would wish to be applied to all his music. The works which lack them are for the most part unpublished works (the *Chant des chemins de fer* was only published in vocal score). So long as Berlioz retained exclusive use of his own music, as he repeatedly insisted upon in the 1830s after the bad experience with the Overture to *Les Francs-Juges*, he felt no need for MMs, but issued them, with the printed scores, as guides to other musicians.[3] What we do find in his autographs are the traditional, generally Italian, tempo indications – allegro, andante and so on – and verbal directions presumably entered at the time of composition which describe the relationship of one tempo to another.

But there are puzzling exceptions. Why is there just a single MM in the published score of the *Symphonie funèbre et triomphale*?[4] Why is there a single unexplained MM in *La Mort d'Orphée*? Why is there no MM for the main Allegro of *Waverley*? The most striking exception of all is *Herminie*, whose autograph is carefully provided with MMs at every speed change including a very rare case of an MM without any supporting verbal direction.[5] The second Air in *Herminie* is extraordinary not just for the intricate network of tempo instructions and MMs that govern its speeds but also for the fact that a work that was never published or performed should have MMs at all. In his next Prix de Rome cantata, *Cléopâtre*, Berlioz wrote no MMs.

At times MMs inevitably conflict with verbal instructions and with common musical sense. Some movements seem unreasonably fast or slow, some are simply impossible. But such problems were not gradually overcome with the passing years. There are some apparently crazy markings in the early works, suggesting perhaps inexperience with the machine (I cannot establish if or when Berlioz acquired his own) or even

---

3 It is curious that Schumann, like Berlioz a firm believer in the virtues of the metronome, also omitted MMs from many manuscripts and entered them at the time of publication. See Brian Schlotel, 'Schumann and the Metronome', *Robert Schumann: the Man and his Music*, ed. Alan Walker (London, 1972) 109.   4 See *NBE* 19, xi–xii.

5 The Breitkopf & Härtel score is misleading on this point. At bar 6 of the recitative following the first Air (Vol. XV, p. 14) the tempo is increased with the plain mark ♩ = 96 (previously ♩ = 84). The unsupported ♩ = 60 found on page 29 of the Breitkopf score should be marked 'Moderato'. There is an unsupported MM also in the *Tempête* Fantasy in *Lélio*.

a mechanical fault. At the midpoint of his career Berlioz used the metronome sagely and helpfully in the abundant MMs of *Benvenuto Cellini*, for example. But in 1861, as he prepared the vocal score of *Les Troyens* for printing, he committed some of the strangest errors of his career. Although most of the opera's MMs are perfectly judicious, there are more cases of impossible figures there than anywhere else in his work.[6]

Another respect in which *Les Troyens* differs from his earlier practice is the sudden inexplicable rash of very high MM figures. The first metronomes were calibrated from 50 up to 160, with set figures at intervals of two from 50 to 60, three from 60 to 72, four from 72 to 120, six from 120 to 144 and eight from 144 to 160. This was soon expanded to a range from 40 to 208.[7]

The available figures were thus the following:

40	60	72	120	144
42	63	76	126	152
44	66	80	132	160
46	69	84	138	168
48		88		176
50		92		184
52		96		192
54		100		200
56		104		208
58		108		
		112		
		116		

Berlioz first stepped outside the original range with the publication in 1840 of *Le Roi Lear*, whose Allegro goes at ♩ = 168. This figure is again found in the *Reine Mab* Scherzo and in the *Chanson de Méphistophélès*. The 1856 vocal score of *Benvenuto Cellini* hit the 184 mark with the *Chœur des ciseleurs*. Nothing however reaches the stratosphere so boldly as the first act of *Les Troyens*, where the scene between Cassandra and Chorebus goes from ♩ = 144 up to ♩ = 176 and then to ♩ = 192 before falling back through ♩ = 176 and ♩ = 160 to the reprise of Chorebus's Cavatina at

---

6 See NBE 2c, 758–9, where eight problems arising from the opera's MMs are set out.

7 An invaluable history of the metronome is found in David Fallows's article 'Metronome' in *The New Grove Dictionary of Musical Instruments*, ed. S. Sadie (London, 1984) II, 645–51. I am indebted to Dr Margaret Seares of the University of Western Australia for assistance with an early Maelzel metronome of French manufacture in that university's collections.

$\eighthnote = 126$, a clear rising and falling pattern.[8] Soon afterwards Cassandra leads off their duet 'Quitte-nous dès ce soir' at a record-breaking $\quarternote = 200$. The *Combat de ceste* is marked $\eighthnote = 176$, Sinon's scene opens 'Allegro féroce' at $\quarternote = 192$, and Laocoon's death is recounted at $\quarternote = 200$.[9] Nothing elsewhere in *Les Troyens* or any other work approaches this surge of very high metronome marks.

At the lower end of the scale the figure of 44 is reached in *Sara la baigneuse* and 'Absence', and the lowest figure of all is the $\dottedquarternote = 42$ for part of the Trio for two flutes and harp in *L'Enfance du Christ*.

Despite some very high figures the MM nearly always gives the prevailing beatable pulse of the music, in practice quavers, crotchets or minims. In Berlioz's early music the MM sometimes gives a semibreve pulse (twice in both the *Resurrexit* and the *Scène héroïque*, once in the *Francs-Juges* Overture and the *Symphonie fantastique*), perhaps implying that the conductor should beat one in a bar. This is certainly possible, since the MMs range from 66 to 96. But when the $\whole = 66$ in the *Resurrexit* was self-borrowed into the carnival finale of *Benvenuto Cellini*, the music was accelerated and the MM transcribed as $\quarternote = 160$. Berlioz's tendency was rather to indicate too small a note-value for the MM, not too large, as the very high MMs in Act I of *Les Troyens* show. The first appearance of Cassandra is marked $\eighthnote = 160$, an extraordinary choice when Berlioz also instructs the conductor to beat quavers. It is, furthermore, the only example of a semiquaver MM. The setting of a quaver MM when crotchets seem to be the main pulse will go some way towards explaining some apparently slow tempos. Conversely, Berlioz insists that the conductor beat quavers for the $\frac{3}{4}$ section of *Roméo seul* (the oboe solo), but gives the MM $\quarternote = 58$, not $\eighthnote = 116$. Instructions to the conductor found in *La Damnation de Faust*, *Les Troyens*, *Le Chef d'orchestre* and elsewhere nearly always require a more rapid, subdivided beat than would be normal in modern practice (the *Invocation à la nature* in nine, for example), yet the MMs vary from indicating too few beats to indicating too many. They do not, in other words, tell the conductor how to beat or even the performer or reader how to sense the pulse of the music.

The metronome's calibrations cover fine differences of speed, so that intermediate settings are not required. Any MM not found on the calibration is therefore suspect. There are several in Berlioz's work, the

8 *NBE* 2a, 53, 56, 61, 62 and 63.   9 *NBE* 2a, 72, 109; 2c, 875; 2a, 123.

most notorious being the 𝅝 = 67 found in the Breitkopf & Härtel score of the *Symphonie fantastique* at bar 29 of the last movement, a palpable error for 𝅝 = 76. But such misprints could also escape Berlioz's own scrutiny, not to mention that of the editors of the *New Berlioz Edition*, to my regret. The ♩ = 125 given for Brander's song in the 1854 scores of *La Damnation de Faust* (and in NBE 8a, 136) must be an error since there is no such figure on the metronome. Rather than 126, which *is* a standard figure, I suggest 152, very close to the 144 given in the *Huit Scènes de Faust* and supported by the insistent footnote quoted above. A similar misprint occurred in the 1863 vocal score of *Béatrice et Bénédict*, where the slow section of the Overture is marked ♩ = 25. This is far off the scale, and demonstrably an error for 52, since the music recurs later at that speed.

Other off-scale figures are harder to judge. There is no 90 on the scale, yet ♩. = 90 seems a good tempo for the *Chant des Bretons*, where it is found. In view of the overwhelming majority of on-scale figures I think it unlikely that Berlioz would have had occasional recourse to intermediate figures of this kind, so we should probably assume that 90 is a misprint for 80. The marking ♩. = 62 (why not 63?) is a good tempo for the Trio 'Me marier?' in Act I of *Béatrice et Bénédict*, but could ♩. = 72 be meant? The same can be observed of the ♩ = 118 for the four bars preceding Fieramosca's Air 'Ah! qui pourrait me résister?' in *Benvenuto Cellini*, although since the Air itself runs at ♩ = 108, 118 may be ten too high. The marking 118 is also found for Herod's outburst 'Eh bien! eh bien! par le fer qu'ils périssent!' in *L'Enfance du Christ*. What about ♩. = 156 for the *Carnaval romain* (the same music went at 152 in *Benvenuto Cellini*)? That must be an error too.

The ♩. = 110 for the *Ronde de paysans* at the beginning of *La Damnation de Faust* is a more complex problem. The figure 110 is not on the scale, and Berlioz explains in the score that the new quavers go at the same speed as the previous semiquavers, which would strictly require an MM of ♩. = 100.66. Thus 110 could be an error for 100, especially since the same music was marked ♩. = 80 in the *Huit Scènes de Faust*. To complicate matters further, a letter to Samuel of December 1855 insists that the mark for the *Ronde de paysans* should be ♩ = 88.[10] The minim confirms that this reference is to the $\frac{2}{4}$ section, not to the $\frac{6}{8}$ *Ronde*, but it contradicts the published score's ♩ = 152 by three calibrations.

The *Danse des esclaves* in Act IV of *Les Troyens* is marked ♩ = 122, an enigmatic entry since the music is in $\frac{6}{8}$ and there is no 122 on the scale. The

10 CG V, 227.

music simply cannot be played at ♩. = 122, so it is not a question of a missing dot (such an error could easily arise since Berlioz always expressed his MMs in the form 122 = ♩. with the note-value, not the metronome number, last; the dot could be mistaken by an engraver for a full stop and omitted). If we suppose that Berlioz correctly gave the note-value as a crotchet, the speed could then be expressed as ♩. = 81, a fast but credible tempo for this music, marked 'allegro moderato' (Colin Davis's tempo is ♩. = 66). If the crotchet in the MM should be a quaver, the most likely reading would then be ♪ = 192, a very high, but possible, alternative.

Other MMs are correctly calibrated but musically suspect or even impossible. The worst cases are again found in *Les Troyens*. Chorebus's beautiful pastoral passage in Act I, 'Mais le ciel et la terre', is marked 𝅗𝅥 = 138, Andante, in ¾. Even if the crotchet is taken to mean a quaver, the tempo seems too fast (Colin Davis's tempo is 𝅗𝅥 = 63). Iopas's song in Act IV is similarly difficult at ♩. = 132, more of a saltarello than an idyll of the fields; even at ♪ = 132 the tempo is too fast (Colin Davis's tempo is ♪ = 96). Could Berlioz have wanted an off-scale ♩. = 32?

Metronome marks which seem to me unattainably fast are the following:

> *Scène héroïque*, first movement, 𝅗𝅥 = 80
> *Scène héroïque*, second movement, bar 323, 𝅝 = 96
> (with an *animez* to follow)
> *Herminie*, No. 2, Air, Allegro assai agitato, 𝅗𝅥 = 152
> (Breitkopf & Härtel, p. 23). (Colin Davis's speed is 𝅗𝅥 = 126)
> *Herminie*, No. 3, Air, Allegro impetuoso vivace, 𝅗𝅥 = 138
> (p. 30). This movement accelerates to 144 and 152.
> (Davis's speed is 116, reaching a maximum of 120)
> *Le Roi Lear*, Allegro disperato ed agitato assai, ₵, 𝅗𝅥 = 168
> *Les Troyens*, Act IV, Duo for Anna and Narbal, Allegretto, ⅜,
> ♩. = 88 (Davis's speed is ♩. = 58)
> *Béatrice et Bénédict*, Act I, Duo, bar 168, Andantino, 𝅗𝅥 = 132
> (Davis's speed is 𝅗𝅥 = 112)

Metronome marks that seem uncomfortably slow are the following:

> *Harold en Italie*, opening, Adagio, ¾, ♪ = 76
> *Te Deum*, Te ergo, Andantino quasi adagio, ¾, 𝅗𝅥 = 50

The *Harold* case is particularly testing since the opening itself can go satisfactorily at ♪ = 76 without any question. But when the solo viola

23

introduces the main Harold theme (often mis-called an 'idée fixe') at bar 38, the slow tempo is impossible to sustain. This is clearly the result of grafting pre-existing music on to the opening fugato, but Berlioz rather surprisingly allows no quickening at that point. Nearly all performances get quicker here, it seems.

The *Te ergo* is simply a case where no performance ever seems to attain the slow speed Berlioz specified. Is ♩ = 50 a mistake for ♩ = 60, perhaps?

There is a much longer list of movements that seem remarkably fast or slow, each item of which may be disputed by each individual. The following are not unattainable, but they need special effort and will usually cause some surprise when played correctly:

FAST: *Francs-Juges* Overture, Allegro assai, $\frac{2}{2}$, 𝅝 = 80

Huit Scènes de Faust, Histoire d'une puce, Allegro, $\frac{3}{4}$, ♩. = 72

Huit Scènes de Faust, Le Roi de Thulé, Andante con moto, $\frac{6}{8}$, ♩. = 72

Huit Scènes de Faust, Sérénade, Allegro, $\frac{3}{4}$, ♩. = 72

Roméo et Juliette, opening fugato, Allegro fugato, ₵, ♩ = 116

Les Troyens, Act IV, Quintet, Allegro moderato, C, ♩ = 116

SLOW: *Scène héroïque*, Air, Lento, $\frac{3}{4}$, ♩ = 60

Waverley, opening Larghetto, $\frac{3}{4}$, ♩ = 56

Huit Scènes de Faust, Paysans sous les tilleuls, Allegro, $\frac{6}{8}$, ♩. = 80

'Le Coucher du soleil', Larghetto, $\frac{6}{8}$, ♪ = 126 (Robert Tear's speed is ♪ = 180)

Requiem, Rex tremendae, Andante maestoso, C, ♩ = 66

Requiem, Sanctus, Andante un poco sostenuto e maestoso, C, ♩ = 52

Roméo et Juliette, Père Laurence's Air 'Pauvres enfants', Larghetto sostenuto, 3, ♩ = 54

Le Corsaire, Adagio sostenuto, C, ♪ = 84

La Damnation de Faust, opening of Part II, Largo sostenuto, C, ♪ = 72

La Damnation de Faust, Part III, Faust's Air 'Merci doux crépuscule', Andante sostenuto, $\frac{3}{4}$, ♩ = 66

Te Deum, Tibi omnes, opening, Andantino, $\frac{3}{4}$, ♩ = 50

Te Deum, Marche, Allegro non troppo, C, ♩ = 92

L'Enfance du Christ, 'Entrez, entrez, pauvres Hébreux!', $\frac{3}{8}$, ♪ = 80

Les Troyens, Act III, Duo 'Sa voix fait naître dans mon sein', Andantino, $\frac{6}{8}$, ♪ = 76

Béatrice et Bénédict, Air 'Il m'en souvient', Andante un poco sostenuto, 3, ♩ = 52

A surprising portion of La Damnation de Faust, the Te Deum and L'Enfance du Christ is slower than we have become accustomed to, although that may simply reflect the performing habits of recent generations. The slow tempos of the Te Deum may be ascribed to its purpose as a work for monumental spaces; at the same time there are strikingly slow tempos in an intimate work like Les Nuits d'été too. 'Villanelle' (♩ = 96), 'Le Spectre de la rose' (♪ = 96) and 'Absence' (♩ = 44) are customarily sung much faster than they should be.

From these lists it is clear that Berlioz's music can be unexpectedly slow or fast, ranging more widely in the tempo spectrum than his interpreters (with a few exceptions) have been prepared to accept. His youth was impetuous in the sense that certain markings in the Scène héroïque, Herminie and the Huit Scènes de Faust call for meteoric speeds, while his late maturity was mellow in the sense that L'Enfance du Christ is broad and spacious. But parts of Les Troyens are unnervingly fast and we have pointed to early works that are much slower than we might expect.

Another approach to this may be explored by comparing the MMs of the same music used more than once. This produces the much more decisive conclusion that Berlioz liked slower speeds as the years went by. La Damnation de Faust overwhelmingly slowed down the music of the Huit Scènes de Faust, and there are other suggestive examples. The following all slowed down the tempo:

(1)　The second edition of 'La Belle Voyageuse' (Allegretto non troppo, $\frac{6}{8}$) reduced the MM from ♩. = 84 to ♩. = 76, a decided improvement.

(2)　The second edition of the 'Chanson à boire' (Allegro frenetico) revised the too fast ♩ = 66 to ♩ = 112.

(3)　The Prière in Herminie (Largo, $\frac{3}{4}$) is set at ♩ = 60, a satisfactory tempo. When the theme returns in the final Allegro of the cantata it is made to move faster at the equivalent of ♩ = 76. But when it was adapted as the 'Chant sacré' (in the Neuf Mélodies) this music was marked at ♪ = 88 (Largo religioso), the equivalent of ♩ = 44 and extremely slow.

(4) The 'idée fixe' in the *Symphonie fantastique* is marked ♩ = 132 at its first appearance. In *Herminie* it had been faster at the equivalent of ♩ = 144. In both works it is later slowed down with the function of reminiscence, in *Herminie* to ♩ = 120 and in *Lélio*, the sequel to the *Symphonie fantastique*, to ♩ = 108.

(5) The *Tableau musical*, the only section of *La Mort d'Orphée* to bear an MM, is shown as ♩ = 72 (Larghetto, $\frac{3}{4}$), a tempo on the fast side for comfort. As the fifth movement of *Lélio*, entitled *La Harpe éolienne*, it has the much lower speed of ♩ = 46, wonderfully effective if skilfully done. (The revision was made in 1855 for the published scores; the autograph is still marked ♩ = 72.)

(6) The passage in the 1824 *Resurrexit* revised as the *Tuba mirum* in the *Requiem* was originally set at ♩ = 76 (Andante maestoso, **C**). The fanfares reappear at ♩ = 72 in 1837, while the entry of the bass voices, simply 'très large' in the *Resurrexit* without any MM, is 'plus large' ♩ = 56 in the *Requiem*.

(7) A great number of tempos were reduced when the *Huit Scènes de Faust* were incorporated into *La Damnation de Faust*. The *Chant de la fête de Pâques* went from ♩ = 80 (Religioso moderato) down to ♩ = 69 (Religioso moderato assai); the *Chanson de Méphistophélès* went from ♩. = 72 (Allegro), a very fast speed, down to ♩ = 168 (or ♩. = 56) (Allegretto con fuoco), almost slow. The scene by the banks of the Elbe was ♩ = 58 (*Concert de sylphes*) in its first version, but ♩ = 54 in the revision. The music of the retreat at the beginning of Part III was originally marked at ♩ = 58 (i.e. ♩ = 116), reduced to ♩ = 104 in 1846 (or perhaps for publication in 1854). *Le Roi de Thulé* was very sharply slowed in the revision, from ♩. = 72 (Andante con moto, $\frac{6}{8}$) to ♩. = 56 (Andantino con moto), a fundamental change in the character of the piece. Marguerite's *Romance* in Part IV was likewise slowed from ♩ = 58 (Lento) to ♩ = 50 (Andante un poco lento).

(8) The passage in the *Resurrexit* that was re-used at bar 95 of the *Christe, rex gloriae* of the *Te Deum* was slowed down from ○ = 88 to ♩ = 76 (halved note-values), although the 'un poco animato' at that point usually brings about a speed nearer to 88 than to 76.

Metronome marks that were increased in later versions are much scarcer than those that were reduced. Of the six examples listed below three show only a marginal increase, barely significant in performance, and one of those is to a suspicious off-scale figure. One revision is of doubtful authenticity, and the figure for Brander's song can only be read as an increase by emending Berlioz's figure. So we are left with only one indisputable case (the *Méditation religieuse*) where Berlioz raised the tempo of a composition at a later date.

(1) *Méditation religieuse* (Adagio non troppo lento, **C**): originally set at ♩ = 54, a very slow tempo, the MM was raised to ♩ = 66 when the work was incorporated in *Tristia*.

(2) The closing section of the *Resurrexit* (in the 1824 Mass) was increased from 𝅝 = 66 to ♩ = 138 (a very slight increase) when removed to the end of the carnival scene in *Benvenuto Cellini*. The big unison tune that follows was marked simply 'animez' in the *Resurrexit* but marked as ♩ = 160 in *Benvenuto Cellini*.

(3) The tiny increase from ♩. = 152 to ♩. = 156 when the ⁶₈ carnival music in *Benvenuto Cellini* was arranged for the Overture *Le Carnaval romain* has been noted already for the occurrence of an off-scale figure, 156.

(4) The Trio for Teresa, Cellini and Fieramosca in the first scene of *Benvenuto Cellini*, with the rather slow mark ♩ = 50, was also marginally increased to ♩ = 52 for the Overture *Le Carnaval romain*.

(5) The *Invocation* in the *Francs-Juges* fragments is marked ♩ = 58. As it appears in the second movement of the *Symphonie funèbre et triomphale* (bar 39) the mark is ♩ = 69, although the hand is not certainly Berlioz's.

(6) Brander's song, in the *Huit Scènes de Faust*, was increased from ♩ = 144 to ♩ = 152 in *La Damnation de Faust* (if that is the correct reading of the suspicious ♩ = 125).

The slowing down of the 'idée fixe' in *Lélio* suggests the distortion and emotional discolouring of memory. This effect, often intensified by the minor key for formerly major-key music, is nearly always reflected, as we would expect, in the MMs. Thus the *Sérénade* in *Harold en Italie* is a little slower when recalled in the last movement, going at the equivalent of ♩. = 52 rather than at its own pace of ♩. = 69; the *Entr'acte* that precedes the third tableau of *Benvenuto Cellini* is a *minore* version of the *Chœur des ciseleurs*, marked at ♪ = 144 as opposed to the ♪ = 184 of the chorus itself.[11] The echo of the Capulets' festivities that precedes the *Scène d'amour* in *Roméo et Juliette* runs at ♩.= 92 as opposed to the ♩ = 108 pulse of the ball; the *Marche troyenne dans la mode triste* that accompanies the arrival of the Trojans at Dido's court is marked down to ♩ = 126 from the ♩ = 138 of the March itself; the delicate transformation of Dido's *Chant national* to which she leads in Aeneas and the court in Act IV is at ♩ = 120 rather than at the ♩ = 132 of the hymn as heard in Act III.

None of this is surprising. But there are two cases where such a recall is shown to be faster than the original passage. One is the 'Souvenir de la marche de pèlerins' in the last movement of *Harold en Italie*, headed 'même mouvement' after the second burst of the brigands' music, and thus moving at ♩ = 104 (often in fact played faster). The *Marche* was marked at ♩ = 96, which is by no means too slow. The other passage is found in Herod's Air 'O misère des rois!' in *L'Enfance du Christ*, marked ♩ = 60 but often taken faster. When Herod later recounts his dream to the soothsayers over a magical accompaniment of divided lower strings and clarinet, the direction is still 'Andante misterioso' but the tempo is slightly and unexpectedly increased to ♩ = 66.

Berlioz's habit of adding MMs at a late stage, usually at the time of publication, produced a number of anomalies which can only call their usefulness into question. When he attempted to express the relationship of one tempo to the next with some kind of proportional formula he must have felt that verbal instructions would serve his purpose better than the cold unaided MMs that we find, for example, in Stravinsky's scores. Perhaps he did not expect all his readers to have metronomes at their disposal. At all events the superimposition of an MM on a clearly expressed verbal instruction causes contradiction on a number of occasions. The formula is usually 'x mesures de ce mouvement équivalent à y mesures du mouvement précédent'. In Table 1 occurrences of this formula are shown with the MM that the verbal instructions imply alongside the actual MM.

In the majority of these cases agreement between words and numbers is near enough, occasionally even exact. But in the *Scène d'amour* in *Roméo et Juliette* and in No. 19 of *Les Troyens* the correlation is so far wrong as to be no help; common sense is a surer guide. There is one further example

---

11 The *Entr'acte* for the fourth tableau of *Benvenuto Cellini* similarly renders Ascanio's $^6_8$ 'Cette somme t'est due' in the minor key. Since it was never published it carries no MM, but something slower than the original ♩. = 60 would be appropriate.

Table 1

Work	Movement	Bar	x	y	Implied new MM	Actual new MM
Sym. fantastique	I	64	1	$\frac{1}{4}$	♩ = 112	♩ = 132
Requiem	*Dies irae*	141	1	2	—*	♩ = 72
Roméo et Juliette	*Scène d'amour*	124	1	2+	♪ = 138−	♪ = 88
Roméo et Juliette	*Reine Mab*	354	1	3	♩ = 138	♩ = 138†
La Damnation	*Ronde de paysans*	1	$\frac{1}{6}$	$\frac{1}{12}$	♩. = 101.3	♩. = 110‡
Les Troyens	No. 2	1	1	8+	♪ = 168−	♪ = 160
Les Troyens	No. 11	1	1	2−	♩ = 104+	♩ = 138
Les Troyens	No. 16	1	1	$\frac{1}{4}$	♩ = 80+	♩ = 80
Les Troyens	No. 19	111	1	4	♩ = 138	♩ = 80
Les Troyens	No. 31	31	3	1−	♩. = 60+	♩. = 66

* The figure cannot be calculated since the previous MM has been overridden by 'animez'.

† The calculation is correct, but Berlioz added the erroneous remark 'Deux fois plus lent que l'autre mouvement', which is not strictly the case at all.

‡ This off-scale figure is discussed above, p. 22.

of the formula in *Les Troyens*, in the original Epilogue abandoned in 1860 and therefore lacking an MM. An 'allegro con fuoco' similar in style to the close of Act II Tableau 1 and presumably moving at about ♩ = 144 is followed by a long Moderato while the curtain is lowered.[12] The new tempo is Moderato, amplified by the formula: 'Une mesure de ce mouvement équivaut à un peu moins de quatre du mouvement précédent'. This gives an approximate MM of ♩ = 72+, which is not necessarily too slow, but it makes this repetitive passage of forty-two bars last well over two minutes. In case it were argued that Berlioz was thus allowing time for the final scene-change to the Capitol at Rome, we should remember that he was normally very inconsiderate to scene-shifters, offering a mere pause over a held chord on a number of occasions in *Benvenuto Cellini* and *Les Troyens*, few of them allowed to survive in definitive versions. This long passage in the *Troyens* Epilogue is surely more intended to suggest the passing of centuries – at heartbeat pulse – though its effect on a patient audience has yet to be tested in the theatre. (In *Béatrice et Bénédict* Berlioz abandoned the 'Une mesure...' formula and resorted to the simpler and more effective note 'Mesure plus courte'.)

12 *NBE* 2c, 900.

Berlioz's MMs occasionally suggest a strategic pattern of tempos which may have structural significance but which would be impossible to observe without them. Between two movements of the *Requiem* the relationship is in fact spelled out, since the *Quaerens me* is marked 'même mouvement que le morceau précédent', the preceding movement being the *Rex tremendae*. Both have the MM ♩ = 66, indeed the *Rex tremendae* is carefully engineered to reach exactly double its original speed at midpoint, ♩ = 132.

It may be no accident that three of the *Huit Scènes de Faust* (the *Chanson de Méphistophélès*, *Le Roi de Thulé* and the *Sérénade*) are all marked at a pulse of 72, and all seem uncomfortably fast. Let us resist the temptation to conclude that Marguerite sings to the accompaniment of her beating heart and that Mephistopheles mocks her by adopting the same pulse in defiance of musical comfort. The first two tempos were reduced to 56 in *La Damnation de Faust*.

There is a similar prevalence in *Les Nuits d'été*, this time of the pulse 96, shared by the first two and the last of the songs. There are some striking cases elsewhere where a movement is marked to continue at the same tempo as the last, as in the *Requiem*. The entry of the Pope in *Benvenuto Cellini* continues the 116 MM of the quintet that precedes it, forming a sextet whose musical character is different but whose basic pulse is the same. This may be why Berlioz expressed the MM as ♪ = 116 rather than the more straightforward ♩ = 58. There may be a purpose behind the 54 MM that links Friar Laurence's Air 'Pauvres enfants' (a strikingly slow tempo) and the *Serment* that concludes the symphony, also moving at 54 pulses to a minute. At the start of *L'Enfance du Christ* the *Marche nocturne* seems to emerge directly from the preceding recitative, both at MM 66.

The most revealing long-range application of MMs is to be found in Act II of *Les Troyens*. The scene in the temple of Vesta has an almost unbroken pulse of 80 from Cassandra's first appearance at 'Tous ne périront pas' to the end. There are other tempos, to be sure, but they all seem to be constructively related to the principal tempo. The first departures are to a march tempo ♩ = 104, then to an 'andantino' at ♩ = 66 which soon speeds up to ♩ = 80 at 'Mais vous, colombes effarées!', a passage whose continuous pulse is emphasised rather than weakened by occasional choral interjections 'un peu animé'. This leads inexorably into the exultant hymn 'Complices de sa gloire', at eighty bars to a minute. When Cassandra addresses the small group who are too weak-willed to follow her, the new half-bar equals the old whole-bar, i.e. an implied 𝅗𝅥 = 80. Then at 'Allez dresser la table' comes an Allegro assai, 'le double plus vite', i.e. 𝅝 = 80. When the remaining virgins assure Cassandra that they will not leave her, the music is Allegro 'presque le double moins vite', i.e. a little more than 𝅗𝅥 = 80, quickly returning to the hymn at its previous 𝅗𝅥· = 80. The party of invading Greeks bring a change of tempo to Allegro assai at 'même valeur de mesure', i.e. 𝅝 = 80, and this is retained to the end. It seems as if Berlioz's plan was to set a basic pulse for the full ten minutes of this scene.

But this analysis is based on his original instructions, to be found in the autograph. In the published vocal score he inserted a series of MMs which contradict the verbal directions and cast doubt on whether he ever had any over-arching sense of tempo at all. Thus at bar 43 of the Finale ('Vous qui tremblez'), where the verbal instruction is 'Une mesure équivaut à deux mesures du mouvement précédent', the MM is given as 𝅗𝅥 = 72, not the 80 that is implied. The 'double plus vite' at 'Allez dresser la table' (bar 68) is marked 𝅗𝅥 = 132, not the 160 implied. And the Allegro 'presque le double moins vite' (bar 106) is not a little over 𝅗𝅥 = 80 as it should be, but ♩ = 152 (i.e. 𝅗𝅥 = 76). What this example reveals is that any temptation to read the numbers as pointers must be subject to the more urgent reality of getting the right tempo for every passage. Berlioz may have chosen the MMs to *avoid* too strong a sense of continuous pulse.

There are many other indications of Berlioz's ideas on tempo besides MMs. We have his timings of certain movements; we have the complex and colourful Italian vocabulary for tempo direction; and we have the evidence of time-signatures. His timings can be simply tabled. We have a note on the timing of the *Offertoire* (in the *Requiem*) in the autograph. There are two sets of timings for movements of *Roméo et Juliette*, the first in the autograph, for the *Scène d'amour*, *La Reine Mab* and the Finale; the second for the first four movements marked on a copy of the first edition in which Berlioz prepared the 1857 second edition. The last page of the autograph of *L'Impériale* is marked 'Durée 10 minutes' in Berlioz's hand. In the copy of the 1861 vocal score of *Les Troyens* in which he made the necessary adaptations of the first two acts as *La Prise de Troie* he marked four timings, possibly indicating optional cuts.[13] These timings may be seen in Table 2, where Berlioz's timing (in minutes) is shown beside the

13 Details of these timings may be found in NBE 9, 151; 18, 365 and 367; and 2c, 774. The autograph of *L'Impériale* is F-Pn ms 1.191.

Table 2

			Berlioz's timing	Actual timing
Requiem	Offertoire		8	7.3
Roméo et	Introduction		17	16
Juliette	Roméo seul – Fête		13	11.1
	Scène d'amour	(autograph):	12	12.6
		(1st edn):	16	15.3
	La Reine Mab	(autograph):	10	6.6
		(1st edn):	11	6.6
	Final		17	17.5
L'Impériale			10	10
Les	Combat de ceste		2	1.3
Troyens	Pantomime		5	5.4
	Marche et hymne (80 bars)		4	2.9
	Otetto (55 bars)		4	3.7

actual timing as computed from the MMs (to one decimal point allowing for pauses, etc.). The two discrepant timings of the *Scène d'amour* can be explained by excluding and including the introductory passage for the Capulets, which lasts about three minutes. Berlioz often performed the movement without it. In general his timings are a little slower than the MM timings; perhaps he was accustomed to players whose abilities did not allow them to attain the ideal speed; perhaps he played his music more slowly in the concert hall than in his head; perhaps his metronome was slightly inaccurate. But none of these explanations will account for the two wildly excessive timings of the *Reine Mab* Scherzo, both almost twice the proper duration. To make the movement last ten minutes requires the pace of a funeral march, ♩. = 90 rather than the 138 marked.

At the end of the 1861 vocal score of *Les Troyens* Berlioz inserted an 'Avis' which gives the complete timing of each act of the opera: 52, 22, 40, 47 and 45 minutes respectively. It is much harder to test these figures against the MMs since there are many passages of recitative and unmarked tempo, especially in the first two acts. None the less Berlioz's timings correspond remarkably closely with those obtained by computation from the MMs. This is an uncomfortable finding for all those, including myself, who find some of the MMs for *Les Troyens* too fast, especially in the faster movements.

Berlioz's choice of time-signature offers a few points of interest and idiosyncracy. He almost always wrote a plain '3' in place of the conventional $\frac{3}{4}$, even though his published scores usually translated this as $\frac{3}{4}$. To find a $\frac{3}{4}$ in Berlioz's hand is extremely unusual. The *Enseigne* in the autograph of *Béatrice et Bénédict* is a rare example; a 3 has been corrected to $\frac{3}{4}$ in the autograph of *Benvenuto Cellini* at the point where the slow 3 of the first-act trio becomes a very fast 3, to the words 'Ah, mourir, chère belle', but whether this is Berlioz's own correction it is hard to say with certainty, harder still to say why. The simple time-signature '2' (for the more conventional ¢) is found twice, the first time in the last movement of the *Scène héroïque* (at bar 60) at the point where the previous tempo, ¢, $\downarrow = 80$, doubles time to $\circ = 80$, 'mouvement double plus vite'; the second case is the opening of *Roméo au tombeau des Capulets*. A plain '4' is rarer still: this is found in the Finale of Act II of *Les Troyens* (at bar 43).

Despite popular belief and the Breitkopf & Härtel edition, Berlioz wrote no music in $\frac{7}{4}$: the 'évolutions cabalistiques' in *L'Enfance du Christ* are carefully notated with alternating bars of 3 and **C**, never permitting a bar of seven beats. Even $\frac{5}{8}$ he wrote only with caution: the *Combat de ceste* in Act I of *Les Troyens* has dotted barlines to divide each bar into $\frac{3}{8}$ and $\frac{2}{8}$. The first sketch for Aeneas's narration of the death of Laocoon, in Act I of *Les Troyens*, is notated with a time-signature '5', although the barlines show alternating $\frac{3}{4}$ and $\frac{2}{4}$ bars. An 'Air de danse de Nègres' sketched for Act IV of *Les Troyens* divides its bars into $\frac{3}{4} + \frac{2}{4}$ with a half-barline and a time-signature $\frac{5}{4}$.[14]

Even the time-signatures $\frac{6}{4}$ and $\frac{3}{2}$, common enough in most composers, are almost unknown in Berlioz. The former is found only, as far as I am aware, in the *Tempête* fantasy in *Lélio*, the latter only in the *Chant national* in Act III of *Les Troyens*.

As for the difference between **C** and ¢, that disputatious area of classical music, Berlioz conforms to the general practice of implying four beats with **C** and two beats with ¢. The signature **C** generally, not always, carries a crotchet MM, ¢ generally, but not always, a minim. Since he never writes $\frac{8}{8}$, **C** is used for metres where the quaver is the pulse, as for example at the opening of Part II of *La Damnation de Faust*. It is used, unusually, with a minim MM in the *Chant guerrier* and for the opening fanfares of the carnival scene in *Benvenuto Cellini*. The signature ¢, conversely, is used of necessity when the MM is given in semibreves,

---

14 See *NBE* 2c, 935 and 938 for these sketches.

and, unusually, when the MM is in crotchets. Two such cases are the opening of the *Francs-Juges* Overture (Adagio sostenuto, ¢, ♩= 72) where a minim pulse at ♩= 36 is unthinkable, and for Aeneas's farewell to his son in Act III of *Les Troyens* (Moderato assai, quasi andante, ¢, ♩ = 96).[15]

The final avenue to Berlioz's thinking on tempo is the variety of Italian terms used by nearly all composers to indicate speed and character. His habits in this regard were far from eccentric, despite his fondness for affecting Italian expressions in his speech and writings. The nearest he came to an Alkan-like profusion of unusual expressions is in the song 'Élégie', where the insertion of an English text alongside the French in the third edition inspired him to some brave English exhortations such as 'with faintness' and 'with transport' as well as the untranslated Italian 'con fremito' and 'ardentemente'. Such strong terms are confined to the early works. The impetuosity of youth is confirmed by finding 'Allegro impetuoso' only in the *Scène héroïque* and *Herminie*; 'con impeto' as a pendant to Allegro is found in *Cléopâtre*, the *Scène de brigands* in *Lélio*, and in the Overture to *Benvenuto Cellini*; 'allegro frenetico' belongs to the 'Chanson à boire' and the *Orgie de brigands* in *Harold en Italie*; 'andante malinconico' covers the middle section of the 'Chanson à boire' and *Roméo seul*.

These pairings may suggest similarities of character that help us to grasp Berlioz's conception. Thus the attachment of the term 'disperato' to three movements puts them in the same gathering: the 'Adagio disperato ed appassionato assai' of the 'Élégie', the 'Allegro disperato ed agitato assai' of *Le Roi Lear* and the 'Allegro agitato e disperato con moto' of *Roméo au tombeau des Capulets*. 'Allegretto grazioso' is found twice: for *Sara la baigneuse* and *Le Repos de la sainte famille*. 'Fieramente' embraces the *Marseillaise*, the *Chant des Bretons*, *La Menace des Francs* and *L'Impériale*, a strongly patriotic bunch of works. Both the *Marche triomphale* of the *Symphonie funèbre* and the *Marche et Hymne* in Act I of *Les Troyens* are 'pomposo'. 'Misterioso' brings together the *Meditation* in *Cléopâtre* (and later in *Lélio*), the *Légende* of *La Nonne sanglante*, Herod and Narbal.

A number of *unica* should be observed: 'grave' in the rejected music for the last scene of *Benvenuto Cellini*; 'mistico' at the end of *L'Enfance du*

---

15 The Allegro non troppo, ¢, ♩= 96 on p. 152 of the *NBE* score of *La Damnation de Faust* (Vol. 8a) is a misprint for ♩= 96.

Christ; 'allegro mosso' for the *Chansonette*; 'placido' at the opening of *La Damnation de Faust*; 'prestissimo' for *La Reine Mab*; 'spiritoso' for 'L'Ile inconnue'; there are others.

The most intriguing problem that these Italian terms present is to determine whether the diminutives 'allegretto' and 'andantino' are faster or slower than their parent terms. Both are exceedingly common in Berlioz. It is often assumed that they are faster and lighter than 'allegro' and 'andante', but it is clear that for Mozart and his contemporaries 'andantino' and 'allegretto' were slower than 'andante' and 'allegro'.[16] In Berlioz's time 'andante' was beginning to lose the sense of briskness it had in the eighteenth century.

A number of the movements I have earlier listed as surprisingly slow are headed 'andantino', such as the music for the Père de famille in *L'Enfance du Christ*, and the opening of the *Tibi omnes* and the *Te ergo quaesumus* in the *Te Deum*. The *Entrée des laboureurs* and 'Sa voix fait naître dans mon sein' in Act III of *Les Troyens* are both 'andantino' and both measured by slow MMs. Most significant of all is the adaptation of *Le Roi de Thulé* from the *Huit Scènes de Faust* to *La Damnation*: its MM was severely cut from $\downarrow\!\!\cdot = 72$ to $\downarrow\!\!\cdot = 56$ and 'andante' was replaced by 'andantino con moto'.

It is tempting to use this example as evidence to doubt the authenticity of the MM $\downarrow = 69$ for the second movement of the *Symphonie funèbre et triomphale*, since its marking 'andantino' replaced its earlier appearance in the *Les Francs-Juges* fragments as 'andante $\downarrow = 58$'. But 'andantino' is not unequivocally slower than 'andante'; *Béatrice et Bénédict* contains two quite brisk passages headed 'andantino': in the Duo for Béatrice and Bénédict in Act I the section at bar 168 is marked 'andantino $\downarrow = 132$', a decidedly jaunty speed; a little later, in the Duo-Nocturne, the main tempo is 'andantino $\flat = 126$' (not as slow as some like to take it). Did Berlioz's sense of 'andantino' speed up in later life, in parallel with the public's perception of the term?

'Allegretto' is in many ways more baffling still. It conveys a suitable lightness for 'Villanelle', at its very steady speed of $\downarrow = 96$. It is still slow – definitely slower than 'allegro' would be – for the *Hamlet* March at $\downarrow = 76$. But how is the *character* of such a piece conveyed by 'allegretto', even disguised as 'allegretto moderato'? It makes no sense. There are even more inappropriate applications. The *Judex crederis* in the *Te Deum*, one

---

16 See Neal Zaslaw, 'Mozart's tempo conventions', *International Musicological Society Congress Report* XI (1972) 720.

of the weightiest of all Berlioz's works, is headed 'allegretto un poco maestoso' when something like 'molto maestoso e non troppo lento' might have been expected. The noisy and pompous *L'Impériale* is headed 'allegretto fieramente', almost a contradiction in terms. *Le Trébuchet*, on the other hand, a piece of diametrically opposite character, is swift and delicate at 'allegretto leggiero e scherzando', ♪.= 88. The 'allegretto non troppo' in Act I of *Les Troyens* before 'Pauvre âme égarée'[17] implies with its MM ♩= 160 that a normal allegretto would be faster still, perhaps ♩ = 176 or so. In a succession of movements in Part II of *La Damnation de Faust* the term 'allegretto' is used for very swift music, unquestionably faster than 'allegro': both *La Cave d'Auerbach* and the *Chanson de Méphistophélès* are marked 'allegretto con fuoco', and at the start of the *Chœur de buveurs* the 'allegretto' is also marked 'lourdement'. In the brief recitative that precedes Mephistopheles's *Sérénade* in Part III the music moves forward from 'allegro non troppo' ♩ = 76 to 'allegretto' ♩ = 112, an unequivocal indication that 'allegretto' is faster than its parent. Or at least it is on this occasion. Elsewhere perhaps something else is implied. For a term that can govern music both heavy and light, pompous and delicate, music for a funeral procession or for a tavern, cabalistic evolutions or the Last Judgement, all things are possible.

We face further ambiguity whenever Berlioz uses the word 'quasi' (in the sense of 'almost'), as he frequently does. 'Andante' can be 'quasi adagio' on the one hand (the opening of the second tableau of *Benvenuto Cellini* at ♪ = 108) or 'quasi allegretto' on the other (the off-stage chorus of monks in *Benvenuto Cellini*). 'Andantino', as we should now expect, is even more widely stretched, being 'quasi adagio' in the *Te ergo* of the *Te Deum* at a very slow ♩ = 50, and 'quasi allegretto' on at least three occasions, bringing together these two elusive diminutives: in the song 'Le Matin' (³⁄₄ at ♩ = 108), in the song 'La Mort d'Ophélie' – where the full direction is 'andantino con moto quasi allegretto', ⁶⁄₈ at ♪.= 63, and in the first part of the Teresa-Cellini duet (1838 version only) – where the direction ambles wordily on as 'andantino con moto ed un poco agitato quasi allegretto', in ³⁄₈, without MM.

When words are as imprecise as this, we need to put our faith in something else. Musical instinct is one helpful but notoriously personal guide; the other, carrying at least the appearance of scientific rectitude, is the metronome.

---

17 *NBE* 2a, 62.

3

Romeo and Juliet
and *Roméo et Juliette*

IAN KEMP

The autograph full score of *Roméo et Juliette* and the first printed scores
of 1847 and 1858 contain a note recommending the suppression of the
Roméo au tombeau des Capulets movement 'every time this symphony is
not performed before a select audience to whom the fifth act of
Shakespeare's tragedy with Garrick's denouement is extremely familiar'.
Setting aside Berlioz's reasons for being prepared to sacrifice the most
extraordinary music he ever wrote, these were the only occasions on
which he stated clearly that for his symphony he had chosen to reject
Shakespeare's tomb scene and depict Garrick's version of it instead. But
he referred indirectly to his preference on several other occasions. In his
Memoirs the Garrick is 'an inspired discovery, incomparable in its
pathos'. Elsewhere in the *Memoirs* it is described as 'the desperate strife
of love and death contending for mastery' and 'extremes of joy and
despair drained to the dregs in the same instant, passion's heat chilled in
the rigour of death'. Again, in his *feuilleton* on Bellini's *Roméo et Juliette*
[*I Montecchi ed i Capuletti*], the tomb scene, 'presented by great English
artists, will remain the most sublime marvel of dramatic art'.[1] Admittedly
these remarks are scattered; but they are emphatic enough. In the present
context their significance lies not in the fact that Berlioz, champion of the
'authentic' text, thought Garrick had improved Shakespeare (in the
Memoirs he had explained that this was the exception that proved the
rule) or that he kept silent on his other Garrick retentions and his further
adaptations of both Shakespeare and Garrick in the symphony. It is rather
that later commentators were not particularly interested in how Berlioz
had actually treated Shakespeare, brushing aside the manifest discrepancies between the two. They ignored the implications of the note above

1 The four quotations are from, respectively, Cairns, 55, 59, 114; and *A Travers chants*, 358.

the *Tombeau* movement, which after all was clearly printed in Malherbe and Weingartner's 1901 full score. Tovey and Barzun were among the commentators who recognised its curiosity but neglected to find out what it meant; Boschot did know but drew no conclusions. It was not until 1964 that Roger Fiske (and ironically not because he had read the note but because the discrepancies prompted him to examine contemporary acting versions of the play) showed how closely the *Tombeau* movement relates to the Garrick version and, in addition, how Garrick sheds light on the *Roméo seul* and *Convoi funèbre* movements.[2] The present article takes Fiske's discoveries as its starting point in another attempt to answer the question, what has *Romeo and Juliet* to do with *Roméo et Juliette*?

I

The overwhelming impact made on Berlioz by Shakespeare at the Odéon in 1827 has been well documented. As for the performance of *Romeo and Juliet* on 15 September, this, it seems, was not only the first but, astonishingly, the last occasion on which he saw the play.[3] What to him was meant by *Romeo and Juliet* centred on that single performance. He cherished its memory for the rest of his life. Of course, one of the reasons why he was so lastingly affected was personal: like Romeo in Garrick's version he too had pined for the unattainable Juliet, and when he had finally won Harriet Smithson he saw himself as 'the real Romeo created by Shakespeare' at the feet of his Juliet.[4] (After their marriage, Harriet was cast as Ophelia, not having the 'passionate fire' of a Juliet.)[5] But the essential revelation was of Shakespeare, so powerful that when writing *Roméo et Juliette* nearly twelve years later Berlioz, in the *Strophes*, was impelled to step outside his work for a moment, in order to apostrophise the genius who had brought it about.

> Premier amour! n'êtes-vous pas
> Plus haut que toute poésie?

2 Roger Fiske, 'Shakespeare in the concert hall', in *Shakespeare in Music*, ed. Phyllis Hartnoll (London, 1964) 189–96.
3 William Cockrell, 'Hector Berlioz and "Le Système Shakespearien"' (Ph.D. diss., University of Illinois, 1978) 281–99, lists all performances of *Romeo and Juliet* given in Paris and England that Berlioz could have attended; but there is no evidence that he saw any more than the one.
4 *CG* II, 60.   5 *CG* II, 127.

Ou ne seriez-vous point, dans notre exil mortel,
　　Cette poésie elle-même,
Dont Shakespeare lui seul eut le secret suprême
Et qu'il remporta dans le ciel!

The 'poetry' there of Berlioz's librettist Emile Deschamps hardly matches its subject; but the sentiment behind it is Berlioz's own. Equating love and poetry like that, as with love and music at the end of the *Memoirs* – first love moreover, which shows that he was thinking of Estelle, as well as of Juliet and Harriet – provides dramatic evidence of the hallowed place occupied by Shakespeare in his sanctuary. This could not have happened without the experience of 15 September 1827.

Contemporary accounts of the Odéon performances, and the texts specially printed for them (in English with an anonymous French prose translation on facing pages, and separately in English and in French), described as conforming entirely to the production, make it clear that what Berlioz saw was a truncated version of Garrick.[6] The most important of David Garrick's 'alterations' of Shakespeare, as published in 1750, can be listed as follows: rhymes, puns and bawdy jokes reduced to an unavoidable minimum; both prologues cut; Rosaline removed (because, as Garrick explained, Romeo's sudden change of affection was a 'Blemish on his Character'), with the result that Romeo is in love with Juliet from the start; Juliet's age increased from nearly fourteen to nearly eighteen; the scenes involving Benvolio, Mercutio and Romeo conflated; the Queen Mab speech bowdlerised; a funeral procession for Juliet with sung 'Dirge' (here Garrick imitated an idea from a rival production and got Boyce to write the music) inserted at the beginning of Act V (to replace the arrival of the musicians at the end of Act IV); and the tomb scene altered, so that Juliet wakes before Romeo dies and there is a final flare-up of passion between them (a reversion to the pre-Shakespearean story by da Porto and Bandello and post-Shakespearean adaptations by Otway and

---

6 Accounts of the Odéon performances are included in *Journal de Delécluze 1824–1828*, ed. Robert Bashet (Paris, 1948) 460–66; J.-L. Borgerhoff, *Le Théâtre Anglais à Paris sous la Restauration* (Paris, 1913) 60–62, 224–7; John R. Elliott Jr, 'The Shakespeare Berlioz saw', *Music and Letters*, 57 (July 1976) 292–308; Peter Raby, '*Fair Ophelia*', *A Life of Harriet Smithson Berlioz* (Cambridge, 1982) 69–78. The texts for the performances are printed in *Théâtre Anglais ou Collection des Pièces Anglaises jouées à Paris, publiées avec l'autorisation des directeurs et entièrement conformes à la représentation / Anglais-Français / Roméo et Juliette / Paris / Chez Mme Vergne [...] / 1827*. A copy is in the Bibliothèque de l'Arsenal, Paris. Copies of the separate English and French translations, printed in the same layout, are in, respectively, the Bibliothèque Nationale, Paris (*The British Theatre*, etc.) and The Shakespeare Library, Birmingham Public Libraries, England (*Théâtre Anglais*, etc).

Cibber).[7] Garrick made other, less radical changes, including the removal of some minor characters and the shortening of scenes, in particular the final one.

The text used at the Odéon accommodated all these changes, with the exceptions of the funeral procession and the final scene, both of which were cut: the play ended with Juliet's suicide. The funeral procession was cut because the French censor did not allow priests on stage. This restriction also accounted for the transformation of Friar Laurence into a hermit – in which guise he was however ill-qualified to marry the lovers.[8] In the event, the scene in which he agrees to do so was also cut, as was the scene with Friar John about the undelivered letter. There were additional changes – little cuts and readjustments, the removal of further minor characters and of Paris in the tomb scene (though he was granted an early entry, after the intervention of the Prince).[9] A few of the insignificant changes derived from John Kemble's version of Garrick (Charles Kemble, his younger brother, played Romeo) but in the main the Odéon changes reflected the limited number and variable quality of the actors available rather than any desire to 'improve' Garrick. Garrick, after all, had made the necessary reforms. Eighteenth-century taste had been appeased with an emphasis on decorum, scrupulous 'nobility' of behaviour, elevated style, and with a reduction of narrative complexity in order to focus on the passions and pathos of the main characters. This was considered more 'natural'. In the nineteenth century it led to a further emphasis on dramatic 'realism' and 'truth', aspects which when added to the revelation of Shakespeare found an immediate response in Berlioz's imagination.

Accounts of the Odéon performances and acting style have been given elsewhere.[10] Here it will be useful to supplement them with just one contemporary description – of the end of the tomb scene – to make it easier to understand why 'realism' and 'truth' meant so much to Berlioz, especially when contrasted with the formality and steady pacing of Classical French drama, and why he preferred this climax to the play, which Garrick's alterations led to rapidly and relentlessly, to the 'less striking end' of Shakespeare.

---

7 [David Garrick] *Romeo and Juliet. By Shakespear. with Alterations, and an additional Scene*: [...] London MDCCL (rpt. Cornmarket Press, London, 1969 – Garrick's 'definitive' text). See Jill L. Levenson, *Shakespeare in Performance: Romeo and Juliet* (Manchester, 1987) 17–31.
8 Borgerhoff, 60–61.   9 *Ibid.* See also *Théâtre Anglais.*
10 See note 6 and Levenson, *Shakespeare in Performance.*

Roméo, dans son amour et dans son égarement, s'approche rapidement de Juliette, la saisit, la presse sur son sein, appuie sur son épaule cette tête chérie, la couvre de baisers; il redouble ces étreintes convulsives, et semble, en s'attachant à elle, s'attacher à la vie; bientôt, déchiré par la violence de ses tourments, il se roule sur la terre, puis se relève avec fureur. Sa raison fuit, ses genoux chancellent, sa vie s'efface, il tourne sur lui-même comme un homme ivre; de ses bras errants, il cherche Juliette , il appelle Juliette d'une langue glacée, il l'appelle, la rencontre, la saisit encore et tombe pour toujours.

Juliette veut quelque temps douter de son malheur, et prend son réveil pour un songe; elle parle à cet ami qui n'est déjà plus, elle cherche quelques restes d'haleine, elle voudrait de son souffle ranimer un cœur qui a cessé de battre pour elle; mais c'est en vain qu'elle veut s'abuser, elle sait tout; elle ira s'unir dans le tombeau avec l'époux qui mourut pour l'y retrouver; l'approche de l'ermite, confidant malheureux de leurs amours, ne fait que hâter le coup qui doit trancher les jours de Juliette; et pour échapper à des secours odieux, pour se soustraire au danger de vivre, elle se frappe d'un poignard, tout à quelques pas de son amant, se traîne avec effort jusqu'à lui, et rend le dernier soupir sur la bouche de Roméo.[11]

[Romeo, in love and in distraction, rushes towards Juliet, seizes her, clasps her to his breast, leans that beloved head on his shoulder, covers it in kisses; he embraces her yet more convulsively and seems, by holding on to her, to be holding on to life itself; then, rent by the violence of his torment, he rolls on the ground and rises again in a frenzy. His reason flees, his knees weaken, his life ebbs away, he turns upon himself like a drunken man; with groping arms he seeks Juliet, he calls Juliet with a chill voice, he calls her, stumbles upon her, seizes her once more and falls for the last time.

Juliet prefers for a while to cast doubt upon her misfortune, and takes her awakening for a dream; she speaks to her friend who is already no more, she seeks some traces of life, she would fain revive with her own breath a heart which has ceased to beat for her; but in vain she strives to deceive herself, she knows; she will go and be wed in the tomb with the husband who died to find her there; when the hermit, the hapless confidant of their loves, approaches, he can but hasten the blow which will bring Juliet's days to an end; and to evade loathsome help, to escape from the danger of living, she stabs herself with a dagger, some few steps away from her lover, crawls painfully to where he is and breathes her last sigh on the lips of Romeo.]

To Berlioz, the fate of the lovers must have swamped almost everything else. It probably would have done so even if Shakespeare's intricate patternings had been retained and not severely distorted. Of the supporting roles that survived, he was fascinated by Mercutio, and to a

---

11 N. P. Chaulin, *Biographie dramatique des principaux artistes anglais venues à Paris précédée de souvenirs historiques du Théâtre Anglais à Paris en 1827 et 1828* (Paris, 1828) 14–15.

lesser extent by the 'cackling' Nurse (unlike most, who found her part detestable) and 'stately' Hermit – as well as by the changes and combinations of tone they brought about. But the fundamental message of Shakespeare lay to him in its truth to life.

II

The only documentary evidence that Berlioz read Garrick in an 'authentic' English text is inconclusive – the similarity between 'my life, my soul, my heart' (in English), in a letter of 5 January 1833 referring to Harriet, and the line 'My life, my love, my soul', the final words of Garrick's second garden (read bedroom) scene. (This line was slightly different in the adapted Garrick texts published in Paris in 1827.)[12] But eventually he must have done so (possibly using Harriet's copy), if for no other reason than that, like his symphony, the 1827 performances and texts omitted references to Rosaline, while all other French translations retained them. It is not clear at what point Berlioz's English measured up to Shakespeare (or Garrick) in the original. In the autumn of 1828 he enrolled on an English course in Paris, leaving it early in 1829 for lack of time.[13] By then he was bold enough to add quotations in English from *Hamlet* and *Romeo and Juliet* to his *Huit Scènes de Faust* (taken from the texts issued for the Odéon performances) and he obviously persevered with the language, if fitfully, not least because he wanted to communicate with Harriet. His progress towards understanding the 'splendours of the poetry' will have gathered pace after his marriage and the first recorded instance of his possessing a complete Shakespeare in English, which is 1835, is unlikely to have marked the first occasion on which he laid hands on a volume.[14] Yet he never really mastered the language and his competence at the time of writing *Roméo et Juliette* can hardly have enabled him to dispense with French translations.

In addition to the translation issued for the Odéon performances, (hereinafter referred to as the Odéon translation), four other prose translations of *Romeo and Juliet* were available to him. These were Pierre Le Tourneur's, published in 1778 in the fourth volume of his pioneering and immensely influential complete translation of Shakespeare, and those in three 'new editions' of Le Tourneur: by François Guizot in 1821, by an

12 See *Théâtre Anglais* and William Shakespeare, *Romeo and Juliet* (London 'and sold at Paris...', 1827).
13 *CG* I, 213 and *CG* I, 167 (the correct date for this letter, No. 79, is 10 January 1829).
14 *CG* II, 240.

anonymous editor in 1822 and by Horace Meyer in 1835.[15] (The translations of Francisque Michel and Benjamin Laroche came too late for *Roméo et Juliette*, though Berlioz seems to have relied on Laroche once it had been published in 1843.)[16] Precisely which of these five sources he drew from and which he drew most from is not easily deduced. He wrote disparagingly of Le Tourneur, presumably referring to the original 1778 translation. Yet his was the only one Berlioz mentioned in print and the only one to include both the funeral procession and Garrick's tomb scene, so it has claims on priority. Le Tourneur followed all Garrick's major changes (except that involving Rosaline), while adding a veneer of authenticity by restoring some of the text cut by Garrick. He enabled Berlioz to realise from the start that the tomb scene was Garrick's for at the end of his translation he said so (as well as listing some of Garrick's other changes) and then provided a translation of Shakespeare's original. Furthermore, he provided a stage direction for the funeral procession (the result of seeing the play in London) which obviously gave Berlioz a crucial musical stimulus: 'On entend une grosse cloche, qui sonne un seul coup de distance en distance' ['We hear a large bell, which rings, once, from time to time'].

The 'new editions' of Le Tourneur were concerned with minor improvements and the gradual restoration of Shakespeare. Thus those of 1822 and 1835 kept the funeral procession, while restoring the tomb scene and the final scene (still shortened in 1822 but complete in 1835). Guizot's translation was the exception to this trend, for he attempted a wholesale restoration. Berlioz certainly used Guizot at one stage. The translation of Gloucester's 'As flies to wanton boys...' from *King Lear* added to the title page of the *Symphonie fantastique* is Guizot's and no-one else's. If he did consult Guizot for the later work it is perhaps surprising that his surviving correspondence contains no reference to the fact, especially since Guizot, in an extended preface, had speculated on the relevance of Shakespeare to future French dramatists in a way that must have been sympathetic to Berlioz.[17]

15 Pierre Le Tourneur, *Shakespeare traduit de l'Anglais*, IV (Paris, 1778); François Guizot [et A. P. Traducteur de Lord Byron], *Œuvres complètes de Shakespeare, traduites de l'anglais par Letourneur, nouvelle édition*, IV (Paris, 1821); *Œuvres de Shakspeare, traduits de l'anglais par Letourneur, nouvelle édition*, II (Paris, 1822); Horace Meyer, *Œuvres Dramatiques de Shakspeare, traduits de l'anglais par Letourneur, nouvelle édition* (Paris, 1835).

16 Cockrell, 19.

17 Raby, 47. Berlioz did not meet Guizot (1787–1874), academic, writer and politician, until 1862 (see François Guizot, *Lettres á sa famille et ses amis* [Paris, 1844] 384), though when Guizot was Minister of the Interior Berlioz had corresponded with him (see *CG* I, 376 and 391).

Table 1

Romeo and Juliet, I.i. 1–35	Garrick, 1750	Le Tourneur, 1778
Sampson Gregory, on my word we'll not carry coals.		S. Gregorio, sur ma parole, je ne l'endurerai pas ;
Gregory No, for then we shall be colliers.		une fois en cholère, nous dégaînerons.
S. I mean, and we be in choler, we'll draw.		
G. Ay, while you live, draw your neck out of collar.		
S. I strike quickly being moved.	S. I strike quickly, being mov'd.	Je suis prompt de la main, quand je suis échauffé.
G. But thou art not quickly moved to strike.	G. But thou art not quickly mov'd to strike.	G. Oui, mais tu n'es pas prompt à t'échauffer.
S. A dog of the house of Montague moves me.	S. A dog of the house of *Montague* moves me.	S. La vue d'un Montaigu me met au champ.
G. To move is to stir, and to be valiant is to stand: therefore if thou art moved thou runn'st away.		G. Se mettre au champ, c'est fuir ; & pour être brave, il faut attendre l'ennemie de pied ferme : mais toi, quand on t'échauffe, tu prends le large.
S. A dog of that house shall move me to stand. I will take the wall of any man or maid of Montague's.		S. Tout visage de cette odieuse famille me verra toujours t'attendre de pied ferme : je prendrai toujours le haut du pavé sur les gens de la maison de Montaigu, hommes ou femmes.
G. That shows thee a weak slave, for the weakest goes to the wall.		G. Et viola la preuve que tu es un poltron ; car le plus foible cherche toujours à s'appuyer de la muraille.

S. 'Tis true, and therefore women, being the weaker vessels, are ever thrust to the wall; therefore I will push Montague's men from the wall, and thrust his maids to the wall.
G. The quarrel is between our masters and us their men.

S. 'Tis all one. I will show myself a tyrant: when I have fought with the men I will be civil with the maids, I will cut off their heads.
G. The heads of the maids?
S. Ay, the heads of the maids, or maidenheads; take it in what sense thou wilt.
G. They must take it in sense that feel it.
S. Me they shall feel when I am able to stand, and 'tis known I am a pretty piece of flesh.
G. 'Tis well thou art not fish; if thou hadst, thou hadst been Poor John. Draw thy tool – here comes of the house of Montagues.

S. Oui, hommes ou femmes, peu m'importe.

G. Mais la querelle n'est qu'entre nos Maîtres, & entre ceux, qui, comme nous, sont à leur service.
S. Cela m'est égal ; je veux me conduire en tyran. Quand je me serai battu avec les hommes, je serai cruel avec les femmes.

G. Allons mon brave, dégaîne : voilà quelqu'un de la maison de Montaigu.

G Draw thy tool then, for here come of that house.

Shakespeare's text is reprinted from the Arden Edition of *Romeo and Juliet*, ed. Brian Gibbons (London, 1980), by kind permission of Methuen & Co. Ltd. In this edition Gibbons elucidates everything that might be obscure to the modern reader.

The verse translation by Emile Deschamps should also come into the reckoning.[18] Berlioz stated that he prepared a prose scenario for *Roméo et Juliette* which Deschamps put into verse. It is difficult to believe however that this scenario was exclusively the work of Berlioz. Deschamps had translated three acts of *Romeo and Juliet* in 1827 and although he did not complete and publish his translation until five years after the symphony's first performance in 1839, close correspondence between, in particular, the distinctly un-Shakespearean symphonic *Final* and Deschamps' equally un-Shakespearean final scene suggest that at least some earlier exchange of ideas had taken place. (Yet Deschamps' retention of the Garrick funeral procession and tomb scene in his 1844 translation, against the current trend, could also confirm that Berlioz was indeed the dominant partner.)

From this short survey of Berlioz's possible French sources it would seem that the most useful to him were Le Tourneur's translation and the Odéon translation (inspired by Le Tourneur but not a direct copy). What all of them – Garrick's changes and Berlioz's own limited knowledge of English – obscured was the vital Shakespearean element of comic bawdy. This presented adapters and translators with some difficulty. Table 1 gives an example of what Garrick evidently thought his audiences would be offended by, how he responded to the problem and how Le Tourneur attempted, scarcely less drastically, to follow Shakespeare and French taste at the same time. In the Odéon translation (and performances) the passage was cut out altogether. It may be doubted that Berlioz ever fully understood Shakespeare's puns and irreverence. But even if he had, they would surely have been out of place in his symphony. That drew its prime inspiration from what he had seen, and was thus to embody a 'Romantic' conception of Shakespeare, concentrating on the internal psychology of the lovers. Equally, if he had seen a comprehensible, unbowdlerised production of Shakespeare's original, he would still have had to cut and adapt in order to mould his ideas to the needs of musical design. There is no point in complaining of an un-Shakespearean bias in the symphony, let alone of prudishness. Berlioz's no doubt assiduous reading of Shakespeare in translation and in the original was not directed towards a revival of *Romeo and Juliet* nor the preparation of a scholarly text for publication. He was re-creating Shakespeare in his own terms.

18 Emile Deschamps, *Œuvres*, I (Paris, 1844).

III

It is not necessary to record here the process by which Berlioz's commitment to some kind of musical *Romeo and Juliet* eventually bore fruit.[19] What is worth underlining is that he was at first unsure whether his work should be a symphony or an opera. If Deschamps is to be believed, Berlioz's initial idea, as early as 1828, was for a symphony.[20] By 1832 he seems to have been considering the more obviously feasible idea of an opera, and had selected scenes and characters which, with the addition of the *Convoi funèbre*, were precisely those which were to appear in the later symphony.[21] So it may be imagined that once he had settled on the genre of symphony with voices (his reasons were eventually revealed in the *Avant-Propos* to the 1858 vocal score), his main compositional problem was how to reconcile the rival claims of a narrative opera of situations and of a symphony with its own purely musical logic – or in other words how to develop his conception of a programme symphony to include singing.

'Music is free; it does what it wants, and without permission'.[22] Berlioz took what he wanted from the Odéon performance, from Shakespeare, Garrick, translations, and doubtless from discussions with Harriet and friends, and added, discarded, altered and expanded – as he wanted. His emphasis lay squarely on the lovers. For the rest, the family feud was to provide a context rather than a continual sense of menace, *La Reine Mab* necessary relief, and the *Final* a conclusion worthy of the scale of his conception. Thus the symphony begins as did the Odéon performance: 'Enter the Montagues and Capulets fighting' – 'Les Montagus et les Capulets entrent en combattant'.[23] The quasi-Shakespearean *Prologue* is placed second. Rosaline is gone. Romeo is understood to be wandering about thinking of Juliet, then drawn to the Capulet house, from which he hears festive sounds including a 'Concert' as well as dance music; masked, he goes in alone. An off-stage chorus now prefaces the balcony scene. The Queen Mab speech is changed in content and significance, and is shifted from before the ball to after the balcony scene. From this latter point in Shakespeare's Act II everything is cut (the deaths of Mercutio and Tybalt, the marriage, Romeo's banishment, Juliet's individual predicament and 'death') until the altered tomb scene, which also excludes Friar

---

19 See *NBE* 18, viii–ix. 20 Deschamps, I, xiv.

21 Cairns, 114; see also Auguste Barbier, *Souvenirs Personnels* (Paris, 1883; rpt. Geneva, 1973) 230.

22 From a report Berlioz made for the Académie des Sciences. See Peter Bloom, 'Berlioz à l'Institut revisited', *Acta Musicologica*, 53 (1981) 197.

23 The first stage direction in *Théâtre Anglais*.

Laurence. Before that Berlioz inserts his funeral procession. His Finale, which amounts to a second prologue and an epilogue in one, does something to explain the missing narrative but gives Friar Laurence an importance out of all proportion to his role in the play; in any case it has very little connection with Shakespeare's final scene – which adds some irony to Berlioz's statement in the *Avant-Propos*: 'This final scene [...] has never been performed in any theatre since Shakespeare's time'.

Berlioz left no direct answers to the questions of precisely why he adapted Shakespeare in the ways outlined above and of whether, in the case of the scenes he did select, there was any correspondence of structure between the scene and the individual movement: the only exception to this latter is contained in the note above the *Tombeau* movement. Answers to these questions must be sought primarily in his music. Some hints about his approach to large-scale design can however be deduced from his interpretation of Beethoven's Ninth Symphony, no doubt the principal *musical* stimulus behind *Romeo and Juliet*.

The first performance of the Ninth Symphony in Paris took place while Berlioz was in Italy so he didn't hear it until 1834, when the second performance took place on 26 January. It can hardly be an accident that *Harold en Italie*, which was begun that month, was originally intended for chorus and orchestra, with Paganini's viola.[24] If that plan misfired, Beethoven's influence is plain enough at the beginning of the Finale of *Harold*. Another four years were to elapse before Berlioz wrote about the Ninth Symphony, but his famous article in the *Revue et Gazette musicale* of 4 March 1838 was obviously the fruit of long study, in particular of Beethoven's approach to the problem of combining chorus and orchestra. Whether his absorption in Beethoven hastened his decision to write a choral symphony himself (and the decision was taken over a busy period of just twelve days after receiving Paganini's gift) remains a matter of conjecture.

In his article on the Ninth Symphony Berlioz reasoned that in order to observe the 'law of crescendo' and set in relief the 'subsidiary' role inevitably placed on his orchestra by the introduction of voices, Beethoven had to start with purely orchestral movements. After that, he was obliged to invent a 'musique mixte' to connect the two major parts of the symphony. He invented instrumental recitative – 'the bridge [...] over which the instruments pass in order to join up with the voices'. Once that

24 CG II, 159.

was in place, Beethoven could use his own words with the actual notes of his instrumental recitative to conclude an oath of alliance (his 'formule de serment') between the two forces, and then go on to the choral part of the symphony with whatever text he chose. Berlioz said curiously little about Beethoven's quotations from earlier movements other than suggesting they atoned for the 'calumny of instrumental harmony' perpetrated in the opening chord of the Finale. He had however already expressed his sympathy with Beethoven's procedure in his own *Harold* Finale and perhaps didn't want to say the same thing again.

The influence of one composer on another is to be measured in terms of idea rather than identity of syntax or procedure. So with Beethoven on Berlioz. Berlioz was writing a narrative as well as a choral work, and Beethoven's actual procedure couldn't be followed anyway. But the 'law of crescendo' could, and one of the most striking features of Berlioz's treatment of his chorus and vocal soloists is precisely that. The *Prologue* begins with a small chorus whose very smallness (fourteen voices) is defined by the focus on solo voices in the middle of it; the prelude to the *Scène d'amour* introduces one of the two large choruses, but with off-stage men's voices only; the *Convoi funèbre* gradually reveals the whole of that one chorus (first *pianissimo* and on a single note, later opening out into full textures) before, in the *Final*, both large choruses, the small chorus and the dramatic bass solo are all employed. The 'crescendo' operates here too, with the bass progressing from recitative, arioso and cantabile to an eventual declamatory style and the large choruses treated sectionally and in recitative before combining with each other, the small chorus, the bass and the orchestra at the end. It also operates in the orchestra, though in reverse, so the two contrasting processes and contrasting sounds interlock: four interspersed 'symphonic' movements progressing from a carefully prepared noisiness (evident also in the *Introduction*, this 'first' movement's timbral preparation), to lyricism and to delicacy, before breaking up in fragments.

Maybe Berlioz didn't need the example of Beethoven to appreciate the 'law of crescendo'. And maybe the 'subsidiary' role ascribed to Beethoven's orchestra and the corrective function of his quotations spurred Berlioz himself to do something different in both cases. But the idea of instrumental recitative was another matter: it instantly provided the 'bridge' between orchestra and chorus and since, after Beethoven, it was no longer necessary to use words to endorse its effect, Berlioz could show that his was to be a choral symphony from the outset. The

49

Introduction contains a passage of instrumental recitative (the 'Intervention du Prince') so conspicuous that were its structural and expressive function not crucial it might seem far too long. Elsewhere the technique is used more subtly. The technique he was particularly proud of, and to which he drew attention on his title pages, was choral recitative. If Beethoven had persuaded him he could make use of the paradoxical idea of instrumental recitative, then Beethoven could have been behind his invention of the equally improbable choral recitative (improbable because it is impracticable with a large chorus – which is why he wrote for an expert small chorus). It remains to observe that Beethoven's 'formule de serment' could have found an echo in Berlioz's final *Serment de réconciliation*, as could Beethoven's hymn to brotherhood in Berlioz's hymn to the same thing.

Example 1 illustrates how these considerations were built into the design of the whole work. Berlioz's own numberings have been altered a little in order to clarify the principal music units (white notes in the example represent major tonalities, black notes minor ones). Number 1 is the *Introduction*, 2 the *Prologue* with its 'quotations' from subsequent movements (whose numbers are given in brackets below), 3 the *Roméo seul* movement, 4 the *Nuit sereine* leading to the *Scène d'amour*, 5 the Scherzo *La Reine Mab*, 6 the *Convoi funèbre* followed by the contrasting and complementary *Roméo au tombeau des Capulets*, and 7 the *Final*. Berlioz reinforced his design by careful control of orchestral resources: the 'crescendo' of voices and orchestra accumulates weight, while the 'diminuendo' of the orchestral movement sheds it (except for the conclusive yet fragmentary 6b). And he reinforced it further with a closed tonal scheme that absorbs both the brawling and final reconciliation of the families (B minor becoming major) and the private worlds of Romeo and Juliet (F, the 'opposite' of B, for Romeo; A, the tonality of springtime, for the lovers).

Berlioz's design is certainly complex. But it also has an elemental strength which suggests that he conceived it in a flash. In fact it was the result of some trial and error, as he revealed in the *Memoirs*, and was not given its definitive form until the Prague performance in April 1846, over six years after its première. The most important changes he made were the removal of a second prologue and consequent revisions to the original first one.[25] Berlioz doubtless wrote two prologues because that had the

25 See *NBE* 18, x and Appendix IV, 400–37.

Example 1

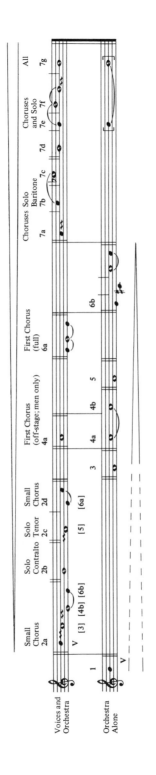

sanction of Shakespeare. An equally strong reason must have been his anxiety to communicate the narrative sequence of the symphony clearly and in a not too compressed form, so that the orchestral movements could be better understood. The original first prologue took the narrative as far as the Mercutio speech (or Berlioz's equivalent of it). Thus the second prologue followed *La Reine Mab*. It began 'Plus de bal maintenant, plus de scènes d'amour! La fête de la mort commence', and went on to explain the *Convoi funèbre*, the *Tombeau* movement and the *Final* with Friar Laurence's role as conciliator. Berlioz cut this second prologue presumably because he felt its continuous 'récitative harmonique' (which featured only one, inconspicuous 'quotation', the *Convoi funèbre* theme) weakened the symphony's musical substance and energy, and because he agreed with the criticism, voiced notably by Stephen Heller, that the opening 'Récitative mesuré' and 'Air' of Friar Laurence in the *Final* forfeited some of their interest since the events they recount had already been made known.[26] Berlioz thus seems to have been persuaded that his narrative did not need so detailed an exposition and could take second place to musical demands. While the simple removal of the second prologue certainly met these points and made the work much tauter, it however left an unresolved contradiction. The revised *Prologue* contains quite detailed preparations, verbal and musical, for the first three orchestral movements. But the brief and very general remarks about death and reconciliation in its new ending contain little preparation for the *Convoi funèbre* and none at all for *Roméo au tombeau des Capulets* – the movement most in need of it. The note at the head of the latter does not solve the problem. But of course this, of all the movements, remains the most vivid, and Berlioz must have felt the texts of the *Convoi funèbre* and *Final* provided sufficient explanation of their place in the narrative.

The original ending of the first prologue provides endearing evidence of Berlioz's devotion to Shakespeare – and of his realisation that this would have to yield to the expressive imperatives of his own music. After the *Scherzetto* on Queen Mab there had been an equivalent to Shakespeare's address to the audience at the end of *his* first prologue:

> ...Is now the two hours' traffic of our stage;
> The which, if you with patient ears attend,
> What here shall miss, our toil shall strive to mend.

---

26 *Revue et Gazette musicale* (19 December 1839) 561.

Berlioz's prologue concluded as follows (and with a rather better tonal connection from the *Scherzetto* than in the revised version):

> Tels sont d'abord, tels sont les tableaux et les scènes
> Que devant vous, cherchant des routes incertaines,
> L'orchestre va tenter de traduire en accords.
> Puisse votre intérêt soutenir nos efforts!

The principal relevance of the original first prologue lies however in its clarification of certain obscurities in the *Roméo seul* movement. For the revision Berlioz gave greater prominence to the 'quotation' of themes, with a consequent reduction of recitative: the dance theme was changed from a brief snatch to extended excerpts, and Roméo's sighs were now expressed musically as well as described verbally. Berlioz's tactics were obviously designed to sharpen the musical focus. His deletion of a considerable passage mostly in recitative resulted however, in the suppression of important information. This passage explained some of the scenario of the movement (see pp. 61–2), which is so different from Shakespeare that it is impossible to guess what it might have been from the music alone. It also set out the episode of Capulet's irritation at the behaviour of Tybalt, with a short 'quotation' of a motif expressing Tybalt's fury and departure. The function of this motif in the movement proper (bar 286) can now be understood as a good deal more than a *basso ostinato* for a coda deriving from a comparable procedure in the first movement coda of the Ninth Symphony. (Bar references here and elsewhere in this article are to *NBE* 18.)

IV

Roméo et Juliette, like several other works of Berlioz, contains instances of his occasional compositional tactic of re-using material from discarded earlier works – here three themes, possibly four. The *Introduction* includes a passage of instrumental recitative very similar to a motif in the *Méditation* in the 1829 Prix de Rome cantata *Cléopâtre* (and thus in the *Chœur d'ombres* in *Lélio*) (see Example 2). Cleopatra, near death, is contemplating the welcome she will receive from the Pharaohs when she is brought to 'sleep in your pyramids'; the Prince is threatening Montague and Capulet with death if another brawl should break out. The correspondence is in itself perhaps not exact enough to prove self-borrowing, though in a letter to Ferrand, Berlioz gave an explanation for the inspiration behind the *Cléopâtre* music which certainly does prove its connection with *Romeo and Juliet*: 'It is the scene where Juliet meditates on her burial in the Capulet's tomb [...] which ends with cries of terror accompanied by an orchestra of double basses plucking this rhythm'.[27] Berlioz then quoted the rhythm of Example 2a, with 'Oh! Shakespeare' added underneath to fit with it. (The rhythm is also very similar to that in the 'Invocation' section of the *Tombeau* movement, where Romeo addresses Juliet in the tomb.)

What Berlioz wrote in the letter to Ferrand could conceivably imply that the *Méditation* in *Cléopâtre* was originally intended for a *Roméo et Juliette* of some sort. The same could be said of the three other themes, all written after *Cléopâtre*, though the question cannot be resolved. The first of these appeared in the withdrawn *Ballet des ombres*, for four-part chorus and piano (see Example 5a). Its text runs: 'Form in ranks, shades, begin the dance, take hands and break this majestic silence that reigns over humanity'. Later, its mode still minor but then, after a long intervening passage, changed to the major, the theme appeared in a rejected choral section of the carnival scene from *Benvenuto Cellini*, where Cellini's theatrical friends are urging the crowd to join the carnival saltarello. Here (shortly after the sudden $\frac{2}{4}$ bars in the saltarello) it was presented first alone, and then in two-part as opposed to the three-part canon of the *Ballet des ombres*, presumably to eliminate the solecisms in the latter. For its permanent home in *La Reine Mab*, at the place where Mab is about to take the young girl to a ball, Berlioz retained the new accompanimental pattern alternating F and A flat, the same initial tonalities of F minor and B flat and the same two-part canon (though greatly widened in texture) that had appeared in the rejected section of the carnival scene (see Example 5b).[28] In all three cases however the music's expressive purpose is the same – an invitation to the dance.

The remaining two themes both appeared in *Sardanapale*, the 1830 cantata with which Berlioz finally won the Prix de Rome. He apparently destroyed most of it, but a fragment of the score survives containing the final 'Incendie' section in which the debauched yet heroic Assyrian king

27 CG I, 270–71.
28 I am indebted to Hugh Macdonald, editor of *Benvenuto Cellini* (NBE 1, forthcoming), for enabling me to elaborate on his remarks in 'Berlioz's self-borrowings', *Proceedings of the Royal Musical Association*, 92 (1965–6) 33.

Example 2 (a) *Cléopâtre, Méditation*

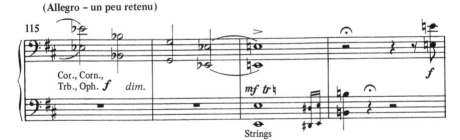

(b) *Roméo et Juliette,* Introduction

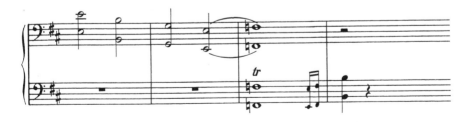

Example 3 *Sardanapale*, 'Incendie'

Sardanapalus sets fire to his possessions, his entourage and himself rather than give up his crown. The 'Incendie', a résumé-cum-coda featuring the work's main themes, includes the passage transcribed in Example 3.[29]

The two thematic ideas in the transcription were first identified by Tiersot as, respectively, the Larghetto oboe melody and a version of the Allegro dance theme from the *Roméo seul* movement. In 1981 Peter Bloom published a reconstruction of the cantata's text and in 1986 the programme for Berlioz's performance on 5 December 1830, which indicate that the Larghetto was the first Aria, called 'Cavatine', and the Allegro theme the main material for a 'Bacchanale'.[30] In the Aria, Sardanapalus is asking his favourite concubine Néhala to arouse his desire; in the symphony, Romeo is persuaded by the sounds of the oboe melody (the 'Concert' of the movement) to venture inside Capulet's palace to see Juliet. The reconstruction in Example 4 of the solo tenor part for the opening stanza of the Aria cannot claim to be what Berlioz actually wrote: for a start its range extends beyond the limits of even his tenor writing, and a transposition down to, say A flat, would simply increase the degree of speculation involved. But the text fits the melody plausibly enough, provides a helpful clue to its expressive meaning and, with the phrase 'prends ta lyre', explains why the oboe is accompanied by pizzicato cellos.

29 The transcription is from the autograph fragment preserved in the Bibliothèque Nationale, Rés. Vm² 178.
30 Julien Tiersot, 'Berlioziana', *Le Ménestrel*, lxxii (1906), 287, 294–5, 302–3. Peter Bloom, 'Berlioz and the *Prix de Rome* of 1830', *Journal of the American Musicological Society*, 34 (1981) 298–9; 'Sardanapale and the Symphonie fantastique', *Berlioz Society Bulletin*, 128 (Summer 1986) 5–6. The reconstruction in Example 4 follows the lead in Tiersot, 302.

Berlioz's 'Bacchanale' was prompted by the stanza in the 'Cavatine' beginning 'Venez, bayadères charmantes' – Sardanapalus's appeal to his dancers to continue the good work of Néhala. In a letter to his father Berlioz wrote that the 'song of the bayadères' was melodically changed in the 'Incendie'.[31] This suggests that it was originally something like, or even the same as the dance theme in the *Roméo seul* movement. Whatever the case the expressive function of the dance theme is the same as the presumed function of the 'Bacchanale' – to intensify passion. (Shortly after its appearance in the 'Incendie', Berlioz combines the 'Bachanale' theme with a melody used earlier in *Sardanapale* – which he would later use in *L'Impériale*, bar 56, at 'Du peuple entier' – in a manner, with full brass, similar to that of the ('Réunion des deux thèmes' in the *Fête chez Capulet*.)

Example 4   'Cavatine' from *Sardanapale* (conjectural)

31 *CG* I, 379.

Whether these four themes' structural functions all fit into place so naturally is less obvious. Certainly some of them do, and Berlioz's command of melodic transformation ensures that they all flow effortlessly into the melodic fabric of their respective movements (for one instance of this see Example 5c). The middle two of them however are associated with radical alterations of Shakespeare and the proposition that they were first conceived as part of the structure of a *Roméo et Juliette* does not therefore carry much weight. This is not to admit the old charge that the symphony comprises a suite of episodes, skilfully interconnected and laid out in a powerful sequence but without the interactions, the driving logic and the inconvenient manifestations of human nature that inform the drama of Shakespeare: a composer may nowadays by gracious general agreement be judged by his own standards. Nevertheless it does open out a central question in Berlioz criticism, which is to what degree the relationship between the programmatic and the 'purely musical' creates the peculiar metabolism of his music. The rest of this article is concerned with the workings of this relationship in *Roméo et Juliette*.

V

The *Introduction* contains three programmatic events – the fighting, the arrival of Montague and Capulet, the intervention of the Prince. By cutting Shakespeare's gradual crescendo from low comedy to highborn violence Berlioz followed the Odéon performance and text; by cutting Benvolio's attempted peace-making and the duel between him and Tybalt he also departed from them. He followed Shakespeare however by representing the somewhat preposterous Montague and Capulet with his somewhat preposterous theme on the trombones, once in the tonic, once in the dominant (bars 44 and 50). Thus his music depends on Shakespeare's narrative sequence yet changes it to suit its own priorities, here an arresting and dramatic beginning whose cardinal function is to set up the element of instrumental recitative. The Prince's speech is therefore given considerably more weight than in the play. In the process Berlioz created the first, Introduction and Recitative, of those unique musical forms that are to be found in each of the work's movements.

The complex texture at the beginning is not really fugal, consisting more of a continual liquidation process, with a very rapid crescendo to a theme (the trombones' theme) not striking enough to pre-empt the effect of the culminating recitative but kept alive by violent rhythmic polyphony

($\frac{3}{4}$ across $\frac{2}{2}$). Although an endeavour to fit words, English or French, to the recitative will fail, there remains a close correspondence between Shakespeare's text and the music. The Prince's speech can be divided into four sections. He attempts to quell the fighting and there is a furious outburst when at first the crowd fails to listen; he continues by telling Montague and Capulet that three brawls are enough; he threatens them with death if another should break out; he commands the crowd to disperse, and Montague and Capulet to appear before him. The recitative can be similarly divided, the triplets of the interruption in the first section being absorbed in the second, the third (see Example 2b) leading into the commanding phrases of the fourth. An added codetta represents the crowd dispersing, muttering and looking daggers at each other: Berlioz returns to the unsettled mood of the beginning and leaves his movement poised on an unresolved dominant seventh. As a whole, the *Introduction* establishes the tone of things and the importance of the orchestra, while demanding an explanation of its eloquent yet unarticulated question. What, exactly, is going on? Thus the apologia for the *Prologue*, which had it come first would have introduced a formality quite at odds with the rest of the work.

Berlioz found a method of structuring the *Prologue* that gave him both flexibility for narrative exposition and strength of musical design – variations on a basic paragraph of choral recitative leading to the prefiguring in the orchestra of one of the main themes of the work. In none of these paragraphs is the procedure quite the same, and Berlioz broke it with *Strophes*. So the *Prologue* is a dramatic and developing organism as well as narrative exposition. The first paragraph is divided into three sections, each signalled by a harp chord: decisive for the first passage of unaccompanied choral recitative, which is marked *mf*, more flowing (arpeggiated) for the second, marked *pp*, thus allowing the contralto soloist to enter with her description of Romeo, and again flowing for the third, marked *f*, with a crescendo leading to the first orchestral 'quotation', the ball music. This latter illustrates how Berlioz responded to the purely musical demand that the constraints of choral recitative should find release, for it is relatively substantial, and especially so when compared with the original prologue. Its dynamic arch leads into the second paragraph, which follows the same basic procedure; it is however in only one section and its 'quotation', of the sighing theme in *Roméo seul*, now has the chorus contributing to it. The third begins with a carefully modulated change of sound, a pizzicato instead of a harp chord, continues differently too, with the orchestra supporting the choral recitative, and finds its culmination in a 'quotation' from the *Scène d'amour* where chorus and orchestra join forces. Together, the three paragraphs make up a burgeoning, completed design, the climax of which marks a high point in the narration, the balcony scene. Berlioz then takes breath – the *Strophes*, his still centre. After that extraordinary moment – a solo contralto *mélodie*, with the harp coming into its own – he could hardly resume as if nothing had happened. In the next paragraph the 'quotation' nimbly absorbs his basic procedure and the new situation, preparing for the tone rather than the material of *La Reine Mab*, at the same time being a solo tenor *ariette* with chorus: a nice variation on a procedure which could have become too predictable. The fifth and final paragraph originally began with another harp chord. Berlioz's revision is a further instance of his aversion to the predictable. Now the orchestra comes in first, with a 'quotation' from the *Convoi funèbre*. The choral recitative is an echo of the same music and the two forces combine in a second 'quotation' from that movement. What this rather cumbersome description of the *Prologue* shows is that even when he had decided it was vital to explain the story to his audience and had devised a scheme allowing for maximum freedom of narrative exposition, Berlioz's musical instincts still forced him to seek out an appropriate form.

He was now ready to enter into the main body of the work. His protagonists are silent, but with their situations outlined he could voice their feelings with the intimacy and suppleness only available in an instrumental language not tied to words. Yet expressive latitude still required technical control and the narrative foundation still had to yield to the more powerful demands of musical structuring; the *Roméo seul* movement shows Berlioz grappling with these compositional problems more deliberately than in any other movement.

His full heading on the printed scores of 1847 and 1858 is *Roméo seul – Tristesse – Concert et Bal – Grande Fête chez Capulet*. The stage direction 'Enter Romeo alone' comes after the ball scene in *Romeo and Juliet* but in the first scene of the play there is already that description of the lovesick Romeo with his 'deep sighs' for Rosaline, avoiding all company save the night, which provided the justification for the second scene of the Odéon production, in which, on his first entry, Romeo was actually seen walking alone. This presumably was the image Berlioz wanted to recapture, not least because it enabled him to paint a portrait of Romeo – indeed a self-portrait in certain respects – gradually emerging from his self-communing and yearning for Juliet until he encounters her at the ball. (In later life Berlioz was surprisingly critical of those who, like himself, had removed Rosaline.)[32]

The *Prologue* presents Berlioz's scenario as follows:

> Le jeune Roméo, plaignant sa destinée,
> Vient tristement errer à l'entour du palais;
> Car il aime d'amour Juliette... la fille
>   Des ennemis de sa famille!...
> Le bruit des instruments, les chants mélodieux
>   Partent des salons où l'or brille,
> Excitant et la danse et les éclats joyeux.--

The original *Prologue* continued:

> Poussée par un désir que nul péril n'arrête,
> Roméo, sous le masque, ose entrer dans la fête, [etc.]

The first two sections of the *Roméo seul* movement thus have him wandering aimlessly, his thoughts fleeting or frozen, until they gather round the exquisite, unattainable Juliet and are articulated in a series of sighs. At that point Berlioz had to get Romeo to the ball, and without confusing the portrait by introducing other characters. So Shakespeare had to be altered anyway. Berlioz's essential solution to the problem – Romeo's wanderings leading him to the Capulet palace from which he hears music and is drawn inside – might conceivably have served on its own, but his actual solution is more true to life. Romeo was surely too timid to have entered the house of his enemies simply on the call of some dance rhythms (bars 63–80). He needed something more persuasive, and what more so than an evocative melody, a 'chant melodieux' drifting across from a 'Concert' elsewhere in the palace (bar 81)? Thus, perhaps, Berlioz's reasons for the final two sections of the movement. In fact there is no other way of explaining his *Concert et Bal* section, especially when it is remembered that his original heading, on the autograph full score, was *Bruits lointains de Bal et de Concert* – an exact description of what his Romeo would have heard in the street outside: distant sounds of dance music, preceding and then mingling with an oboe melody. To suppose that this is meant to *represent* Juliet herself conflicts with this scenario, though Romeo obviously *associates* the theme with Juliet; otherwise he wouldn't have found the courage to enter the palace.[33]

---

32 *A Travers chants*, 350.
33 The heading on the autograph full score for the complete movement is *Roméo seul* [subsequently replaced simply by *Tristesse* – which shows that the oboe melody can't be associated with this section] / *Bruits lointains de Bal et de Concert*: / *Grande Fête chez Capulet*. The autograph

The musical consequence of his scenario meant that he had committed his Introduction before the Allegro to no less than three slow sections. The first two flow into each other naturally enough – a melodic line gradually gaining substance and definition. But the third? His ingenious solution of making it part of the Allegro only in retrospect is not wholly convincing because the oboe theme is too self-contained; it arrests the gathering momentum. Its programmatic function needs underlining somehow (maybe by an at first extremely *lointain* oboe theme and by very pointed definition of the dance rhythms). But when the doors are flung open, Romeo steps inside the ballroom and the music springs to action, the dramatic effect is undoubtedly the greater for having been withheld for so long.

The *Grande Fête chez Capulet* is much more than the necessary Allegro after an Introduction. It sets up a violent contrast, between intimacy and vulgarity, between the profound inner reality of the slow music and the garish outer reality of the ballroom. This is what creates the dynamic of Berlioz's form. As for the *Fête* itself, Berlioz concentrates on the impression Romeo receives of the swirling dancers and dance music and misses out most of Shakespeare's nine little episodes, though his structuring of the section as a thrice-heard rondo theme with two episodes and a coda enables him to retain Shakespeare's shifting planes of focus. The oboe melody seems in its snuffed-out appearances in the second of Berlioz's episodes to represent Romeo momentarily recognising the figure of Juliet through the confusing mass (whether the bass motif in the first episode [bar 157] represents anything is impossible to say), and in its combination with the dance music to represent him stretching out to her in a kind of dumb shout. Shakespeare's episode of their first meeting is not there – unless it is the tiny passage (bar 273) before the Tybalt episode. Capulet's humiliation of Tybalt is given extraordinary prominence, occupying what amounts to the second half of the section. This dislocation of Shakespeare's proportions (which were more or less preserved in Garrick and in the Odéon performances) is a particularly striking illustration of how Berlioz's compositional priorities can override the programmatic. Why he should have needed so unusually extended a coda in the tonic after a previous section also in the tonic could of course be

---

libretto, printed libretto, programme for the first performances and Deschamps' printed libretto have the same (apart from *Bruit lointain*). Berlioz's alteration for the printed scores was presumably made in the interests of simplicity.

understood as programmatic – Romeo not wanting to leave. But it is best understood by saying that had he used a traditional design, with longer and more modulatory episodes and with a much shorter coda, he would have forfeited the flat, two-dimensional effect chosen both to sustain the atmosphere of the ballroom and to contrast with the depth of feeling in the *Scène d'amour*.

The transitional upbeat of the *Nuit sereine* continues Berlioz's scenario (jettisoning Mercutio's conjuration speech) from the vantage point of Romeo in the garden, with the young bloods coming and going, crescendo and diminuendo, singing a version of the dance music prefigured in the *Prologue*. Thus the scene is set. Berlioz's love scene does not have the light-fingered enchantment of Shakespeare's balcony scene. It is more inward, its discoveries more knowing, its course less volatile. Yet a thousand books would fail to explain its secrets, subtleties, compositional mastery and the peculiar alchemy by which the balcony scene is never quite the same once you've heard the *Scène d'amour*. Here the concern is simply to show how closely Berlioz followed Shakespeare. (Garrick and the Odéon performances omitted very little.) Table 2 sets out the correspondences. The verbal cues in the Table are for orientation, to indicate correspondences of mood and dramatic action rather than the literal paraphrase, though sometimes Berlioz is in fact remarkably exact. (Shakespeare's text, here and elsewhere in this article, is drawn from the Arden Edition. See p. 45.)

The four sections of the balcony scene are reflected in the four sections of the *Scène d'amour*. In the first, Romeo is in the garden thinking about Juliet, then seeing her and being frightened to declare himself until she speaks the words she had previously only been mouthing. Berlioz sets up a two-layered texture in the tenor and soprano registers, with motifs which flow musingly and assemble haltingly, until they unite in a single texture. Out of that emerges a real melody in the tenor – what may be called the first subject. This opening musical strophe is then repeated, with variation. Shakespeare's second section is of Juliet's agitation and Romeo's attempts to reassure her. Berlioz's strophe here, again repeated with variation, is of breathless fragments and eloquent instrumental recitative. In Shakespeare's third section, Juliet desperately wishes she had not been overheard, lest she should be thought too forward; but she knows Romeo loves her and she asks that he trust her love for him. Berlioz ushers in his second subject, a long melody in the soprano which shades into his, and Shakespeare's, final section, the love scene proper – where

Table 2

Balcony scene, II.ii.	line	bar	Scène d'amour, 3.124		
			Introduction/Exposition		
			FIRST SECTION		
Romeo in garden. Juliet at balcony			Strophe 1		
R. But soft …	1	125	Aa ⎤	viola/cello ⎤	
It is my lady, O it is my love!	10				A major
She speaks, yet she says nothing.	12	127	Ab ⎦	clarinet/cor anglais ⎦	
J. Ay me.	25				
R. O speak again bright angel …	26	146	B	'First subject': cello/horn; *pp*	C sharp minor to A major
			Strophe 2		
J. O Romeo, Romeo,…	33	155	Ab¹ ⎤	shorter, growing clearer and more sustained	A major
Take all myself.	49				
R. [listens]…shall I speak at this?	37	155	Aa¹ ⎦		
R. I take thee at thy word. [declares himself]	49	172	B¹	cello/viola with cor anglais/ bassoon: *ff*	C major
			SECOND SECTION: transition		
			Strophe 1		
J. What man art thou?	52	181	Ca	motif from Ab	C major to ⎤
R. I know not how to tell thee who I am:	53	205	Cb	cf. B	A major ⎦
			Strophe 2		
J. If they do see thee, they will murder thee.	70	220	Ca¹	shorter	A major to ⎤
R. Alack, there lies more peril in thine eye…	71	228	Cb¹		F sharp minor ⎦
			THIRD SECTION		
J. Thou knowest the mask of night…Fain would I dwell on form; fain, fain deny/What I have spoke.	85 88	250	D	'Second subject': flute/cor anglais	F sharp minor to ⎤
Dost thou love me?	90	264			A major ⎦
I know thou wilt say 'Ay',		266			
Yet, if thou swear'st,	91–2	267–8			
Thou mayst prove false.					
			Rondo		
			FOURTH SECTION		
J. In truth, fair Montague, I am too fond,	98	274	E	'Third subject' and Rondo theme (cf. B and D): violin	A major
But trust me, gentlemen,…	100				

Table 2 (cont.)

Balcony scene, II.ii.	line	bar		Scène d'amour, 3.124	
R. Lady, by yonder blessed moon...	107	280		—Episode 1: viola and cello	
J.R. [dialogue]		286	E¹	Rondo theme: violin/cello with clarinet/ bassoon	
J. I have no joy in this contract tonight:	117	292		—Episode 2: anxious dynamics	unsettled
...Sweet, good night.	120	300		firmer	dominant
This bud of love,...	121	304		growing	
May prove a beauteous flower...	122			violin in triplets	
Good night, good night.	123	307		pause	
R. O wilt thou leave me so unsatisfied?	125	308		inhibited rhythms	
J.R. [exchange of vows]	127–32	318		violin	modulating to tonic
J. My bounty is as boundless as the sea,	133–5	322	E²	Rondo theme: violin	A major
[same speech]		332	E³	Rondo theme: clarinet	A major
Nurse [calls within]	136	332		interruptions: violin	
J. Stay but a little, I will come again. [exit]	138	341	E⁴	Incomplete Rondo theme with first phrase prolonged: violin	A major
R. I am afeard...	139	340		cello added	
J. [returns]	143	350		pause: partial completion of Rondo theme	
J. If...Thy purpose marriage,...all my fortunes at thy foot I'll lay,	143–5 147	355		—Episode 3	into E flat major
N. [calls within]	149	358		—Episode 4: animez; agitato rhythms	modulating to
J. – But if thou meanest not well... ...leave me to my grief.	150–52	362	E⁵	Distorted Rondo theme: flute/oboe/ clarinet	B minor modulating
N. [calls within]	151	363		added string scales	to

Table 2 (*cont.*)

Balcony scene, II.ii.	line	bar		Scène d'amour, 3.124	
J. Tomorow I will send. A thousand times good night.	153–4	367	E⁶	Transformed Rondo theme (cf. B): full orchestra	dominant
[exit]	154	372–5		—Episode 5: *animez*	modulating to
R. A thousand times the worse…	155	373		cello/bass added	
J. [returns] Hist! Romeo, hist! I have forgot why I did call thee back	158 170	375	E⁷	Abbreviated Rondo theme: final phrases only, separated	A major
…Parting is such sweet sorrow.				by pauses	
[exit]	184				
R. Sleep dwell upon thine eyes,	186	382		Codetta	

Berlioz introduces his third subject, a new melody at first also in the soprano.

His third subject is not really new. It amalgamates phrases from both of the previous two and so is heard as fulfilment rather than resolution – an expressive effect underlined by the previous two's tonalities, which reach from different tertial relationships to the same home tonic of A major. The first three sections of the movement together therefore comprise an introduction-cum-exposition, whose principal themes, linked by a transition, are eventually synthesised, and whose function is not, as in the Classical model, to create oppositions, but to lay out a predestined course. To Berlioz, it might be said, the lovers were 'made for each other'. Having found each other, they wanted to stay where they were and didn't want to go anywhere else. All the new situation demanded was room for elaboration. Berlioz's musical metaphor here is a rondo, the rondo theme always coming back to the same thing (his third subject) yet always different, and, in the episodes, allowing for fresh discoveries.

It may be objected that the above presents a crassly literal and cold-blooded account of music that seems to behave spontaneously. Yet how else can its contents be explained? In any case, Berlioz obviously put his own gloss on the emotional substance of Shakespeare, simplified (the four questions and answers in the transition being reduced to two, for example) and altered the proportions (Shakespeare's extended coda being almost eliminated – there's no point in a musical coda when the music has been largely in the tonic). The conclusion to be drawn from the correspondences in Table 2 is not therefore that Berlioz's structure is naive, but rather that it is dramatic, that Shakespeare is musical, and that both derive from the same archetypal source.

In contrast to the *Scène d'amour*, *La Reine Mab* is the most conventionally designed movement in the symphony, a scherzo and trio, its style deriving from the opening sections of the scherzos in the *Eroica* and Ninth Symphonies and bearing a clear if generalised relationship with the contents of the Queen Mab speech. Or so it seems. On closer inspection, Berlioz's scherzo turns out to be as far removed from its models and as deeply influenced by the programmatic as are the other movements. The actual programme is spelt out in the *Scherzetto*. This paints a selective picture of Mab, emphasising the imaginative, the delicate, fleeting, colourful, entrancing, and drawing a veil over Mercutio's increasingly nasty descriptions of her person, equipment and various assignments. These latter are reduced from Mercutio's ten to three. Of the three, the first is adapted, the second authentic, the third freshly invented. Since Berlioz altered Shakespeare to this degree, it might perhaps have been expected that one of Mab's assignments would be of making Romeo dream about Juliet, and indeed the trio section almost sounds like that : its instrumentation, flute and cor anglais, is the same as for the 'second subject' (Juliet) in the *Scène d'amour*. But this section is in fact of Mab galloping 'through a page's brain, who dreams of a mischievous trick or a soft moonlight serenade from under the tower' – instead of Shakespeare's 'Through lovers' brains, and then they dream of love'. Her second assignment is through the soldier's neck; he dreams of 'cannonades, sharp thrusts [...] the drum! [...] the trumpet! [...] he wakes, and swears, and prays still swearing, then goes back to sleep and snores with his comrades'. Apart from the added sounds of drum, trumpet and the snoring, this is faithful enough. The last is of Mab making a young girl dream she is being dressed up and taken to a ball – a charming ending but nothing to do with Shakespeare.[34]

What this scheme of things provided, or rather was engineered to

---

34 Or at any rate nothing to do with 'This is the hag, when maids lie on their backs, / That presses them and learns them first to bear, / Making them women of good carriage'. In Deschamps' 1844 translation the 'maids' become a young girl: Mab 'lui fait entrevoir des mystères, qu'un jour / A son cœur ignorant dévoilera l'amour'. In his translation Shakespeare's 'lovers' are also changed – into a page who dreams of Berlioz's 'espiègles tours et propos amusants'. Berlioz's 'molles serenades' are allotted to a 'dame romaine'.

provide, was a radical modification of the scherzo and trio model in which the music is through-composed and does not stop and start – presumably to keep it in the air as it were. The first scherzo is all Mab: after an introduction (already a departure from the norm) in which she inspects her chariot and waggoner, she sets forth to a classically proportioned sentence, whose subsequent reductions, between episodes, from eighty to forty-four and then twenty-four bars, shift the focus from what she is to what she is up to, or, in musical terms, clears the air for the emergence of new themes in later sections. After the 'moonlight serenade' of the trio with its 'tower' lit up by violin harmonics (the 'mischievous trick' seems to have gone by the board – unless Berlioz was referring to the continuing Mab motifs in subtle gear-change, three- as opposed to four-beat pulse), Mab sets forth again and quickly arrives at the soldier. The horns' theme (fairy trumpets) of this second scherzo modulates from F to A flat and eventually breaks the four-beat pulse, so generating the momentum which leads to the movement's double climax – fanfares of battle, with added drum (bar 564), and the soldier waking up (bar 603), with the violas swearing on their C-strings (bar 609). He prays, modally if rather perfunctorily (bars 611–14), and Mab considers her last assignment with the young girl (bar 615), leaving him snoring on four bassoons (bar 631) and a horn (bar 641), most realistically and with his six-bar patterns oblivious to and rhythmically dissonant from the four-bar patterns of Mab above (see Example 5b). So begins Berlioz's coda.

A coda is not the place for new themes; yet he obviously wanted his to contain some novelty. His solution is to signal the episode of Mab dressing up the young girl for the ball with the new sound of antique cymbals ('which doubtless served in antiquity to point the rhythm of certain dances')[35] and with a motif (Example 5b) that appears new but is actually familiar and conclusive. This motif comprises both the canonic motif from *Le Ballet des ombres* and a transformation of the last phrase in both parts of Mab's principal theme – an extraordinary example of the integrating powers of genius. Then, Mab takes the girl to the entrance of the ballroom and inspects her appearance (bars 716–24, a tiny section deriving, cryptically, from the soldier's prayer and seeming to depict Mab tapping the girl's shoulders with a wand). And then, according to the *Scherzetto*, the cock crowed (bars 725–6), day broke and Mab sped off in a flash – which she does.

---

35 *Grand Traité d'instrumentation* (Paris, 1843) 274.

Example 5 (a) *Le Ballet des ombres*

(b) *La Reine Mab*, Coda

(c) *La Reine Mab* (from the principal theme)

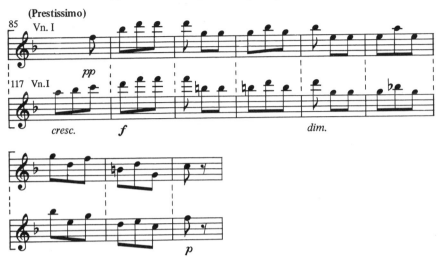

Garrick's justification for his 'Dirge' and funeral procession was Capulet's last speech in Act IV.v.84–90 (which he retained in his version, though it was omitted from the Odéon performances). It ends as follows:

> Our instruments to melancholy bells,
> Our wedding cheer to a sad burial feast;
> Our solemn hymns to sullen dirges change,
> Our bridal flowers serve for a buried corse,
> And all things change them to the contrary.

Berlioz's justification for his *Convoi funèbre* – the funeral procession and 'Dirge' were omitted from the Odéon performances – was doubtless more structural and stylistic. He wanted to effect a gradual transition from the spirit of delight reached in *La Reine Mab* to the stark tragedy of the denouement and in the process to prepare for the operatic style of the remainder of the symphony. As a result the narrative element in the *Convoi funèbre* is minimal, and Berlioz was spared the need to ask Deschamps to translate Garrick's lines 'Rise, rise! / Heart-breaking sighs / The woe fraught bosom swell; / For sighs alone, / And dismal moan, / Should echo Juliet's knell', etc. (which Deschamps later translated only too faithfully). Berlioz's text consists of little more than 'Jetez des fleurs'. Certainly he retained the programmatic, in such features as the choral and then instrumental tolling on one note derived from Le Tourneur (see p. 43), the irregular placing of the choral chants, the instrumental sobs, and the general effect of a procession approaching and receding, crescendo and diminuendo. But his principal brief was expressive and musical – a tortured fugue subject gradually accumulating lines and new harmonies, being allowed a relaxing episode and then intensified by stretto, until the texture flows into full choral harmony in the major, with the initial dispositions reversed. Thus Berlioz's introduction of his choral forces – until attention is re-directed for the last time to the orchestra.

This how Berlioz remembered the reunion of Romeo and Juliet in the tomb scene (the relevant phrases from Garrick are in square brackets):

A ce nom de Roméo, [I'll not wed Paris, – Romeo is my husband] qui s'exhale faiblement des lèvres de Juliette renaissante, le jeune Montaigu, frappé de stupeur, demeure un instant immobile : un second appel plus tendre [Oh my lord, my Romeo!] attire son regard vers le monument, un mouvement de Juliette dissipe son doute. Elle vit! il s'élance sur la couche funèbre, en arrache le corps adoré en déchirant voiles et linceuil, l'apporte sur l'avant-scène, le soutient debout entre ses bras. Juliette tourne languissamment ses yeux ternes autour d'elle, Roméo l'interpelle, la presse dans une étreinte éperdue, écarte les cheveux qui cachent son front pâle, couvre son visage de baisers furieux, éclate en rires convulsifs; dans sa joie déchirante, il a oublie qu'il va mourir. Juliette respire. [there's a sovereign charm in thy embraces that can revive the dead] Juliette! Juliette!... [Romeo's last words in Garrick] Mais une douleur affreuse l'avertit; le poison est à l'œuvre et lui ronge les entrailles!... 'O *potent poison!* [Berlioz here inadvertently quotes from *Hamlet*, V.ii.358] *Capulet! Capulet! grâce!*' [Capulet forbear – Paris, loose your hold] Il se traine à genoux, délirant, croyant voir le père de Juliette qui vient la lui ravir encore [...].[36]

[At the name of Romeo, escaping feebly from the lips of the reviving Juliet, the young Montague, dumbfounded, remains motionless an instant; a second, yet more tender call draws his gaze towards the monument where Juliet lies, dispelling all doubt. She lives! He dashes upon the funeral couch, snatches the beloved body from it, tearing the veils and the winding-sheet, and brings it to the front of the stage where he holds it upright in his arms. Juliet gazes languidly around her with her dim eyes, Romeo calls her by name, hugs her in a distraught embrace, smooths away the hair which is hiding her pale forehead, covers her face with mad kisses, is carried away with gusts of convulsive laughter; in his heartrending joy, he has forgotten that he is about to die. Juliet breathes. Juliet! Juliet!... But a dreadful pain alerts him; the poison is working and devouring his entrails!... He drags himself along on his knees, delirious, seeing, as he thinks, Juliet's father coming to snatch her away again.]

Considering this was written thirty-two years after Berlioz had seen the performance, it is astonishingly vivid (compare with the contemporary

36 *A Travers chants*, 358–9.

description given on pp. 40–41): to him the essence of the scene remained in those sudden, delirious embraces. Knowledge of Garrick's tomb scene does not however provide the whole answer to the unrevealed programme of *Roméo au tombeau des Capulets*.

Garrick removed the passage in which Romeo addresses the body of Tybalt; but apart from that, and a few other minor cuts, he preserved Shakespeare's text until Romeo kisses the drugged Juliet. The Odéon performances followed Garrick/Shakespeare, with the important difference that the episode with Paris was omitted. In Berlioz's second prologue it wasn't mentioned either. But the *Tombeau* movement is surely clear. The episode with Balthazar is cut. Romeo arrives (bar 1), 'More fierce and more inexorable by far / Than empty tigers or the roaring sea,' (V.iii.38–9) and wrenches open the tomb (bars 15–17). He encounters Paris and after 'three swift strokes' (as Berlioz describes it,[37] though his music gives four) kills him – and draws the sword out. (In Example 6 Berlioz's original barlines have been altered in order to illustrate his remarkable use of rhythm for expressive effect.)

Romeo surveys the tomb: dominant chords in C sharp minor, shading from trombones and horns, to wind, to strings. He sees three bodies: interposed, different chords, on trombones and horns, for each of them, Paris (bar 36), Tybalt (bar 40) – and Juliet (bar 44), where an added oboe

Example 6 *Roméo au tombeau des Capulets*

37 Cairns, 115.

links with Romeo's last dominant chord. In fact Romeo sees Juliet before Tybalt in Shakespeare; but if this interpretation of the music is allowed so will Berlioz's smooth transition. Romeo addresses Juliet: a long melody in C sharp minor – 'O my love, my wife, / Death that hath suck'd the honey of thy breath / Hath no power yet upon thy beauty' (V.iii.91–115); he drinks the poison (pause, bar 68), kisses her (rests, bar 70), and sinks to the ground.

This is the point at which the Garrick scene proper begins – Juliet recovering, and the entry of Friar Laurence therefore postponed. With a surge of energy Romeo stumbles to his feet, takes her hand and drags her towards him, wanting to flee the tomb together. The drowsy Juliet thinks at first that he is someone come to take her away to marry Paris; she suddenly realises who he is and they embrace wildly. Romeo is now losing his powers of speech and cannot support the reeling Juliet; but he is able to explain what has happened before he dies, his mind wandering and imagining that Capulet and Paris have come to take *him* away. Juliet faints over his body. The frightened Friar Laurence appears, as in Shakespeare quickly gives up his attempt to hide her away in a convent, and Juliet is left alone (now also as in Shakespeare) to try to suck poison from Romeo's lips before noises off drive her to stab herself with Romeo's dagger.

For this final part of the scene Berlioz depicts the recovery of Juliet with the melody of her awakening love from the opening of the *Scène d'amour*, altered minutely to absorb her fear of being taken away (*sforzando* accents, which dramatise the beauty of her last phrase as she recognises Romeo). Romeo's own recovery is graphically present in cellos and basses. The desperate passion of their embraces is as unmistakable as its subsequent disintegration – Juliet's realisation ('And did I wake for this!': ghastly echoes of the tolling funeral music) laid over Romeo's attempt to speak (trombones), her distraction (violins), his lurching to the ground, and death. With calculated certainty Juliet decides what she will do, and does it. Berlioz's focus is entirely on the lovers. Words are subsumed within action and emotion. Friar Laurence is dispensed with, as are the interruptions off-stage.

The electrifying impact of the *Tombeau* movement can be ascribed to the precision of Berlioz's musical narrative and its sheer presence. Yet by themselves these prescriptions are a recipe for incoherence and they hardly account for the phenomenon by which the music is so much more than it seems to be. The crucial question therefore is what is its impact if you have no idea of the programme? Berlioz himself evidently thought none (see p. 37). But the startling modernity of its style constitutes a vindication of its own. More relevant here is his shaping of the movement as a metaphor of its complex structural function – a turning-point marking the disintegration of the inner, orchestral line of the symphony's argument and the continuing rise of the outer, more operatic line. As for the latter, the changeable and almost visual gestural language and in particular the central instrumental 'Air' (as the *Invocation* might be called), which incorporates the only strictly new material in the movement, leaves no doubt that Berlioz is entering a new world of expression. At the same time he is concluding his existing one. Apart from the 'Air', the movement comprises a kind of recapitulation, in which the material does not reach an apotheosis but is wrenched askew, fragmented and then eliminated altogether. In the first Allegro, material from the *Introduction* is transformed; in the second, material from the *Grande Fête chez Capulet* (with a snatch from the *Prologue*), the *Scène d'amour* and the *Convoi funèbre* is transformed, extended and liquidated – in a sequence where the course of the symphony (or of the love of Romeo and Juliet) flashes past like a distorted echo.[38] Berlioz structures all this as two Allegros enclosing a largo, with slow bridge passages in between. The Allegros are in the same tempo but of vastly different lengths and textures, so that the fundamental effect is of an introduction to a slow, low, sombre and continuous melody which is answered by fast, high, feverish and disjunct thematic fragments – a profoundly satisfying if precarious equilibrium that creates its own finality.

It may be argued that after so final an ending to that part of his symphony Berlioz needed the injection of a new sound to enable it to continue. Thus perhaps one reason for the appearance so late in the work of his bass solo. At the same time it is surprising that Berlioz, the anti-clericist, should have chosen to give this role to Friar Laurence, inverting the character of Shakespeare's bumbling humanist who is eventually shown to be a coward, and turning him into a figure of pious rectitude. Maybe Berlioz's reasons for his new soloist, and for his radical alteration of Shakespeare's final scene, were in fact more straightforward and

---

38 The transformations can be seen in the following comparisons between earlier movements and the *Tombeau* movement. Bar 1 of the *Introduction* and bar 1; bar 129 (rhythm) of the *Grande Fête* and bar 90 (rhythm); bar 276 (melodic motif) of the *Scène d'amour* again with bar 90 (melodic motif); bar 48 of the *Prologue* with bar 96; bar 35 of *Nuit sereine* with bar 101; bar 146 of the *Scène d'amour* with bar 107; bar 126 of the *Convoi funèbre* with bar 158.

practical. He needed someone to explain things at the end, and the only other candidate, the Prince, would have been too quick-witted and authoritarian a character to have allowed him the room to develop an appropriately large-scale conclusion to the work.

In Shakespeare's final scene there are seven episodes. (1) Watchmen appear, discover the bodies, send for the Prince and families, and arrest Balthazar and Friar Laurence. (2) The Prince arrives with the families and demands to see the suspects. (3) Friar Laurence accepts that he is the prime suspect and at great length confesses the whole story. (4) Balthazar and the page confirm it. (5) The Prince says all are punished. (6) Montague and Capulet make peace, vowing to erect statues to Romeo and Juliet. (7) The Prince dismisses everybody in terms of solemn regret.

Garrick cut the first and fourth of these episodes, reduced the third and fifth, and altered the last to draw a moral, namely that Montague and Capulet have reaped what they have sown. Kemble's version of Garrick cut much more, and of course at the Odéon the scene was cut altogether. All this was no doubt what induced Berlioz to say that the 'final scene of the reconciliation between the families [...] has never been performed on any stage since Shakespeare's time' – though it hardly accounts for his imagining the last scene of his proposed *Romeo* opera as 'the solemn oath sworn by the warring houses [...] to abjure the feud' or, in other words, for what he actually wrote in his *Final*.[39] This is conditioned by the musical demands of a culminating tableau and is ruthless in its indifference to Shakespeare, from whom Berlioz 'took what he wanted, without permission'.

He wanted a dramatic scenario in which the chorus would be present sufficiently often to justify their eventual crowning of the whole work, and in which his bass soloist could in a similarly unhurried way be shown as integral. Thus his *Final* begins with the feuding families, a state of affairs that is never depicted in the last scene of the play, though Shakespeare does allude to it when Lady Capulet says 'all run / With open outcry toward our monument' (V.iii.191–2). Friar Laurence proudly recounts the full story and apostrophises Romeo and Juliet – a 'Récitative mesuré' and 'Air', the latter taking its cue from Shakespeare's sixth episode, the two together appealing to the families' sense of pathos. After this period of sentiment, action is called for. The Friar assumes the authority to command the families in the name of God to cease feuding. That they

39 Cairns, 114.

refuse to do so, despite threats of divine vengeance, enables Berlioz to recapitulate the opening of the whole work and so to dramatise his extraordinary change of direction. Friar Laurence suddenly switches from impotent rage to prayer. Whatever Berlioz himself may have thought of appeals to the deity, there is no doubting the aptness of his psychology here. The prayer (called 'Invocation' at the first performances) is answered by a miracle: the families' hate evaporates. And the music leads into the final 'oath of reconciliation'.

Whether Berlioz was the sole author of this scenario remains an open question, for Deschamps' translation of the play includes all the most extreme of the Finale's 'alterations' – the feuding families and versions of the *Air*, *Invocation* and *Serment*, though in a different order. There can be no doubt however that Berlioz's musical scheme and style quickly dispel any reservations about their place and function in the total design. The powerful sweep of the *Final* (even the *Air* and *Invocation* are through-composed) and its operatic realism are not simply the lineaments of a grand ending: they define the intimacy of the love story at the centre and allow its wider meaning to be absorbed. The real miracle of the *Final* is that the grandeur of its *Serment* also has regret in it.

So Berlioz did not betray Shakespeare. He paid him the compliment of showing how fruitful his work could be.

4

In the shadows of *Les Nuits d'été*

PETER BLOOM

> Allons la belle nuit d'été   (Alfred de Musset)
> ...cette délicieuse harmonie, pure, calme et sereine
> comme une belle nuit d'été...   (Hector Berlioz)[1]

In the shadows of Berlioz's *Nuits d'été* are persons, places, paintings and poems once a part of the richly textured fabric of its genesis, now obscured, in the musical world, by the brilliance of the aesthetic object, the enduring artistic entity itself. This is not always the case. Many listeners know something of the 'scandale' surrounding *Le Sacre du printemps*, for example, but nothing of its substance; many shudder at Schoenberg prior even to the sounding of the 'set'. It is my intention here to examine some of the paths that lead to and from a work whose prior reputation provokes no such aural paralysis for it is 'one of Berlioz's works to treasure most', in Hugh Macdonald's words, though one about which Berlioz himself was 'shy to the point of silence', the song cycle *Les Nuits d'été*.[2] I wish to consider not the orchestral version – frequently performed, often recorded, rather well known – but the original version for voice with piano accompaniment – rarely performed, rarely recorded, little known indeed. Not yet appreciated in historical context, not yet exhausted by the 'new Berliozians', it invites critical enquiry. In the six sections that follow, I consider in section I the question of the date of *Les Nuits d'été*; in II, I comment on the autograph manuscripts; in III, I

---

1 The quotation from Musset stands as an epigraph in Théophile Gautier's *Poésies* (Paris, 1830) 71. The phrase from Berlioz appears in his review of a concert given by former students of Alexandre Choron, in *Le Rénovateur*, 4 (17 March 1835) 1.
2 Hugh Macdonald, *Berlioz* (London, 1982) 125, 38.

outline the relationship between Berlioz and Théophile Gautier; in IV and
V, I take note of the reviews of the cycle and consider what they tell us of
the work's *raison d'être*; and in VI, I look more closely at the third song
of the cycle, 'Sur les lagunes', in the attempt to construct what Berlioz
might have called an 'admirative' critique.

I

The nineteenth-century French 'song', as opposed to the German Lied, is
a genre against which many hold a certain prejudice: ditties produced by
composers of the second rank to satisfy the demands of an increasingly
middle-class public for a music readily performable at home. The genre
surely deserves a second hearing: it was a vehicle for certain political
sentiments that in other guises might have been subject to censure; it was
a favoured outlet for the sometimes formidable creative energies of
women composers who did not compete in other musical arenas; and it
was the music of the people in the very real sense of the sounds many
Frenchmen thought of when they thought, if at all, of the art of music
itself.[3] I use the word 'genre' here because the distinctions between the
commonly employed terms 'romance' and 'mélodie' simply do not hold
firm. Schubert's Lieder were generally published in France in the early
nineteenth century as 'mélodies'; but Mendelssohn's celebrated 'Lieder
ohne Worte' became, in French, 'romances sans paroles'. Berlioz, who
made some forty contributions to the category, used both terms without
pedantic distinction.[4] The term 'mélodie', in principle, suggests an
element of musical seriousness that was lacking in the more light-hearted
and often sentimental 'romance'. This new seriousness was inspired by
the choice of more substantial poetry, of which there was a great flowering
from the Romantic generation in France. But for the musical term alone,
we might simply consider the title page of the first edition of Berlioz's
Opus 2: 'Neuf mélodies imitées de l'anglais (Irish Melodies) pour une et

3 See Ralph Locke, 'The music of the French chanson, 1810–1850'; and Austin Caswell, 'Loïsa
Puget and the French *Romance*'; both essays in Peter Bloom, ed., *Music in Paris in the Eighteen-Thirties* (New York, 1987).
4 His *Nuits d'été* were announced in the *Allgemeine musikalische Zeitung* as 'Gesänge
(balladenartig)' – ballad-like songs: 'Von Hektor Berlioz sind sechs Gesänge (balladenartig) für
Mezzosopran oder Tenor under dem Titel: Les nuits d'été erschienen, welche sehr gepriesen
werden. Bekanntlich hat Berlioz bis jetzt nur grössere, und zwar meist Orchesterwerke,
geschrieben'. *Allgemeine musikalische Zeitung*, 43 (1 September 1841) 718. Berlioz's earlier song
publications were obviously unknown to the writer of this notice.

deux voix, et chœur, avec accompagnement de piano/[...]/dédiées par les auteurs à Thomas Moore [...]'. The word 'mélodie', in this issue of 1830, is used in the primarily literary sense of a poetic text intended for recitation or singing.[5] It is partly for this reason, then, that Berlioz and his collaborator, Thomas Gounet, received equal billing as 'les auteurs', and, more important, it is for this reason that the phrase 'avec accompagnement de piano' was obligatory. When the second edition of these songs was published, in 1849, the word 'mélodie' had become widely understood in its purely musical sense: the phrase 'avec accompagnement de piano', now superfluous, was stricken. In fact, a leading French dictionary takes Berlioz's Irish Melodies of 1830 as the 'point of departure' for the new genre of *mélodie*.[6] The path eventually leads, ten years later, to *Les Nuits d'été*.

'Ten years later' takes us to 1840, the year during which these small compositions were conceived. Oddly enough, for a composer whose life is known in such precise detail, we cannot date *Les Nuits d'été* with greater exactitude. In his correspondence of 1840, Berlioz does not mention the work. The original autograph manuscripts of the songs are not dated. We know only that the titles 'Absence' and 'Le Spectre de la rose', the eventual fourth and second numbers of the cycle, appeared in the *Revue et Gazette musicale* on Thursday, 5 November 1840, as items on the programme of the concert, sponsored by that journal, to be given on the following Sunday, 8 November.[7] But when the journal appeared on Sunday morning, these two songs did not figure on the printed programme. From the detailed reviews of this concert that appeared in the *Revue et Gazette musicale* itself, and in the elegant magazine *L'Artiste*, reviews that discuss every item on the printed programme of 8 November, we can assert with confidence that the songs were not performed.[8] It is arguably the case that they were not performed because they were not yet written. There is one piece of evidence which suggests, however, that

5 In the dictionary appended to the second edition of *La Musique mise à la portée de tout le monde* (Paris, 1834), F. J. Fétis makes no mention of the 'mélodie' in his otherwise thorough treatment of the sub-categories of the 'air'.

6 *Dictionnaire de la musique*, ed. Marc Honegger (Paris, 1976) *s.v.* '*mélodie*'. None the less, when he offered to publish *Les Nuits d'été* in February 1856, J. Rieter Biedermann called the songs 'délicieuses romances' (*CG* V, 252).

7 *Revue et Gazette musicale*, 7 (5 November 1840) 519. This issue of the *Revue* is misdated: 'Jeudi', dated the 4th, in fact fell on the 5th.

8 *Revue et Gazette musicale*, 7 (12 November 1840) 539–40; *L'Artiste*, 2ème série, 6/20 (November 1840) 316.

Berlioz had indeed begun to set a series of poems by Théophile Gautier as early as March 1840: an autograph fair copy of the eventual first song of the cycle, 'Villanelle', now preserved in Darmstadt, in the Hessische Landesbibliothek.[9] This manuscript is signed and carefully dated 'Paris, 23 mars 1840'. It was reproduced some two and a half years later by the *Allgemeine musikalische Zeitung*, in the journal's intermittent series of facsimiles of composers' manuscripts, on 16 November 1842 – with the signature, but without the date.[10] Berlioz was not in the habit of putting precise dates on his autograph manuscripts; when he did so, it was sometimes after the fact, and inaccurately. The date of 23 March 1840 on the Darmstadt manuscript looks somehow suspicious to me, as though it were added to commemorate something important, I know not what, at the time he sent the manuscript off to Carl Ferdinand Becker, editor of the *Allgemeine musikalische Zeitung*, in 1842. Becker had good reason to reproduce Berlioz in November of that year: in the issue of the 16th, he printed an excerpt from Karl Gutzkow's *Briefe aus Paris* (Leipzig, 1842) which had just appeared, apparently with a splash.[11] Gutzkow was one of the important figures in the *Junges Deutschland* movement, one of the more faithful painters of the Parisian scene, along with his better-known contemporaries Ludwig Börne and Heinrich Heine, and one of Wagner's associates in Dresden in the 1840s; he writes in this excerpt of the dramatic contrast he finds between the mind and the music of Hektor Berlioz:

His brow lacks the imprint of daring enterprise and the smoothness of serene resolve, though it expresses rather nobly a pensive seriousness and a certain brooding, melancholy spirit. [...] To express the other-worldly harmonies that sound in his soul, he has been unable to find the right worldly technique, the right measure, the right notes.[12]

---

9 I should like to thank Dr Oswald Bill, of the Hessische Landes- und Hochschulbibliothek, Darmstadt, for providing me with information about this manuscript.

10 The *Allgemeine musikalische Zeitung* reproduction, by careful cutting and pasting, very subtly reduces the first six systems of Berlioz's manuscript to five – in order to allow for the printed title, 'Beilage No. 8 zur Allgemeine Musikalischen Zeitung 1842./Facsimile der Handschrift von H. Berlioz'. The rest of Berlioz's manuscript is reproduced with absolute fidelity. (In the modern reprint of the *AmZ* [Amsterdam, 1966], the Berlioz facsimile is erroneously bound after col. 176; it should follow col. 928.)

11 See J. Dresch, *Gutzkow et la Jeune Allemagne* (Paris, 1904).

12 *Allgemeine musikalische Zeitung*, 44 (16 November 1842) col. 925. Was the paper on which Berlioz copied 'Villanelle' – three single sheets sewn together, of a size and watermark ('GFJ') unknown elsewhere in his œuvre – sent to the composer, in 1842, for the express purpose of facsimile reproduction? It is, after all, not immediately evident how the *AmZ* facsimile was made, for in 1842, photography was in its infancy, and not yet used for making copies of

In March 1840 Berlioz himself had no reason to make the kind of careful fair copy of 'Villanelle' that later served the editor of the *Allgemeine musikalische Zeitung*. He did in that month have time for small-scale composition: he wrote nothing for the *Journal des débats* between 17 March and 12 April of that year; and for the *Revue et Gazette musicale* he reviewed only the orchestral concerts at the Conservatoire (on 12 and 29 March and 9 April). He had finished *Roméo et Juliette* in September 1839 and would not receive the commission for the *Symphonie funèbre et triomphale* before April 1840. I conclude, then, that the Darmstadt manuscript was prepared in the autumn of 1842, shortly before its facsimile reproduction, and that the date inscribed on it of March 1840 represents Berlioz's best recollection of the moment at which he had composed the song. Furthermore, the title of the work as a whole – Berlioz's, not Gautier's, and thus a bit of evidence by no means too obvious to consider – may tell us something of the season of its main composition. In any event, the only certainty as to the date of completion of the entire cycle, *Les Nuits d'été*, is provided by the date of publication of the first edition, for voice and piano.

It is, of course, not easy to establish with precision the dates of many kinds of nineteenth-century French publications. Literary scholars often have recourse to the *Bibliographie de la France* – and this did have, as well, a regular section for artistic productions, including music. *Les Nuits d'été*, however, figures nowhere in that semi-official periodical. Berlioz's publisher, Adolphe Catelin, seems not to have bothered to advertise his client's newest collection. Catelin had had dealings with Berlioz since 1836, bringing out a number of his songs, the piano reduction of the cantata *Le Cinq Mai*, and the full score and parts of the overture *Le Roi Lear*. In a letter of 9 November 1840, Berlioz chastised Catelin for not advertising his works, saying that after all, 'the public cannot divine their existence'![13]

Like many French publishers of the period, Catelin in the early 1840s

---

manuscripts. It is my assumption that the facsimile was produced by the process of transfer lithography, which requires special ink and special paper. These materials were readily available in Paris, of course, since the city was home to hundreds of lithographic shops and to the printing business in general; but given the high cost of fine quality paper at the time, Berlioz might have appreciated receiving the necessary materials from abroad, and free of charge.

13 'Le public ne peut pas le deviner' (CG II, 664). When Simon Richault took over Berlioz's publications from Catelin, in 1843, he did place an advertisement that included *Les Nuits d'été* in *La France musicale* of 26 November 1843.

kept changing addresses; for a time, had more than one.[14] From a plate number near to that of the Berlioz, it can none the less be established that *Les Nuits d'été* appeared no later than August 1841.[15] Indeed, though no advertisements have been found, *Les Nuits d'été* is mentioned in the *feuilleton* of the *Allgemeine musikalische Zeitung* of 1 September 1841.[16] More important, a review of the collection appeared in Paris as early as 4 July 1841, in the capital's leading music journal.[17] I shall say a word about the substance of this review below. Here let me note simply that the author was Berlioz's friend, the pianist-composer Stephen Heller. Though it is likely that Heller was working from an advance edition of the score and thus logical to conclude that the Catelin edition appeared in the mid-summer of its title, in July 1841, it is at least possible – since the publisher is not mentioned in the review – that he had only Berlioz's autographs before his eyes.[18]

II

Let me follow these comments on the dating of *Les Nuits d'été* with a word about the autograph manuscripts, five of which are to be found in the Fonds du Conservatoire of the Bibliothèque Nationale.[19] The sixth was sold at Sotheby's in 1947 and is listed in the *New Berlioz Edition* as untraced.[20] I was pleased to locate it in the little-explored music collection of the Fondation Martin Bodmer, in Cologny, near Geneva, Switzerland.[21] These autographs, undated, tell us nothing of the precise moment of composition. But they do suggest something of the order of composition, and they do, as always, offer fascinating glimpses of the composer in the

14 See Cecil Hopkinson, *A Bibliography of the Musical and Literary Works of Hector Berlioz*, 2nd edn, ed. Richard Macnutt (Tunbridge Wells, 1980) 194–5; and Hopkinson, *A Dictionary of Parisian Music Publishers* (rpt., New York, 1979) 23.

15 The plate number of the Berlioz is Ad.C. 872. Plate number Ad.C. 841, for a 'Menuet dans les bois' by Alexis Roger, is listed in the *Bibliographie de la France* of 28 August 1841. The *Bibliographie de la France* is useful, of course, for only a *terminus ad quem*; the arts listings in particular were not always up to date.   16 See note 4.

17 *Revue et Gazette musicale*, 8 (4 July 1841) 328–9.

18 A copy of the Catelin edition preserved in the Bibliothèque Nationale carries the dedication: 'A. M. St. Heller, témoignage d'amitié et d'une vive admiration pour son grand et noble talent. H. Berlioz' (Musique, Rés. F. 1432 [27]). The orchestral indications in pencil on Heller's copy of 'Villanelle' are, I think, in spite of the opposite assertion in the card catalogue of the Département de la Musique, *not* in Berlioz's hand.

19 Musique, mss. 1179 ('Villanelle'); 1180 ('Absence'); 1181 ('Le Spectre de la rose'); 1182 ('Barcarolle' ['L'Ile inconnue']); 1183 ('Au Cimetière. Clair de lune').   20 *NBE* 13, 122.

21 I should like to thank M. Braun, curator of the collection, for his kindness during my visits to the Fondation Bodmer.

workshop. The five Paris manuscripts are all of the same twenty-four-staved paper carrying the embossed octagonal emblem of Dantier fils, the man from whom Berlioz began purchasing materials in 1838.[22] The Geneva manuscript – 'Sur les lagunes', the eventual third song of the cycle – is of larger, thirty-staved paper, embossed with a somewhat different emblem from the same dealer. The Paris manuscripts (each a separate bifolium) are numbered at the tops of the first pages of their respective bifolia, and while the titles of the poems are written out, the name of the poet is not. The Geneva manuscript, on the other hand, is headed 'Lamento/Paroles de Th. Gautier'. From this admittedly limited evidence, it is my supposition that the initial project included four songs: 'Villanelle', No. 1 (I follow the numbering of the Paris manuscripts); 'Absence', No. 2; 'Le Spectre de la rose', No. 3; and 'Barcarolle' ('L'Ile inconnue'), No. 4. 'Au Cimetière' ('Clair de lune') is numbered with a 6 in the Paris collection, but by a different hand, or at a different moment. The Geneva manuscript – without number, with the poet's name – would seem originally, if only for a short while, to have been conceived for separate publication. It was not long, apparently, before Berlioz decided to make a six-song compilation, or 'recueil', as he later called it, keeping 'Villanelle' as overture, removing the coda, 'Barcarolle', from fourth to sixth position, and arranging the interior songs in what became their definitive order. Such rethinking, however rapidly it might have taken place, provides strong evidence, in my view, that the work (whose original version, let us not forget, was presumably to be performed by only one singer) may be viewed as a 'cycle' – that is, as a grouping together of songs that unfolds in a fashion that is to be heard as logical from the point of view of both poetic discourse and musical continuity.[23]

Two further comments on these scores: in his authoritative catalogue of Berlioz's autograph musical documents, D. Kern Holoman calls the Paris manuscripts 'autograph fair copies'.[24] My examination suggests, from placement and penmanship, that 'Reinschrift' is a fair description of 'Le Spectre de la rose' and 'Barcarolle'; but that the other manuscripts are 'Urschriften', carefully corrected with paste-overs for subsequent use by the publisher. And – the point is unrelated – whereas the manuscript of 'Le Spectre de la rose' is headed 'Andante un poco lento e dolce assai', a

---

22 See D. Kern Holoman, *The Creative Process in the Autograph Musical Documents of Hector Berlioz* (Ann Arbor, 1980) 98.

23 This question is considered in detail in the article in the present volume by Julian Rushton. Berlioz spoke of his 'recueil' to Baron von Donop, in 1858 (CG V, 602).   24 Holoman, 220–31.

later album leaf with the opening nine bars of this song was simply marked 'Adagio' by the composer.[25] The slower marking may well represent his definitive conception of its tempo – the result of having heard the song in performance.

III

In order to enter the mainstream of history, the poet Wilhelm Müller needed Franz Schubert, *Die schöne Müllerin* and *Winterreise*. Théophile Gautier needed no such help from Berlioz. In fact he rose to prominence on the shoulders of Victor Hugo, to whom he was introduced by Gérard de Nerval in 1829, for whom he organised the claque at the famous première of *Hernani* in 1830, and with whom he was closely to associate in the literary world, though always as a junior partner, for more than forty years. It was most likely at the 'bataille d'*Hernani*', on 25 February 1830, or shortly thereafter, that the flamboyant nineteen-year-old poet, whose 'Opus 1' (*Poésies* [Paris, 1830]) went on sale on 28 July of that year, met the 'enfant terrible' of the musical world, who was writing the winning Prix de Rome cantata at the Institut de France at precisely the same moment, during the three-day revolution at the end of July. Berlioz speaks relatively little of Gautier in his letters; and in Gautier's recently published *Correspondance générale*, the first three volumes of which take us to 1848, there is similarly little mention of the composer of *Les Nuits d'été*.[26] It is none the less apparent, from the letters which do exist, that the two had many interests in common and that, while they had little occasion to correspond in writing, they saw each other frequently: two working journalists who found criticism 'pénible' while raising the genre to new levels of perfection.

Gautier was probably among those who came to Berlioz's lodgings in Montmartre in 1835 for the grand celebration of his son Louis' first birthday; Louis Berlioz's mother, Harriet Smithson Berlioz, was long admired by the young writer; and in his *feuilletons* that appeared regularly in Emile de Girardin's new, inexpensive and thus for the first time widely circulating newspaper, *La Presse*, Gautier – no doubt with cues and clues from the composer – regularly praised Berlioz's concerts

---

25 Bibliothèque Nationale, Musique, ms. 382. On this sort of discrepancy see the article in the present volume by Hugh Macdonald.

26 Théophile Gautier, *Correspondance générale*, ed. Claudine Lacoste-Veysseyre (Geneva, 1985 [I], 1986 [II], 1988 [III]).

and compositions. When the popular song composer Hippolyte Monpou died suddenly in 1841, at the age of thirty-seven, Gautier praised him as 'Le Berlioz de la Ballade'; when Berlioz himself died, Gautier prepared a long and laudatory article for the *Journal officiel*, an article shortly thereafter reprinted in his celebrated *Histoire du Romantisme* (Paris, 1874). For Gautier, Berlioz was 'the most literary musician in existence'; he formed, with Victor Hugo and Eugène Delacroix, the great trinity of French Romantic art.[27] For Berlioz, Gautier was surely a poet of moonlight, melancholy and, to paraphrase Henry James, a clear and undiluted strain in the minor key. In 1844, when Gautier was negotiating a new contract with Alexandre Dujarier, owner of *La Presse*, he said that he was, after all, the journal's Jules Janin (drama critic), Etienne Delécluze (salon critic) *and* Hector Berlioz (music critic).[28] In 1847, when Berlioz was engaged by the half-mad impresario Louis-Antoine Jullien as conductor of the concerts at the Drury Lane Theatre, in London, he requested a new ballet scenario from Gautier, whose excellent reputation in the genre had been earlier created by *Giselle* (1841). Gautier prepared a scenario, based on Goethe's *Wilhelm Meister's Apprenticeship*, but with the demise of Jullien's enterprise, the project – for which Berlioz himself was presumably *not* going to compose the music – came to naught. Apart from this non-venture, their only artistic collaboration occurred with *Les Nuits d'été*.

In fact, 'collaboration' may not be the appropriate word. Gautier left Paris for Spain on 5 May 1840 and returned to the French capital five months later, on 7 October. He and Berlioz could have spoken about the settings before Gautier's departure, in March or April, if not months, or even years earlier, and it is my assumption that they did. In August 1837, Victor Hugo wrote a note to Berlioz which introduces 'some lovely verses that a young poet, my neighbour, has written for you and asked me to send along'. The neighbour in question may well have been Gautier; the verses, some of those later set as *Les Nuits d'été*.[29] Apart from this letter, however, from which one can draw no definitive conclusion, there is no document that attests to Berlioz and Gautier having worked actively together.

As to Gautier's way of working with musicians, however, documents there are. A number of his poems were written expressly for musical

27 Gautier, *Correspondance générale* I, 271 n.; III, 298; and III, 119n.   28 *Ibid.*, II, 195.
29 Hugo's note is printed without precise date in CG II, 311–12. To Katherine Reeve I am indebted for the information that this letter is postmarked 3 August 1837, and that the Hugo specialist Jean Gaudon identifies the 'young poet' as Gautier.

setting, including the 'Barcarolle' that eventually became the finale of Berlioz's cycle. This poem, drafted in 1834 for the composer Allyre Bureau, was several times revised by Gautier before its definitive publication in 1838 in the collection *La Comédie de la mort* (Paris: Desessart, 1838) – a collection to which Berlioz would surely have been attracted by the irony of the title alone,[30] and from which he would make his own selections in 1840.[31] For Bureau, the first musician with whom Gautier collaborated, the poet drafted what he called his 'chanson' in two ways, with and without refrain; he told the composer to use the version he thought the more suitable for musical setting.[32] Gautier was later more explicitly 'liberal' with his friend François Bazin (winner of the Prix de Rome in music in 1840), to whom he sent a poem with the following advice: 'treat my poetry as you wish; if something [in the text] displeases you, I shall change it. I am sending it in two versions, with and without refrain. You choose. And write to me if you have any other particular

---

30 Berlioz once quipped, after all, that the *Dies irae* was a 'jolly refrain' (*Les Grotesques de la musique*, 311). The title of Berlioz's *Les Grotesques* (1858) may well have been inspired by Gautier's *Les Grotesques* (1844).

31 The title of the first edition of *La Comédie de la mort* (1838) applies to the long, two-part poem that opens the volume ('La Vie dans la mort', pp. 13–37; 'La Mort dans la vie', pp. 39–84). There follow, with no overall title, some fifty-seven poems, unnumbered. For musical setting, Berlioz chose [No. 27] 'Le Spectre de la rose'; [No. 28] 'Lamento. La Chanson du pêcheur'; [No. 38] 'Absence'; [No. 44] 'Lamento'; [No. 45] 'Barcarolle'; [No. 56] 'Villanelle rythmique'. It is noteworthy that Berlioz's selection includes two 'pairs' of poems, Nos 27–8 and 44–5, and that the final ordering of his song cycle follows Gautier's – except for the removal of 'Villanelle' from last position to first. It is as though Berlioz warmed gradually to the idea of making musical settings as he read progressively through Gautier's volume, and began to compose – as he did the music of *Les Troyens* – with the 'scene' towards the end that inspired him the most.

32 'Tu prendras celle que tu trouveras la plus favorable à la musique'. Gautier, *Correspondance générale* I, 42–3. It may be from the date of Bureau's setting of 'Barcarolle', 1834, that the notion arose of Berlioz having begun to compose *Les Nuits d'été* in that year. This notion, as far as I can tell from the published letters and autograph manuscripts, has no basis in fact. It is true that three or four of the six poems eventually selected by Berlioz appeared prior to the 10 February 1838 publication of *La Comédie de la mort*: 'Barcarolle', in 1834; 'Le Spectre de la rose' (in the magazine *Don Quixote*, on 7 May 1837; 'Villanelle rythmique' (written for Xavier Boisselot and set by him – according to a note on the autograph manuscript [Bibliothèque Nationale, Musique, ms. 4383] – in 1837); and 'Lamento', which, according to René Jasinski, ed., *Poésies complètes de Théophile Gautier* (Paris, 1970) I, lv, appeared in 1837 under the title 'Sur la mer', with music by Hippolyte Monpou. (I have been unable to find a copy of this song in the collections of the Bibliothèque Nationale.) However, if Berlioz were responding to something *earlier* than the 1838 edition, he would probably not have entitled the eventual sixth song of his cycle simply 'Barcarolle' – as he wrote on the autograph manuscript. The original title of Gautier's poem (1834) was 'Le Pays inconnu'; when it first appeared in print (1835) its title was 'Mirage (Barcarolle)'. Both earlier titles are more colourful and suggestive and thus more likely to have been used by Berlioz than the one-word title of Gautier's 1838 edition. See Spœlberch de Lovenjoul, *Histoire des œuvres de Théophile Gautier* (Paris, 1887) I, 77–9. Let it be noted here that a nearly complete manuscript of *La Comédie de la mort* had existed since 1835, when the title was announced in the catalogue of the publisher Renduel. Gautier continued to modify and correct this manuscript until its publication in 1838. (See Jasinski I, vi.)

musical idea to which my poetry might be adapted'.[33] When he sent a poem to Meyerbeer, in the spring of 1839, Gautier went so far as to indicate the scansion of the text, dividing the lines into poetic feet and showing the long and short syllables of each – something rarely done in French poetics, where analysis is based on syllable count and on the rhythm and intensity of the line as a whole. To the German composer, Gautier added: 'If you find this pattern acceptable, I shall try to improve the verses while maintaining the present form. If you would prefer some other metre, please let me know. I have maintained a rigorous symmetry in these lines; if they are not yet worth much as poetry, they are, I think, appropriate for musical setting'.[34]

From these examples – one could give more – it is clear that Gautier did not belong to that group of poets whom Berlioz considered completely lacking in musical sensibility.[35] On the contrary, Gautier was well aware of what he called the 'double exigencies of poetry and music';[36] he was willing to adapt his poetry to the needs of the musician (though he generally wished to do the adapting himself); and unlike Goethe, who preferred music that in no way challenged the supremacy of his verses, Gautier saw the *mélodie* as a mutually creative venture. It is for this reason, no doubt, that so many composers, including Bizet, Fauré and Duparc, found inspiration in the poems of *La Comédie de la mort*.

Of the fifty-seven poems in his collection, sixteen were sooner or later set by one or more composers during the nineteenth century. 'Villanelle', written expressly for Xavier Boisselot,[37] was set by Berlioz and at least

33 'Agissez à votre aise avec ma poésie; si quelque chose vous gêne je le changerai. Je vous l'envoie de deux manières: avec refrain et sans refrain. Choisissez. Ecrivez-moi si vous avez quelque idée particulière où ma poésie puisse s'adapter.' Gautier, *Correspondance générale* I, 248.

34 'Si cette forme vous convient je tâcherai d'adjuster des vers un peu mieux tournés que ceux-ci sur les longueurs que je vous envoie – si toute autre mesure vous agrée davantage faites-moi savoir. J'ai mis une grande rigueur de symétrie dans ces lignes et si elles ne valent rien encore comme poésie je les crois favorables à la musique' (*ibid.*, I, 146). See also the facsimile of this letter, after p. 366. (It seems that Meyerbeer never made a setting of Gautier's poem 'Josué arrêtant le soleil'.) Berlioz, of course, would not have needed (or appreciated) any such *monstre* (the marvellous French word for a schematic outline). Indeed, in another context, he remarked, 'plutôt que d'altérer le rythme musical, il vaut mieux gêner un peu la marche de la poésie'. See his letter to Ferrand of 16 May 1834 in CG II, 183.

35 CG II, 285: 'Hugo s'attend à un grand succès, il juge la musique comme tous les poètes, c'est-à-dire que le sens de cet art lui manque complètement'. For a further appreciation of Gautier's 'très-grande sensibilité musicale', see Ernest Reyer, *Notes de musique*, 2nd edn (Paris, 1875) 408–13.

36 *La Presse* (11 December 1839) – Gautier's review of Berlioz's *Roméo et Juliette*.

37 Boisselot and Gautier were colleagues at the newspaper *La Charte de 1830* in 1837–8. Berlioz had known Boisselot (who married Lesueur's second daughter in 1833) since his student days. Boisselot's review of the première of *Benvenuto Cellini* (*Revue et Gazette musicale*, 5 [16 September 1838] 569–72) is admirable (and admiring of the work). Berlioz was to return the

twenty-three others.[38] 'Le Spectre de la rose' was set by eight others; 'Sur les lagunes', by twenty others; 'Absence', by sixteen others; 'Au Cimetière', by only three others; 'Barcarolle', by eighteen others. Two further poems from *La Comédie de la mort*, entitled 'Romance' and 'Les Papillons', were set by eleven and twenty-one composers respectively. These dry-as-dust statistics tell us that, except for 'Au Cimetière', Berlioz chose poems that were or became widely considered appropriate for musical setting. Indeed, they lead us to ask (since he was doing what everybody else was doing, or would do) why he didn't set 'Romance' and 'Les Papillons' as well as, or instead of, 'Au Cimetière'.

A partial answer is provided by our knowledge of Berlioz's own thoughts about composing a *mélodie*, or *romance*, expressed most succinctly in a letter to a fashionable journal whose editor had asked him to set a poem by Léon Guérin. Writing on 10 October 1834, Berlioz turned down the editor's request, saying (if I may translate loosely) that 'the character of each couplet [of the poem] would require a different music – something that would make the dimensions of the piece simply incompatible with those of a work appropriate to your journal'. 'Furthermore', he adds, 'I am at the moment so busy that I simply do not see how I could find an entire day and devote it exclusively to this little composition'. And he concludes with a credo: 'Such things ought really to be *improvised*, so to speak, and when one fails [to find the appropriate setting] on first encountering the poem, in my opinion one really ought to abandon the effort' (my emphasis).[39]

Here, then, is indirect evidence of Berlioz's presumably immediate attraction to Gautier's poetry. We have no evidence, however, as to why Berlioz selected the title of 'Nuits d'été' for his collection, though he may have desired a summer publication, and he may simply have found the expression euphonious and appropriate to the theme of melancholy

favour in his review of Boisselot's opera *Ne touchez pas à la reine*, in the *Journal des débats* (24 January 1847).

38 Mme J. Bernard, J. Baudot, H. Bizalion, Allyre Bureau, M. Barty, A. Canivet, A. Coedès, G. Costa, Duprato, E. Durand, G. Gragerolle, Ed. Garnier, E. Gautier, Vicomte de Kervéguen, C. Lefebvre, Ernest Louis, Ed. Pascal (four versions), Ch. Poisot, Th. Radoux, F. Raynal, H. Réber, J. De Riu, M. Weckerlin. These names, and the numbers given in the text, may be found in Spoelberch de Lovenjoul, *Histoire* (see note 32).

39 'Le caractère de chaque couplet exposerait une musique différente, ce qui donnerait alors à ce morceau une extension incompatible avec les formes qui conviennent à votre journal. Je suis en outre tellement occupé en ce moment, que je ne saurais comment faire pour disposer d'une journée entière et la consacrer exclusivement à cette petite composition. Ces choses-là doivent être pour ainsi dire improvisées, et quand on ne réussit pas de prime abord, mon avis est qu'il faut y renoncer' (*CG* II, 203). To Liszt, in 1836, he spoke again of the recalcitrance of his muse for such 'petites compositions' (*CG* II, 412).

longing that runs through these poems. One must assume that considerations of euphony were likewise important to his choice of titles for the six individual songs: Gautier's 'Villanelle rythmique' became Berlioz's 'Villanelle'; 'Le Spectre de la rose' was unchanged by the composer; what for Gautier was 'Lamento. La Chanson du pêcheur' became Berlioz's 'Lamento' (in the Geneva manuscript) and 'Sur les lagunes. Lamento' (in the printed edition); 'Absence' remained unchanged; Gautier's second 'Lamento' was entitled 'Au Cimetière. Clair de lune' by the composer (though the second part of Berlioz's title seems to have been an afterthought). For the final song of the collection, Berlioz used Gautier's title, 'Barcarolle', in the manuscript, but changed it to 'L'Ile inconnue' in the printed edition. It is furthermore possible – the point is of no small significance – that some of these emendations ('Sur les lagunes'; 'Au Cimetière'; 'L'Ile inconnue') were made by the composer with a view towards inspiring the scenic imagination of the artist who might eventually be charged with making title-page illustrations which, as the reviews of the day make abundantly clear, were objects of appreciation equal in importance to that of the songs themselves. Unfortunately, *Les Nuits d'été* appeared from Catelin, and later from Richault, with neither engraved portraits nor lithographed vignettes. Those by Louis Boulanger and Barathier that grace the Boieldieu jeune edition of Berlioz's *Le Montagnard exilé* (1823) and the Schlesinger edition of *Neuf Mélodies* (1830), for example, to say nothing of the later ones by Frédéric Sorrieu and Georges Staal that enhance the Richault editions of Berlioz's *La Captive* (1849) and *Sara la baigneuse* (1850), provide a treat for the eye that some might find as delightful as the music inside.[40]

IV

I have earlier mentioned the review of *Les Nuits d'été* that appeared in July of 1840 in Maurice Schlesinger's *Revue et Gazette musicale* over the signature of Stephen Heller. (Heller, whom Berlioz had met in 1838, was later to become one of the composer's closest friends.) This is the only contemporary review of the collection I have been able to find. In the *Journal des débats*, Joseph d'Ortigue would write at length of Berlioz's songs on the occasion of the publication of *Tristia*, in 1852.[41] These

40 Many of these illustrations are reproduced in Adolphe Jullien, *Hector Berlioz, Sa vie et ses œuvres* (Paris, 1888). See the 'Table des gravures', pp. 381–4.
41 *Journal des débats* (1 July 1852).

reviews provide us with important information about the work and its *raison d'être*. From Heller's article, a spirited defence of Berlioz's work in general, I should like to quote only two sentences: 'In effect', wrote Heller, 'could anything have been easier for Berlioz than to write some of those insipid and perfumed melodies sought out by singers who are "à la mode" and their fashionable clientèle?' (Heller uses the English word 'fashionable', which was fashionable in French at the time.) 'But Berlioz has never wanted to dishonour his art', Heller goes on; 'he venerates it as a sacred object, and with religious zeal pays it homage with his most profound thoughts'.[42] From d'Ortigue's article, rather less defensive, rather more analytical, I cite the following lines: 'Several of these mélodies have been orchestrated, after the fact, by the composer. I say "after the fact" and you can easily see why. Monsieur Berlioz's musical imagination is constantly nourished by orchestral timbres. One will perhaps say to him, do for all what you have done for [some – that is, orchestrate them]. For my part, I would not be pleased, for I prefer the simplicity of the initial inspiration to the embellishment, though fully genuine, of the second thought. *Parvoque potentem*'.[43]

It is generally assumed that aside from 'Absence', orchestrated by Berlioz for performance by his then mistress, Marie Récio, in 1843, the other five songs of *Les Nuits d'été* were orchestrated shortly prior to publication in 1856. D'Ortigue's remark allows for the possibility that more than 'Absence' had been orchestrally 'embellished' by 1852, if not before.[44] As for the thrust of his comment, that the voice and piano version has an inspirational freshness worth preserving, it is of course not to be underestimated, in spite of the historical appreciation with which Berlioz's orchestration has been favoured. Berlioz himself implied, as D. Kern

---

42 'Rien lui serait-il plus facile, en effet, que d'écrire aussi des mélodies fades et parfumées, telles que recherchent les chanteurs à la mode et leur fashionable clientèle? Mais jamais Berlioz n'a voulu déshonorer son art, il le vénère comme chose sacrée; et c'est plein d'un zèle religieux qu'il lui consacre le tribut de ses meilleures pensées.' See note 17.

43 'Plusieurs de ces mélodies [he mentions five of the six songs] ont été instrumentées après coup par l'auteur; je dis après coup, et cela se conçoit: la pensée musicale de M. Berlioz est sans cesse bercée par les timbres d'orchestre. On lui dira peut-être de faire pour toutes ce qu'il a fait pour *le Pâtre*, *la Captive*, *Sara la baigneuse*, *l'Absence*. Pour mon compte, j'en serais fâché, et je préfère la simplicité du premier jet à l'embellissement, quoique très réel, de seconde main. *Parvoque potentem*' (see note 41). The Latin quotation here (from the *Aeneid* VI, 843) may be rendered 'and be a master through small things'.

44 See also item 15 in Berlioz's letter to the members of the Académie des Beaux-Arts, 6 March 1851, in *CG* IV, 37: '*Les Nuits d'été*, six morceaux de chant avec piano; *quelques uns* avec orchestre' (my italics).

Holoman puts it, 'that the orchestration of a work occurred subsequent to what [he] believed to be its completion'.[45] In prompting d'Ortigue to write something about his collection of songs, Berlioz said that he wanted 'only that their existence be known, that they are not shoddy goods, that [the composer] in no way has *sales* in mind, and that these "petites compositions", which have nothing formally or stylistically in common with Schubert's, require for proper execution singers and pianists – *musicians* – of consummate artistry'.[46] He would later commit the same notion to print:

The unfortunate thing about salon compositions such as these [praiseworthy songs by Jakob Rosenhain] is that to play the piano part you need a pianist, and to sing the voice part you need a singer. And – what makes the composer's requirements even more obviously intolerable – this pianist and this singer must both be *musicians*.[47]

For Berlioz, then, small-scale compositions required more than small-scale musicianship. 'Parvoque potentem' indeed.

V

Are we to believe Berlioz when he says of his songs that they were not *commercially* inspired? Some publishers at the time – Catelin was one – seem to have existed on such publications; their stable of composers was presumably fed as well by such staples of the repertory. What other reasons might Berlioz have had for departing from his passion for the grandiose and taking up a genre in miniature? Beyond Ian Kemp's suggestion that the work 'must be regarded simply as a characteristic product of the Romantic temperament',[48] I should like to try out five possible specific reasons for Berlioz's undertaking *Les Nuits d'été* for voice and piano in the spring of 1840.

45 See Holoman, *The Creative Process*, 173. The title page of 'La Belle voyageuse', for example, published separately by Richault, would seem to confirm this: 'Musique de Hector Berlioz; instrumentée pour orchestre par l'auteur'. It was only natural that Berlioz himself, after orchestrating *Les Nuits d'été*, would embrace the new version (see CG V, 602).

46 'Je veux seulement qu'on sache qu'ils existent, que ce n'est point de la musique de pacotille, que je n'ai point en vue *la vente* et qu'il faut être musicien et chanteur et pianiste consommé pour rendre fidèlement ces petites compositions, qu'elles n'ont rien de la forme ni du style de celles de Schubert' (CG IV, 150–51 – a letter to d'Ortigue dated 5 May 1852).

47 'Le malheur des compositions de salon telles que celles-ci, c'est que pour en jouer la partie du piano il faut un pianiste, et pour en exécuter la partie du chant il faut un chanteur. Et, ce qui rend plus manifeste et plus intolérable encore l'exigence de l'auteur, il faut que ce pianiste et ce chanteur soient tous les deux musiciens' (*Journal des débats*, 25 November 1854).   48 NBE 13, xi.

(1)   He wished to write something for a particular singer whom he admired. As in literature, where so many fictional characters are modelled on friends and acquaintances of the author, here, too – and especially in vocal music, characteristic performers may be 'inscribed' into the characteristics of a score. The Catelin publication of 1841 is marked for mezzo-soprano or tenor, but Berlioz – a self-described 'second-rate baritone' but a practised vocal coach[49] – surely had a preference for the former: Marguerite, in *La Damnation de Faust*, is a mezzo; so, too, are his greatest heroines, Cassandra and Dido, in *Les Troyens*, to say nothing of Béatrice, in *Béatrice et Bénédict*. In July 1840 Berlioz criticised the hiring practices of the management of the Opéra by saying that 'if [at this theatre] there continue to be [...] only super-high sopranos, with no medium or lower registers, then I think it will be necessary to give up passionate scenes and dramatic music entirely'.[50] Gautier, too, favoured the lower female voice, which he praised in his 1847 poem 'Contralto', probably written for his long-time mistress, the contralto Ernesta Grisi. The Paris manuscripts of *Les Nuits d'été* specify no vocal type, but the Darmstadt fair copy of 'Villanelle' is carefully marked 'Mezzo Soprano'.

Berlioz's ideal mezzo was Pauline Viardot (1821–1910), who was only nineteen years old in 1840 but who was even then recognised by connoisseurs as an artist. Meyerbeer would soon suggest that she be engaged by the Opéra, and Berlioz (who in 1838 called her a 'diva manquée', though more for her repertory than for her vocal resources) would later consider her one of the greatest artists in the history of music.[51] The reigning mezzo at the Opéra at the time was Rosina Stoltz (1818–1903), who created the role of Ascanio in the 1838 production of *Benvenuto Cellini* (and who created a stir after 1840 as the mistress of the new director of the Opéra, Léon Pillet). It may be that Berlioz's relations with Stoltz were on the wane at the time of *Les Nuits d'été* – and personal relationships, to say nothing of romantic attachments, were obviously of no small consequence in the artistic world at the time. Cornélie Falcon

49 See Cairns, 36; and *CG* II, 699.
50 'Ma foi! s'il n'y a plus à l'Opéra que des *soprani* sur-aigus, sans *medium* ni cordes graves, je crois qu'il faudra renoncer à la musique de caractère et aux scènes passionnées' (*Journal des débats*, 19 July 1840).
51 See Meyerbeer, *Briefwechsel und Tagebücher*, III, ed. Hans and Gudrun Becker (Berlin, 1975) 312; *CG* III, 531; and Berlioz's review of Meyerbeer's *Le Prophète* in the *Journal des débats* of 20 April 1849. In 1838 one reviewer called her voice a 'mélange de soprano et de ténor'; in 1839 Gautier called her 'une étoile à sept rayons [qui] a fait briller sa charmante lueur virginale'. See Yvette Sieffert-Rigaut, 'Pauline Viardot: femme et artiste', *Romantisme*, 57 (1987) 18, 19, and the article in the present volume by Joël-Marie Fauquet.

PETER BLOOM

(1814–97), who sang the first performance of the orchestral version of Berlioz's *La Captive* in 1834, was also a leading mezzo of the period and, according to Berlioz, the repository of the current Opéra director's hopes for success.[52] One must of course also mention the apparently mediocre mezzo who became Berlioz's second wife, Marie Récio. But she seems not to have appeared on the scene – at least that of the Opéra – until 1841, well after the composition of *Les Nuits d'été*. Indeed, the archives of the Opéra clearly indicate that Récio was hired on 9 October 1841; her contract was terminated on 8 September 1842, when she left Paris, for Brussels, with Berlioz. In these eleven months she sang in the Opéra's productions of Rossini's *Comte d'Ory* and Donizetti's *La Favorite*.[53] That so little is known about this 'devoted and intelligent woman' who, though ungraciously excluded from the *Mémoires*, shared some twenty years of the composer's life, 'never for a day ceasing to lavish upon her husband the most tender and delicate attentions', is one of the real lacunae of modern Berlioz scholarship.[54]

(2) He wished to write something for a particular concert in the spring of 1840. We have already noted the scheduling of two of the songs for performance in November. (Berlioz had earlier directed another concert sponsored by the *Revue et Gazette musicale*, on 6 February 1840.) Perhaps he had in view a performance at one of the soirées offered in the spring of that year at the Palais Royal by the Duc d'Orléans. Berlioz had had regular contact with the royal family since the early 1830s, and like many other artists of the time, including Théophile Gautier, he was especially fond of this duke – that is, Ferdinand-Philippe, King Louis-

---

52 See *CG* III, 635.

53 See Archives Nationales, AJ[13] 229 and 308; Archives de l'Opéra, AD 60 (632) (27 August 1842) and PE 3 (699), pp. 212, 230. Pierre Citron's assertion that Marie was not a 'regular' employee of the Opéra (*CG* III, 11, note 3) is incorrect. She was engaged with an annual salary of 1,328 francs, and was paid 110.66 francs per month, plus 'feux' of seven francs for each performance in which she participated (usually eight per month). In September 1842 she received her salary, but no 'feux', and was accorded a one-month terminal leave, to 8 October. The September payment records for Marie are marked 'dernier payment [*sic*]', though when she returned her costumes on 11 November 1842, she received a further payment of 29.44 francs.

The moment at which Marie appeared 'on the scene' of Berlioz's *life* is simply not clear. When he later wrote to his son Louis in order to justify his marriage to Marie, he said that he could neither live alone nor abandon the person who had been living with him for fourteen years: 'je ne pouvais ni vivre seul, ni abandonner la personne qui vivait avec moi depuis quatorze ans' (*CG* IV, 596). This letter was written on 26 October 1854; read literally, it means that Marie had been living with him since sometime in 1840. (Was he already thinking of her when he suggested in 1840 that the Opéra should hire other than super-high sopranos?)

54 The quotation is from the obituary that appeared in *La France musicale* on 22 June 1862. In Eduard Hanslick's *Aus meinem Leben* (Berlin, 1894) I, 57, Marie is referred to as Berlioz's tight-fisted financial manager; Berlioz himself called her his '*homme* d'affaires' (*CG* V, 30).

Philippe's eldest son and the heir to the throne of France. Indeed, the Duc d'Orléans attended a performance of Berlioz's major work of the year 1840, the *Symphonie funèbre et triomphale*, and shortly thereafter accepted the dedication of the published score. The possibility of music by Berlioz having been performed at one of these soirées is thus real, since the programmes, often featuring some of the most celebrated artists of the capital, ranged from *romances* to quartets by such luminaries as Beethoven and Baillot.[55] (The Duc d'Orléans' accidental death on 13 July 1842 was a national calamity; he had been popular with all groups of society.) There were, of course, numerous chamber music concerts in 1840 in the salons of Erard, Herz, Pape, Bernhardt, Richter, Petzold, Couder and others who had the requisite room and riches. Such soirées, however, though he clearly liked the beverage, may not have been Berlioz's cup of tea.[56]

(3) He wished to write something for reasons of friendship: his colleague Gautier was going off to Spain, and Berlioz wished artistically to say farewell. (Gautier, like Berlioz, was to travel widely during his career, something rather unusual for a Frenchman. Was this *Wanderlust* an important element of their friendship?) More plausible, he wished to embody in music an emotional farewell to his wife, Harriet Smithson, who by 1840 was becoming increasingly dependent, isolated, prone to illness, sensitive, frustrated, resentful and demanding.[57] Perhaps he wished simultaneously to commit to music his new feelings for Marie Récio: that oddly specific date on the Darmstadt manuscript might even be the date of their first encounter – though as I have stated, the chronology of her employment at the Opéra suggests otherwise. Furthermore, for Berlioz,

55 Precise information about the specific music played in the salons is difficult to obtain. See Joël-Marie Fauquet, 'Les Salons', in *La Musique à Paris en 1830–1831*, ed. François Lesure (Paris, 1983) 123–4; and Jean Mongrédien, *La Musique en France des Lumières au Romantisme* (Paris, 1986) 237–43.

56 One of the regular participants in such soirées at the time (and another figure in the shadows of *Les Nuits d'été*) was the pianist Jakob Rosenhain, who came to Paris in 1837 and who was active there for some thirty-three years. On p. 2 (recto) of the Paris autograph of 'Villanelle', Berlioz signed the manuscript ('H. Berlioz') and the pianist wrote: 'Manuscript [*sic*] de H. Berlioz/Paris 1852. J. Rosenhain'. On p. 2 (verso) of the Geneva autograph of 'Lamento', Berlioz wrote 'C'est à Mr Rosenhain'; and the pianist wrote, 'Autographe de H. Berlioz/donné par lui à J. Rosenhain/Paris 1852'.

Berlioz, who had a high regard for Rosenhain's artistry (see the *Journal des débats of* 27 March 1851 – 'un de nos plus habiles pianistes' – and of 25 November 1854, mentioned in the text above and in note 47), gave these manuscripts to Rosenhain, perhaps after the evening of piano trios (of which Rosenhain wrote several) at Berlioz's home in late December 1852 (CG IV, 244). None the less, though his name figures on two of the autographs, Rosenhain seems not to have been in Berlioz's mind when he composed *Les Nuits d'été*.

57 See Peter Raby, *Fair Ophelia. A Life of Harriet Smithson Berlioz* (Cambridge, 1982) *passim*.

life imitated art more often than the reverse: like Wagner, who pursued an affair with Mathilde Wesendonk because he was artistically consumed (in *Tristan*) with the idea of love, Berlioz, too, may have found in Gautier's poems the expression of a kindred aesthetic, and subsequently, in Marie, albeit briefly, a kindred soul. Finally, one must seriously consider the possibility that Berlioz's thoughts were directed in the amicable if not amorous direction of the dedicatee of the printed edition of *Les Nuits d'été*, Louise Bertin, poet, composer and member of the influential family that long supported Berlioz's musical endeavours.

(4) He wished frankly to make some quick, cold cash. Berlioz had lifelong financial problems. To the dismay and embarrassment of his middle-class family, these problems were sometimes emphasised by those who wrote about the composer, including Gautier, in the daily and weekly press. In 1841 Berlioz wrote to his sister that 'la grande musique' was ruining him.[58] Perhaps he wished to recoup his losses with some potentially remunerative music that was 'petite'. But the publisher of *Les Nuits d'été*, Adolphe Catelin, was in marketing neither inventive nor aggressive. He went out of business only two years later. Furthermore, the Berlioz of the *Mémoires* was never in the music business for profit: his regard for the sanctity of art – explicitly mentioned in Stephen Heller's review of the song cycle – was surely genuine.

(5) He wished to demonstrate that he was essentially a 'normal' composer – normal, that is, in the sense of one prepared not only to moderate his means, but also to submit to the supremacy of 'words', and in so doing, to recognise or acknowledge a desire to 'entertain'. To me, this would seem to be a primary reason for Berlioz's attention to song in 1840. For more than ten years, ever since the premières of the overture to his first opera, *Les Francs-Juges*, in 1828, and, of course, of the *Symphonie fantastique*, in 1830, he had been considered an oddity, an exception, a fantastic extremist. Throughout his career, but particularly in the autumn of 1840, when he organised a 'festival' at the Opéra, the first of its kind, Berlioz was reviewed in the press as a noise-maker and a madman. In October, the satirical *Charivari* launched repeated diatribes against him. And in November and December, the *Revue des deux mondes*, a most respectable journal, treated Berlioz with a no-holds-barred viciousness. Vindictive reviews and what we would consider to be libellous personal attacks in the press were not limited to Berlioz, of course; Balzac, for one, suffered more than his fair share. Furthermore, in the same year, one of

58 *CG* II, 685.

the most thoughtful contemporary journalistic analyses of any work by Berlioz appeared in the socialist newspaper, *La Phalange*, from the pen of the aforementioned Allyre Bureau, the violonist-composer who was one of Gautier's close friends and who, after playing an active role in the Revolution of 1848 (as well as the violin at the Théâtre Italien), finished his days in the utopian socialist colony at Kellum Springs, Texas. Bureau wrote that Berlioz is a composer 'whom France would do well to glorify rather than to have fun degrading and diminishing as much as possible. I suppose', he said, 'that we are waiting until after he is dead to discover that he just possibly had a touch of genius'.[59]

These reviews, positive or negative, were personally or politically inspired. That is to say, they were prepared directly on the nudging of those who knew the critic or the object of his notice, and were in a position to tender thanks for services rendered. Or they were motivated by envy, by competition, by clique-ism. No opinion expressed in nineteenth-century French newspaper print was unprimed: 'critics' ideologies, and more specifically their political attitudes and personal acquaintances played a singularly important role in aligning them "for" and "against" an artist'.[60] This is the overmastering message of the newly published correspondence of Théophile Gautier; it is the message of some of the letters of Berlioz published for the first time in the latest volumes of his *Correspondance générale*; it is the message Karl Gutzkow conveyed to German readers in his *Letters from Paris* of 1842, when he said that it is impossible for a critic in Paris 'to be completely independent, or, what is the same thing, to be completely honest';[61] and it is a message of which one is constantly reminded in the France of the 1990s as well: life and culture are and always have been 'politicised' in France to a degree difficult for Americans, for example, to imagine or accept. The great cultural philanthropist in France has long been the government, the administration, 'officialdom'. (As a French journalist remarked recently, 'L'Administration y fait toujours la pluie et le beau temps'.) In the nineteenth century, it was not 'grants' for the arts that the government was handing out, but rather indemnities or administrative posts, sinecures and the like, which permitted artists to work much, if not most, of the time for themselves. (Dumas was librarian at the Palais Royal; Nodier

---

59 'Berlioz est sans contredit une belle et puissante organisation; c'est un compositeur dont la France ferait mieux de s'enorguellir que de s'amuser à le détracter et à le rapetisser autant que possible. On attend sans doute qu'il soit mort pour trouver qu'en effet il pouvait bien avoir quelque génie.' *La Phalange* (1 January 1840) 16.

60 David Bellos, *Balzac Criticism in France* (Oxford, 1976) 189.   61 See note 12.

was librarian at the Arsenal; Musset was librarian at the Ministry of the Interior; Berlioz was librarian at the Conservatoire; in 1868 Gautier became librarian for the Princess Mathilde. Filling out book orders and catalogue cards was for none of these men a primary occupation.) Notices in the press, with the potential they offered of reaching 'les dames du grand monde', as Berlioz called them,[62] and a host of others in high places,[63] were crucial: the talked about were on the road to success. We must try to read those notices against a political backdrop, and with political questions – the force of central authority – in mind.

With *Les Nuits d'été*, Berlioz's detractors were now asked to reconsider.[64] This is the purport of Stephen Heller's review – a review whose content, we can be certain, was prompted, if not dictated, by the composer. 'Do not accuse Berlioz of conspiring against the rules of art', wrote Heller. 'He does not work according to a system; he is neither an abolitionist nor a blind slave bound to ancient theories. Pre-eminent in his work is inspiration: he listens to what he thinks; he paints what he feels.'[65] Joseph d'Ortigue opened his review with irony:

---

62 *CG* II, 722.

63 Such as the Ministry of the Interior. Indeed, the notices in the press were sometimes *dictated* by the Ministry of the Interior. To give but one example: in a note to Eugène Scribe, Jules de Wailly – an official in that ministry – says that he has asked J. E. Duchesne (Berlioz's occasional replacement as arts columnist for the *Journal des débats*) to include in a forthcoming article a comment Scribe himself hoped to have published. 'M. Duchesne [...] est un de mes meilleurs amis [...]: vous pouvez donc être bien sûr que ce sera fait, et bien fait'. (Bibliothèque Nationale, Manuscrits, N.a.fr. 22552; the letter is undated, but the postmark, barely legible, seems to indicate 1845.)

64 Indeed, as early as 1830, when Berlioz's first efforts in the genre of song appeared (the *Neuf Mélodies*), his first important critic, F. J. Fétis, did precisely that: 'Nous ne pouvons que féliciter M. Berlioz de ce qu'il entre dans un système mélodique beaucoup plus gracieux dans cet ouvrage que dans ces autres compositions. Il y a du charme dans ce recueil de mélodies, et l'on voit clairement que M. Berlioz n'a qu'à vouloir pour entrer dans une route naturelle, la seule qui conduise à des succès durables'. *Revue musicale*, 7 (6 March 1830) 160.

65 'N'accusez donc pas Berlioz de conspirer contre les règles de l'art. Il ne travaille pas d'après un système; ce n'est ni un démolisseur, ni un esclave aveugle des vieilles théories; ce qui préside à ses œuvres, c'est l'inspiration: il s'écoute penser, et peint ce qu'il sent.' See note 17. Heller later returned to this theme when he recalled telling Berlioz he wanted too much: Berlioz despised the larger public, yet sought its admiration! 'Mon cher ami, vous voulez trop avoir, vous voulez avoir tout. Vous méprisez le gros public et vous voulez cependant être admiré de lui. Vous dédaignez les applaudissements de la foule, – c'est votre droit d'artiste à l'esprit noble et original, – et cependant vous en avez l'appétit ardent.' See 'Une Lettre de Stephen Heller sur Berlioz', *Revue et Gazette musicale*, 46 (1879) 73.

Heller's defence of Berlioz should be seen in the light of one of the major musical issues of the spring of 1840, the prominence of Donizetti's music at four Parisian theatres and Berlioz's public resentment of it. Replied Donizetti (in a letter to a friend, dated 20 April 1840): 'everyone is laughing and everyone is whistling [at Berlioz's music and articles]. I alone feel compassion for him...he is right...he has to avenge himself'. Cited in William Ashbrook, *Donizetti and his Operas* (Cambridge, 1982) 147.

'What?' some will say, 'Monsieur Berlioz has composed *mélodies*? How odd indeed!' Yes, Monsieur Berlioz has indeed composed *mélodies*, even *romances* – agreeable, pure, tender, majestic and melancholic, they express with truth and nobility a particular state of mind. […] Whatever opinion one may have of the poetic talents of Monsieur Théophile Gautier, one cannot deny the richness of his imagery and his feeling for form, manifested in vivid colours and a prodigiously instinctive vocabulary, the one reflected by the other. Nothing of this – image, tone, form, reflection – has escaped the composer […].[66]

VI

Let us turn to one of the poems of Gautier set by Berlioz and test the validity of d'Ortigue's assertion. From the syllable count and rhyme scheme of 'Lamento. La Chanson du pêcheur' (printed here in the Appendix), it is readily apparent that this poem, by no means an exception in the collection from which it comes, maintains a three-stanza structure of absolute regularity – something Gautier obviously felt was appropriate for song composition. Indeed, the third line of the third stanza explicitly invites musical setting, using that fashionable word 'romance' as bait. Most notable here, in a text whose vocabulary is simple and whose imagery is transparent, is the thrice-given refrain with the graceful assonance and alliteration of the words 'sort', 'sans', 's'en' and 'sur'. These were lines and sounds to give flight to the composer's imagination. As a point of comparison we may look at the setting of this poem made by Berlioz's younger contemporary Félicien David, a setting published several months prior to Berlioz's, in December 1840[67] (see Example 1). The setting by David, not without interest for its 'ad libitum' treatment of 'Que mon sort est amer!', is purely and unimaginatively strophic; Berlioz's is through-composed with an expressive refrain. David's choice of the key of G minor may be appropriate, but the tempo marking, 'poco allegretto', in $\frac{6}{8}$, seems a shade too dance-like for what is, after all, a lament. Berlioz's setting is likewise in $\frac{6}{8}$ metre; so is the later, F minor setting (1870) by Charles Lenepveu, marked 'andantino'. Charles

---

66 'Comment! diront quelques-uns, M. Berlioz a donc fait des *mélodies*? c'est fort singulier!… Oui, Messieurs, M. Berlioz a composé des *mélodies*, des *romances* même: ce sont des chants suaves, purs, tendres, fiers ou mélancoliques, qui expriment avec noblesse et vérité une certaine situation de l'âme. […] Quelque opinion que l'on se forme du talent poétique de M. Th. Gautier, on ne saurait contester à cet écrivain la richesse des images, un sentiment de la forme qui se manifeste par un coloris très vif, un instinct prodigieux des mots et de la manière dont ils se reflètent les uns dans les autres. Rien de tout cela, images, coloris, formes, reflets, n'a échappé au compositeur.' See note 41.

67 David's 'Lamento' was listed in the *Bibliographie de la France* on 2 January 1841.

Example 1   Félicien David, 'Lamento. La Chanson du pêcheur'

- mours. Dans le ciel, sans m'at - ten - dre, El -

- le s'en re - tour - na; L'an - ge qui l'em - me-

na Ne vou - lut pas me pren - - dre.

Gounod's E minor setting (1872) is also in compound metre ($^{12}_{8}$) and is marked 'lento'. Like David's, Berlioz's setting (marked 'andantino') is in G minor, the only song of *Les Nuits d'été* in the minor mode. In the published cycle it follows in logical harmonic order from the close in D major of the previous song.[68] Berlioz's 'Lamento' is built upon a recurring motif – an ostinato, or, one might even say, a leitmotif; this is Berlioz's musical response to Gautier's haunting poetic refrain, 'Ah, sans amour, s'en aller sur la mer' and the embodiment of the 'expression passionnée' of which the composer later spoke, in the Post-Scriptum of his *Mémoires*, as one of the chief characteristics of his music.[69] The leitmotif occurs some fourteen times in the piano part; though echoed in the vocal line, it occurs there literally only twice – at 'pleure, pleure' (bars 57–8), one of the few words of the original poem repeated by the composer, and at the final sigh, 'Ah', another Berliozian textual addition and a dramatic touch that is both fitting and lovely.

The linear half-step motif is presented as a sustaining of the fifth degree of G minor briefly inflected by the (flattened) sixth. In the course of the song the sustained D functions variously as the fifth, third (major and minor) and root of a triad.[70] 'Sur les lagunes' is a member of that

---

68 In the orchestral version, the harmonic change from 'Le Spectre de la rose' to 'Sur les lagunes' – from B major to F minor – seems more a disjunction than a progression.
69 *Mémoires*, 561.
70 Its most subtle occurrence is at 'Sous la tombe elle porte/Mon âme et mes amours' (at bars 9–16 of the score); to describe this passage with the Roman numerals of functional analysis would be to bury Berlioz's smooth progression under strained verbiage.

privileged group of movements, or moments, controlled by a systematically repeated gesture that by its very strictness calls attention to all that is free and imaginative in Berlioz. This expressive scenario – something of a restrained lyrical response to, if not a reaction against, the German tradition of motivic development – is used to sublime effect in the septet in Act IV of *Les Troyens*, which is linked to the love duet that follows, in G flat major, by the insistent oscillation of the fifth and flattened sixth degrees of F major. It was used by Berlioz as early as 1834, for the tolling of the evening bells in the Pilgrims' March of *Harold en Italie*; it was used again in the Funeral March of the dramatic symphony, *Roméo et Juliette*; and it was used in what is the true forerunner of the compositional procedure employed in 'Sur les lagunes', the Offertorium of the *Requiem*, which won for Berlioz the 'priceless approval' of Robert Schumann: 'This Offertorium', said Schumann to the composer, 'surpasses everything'.[71] The choral psalmody here, which Berlioz called a 'chorus of souls in Purgatory',[72] surely has a direct bearing on the significance, for the composer, of the ostinato in 'Sur les lagunes'. The significance would likewise be similar to that of Juliet's *Convoi funèbre*, whose ostinato Berlioz also called a psalmody: it is a kind of religious significance, suggested by the 'heavens' and 'angels' of Gautier's poem, which adds the deity to the typically Romantic constellation of night, death and love that motivates this lamentation on the soul of the departed lover.

At the end of 'Sur les lagunes' we are left poised on the dominant, longing until 'infinity' for our 'belle amie'. Only on one other occasion did Berlioz end a movement with such an obviously unresolved harmony – in *La Harpe éolienne. Souvenirs*, the instrumental movement from *Lélio ou Le retour à la vie*, the sequel to the *Symphonie fantastique*, revised in 1855.[73] The poetic, or dramatic, circumstances there are similar, and there, as in the song, Berlioz reworked the ending with particular care. Indeed, for 'Sur les lagunes', there are even slight differences between the corrected autograph and the first edition, suggesting further adjustments to the ending in proof.

Chopin and Schumann essayed unresolved endings in certain multi-sectional works (e.g. the Prelude in F major from Op. 28; and 'Bittendes Kind' from *Kinderszenen*), and in this case, as in those, the technique of

---

71 *Mémoires*, 350 ('me valut un suffrage inestimable, celui de Robert Schumann'); and Cairns, 243 and n.   72 See Holoman, *The Creative Process*, 259.
73 On this movement, see Peter Bloom, 'Orpheus' lyre resurrected: A *Tableau musical* by Berlioz', *The Musical Quarterly*, 61 (1975) 189–211.

avoiding closure – in a sense the most obvious of all representational practices of the Romantic era in music – signals the composer's larger structural conception. I have earlier suggested, on the basis of differences among the Paris and Geneva manuscripts of *Les Nuits d'été*, that 'Sur les lagunes' was separately composed and subsequently incorporated into the six-song collection published in 1841. It is on the one hand logical to assume that the decision to end this song on the dominant was a part of the larger determination to publish the six songs in what became their final, progressive arrangement as – there is no other word for it – a 'cycle'. On the other hand, *this* ending on the dominant is not as expectant, or anticipatory, as others. The seventh degree of the final chord is not present. The chord, with the third in the tenor register,[74] has a life of its own. Its 'yes and no' quality, which might well have prompted the exquisite closing of the slow movement of Mahler's Fourth Symphony, for example, is as expressive as it is vague; its message could be one of irony, or of hope, or of despair.

Indistinct and ambiguous though it may be, there *is* none the less a message here, which filters through the works of artists as diverse as Carl Wilhelm Kolbe the Younger, E. T. A. Hoffmann, Lord Byron, Eugène Delacroix, Casimir Delavigne and Gaetano Donizetti. Let me be precise: that lovely, incantatory line, the line that encapsulates the gloom of life in the shadow of death and thus a quintessential element of Gautier's collection – 'Ah, sans amour, s'en aller sur la mer' – did not come to Gautier simply from the recesses of his poetic imagination. It is in fact a translation of the first two lines of what is apparently an old Venetian verse:

Ah! senza amare,	Ah, without love,
andare sul mare,	to wander on the sea,
col sposo del mare,	with the spouse of the sea,
non puo consolare.	is no comfort to me.

This verse was inscribed on the frame of a painting by C. W. Kolbe that was exhibited in Berlin in 1816; the painting and the story it represents is the subject of a tale by E. T. A. Hoffmann called 'Doge und Dogaresse' ('The doge and the dogess'), a tale first published in 1818 (and subsequently incorporated into *Die Serapions-Brüder*), a tale that first appeared in French translation in the Parisian newspaper *Le Globe* in July 1829. The doge in question is the historical figure of Marino Faliero, who

---

74 The Geneva autograph shows a flirtation, abandoned, with the third in the lower register.

is likewise the subject of the drama by Byron that was published in 1820 and played in Paris, in French, in 1821, at both the Comédie française (in verse) and the Théâtre de la Porte Saint-Martin (in prose). Byron's drama in turn inspired Delacroix's famous painting of 1826, 'The execution of Marino Faliero'; and it inspired the tragedy by Casimir Delavigne, published in 1829 as *Marino Faliero*. Finally, the play by Delavigne served Emanuele Bidera when he prepared a libretto for an opera of that title by Donizetti, to be given in Paris at the Théâtre Italien, in 1835.

It is obvious, then, that the subject – the arrogant old doge who is executed for breaking with his patrician class and favouring 'the people'; the aged aristocrat who is married to the young and beautiful daughter of one of his former comrades-in-arms – was in the air. The obscure relationships among these many transformations of the legend and the historical reality are not the province of the present study. (I leave intertextuality and 'the anxiety of influence' to the famous Bloom – Harold.) Suffice it to say that for Byron and for Delacroix, the high tragedy of the political figure is pre-eminent – and the wife of the doge remains faithful. For Delavigne, the wife of the doge succumbs to a young lover and later asks her husband's forgiveness just prior to his execution. For Bidera and Donizetti, it is simply not clear whether the young lovers consummate their guilty passion.[75] For Hoffmann, the love intrigue takes precedence: the wife of the doge returns the affections of her youthful admirer but remains faithful to the old man until his demise. Then, in a kind of pre-Wagnerian 'Liebestod', the lovers are united – only to have their gondola swallowed up by a storm that arises in the aftermath of the doge's execution. The lovers are drowned in revenge by what is, of course, the metaphorical and traditionally 'real' wife of the doge, the sea.

It is earlier, while riding with the doge in the channel before St Mark's Square, that the dogess hears 'the notes of a soft male voice, gliding along the waves of the sea', and singing the verses 'Ah! senza amare, andare sul mare' – 'Ah, sans amour, s'en aller sur la mer'.[76] In Hoffmann, these verses crystallise the young woman's emotions: it is upon hearing them that she feels the anguish of the lovelessness of her marriage to the doge and the temptation of lust for her handsome young admirer.

75 See Philip Gossett, 'Music at the Théâtre Italien', in Bloom, *Music in Paris*, 347. In 'Les Martyrs ignorés', Balzac has a character praise Byron for having Faliero's wife remain faithful, and criticise Delavigne for having her poison the old man's final days with the admission of her infidelity. See *La Comédie humaine* (Bibliothèque de la Pléiade; Paris, 1981) XII, 731.
76 See Hoffmann, *Weird Tales*, trans. J. T. Bealby (New York, 1928) 57.

We know that Théophile Gautier was familiar with these lines from Hoffmann's tale.[77] We know that Berlioz devoured Hoffmann when the tales first appeared in French in 1829.[78] Furthermore, he knew the play by Byron; and he might well have seen both the Delavigne and the Delacroix.[79] He reviewed the Donizetti in March 1835 and said of the subject that it was too well known to require retelling.[80] The sea, finally, had always been the image of his dreams.[81] We may safely assume, then, that Berlioz took up these lines – not a tale of a doge, but an encapsulation of the emotions of a dogesse – with a full awareness of their historical, poetic and musical resonance.

In 'Sur les lagunes', with its musically open-ended conclusion and its ostinato so effortlessly demonstrating 'the complex character and function' of only one note, achieving a myriad of expressive possibilities with a miraculous economy of means, Berlioz, in what I have called a privileged moment, reveals 'something of the inner process of Romanticism itself'.[82] He begins with a text that calls itself a 'romance'. But instead of doing with it what a 'normal' composer might have done, and in spite of what I believe was the primary reason for turning his attention

---

77 In *Partie carrée* (1851), Gautier quotes the line: 'La chanson vénitienne, dans son admirable mélancolie, dit qu'il est triste de s'en aller sur la mer sans amour. C'est vrai et c'est beau; l'amour seul peut remplir l'infini' (Paris, 1914; 226). It should be noted here that 'Ah, sans amour' is not the only 'borrowed' phrase in Gautier's collection. Indeed, the expressions 'la vie dans la mort' and 'la mort dans la vie', the titles of the main poems in the book, occur in Balzac's *Physiology du mariage* of 1829. See David G. Burnett, 'A Study of Selected Poems from La Comédie de la mort' (Ph.D. diss., Indiana University, 1973) 115.

78 'Hoffman [*sic*], ses *Contes fantastiques* m'ont beaucoup plu' (28 December 1829); 'Avez-vous les *Contes Fantastiques* d'Hoffmann? C'est fort curieux!' (2 January 1830). One of Berlioz's close friends in 1929–30 was Richard, a translator of the *Contes*. See CG I, 293, 301, 348.

79 Based on the execution scene from Byron's play, and exhibited at the salon of 1827. 'La foule se passionnait pour ce tableau'. See Hugo, 'Exposition de tableaux au profit des Grecs: la nouvelle école de peinture', in *Œuvres complètes de Victor Hugo* (Paris, 1967) II, 984; cited by Lee Johnson, *The Paintings of Eugène Delacroix* (Oxford, 1981) I, 99.

80 'Le sujet du libretto est trop connu pour que je ne puisse, cette fois, en esquiver l'analyse.' *Le Rénovateur* (29 March 1835) 1.

81 See, for example, CG III, 644: 'Oh! la mer; la mer, un bon navire! un bon vent! [...]'

82 See Brian Primmer, *The Berlioz Style* (London, 1973) 97.

to song in the spring of 1840 – namely the explicit desire to show a certain public that in fact he was a 'normal' composer – Berlioz rather applies to that text a compositional technique of both obvious premeditation and apparent spontaneity, thus creating the kind of *chef d'œvre* that causes us now to view 'normal' works in the shadows of *Les Nuits d'été*.

APPENDIX

Lamento	Lament
La Chanson du pêcheur	**Song of the Fisherman**

Ma belle amie est morte:	My lovely one is dead;
Je pleurerai toujours;	I shall weep [for her] forever.
Sous la tombe elle emporte	She carries my heart and soul
Mon âme et mes amours.	With her into the grave.
Dans le ciel, sans m'attendre,	Without waiting for me,
Elle s'en retourna;	she has returned to heaven.
L'ange qui l'emmena	The angel who led her there
Ne voulut pas me prendre.	wished not to take me along.
Que mon sort est amer!	How bitter my fate is!
Ah! sans amour,	Ah, without love,
s'en aller sur la mer!	to set out on the sea.
La blanche créature	The white creature
Est couchée au cercueil.	is lying in her coffin.
Comme dans la nature	How everything in nature
Tout me paraît en deuil!	seems to me in mourning!
La colombe oubliée	The forgotten dove is weeping
Pleure et songe à l'absent;	and thinking of her who is gone;
Mon âme pleure et sent	my soul is weeping
Qu'elle est dépareillée.	and feels deserted.
Que mon sort est amer!	How bitter my fate is!
Ah! sans amour,	Ah, without love,
s'en aller sur la mer!	to set out on the sea.

Sur moi la nuit immense	All-encompassing night spreads
S'étend comme un linceul;	itself over me like a shroud;
Je chante ma romance	I sing my romance
Que le ciel entend seul.	which is heard by heaven alone.
Ah! comme elle était belle	Ah, how beautiful she was;
Et comme je l'aimais!	and how I loved her!
Je n'aimerai jamais	I shall never love another woman
Une femme autant qu'elle.	as much as I loved her.
Que mon sort est amer!	How bitter my fate is!
Ah! sans amour,	Ah, without love,
s'en aller sur la mer!	to set out on the sea.

(Théophile Gautier)

Jacques Barzun read the first version of this article and provided me with detailed criticism and encouragement for which I am deeply grateful. To subsequent readers of various drafts, Ralph Locke, Louise Litterick, Ruth Solie, Katherine Reeve, Raphael Atlas and Julian Rushton, I should also like to extend my appreciation for many wise and generous 'corrections et perfectionnements'.

5

Les Nuits d'été: cycle or collection?

JULIAN RUSHTON

This essay addresses a critical question: is the group of songs published by Berlioz as *Les Nuits d'été* simply a collection of songs by one poet and one composer, or should it be called a cycle, with all that the latter term implies for our understanding of it as a whole? In this discussion broadly historical considerations, including compositional processes, must be secondary to the critical end. As it happens, information on the genesis of the songs is unusually sparse for Berlioz, and our knowledge of his intentions is even more so.[1] My conclusion, which is intended to owe more to critical reasoning than to wishful thinking, is that *Les Nuits d'été* is indeed a cycle, but of a kind which may be peculiar to itself and to Berlioz.

One historical point, however, is germane to the argument and, it must be said, potentially damaging. *Les Nuits d'été* exists in two distinct versions. The first, composed in 1840 and published the following year, is for voice or a sequence of voices and piano; the second, of which the instrumentation was undertaken at various times, was published in 1856 for a different sequence of voices and orchestra.[2] In discussing the orchestral version Hugh Macdonald remarks that 'the set of six songs is not necessarily to be considered a cycle';[3] it is this version which makes the designation 'cycle' especially problematic. In 1841, the songs were set for mezzo-soprano or tenor, except No. 5 which is simply for tenor. In 1856, doubtless to suit the dedicatees, Berlioz transposed Nos. 2 and 3

---

1 There is no mention of *Les Nuits d'été* in Berlioz's letters from the period of composition. On its composition see the article in the present volume by Peter Bloom; *NBE* 13, xi; and Holoman, *Catalogue*, 217.
2 In 1856 the version with piano was issued in a revision corresponding to the orchestral version; the principal change is the new introduction to No. 2, but there are numerous detailed alterations.
3 Hugh Macdonald, *Berlioz* (London, 1982) 125.

down by different intervals and indicated a preference for male voices in Nos. 2 and 5. If the dedicatees – six singers from various German courts – are classified into voice-types, four singers are required: soprano (Nos. 1, 4, 6), contralto (No. 2), baritone (No. 3) and tenor (No. 5). Alternatives are offered but two singers are the minimum for an authentic performance.[4] The instrumentation, moreover, is different in every song.

Berlioz did express a preference for having all six songs published in a single score, but he acknowledged that it would be necessary, as in 1841, to make the (revised) piano versions available separately.[5] His actions otherwise suggest little concern for the cyclic qualities of his composition. From 1856 he promoted performances of 'Le Spectre de la rose' (as he had earlier of 'Absence'), but not of the whole set; he apparently never heard the other four songs. Thus while the importance of *Les Nuits d'été* in the history of the orchestral song should be assured, its place in the history of the orchestral song cycle is more doubtful.

I do not intend a critique, still less a taxonomy, of definitions of 'song cycle', but some reference to them may be useful in clarifying what the term implies for the purposes of this paper. *The New Grove* calls a song cycle a 'composite form of vocal music consisting of individually complete songs for solo or ensemble voices... It may relate a series of events, or a series of impressions, or it may simply be a group of songs unified by mood. The text may be by a single author or from several sources'.[6] This is one of the more inclusive of published definitions; others, however, broadly agree with Sir George Grove himself in insisting that a cycle forms 'one composition'.[7] For the purposes of this discussion, at least, Orrey's definition (in which the music 'may or may not reveal an over-all coherence') seems too permissive to be useful, for it fails to distinguish between a cycle and a collection.[8] For Peake, however, 'cycle' implies

4 In practice the cycle is usually sung by sopranos who transpose Nos. 2 and 3 back to their 1841 pitches, with a disturbing effect upon the orchestral layout. I am only aware of one recording which uses mixed voices and Berlioz's keys (conducted by Colin Davis; Philips CD 416 961–2).
5 CG V, 306. On the dedicatees see *NBE* 13, 135–6.
6 Louise Eitel Peake, 'Song cycle', *The New Grove Dictionary of Music and Musicians*, ed. Stanley Sadie (London, 1980) XVII, 517.
7 Sir George Grove, in *Grove's Dictionary of Music and Musicians*, 5th edn, ed. Eric Blom (London, 1954) VII, 962.
8 'A group of songs with a common theme, the poems usually, but not necessarily, by one poet. The music may or may not reveal an over-all coherence, of key schemes, form, and so on; or it may present little more than a unity of mood; or it may simply follow the dictates of the poems, with little or no attempt at organic unity.' Leslie Orrey, 'Song-cycle', *The New Oxford Companion to Music*, ed. Denis Arnold (London, 1983) II, 720.

greater unity than can be detected in 'collections' such as Schumann's Spanish songs or Brahms's *Liebeslieder* waltzes.[9] This distinction appears useful; it is similar to that between a 'collection' and a 'multi-piece', made with reference to Brahms's piano sets by Jonathan Dunsby.[10]

'Multi-piece', perhaps more precisely than 'cycle', implies a deliberate grouping of separable pieces which display some kind of coherence, or group identity, beyond what is supplied by such external factors as their being gathered in a single publication, and beyond such facts of reception as their forming a pleasantly modulated sequence in performance. In a group of instrumental pieces the demonstration of this coherence (or, as it is usually called, unity) is a matter purely for musical analysis. In a group of songs, the verse merits separate consideration. Mere selection from a single poetic source, while it may be a contributory factor, is not enough to justify naming a set of songs a cycle.[11]

On the surface, there is no question of a narrative in *Les Nuits d'été*, nor even of identifying the poetic *persona* of one poem with that of any other. Sexual love is the predominating theme of Théophile Gautier's collection *La Comédie de la mort*. But even if we assume a male *persona* (despite Berlioz's choice of voice-types), he and his lover continually change. In the two songs subtitled 'Lamento' the protagonists are a fisherman facing the illimitable ocean (No. 3) and a neurotic lover suffering claustrophobia in a churchyard (No. 5). The more happily situated lovers of Nos. 1 and 6 cannot be identified with each other or with the lover of the absent one in No. 4; while the singer in No. 2 is ostensibly a dead rose.

It would be easy to argue that Berlioz chose these poems less with a view to their narrative coherence – there is no question of death (Nos. 3 and 5) followed by resurrection – than for the sake of musical contrast. Indeed, one of the most remarkable aspects of the set is the variety achieved in the central sequence of four slow songs. If we sense the presence of a narrative element, it is by metaphor: the songs could each represent the stages in a

9 Peake ('Song-cycle') makes no mention of Berlioz, whose *Mélodies irlandaises* (1829) form a one-poet collection rather than a cycle, and only mentions France in the context of cycles, like Fauré's, influenced by Schumann. The preceding article in *The New Grove* ('Song', by Geoffrey Chew) also omits Berlioz. Yet its bibliography includes Noske, *French Song from Berlioz to Duparc* (New York, 1970), in which Berlioz is seen to have contributed to establishing the *mélodie* as a serious form at least a decade before Chew's suggested date of 1850.

10 Jonathan Dunsby, 'The multi-piece in Brahms: *Fantasien* Op. 116' in *Brahms*, ed. R. Pascall (Cambridge, 1983) 167–89.

11 Certainly Gautier had no cyclic intention. He did not group the six poems chosen by Berlioz, although as it happens Nos. 2 and 3, and 5 and 6, follow each other in the poet's collection. It is not certain that this affected Berlioz's final ordering of the cycle. See Bloom, 'In the shadows', esp. note 31.

relationship, perhaps that of Berlioz and his first wife. Such a covert programme would account both for the intensity of expression in the laments, and for the fact that Berlioz never brought the cycle to performance. But so deep-laid, and possibly unconscious, a metaphor does nothing to impair the individual integrity of the songs.[12]

A summary of the comparative structures of the poems and songs, together with their prevailing moods, is contained in Table 1. Berlioz's own title 'Summer Nights' offers no clue to the scope or the unity of conception of the set, and on the literal level it is mildly confusing. 'Villanelle' is a spring song. 'Le Spectre de la rose' and 'Au Cimetière' mention summer flowers, but whereas the poet gives the time of the latter as sunset, Berlioz added the subtitle 'Clair de lune'. 'Sur les lagunes' refers to 'nuit immense'; is it a long winter night (when the fisherman might miss his lover), or a summer night (when the immensity of space becomes palpable)? If so there is a link with 'Absence', whose theme is spatial distance. Neither time nor season, however, may be assigned to 'Absence' or 'L'Ile inconnue'.

Recurrent imagery is not a major feature of the chosen poems. Flowers, perfumes, pearly dewdrops, have no obvious musical analogues (except that the dew twice brings F major: No. 1, bar 26, and No. 2, bar 19). The lament of the dove in 'Sur les lagunes' (bars 54–60) is a metaphor for the lover's complaint, while in 'Au Cimetière' the dove is real, its song giving rise to the phrase 'Sur les ailes de la musique' (from bar 68). A musical cross-reference is just detectable, since both passages spread an ascending major arpeggio and follow it with semitonal sighs, but it is surely too tenuous to function as a sign or enhance the unity of the set. Berlioz omitted verses of 'Absence' in which the poet conceives himself as a wounded dove whose soul flies into the beloved's mouth.

The sequence of moods may be clarified by reference to musical parallels in earlier works, mainly, though not entirely, dealing with the theme of love. In 'Villanelle' love appears joyful, but the musical texture bespeaks fragility as well as freshness; the staccato woodwind, the quicksilver modulations, and the incomplete imitations which freshen the second and third stanzas are reminiscent of episodes in the Ball scene and

---

12 I am indebted to Ian Kemp for the idea of a metaphorical narrative. The lack of performances cannot entirely be explained by external factors. If the orchestral song cycle was not a fashionable genre, the individual song certainly was. Neglect might plausibly result from a painful association between the music and an episode in Berlioz's life. Probably for this kind of reason he never promoted performances of the 'Elégie en prose' (see Berlioz's *Mémoires*, chapter 18) or the *Marche funèbre pour la dernière scène d'Hamlet*, although he published both.

Table 1

	Berlioz's title [Gautier's title where different]	Gautier's form	Berlioz's form	Mood
1.	Villanelle [Villanelle rhythmique]	3 strophes	Strophic	Spring song: love, hope
2.	Le Spectre de la rose	3 strophes	Through-composed, each verse same at opening	Dream: languor after the ball; tender, haunting
3.	Sur les lagunes [Lamento: (La Chanson du pêcheur)]	3 strophes	Through-composed, verse 3 like 1, verse 2 contrasted, each verse ending with the same refrain	'Nuit immense': a dead lover; loneliness
4.	Absence	8 strophes	3 strophes set as a rondo, ABACA; the rest omitted	Loneliness: distance of lover
5.	Au Cimetière (Clair de lune) [Lamento]	6 strophes	6 arranged as 3 large strophes, in ABA pattern	Sunset in poem, 'Clair de lune' in music; a dead lover; flight from the graveyard
6.	L'Ile inconnue [Barcarolle]	4-line refrain 6-line verse, A B A C A D	Rearranged to close the form: A B A C A (lines 1–2) D A (lines 2 and 4)	Ebullient, colourful yet ironic

▌ Table 2

Roméo et Juliette (*Scène d'amour* from bar 124)	'Le Spectre de la rose' (orchestral version)
$\frac{6}{8}$ Adagio in A	$\frac{9}{8}$ Adagio in B (originally D)

CONTRASTS

Dramatic	Lyric
Ambiguous form despite use of refrain	Clear returns to opening

Harmonic contrasts

Little structural modulation	Clear cadences in other keys
Static harmony to main melody (pedal)	Mobile harmony of main melody

PARALLELS

Harmonic parallels

Dissolve in opening Andante (bars 1–35)	Dissolve in bars 37ff.	
(bar 352) A–E♭–b–c♯–E	Remote modulations before the climax	(bar 28) B♭–B–c♯–g♯–F♯
(bar 368)	Late appearance of the dominant at a climax	(bar 47)

Instrumental and melodic parallels

(bar 125ff.)	(bar 1ff.)	
Divided cellos	Divided violas	
Melody in violas, violins	Melody in cellos	
(bar 127)	Wind melody	(bar 2)
(bar 131)	Strings accompany, with violin trills	(bar 9)
(bars 243–55)	New melodic ideas generated in relative minor	(bars 55–60)
(bar 308ff.)	Rhythmic syncopes, offbeats	(bars 37 and 45ff.)

Queen Mab Scherzo in *Roméo et Juliette*, composed only months before. After the four slow songs, 'L'Ile inconnue' treats a relationship matured by irony; the girl cannot believe in what she asks for (the land where loves last for ever). The exotic images of the text are reflected not in word-painting but in the restlessness of the music's explorations, a product of the same mind as the 'Elégie en prose'. The sense of unlimited space in 'Absence' is achieved partly by the diffusion of a very simple musical idea over a wide pitch-spectrum at a slow tempo: a miniature version of parts of the *Grande Messe des morts*, notably the *Hostias*. The *Offertoire* from the same work anticipated the intermittent semitone motif of 'Sur les

117

lagunes'. What in the choral work is hieratic, however, becomes secular, or even nihilistic, in the songs.

'Le Spectre de la rose' may be more closely associated with the love scene in *Roméo*. Much of Berlioz's love music is in compound time, here $\frac{9}{8}$ rather than the usual $\frac{6}{8}$. Like the *Scène d'amour*, 'Le Spectre' concerns the aftermath of a dance; the rose is a surrogate lover (male despite Berlioz's confining the orchestral version to contralto). But when this Romeo leaps into the orchard, he finds Juliet already asleep. The parallels in musical technique are shown in Table 2. There is also some correspondence between the *Scène d'amour* and 'Sur les lagunes'. Both are in a slow $\frac{6}{8}$; both are ambiguous in design, despite being bound together by a refrain; and 'la blanche Juliette' in musical terms is not unlike the 'blanche créature' of the song, using the diminished triad on the supertonic (C–E flat–G flat: see Example 1) in a context of strong emphasis on the third degree (connected by lines in Example 1: the excerpt from *Roméo* is transposed for convenience of comparison).

One important feature of such undoubtedly cyclic works as *Die schöne Müllerin* and *Dichterliebe* is a progressive expansion and complication of musical forms employed. Berlioz's original intention may have been to organise four songs on this basis, proceeding from the clearly strophic 'Villanelle' to the lucid refrain form of 'Absence', followed by the varied strophic form of 'Le Spectre de la rose', and concluding with the less easily definable form of 'L'Ile inconnue'.[13] His published order suggests a division of the songs into parallel halves, each beginning with a simple form ('Villanelle', 'Absence') and proceeding to greater complexity through the explicitly nocturnal 'Le Spectre' and 'Au Cimetière' to the most complex forms, 'Sur les lagunes' and 'L'Ile inconnue'. This division

Example 1

No. 3 ('Sur les lagunes'), bars 36–43

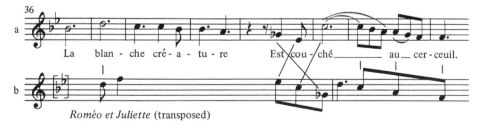

Roméo et Juliette (transposed)

13 Holoman, 217; cf. Bloom, 'In the shadows', p. 86.

is supported by other factors, although not, as will become apparent later, unequivocally.

Berlioz set every verse in the chosen texts except in 'Absence', but only in 'Villanelle' did he follow the strophic form of the poem. Even here the result is far from simple, and the harmony, in particular, removes the song from the drawing-room style of the *romance*. An interesting feature of the working autograph (F-Pn ms 1179) is that the second part of the first verse (Example 2b) is superimposed on an earlier and simpler version which, however, Berlioz used for the equivalent passage in verse 2 (Example 2a). A significant consequence of this afterthought is a third passage of emphasis on the flattened sixth degree (in verse 1, bar 30), to which verse 3 returns (bar 114); it reinforces, at a moment of climax, an element already in the music. The strophic variations may be primarily musical in impulse; certainly they are not all dictated by the poetry. But the conflict of the flattened and diatonic sixth degrees is crucial in this song (it persists in at least some of the others). The growing complexity of the human relationship in the poem is hardly enough to account for the imitative counterpoint so much admired by Noske.[14] Where in the first strophe the F natural in the melody could be a response to 'froids' and 'trembler', it corresponds less directly to 'amants béni' and 'lapin caché' in the second and third. Yet in strophe 2 the ascent to F sharp where the second F natural is expected (bar 70) arrives appositely at 'beaux amours'. The effect results from the song's chromatic norms; diatonicism becomes an expressive nuance.[15]

Example 2   No. 1 ('Villanelle')

a   (Verse 2)   Pour par - ler de nos beaux a - mours _____

b   (Verse 1)   Que l'on voit au ma - tin trem - bler _____

14 Noske, *French Song*, 107.
15 The classic purity of 'Villanelle' is enhanced by the asymmetry Berlioz produced by the four-bar interlude before the third strophe (judging from the same manuscript, another afterthought), and by his short coda. Instead of three verses of forty bars each, the proportions are 40:40:52 (the last two bars being the final tonic), placing the interlude on the Golden section (see Julian Rushton, *The Musical Language of Berlioz* [Cambridge, 1983] 183 ff.).

For all its subtlety, 'Villanelle' remains a strophic song. For the three-stanza poems of 'Le Spectre de la rose' and 'Sur les lagunes' Berlioz still further eroded a strophic design. In 'Le Spectre' each eight-line stanza begins with the same arching melody, but the second verse reduces the phrase by a bar and modulates in doing so (see Example 3). The musical setting suggests six quatrains rather than Gautier's three eight-line stanzas. The second half of each stanza involves a radical departure, the first to an extraordinary key (the flattened tonic), the second by harmonic chemistry of even greater potency to a less curious goal, the dominant. Only the third, by way of a poised phrase in the relative minor (bars 55–61), resolves fully in the tonic. The three stanzas of 'Sur les lagunes' end with the same haunting refrain, but this pattern is in conflict with an overall ternary design formed by the contrasted musical character of the second stanza. The words did not compel Berlioz to adopt this solution; Fauré in his beautiful setting (Op. 4 no. 1) uses the same melody for both stanzas.

Berlioz completely altered the poetic form of 'Absence', not only to shorten the text but to make a fully cadenced refrain form with two episodes (themselves a model and variation). The result is as direct as a strophic form. 'Au Cimetière' displays the opposite tendency to 'Le Spectre de la rose': six stanzas are made to sound like three. Berlioz treats the first two as a model and the last two as a variation, altered to form a conclusion. The middle section is markedly different in texture, so that the overall form reproduces the ternary design of the other lament, 'Sur les lagunes'. Finally, in 'L'Ile inconnue' Berlioz more discretely subverts the poetic form. The addition of a fragmentary refrain to the coda (from bar 119) is not arbitrary: Gautier suggests it by introducing the four-line first stanza three times. Berlioz could have treated this device literally, but instead he provides variation in the first reprise (bar 44), and alters and abbreviates the second (bar 76). The lover's response is picked out by a

Example 3   No. 2 ('Le Spectre de la rose')

Table 3

	1	2	3	4	5	6
1841	A	D	g	F♯	D	F
1856	A	B	f	F♯	D	F

prolonged use of the dominant. With the poet's dismissal of the earthly paradise, Gautier simply stops; in Berlioz's coda, the poet is still gently urging his lover to name her desire.

The most obvious difference between the two versions of *Les Nuits d'été* is the altered key-scheme. Tonal rounding is not a necessary condition of a cycle: Beethoven's *An die ferne Geliebte* and Schumann's *Frauenliebe und Leben* are exceptional in clinching a tonal reprise by reverting to the music of the first song. But some kind of tonal organisation may be considered normal for a cycle. Table 3 superimposes the keys of the two published versions. The 1841 keys reinforce the equal bipartite division of the work. The first part proceeds by descending fifths (Nos. 1–3), then after a shift of focus the second part moves by thirds. The chromatic shift from D to F, with its implied mixture of major and minor modes, and the more remarkable move from G minor to F sharp, are both common enough in Berlioz.[16] In any case, 'Sur les lagunes' ends on its dominant, so the foreground progression between the third and fourth songs (reversed between the fourth and fifth songs) is from D to F sharp.

The 1856 keys apparently disrupt this lucid scheme. Kemp observes that 'the inconsequence of the initial key relationships (A to B, B to F minor, F minor to F sharp) is disguised by the unexpected and dramatic sequence of voices'; nevertheless he suggests that orchestral performance with the 1841 keys may be 'a legitimate attempt to restore his original conception'.[17] But the new tonal relationships may be viewed, indeed relished, in a more positive way. Shifting from A to B for No. 2, I–II rather than I–IV, enhances the languor of the newly entered world of dreams. Moreover the pitch F sharp, whose resolution alongside F natural to the dominant E has been recollected at the end of 'Villanelle' (bar 122), is

16 See Rushton, *The Musical Language*, 30–37.
17 *NBE* 13, xiii, xii.

heard at the start of 'Le Spectre' as the new dominant. Rather than being inconsequential, this might be heard as the replacement of a banal progression by a richly evocative indirect relationship.

The more extreme shift of a tritone from B to F minor (Nos. 2–3) may itself be experienced as an analogue for the harsh awakening to bitter reality in the 'Lamento'. Berlioz is careful to bridge this tonal chasm, partly by orchestral timbre: No. 3 begins with strings in the same register as the cadence of No. 2 (although the double basses change from pizzicato to arco); the solitary clarinet is replaced by the horn. And absolute pitch still provides continuity: when the songs are heard consecutively the D sharp on top of the final chord of No. 2 recurs as E flat in the third bar of 'Sur les lagunes'. The same kind of continuity in contrast appears at the end of No. 3. The foreground is in fact another tritone, from the final dominant of 'Sur les lagunes' (now C major) to F sharp; but the recently heard and very expressive Neapolitan harmony (G flat in No. 3, bar 107) is enharmonically equivalent to the new tonic. There is more continuity of timbre between the two songs (clarinets, horns, strings), and the higher pitch of the principal motif of 'Sur les lagunes' (D flat) is reproduced in the opening C sharp of 'Absence'.

The remaining key-relationships are unchanged, but even the relatively conventional move (in nineteenth-century terms) from F sharp to D is smoothed by the position of the pitch F sharp as the treble, and on violins, at the end of 'Absence' and the first chord of 'Au Cimetière'. There is also continuity of metre and instrumentation (flute, clarinet, strings). Berlioz clearly wanted a big contrast between the last two songs, but he also wanted to round off the set. In 1841 the tonic which occurs twice (D) returns in the penultimate song; in 1856 the tonic which recurs is F, in the final song. This key is carefully prepared in the course of 'Au Cimetière' by the first decisive shift away from its key centre (D), which is to a Berliozian favourite, the flat mediant, in this case F (bars 25, 122). The melodic shift of these bars (from D to C) bridges the songs in the bass, since 'L'Ile inconnue' opens on a six-four.[18]

18 Pitch-relations in Les Nuits d'été are generally characteristic of Berlioz; for example, the prevalence of modal mixture including the melodic use of the flattened sixth (F natural in 'Villanelle', D flat in 'L'Ile inconnue', etc.). That an element is characteristic of the composer does not preclude its assisting a collection to become a cycle, but only if it saturates the whole set. There is, however, no real modal mixture in 'Absence', since the D natural supporting F sharp in the first episode (bar 16) does not imply a tonic D to match the subsequent D sharp minor. 'Le Spectre de la rose' strongly features the natural rather than the flat sixth. ('Villanelle', of course, featured both.)

One consequence of the new key-scheme is an asymmetrical division into two plus four songs rather than three plus three, the tonal tritone after No. 2 being a stronger division than the chordal tritone after No. 3. In the second part (Nos. 3–6) the internal key-relations are rounded by the F minor–F major of Nos. 3 and 6. This tonal design may be summarised in terms of fundamental lines, which in each song except 'Au Cimetière' start on the fifth degree.[19] There is, however, some significant variation in the way in which the lines are resolved. Whereas 'Le Spectre de la rose' and 'L'Ile inconnue' proceed by step to the tonic in the voice, 'Villanelle' and 'Absence', the simplest forms, do so only in the orchestra, without additional emphasis in the closing bars. The coda of 'Villanelle' actually reinforces the fifth in the treble. Its fundamental line is confided to the bassoon, an octave below the expected register (when the song is sung, as it usually is, by a mezzo-soprano); such displacements are an important feature of some of the other songs (see Example 4). The vocal part of 'Au Cimetière' expresses no fundamental line, but prolongs the tonic, enhancing the claustrophobic atmosphere of the song; the orchestra, however, articulates a descent from F sharp, the keynote of 'Absence'. 'Sur les lagunes' establishes the fifth securely, but never resolves it, ending with C as the overtone of the final dominant chord. These and other pitch connections are outlined in Example 4. It is only in the orchestral version that No. 2 picks up and resolves the prominent sixth degree of No. 1. The semitonal shift in the treble before No. 3 marks the strongest break, corresponding to the key-change. The C sharp of No. 4 harks back to the fifth of No. 3's Neapolitan. The remoteness of this relationship enhances the mood of 'Absence'; the resulting shift, tonally by a semitone, is as expressive as the move from F to G flat for the love duet at the end of Act IV of *Les Troyens*, and is brought about by similar means.

For all the variety of melodic shapes in *Les Nuits d'été*, there appear to be simple melodic archetypes to which a number of passages may be referred (see Example 5).[20] These archetypes govern short phrases rather than whole melodies and often appear at significant junctures, notably the beginnings of stanzas. The emotional significance of 'Au Cimetière' within the cycle is reflected in the nature of its melody, the most restricted

19 See Rushton, *The Musical Language*, 178.
20 On Berlioz's use of such sub-motivic archetypes see Walter Schenkman, 'Fixed ideas and recurring patterns in Berlioz's melody', *The Music Review*, 40 (1979) 25–40, and Rushton, *The Musical Language*, 146.

Example 4

Berlioz ever wrote: an example 'of the concentrated, passionate melancholy that [...] will act on the mind with the effect of a powerful drug –
if the listener is prepared to yield'.[21] For twenty-five slow bars the melody
consists of a fourfold rise and fall over a third (motif X), varied only by the
mixture of modes. The second and fourth statements fall by one more step
(motif Y). (See Example 6.) The concentrated development begins with
the harmonically ambiguous resolution of the C natural to B and back, a
passage based on X^1. At bar 31 ('maladivement tendre') the motif ends for
the first time on its middle note, and the next phrase uses X^a in isolation,
introducing the last pitch (E flat) needed to fill the chromatic space
between B and F sharp. Reduplication of the contour of X^1 attains the
enharmonic equivalent of F sharp; the returning tritone G flat–C closes a
large X^2. The falling Y^b then complements the ascending X^a of bar 33 and
leads to a complete statement of Y^1.

The rising arpeggio of bars 42–3 seems to jeopardise the basic shape, yet
it is an ampler version of bars 34–6. The derivation of bars 44–6 is clear,
but the cadence is tenuously connected: its rise to F sharp corresponds to
the first poetic suggestion of the supernatural ('comme en soupire aux
cieux / L'ange amoureux'). Berlioz reproduced this tender arc of melody
virtually unaltered for verse 3, but the cadence now folds in to end on the
tonic. The middle section forms a contrast, beginning from a vocal
monotone; but at the melodic flowering ('Sur les ailes de la musique') the
main motif is again X^a.

Example 5

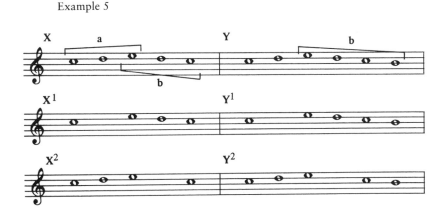

21 J. H. Elliot, *Berlioz* (London, 1938) 153.

Example 6   No. 5 ('Au Cimetière')

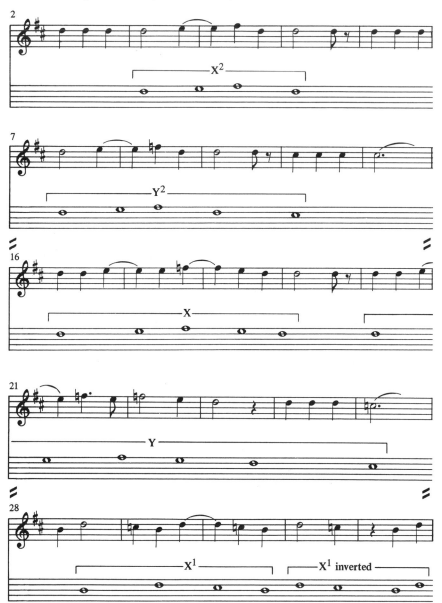

A complete paradigmatic analysis would be needed to determine the relationship between textual detail and the use of either closed melodic patterns (X, X^1, X^2) or open ones (like the replication of X^a at 'Sur les ailes de la musique': E–F–G: G sharp–A–B). Motif X folds in on itself; motif Y represents a slight opening out of X. From a semantic point of view it is noteworthy that closed motifs are particularly concentrated in the two songs subtitled 'Lamento' (Nos. 3 and 5) whereas, despite its subject, the motifs of 'Absence' are particularly open and one-directional. Example 7 shows the rising fourth partly filled by a third on repetition. The responding phrases invert the contour while extending the range. When the scale over a ninth, inevitably open, has recovered the high F sharp, the matching (mainly arpeggio) descent ends by curling in on itself, for the only time, with an inversion of X at the cadence. The first episode contains a complete statement of Y (Example 8a), perhaps significantly at the despairing 'O sort amer, ô dure absence!', as the radiance of the refrain,

127

Example 4   No. 4 ('Absence')

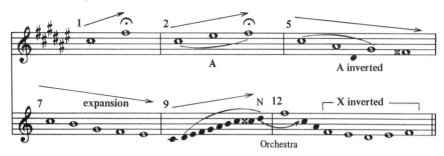

resonant with hope, is replaced by the terrible recollection of separation (cf. bars 46–51, lying a third higher).

The final phrase of each episode is open, a falling fourth, an interval which is prominent in 'Villanelle' and still more in 'Le Spectre de la rose'. Both these songs concentrate upon open motifs. 'Le Spectre' is filled with falling scales (extending Y^b), and contains Y in a form virtually identical to that of 'Absence' (Example 8b). The falling shapes contribute an elegiac quality, but they are balanced by closed phrases, of less restricted range than X (bar 19, 'Des pleurs d'argent'). The influence of X is comparatively reduced in this phrase which launches the wonderful modulation to B flat. The continuation of verse 2 uses closed (but not X-related) shapes ('Toute la nuit mon spectre rose', bar 34), only to open out for the cadence (bar 37). At bar 40 ('Ni messe ni de profundis') X is appropriately inverted, and in the superb phrase which follows ascending thirds seem to lead the rose into paradise. Here the juxtaposition of fundamental shapes gives point to the text (closed: *de Profundis*; open: paradise).

Behind the melodic richness of its foreground *Les Nuits d'été* possesses a measure of background similarity. Its basis, reducible to a number of contrasting archetypes, represents compositional thought reasonably specific (though not unique) to this group of pieces. If using such patterns is a method of composition, it is consistent with the conception of the more exposed *idée fixe* and its permeation of other themes.[22] Its prevalence here is reinforced by an examination of the two songs whose motivic content has not so far been discussed.

22 See Edward T. Cone, 'Schumann amplified: an analysis' in *Berlioz: Fantastic Symphony*, ed. Cone (Norton Critical Score; New York, 1971) 249 ff.

128

Example 8   (a)   No. 4 ('Absence')

               (b)   No. 2 ('Le Spectre de la rose')

A complementary relationship between the overtly contrasted 'Sur les lagunes', the first lament, and 'L'Ile inconnue', the second cheerful song, makes the revised tonality of the former seem more than coincidental. Number 6 is not only the harmonic completion of the open (dominant) ending of No. 3 (it begins on a dominant of F, which is quickly resolved); it makes this point despite the intervention of two other songs by perceptible motivic connections. In addition, both songs are about the sea; both are in $\frac{6}{8}$ (the only songs in this metre); both make extreme use of the semitone above the dominant. Despite its exuberant character, the modal mixture of 'L'Ile inconnue' is particularly rich: nearly half of its 135 bars suggest F minor rather than F major. The pitch D flat appears frequently on strong beats, in various harmonic contexts, but often with a grating tritone appoggiatura (G natural, notably at bar 108, where it comes as a shock after a period of tranquil diatonicism). The use of the Neapolitan (bars 39, 114) is another cross-reference to the end of No. 3.[23]

There is also a formal parallel: both songs have a refrain which does not (as it does in 'Absence') constitute a complete musical section. While they return clearly to their openings, they deploy a greater range of intermediate ideas than the other songs; and there are enough motivic connections to justify the suggestion that these songs represent the negative and positive aspects of a common theme – frustration in a human relationship. Both lovers are divided from their loves by more than the sea: the fisherman by death, the gondolier by incompatibility.

Particularly striking in 'Sur les lagunes' is the disguised reminiscence of the first shape in the voice in the completely contrasted second verse ('La blanche creature'; Example 9). More obvious is the development of motif X (which also forges a link with 'Au Cimetière'). Motif X at its purest begins in the refrain: 'Que mon sort est amer!' (bars 28; 67 [orchestra] and 69; 98–101; Example 10a). The rhythm and contour of Example 10a are reproduced in 'L'Ile inconnue', extended into motif Y, at the questioning episode ('Est-ce dans la baltique', bar 62) and the rejection of

23 Bars 9–17, 21–33, 37–40, 44–58, 62–4, 108–17 and 123–6 of No. 6 suggest F or B flat minor, and 65–75 their diatonic relations such as A flat; hence by contrast the luminosity of the girl's words, using C major, and the brightness of the 'true' relative minor, D minor, when C sharp, not D flat, leads to D minor. D flat appears on the first beat of bars 9, 10, 12, 14 to 17, 22–8, 30, 32, 37, 39, 40, 45, 47, 50–58 as 9–17, 63 and 65 (delayed by appoggiaturas), 66, 67, 72, 74, 95, 108, 110, 114, 116, 123–6. G is heard above D flat in the refrain (15–17; 56–8) and throughout most of bars 23–32, etc. As for 'Sur les lagunes', it less surprisingly introduces the major for its second verse, only to qualify it at once with the flat sixth (bar 40); then it modulates there (48) and beyond, to ♭VI of VI (from B flat, E double flat or D major)!

Example 9   No. 3 ('Sur les lagunes')

Example 10 (a) No. 3 ('Sur les lagunes')

(b) No. 6 ('L'Ile inconnue')

the girl's dream: 'Cette rive, ma chère, / On ne la connaît guère' (Example 10b).

Is it idle to speculate on the appropriateness of this identity of motif? How bitter is the fate of the lovers who cannot find eternal love? How much is the eternal longing of the fisherman the product of his lover's death, and how much the longing of the Romantic poet after the unattainable? Both songs suggest the impossibility of perfect happiness on earth, a theme dear to Berlioz which forms a vital strand in such diverse works as his instrumental symphonies, *La Damnation de Faust* and *Les Troyens*. The harrowing refrain of No. 3 – 'Ah! sans amour s'en aller sur la mer!' (Example 11a) – responds to motif X by sweeping down an eleventh: an open motif, but one which expresses the inalienable distance of the beloved (beyond death). Its tender counterpart is the ascending fourth of 'Absence'; its exuberant twin is the main idea of 'L'Ile inconnue', which also descends the octave but then changes direction to end a fifth above rather than a fourth below the lower tonic (Example 11b).

Example 11 (a) No. 3 ('Sur les lagunes')

(b) No. 6 ('L'Ile inconnue')

While each song of *Les Nuits d'été* is complete in itself, and each can be as effective on its own as an independent piece, like *La Captive*, I hope enough has been said to show why a whole performance should be greater than the sum of the parts. The evidence points to a cyclic organisation typical in its mingling of various types of connective tissue of nineteenth-century cycles in general, whether instrumental or vocal.[24] Berlioz ordered his material with care. The 1856 version destroys timbral unity (varied instrumentation replaces the piano; different voice-types replace one), tonal order and symmetrical grouping; but it introduces a richer configuration of key-relationships which tends to enhance underlying pitch-connections, together with alternative and subtler forms of asymmetrical subdivision. My motivic analysis suggests yet another binary division within the set, into interlocking groups. Numbers 1, 2 and 4 are in sharp major keys and use open and scale motifs; Numbers 3, 5 and 6 are in flatter keys (especially since so much of No. 5 can be referred to D minor), and are most obsessed with motif X.[25]

Each song has some unique element, some individual colouring which draws it apart from the rest. Such features are the final argument that this is a cycle, not a mere collection. A collection, suggests Dunsby,[26] will often exhibit less contrast than a cycle, because its author, not expecting it to be experienced as a whole, is not concerned to avoid repetitiveness. A cycle possesses all the virtues of a collection and others, since the interplay of contrast and coherence forms a more complex entity.

Berlioz's evident concern for contrast appears in the arrangement of

24 Dunsby, 'The multi-piece', 168–9.
25 Whether this further subdivision strengthens the cyclic chain or weakens it through indeterminacy remains an open question.
26 Dunsby, 'The multi-piece', 180.

metre and tempo. The metrical sequence is $\frac{2}{4}$, then $\frac{9}{8}$, a maximum contrast added to the tempo change which balances the pitch connections existing with either transposition of No. 2. There follow two songs in $\frac{6}{8}$ in contrasted tempi (Nos. 3 and 6) framing two slow songs in $\frac{3}{4}$. Yet 'Absence' is lucid in its metrical structure whereas 'Au Cimetière' is as ambiguous here as in its harmony: much of its melody, supported by chord-change over a pedal, could be barred in duple groups (refer to Example 6). The individuality of each song also appears in the following features:

(1) 'Villanelle' alone is strophic and makes use of imitative counterpoint. Its metre and rhythmic patterns are the simplest; there is not a single qualifying triplet.

(2) 'Le Spectre de la rose', despite its semitone appoggiaturas, is not obsessed with the flattened sixth, preferring the diatonic sixth; it alone employs a harp.

(3) 'Sur les lagunes' is the only song in the minor, and ends on the dominant.

(4) 'Absence', the only song not to set a whole poem, has a uniquely simple relationship of voice to orchestra (the latter is hardly independent at all, though as in 'Villanelle' it provides the resolution of the fundamental line). It is free of chromatic key-relations.

(5) 'Au Cimetière' has a different fundamental line ($\hat{3}$–$\hat{2}$–$\hat{1}$ in the orchestra; static in the voice), and makes extreme use of harmonic and tonal ambiguity; it is also the most motivically concentrated.

(6) 'L'Ile inconnue' opens on a dominant and has a full (tonic prolonging) coda. It has the fullest orchestration (ten winds), and its constant surge of string semiquavers (in 1841, unpianistic tremolos) makes it a true finale. The use of the dyad D flat–G is particularly remarkable.

If these features distinguish the individual songs, however, they also reinforce the position of Nos. 5 and 6 at the end. These two contribute much to the cyclic sense by exploitation and resolution of features accumulated in the first four. They both adopt metres used already. Number 5 is the second lament, and the fourth slow piece, whose ambiguities result from a saturation with elements heard before; No. 6 acts as a resolution of previous problems. Elements such as the flat supertonics, which even in No. 2 would have led to an agonised departure from the home key, here find resolution no further away than the minor subdominant, which can also act (e.g. in bars 9–12) as a consonant basis for the usually disruptive D flat. Besides its special relationship to the otherwise very distinctive 'Sur les lagunes', 'L'Ile inconnue' rounds off the cycle by a return to a fast tempo (cf. 'Villanelle') and uses syncopation, otherwise mainly confined to 'Le Spectre de la rose'. From 'Absence' and 'Sur les lagunes' comes the last song's powerful articulation of the high tonic. The relationship to Nos. 3 and 5, and the function of No. 6 as resolution of their peculiar intensities, needs no further underlining.

The philosophic reader will have noted my assumption that unity, uniqueness and their reconciliation, are artistic virtues. Variety, perhaps, needs no defence; coherence, however, suggests the ideology of organicism, much questioned today and (many would say) less relevant to Berlioz than to his German contemporaries. My own view is simple: it is that the construction of rich sets of relationships, of significant complexity and the reconciliation of opposites, is what distinguishes great from run-of-the-mill art. My claim that *Les Nuits d'été* is a cycle is motivated by my sense of its artistic greatness.

The basis for this claim extends beyond the more readily analysable pitch and tonal relations to other musical variables, although such a claim must clearly rest on factors independent of vagaries of performance. Even in the piano version, and however many singers take part in an orchestral performance, the last two songs will gather elements from the earlier ones and show them in a new light. The elements which the last song particularly develops are, moreover, those which distance Berlioz's cycle from monotony or blandness. *Les Nuits d'été* does not aspire to the continuity of *An die ferne Geliebte*, nor (to consider cycles which are certainly not narratives) the intensity of purpose of Brahms's *Vier ernste Gesänge* or Mahler's *Kindertotenlieder*. If by some notions of 'cycle' its claim to be more than a mere collection may seem tenuous, this may be less the result of any lack of 'unity' in the work itself than of the inadequacy of these particular notions.[27] Comparison of the two versions of *Les Nuits d'été* shows how the orchestral transcription and designation for different voices actually produce new relationships; but these only arise because the internal cohesion of the material shared by both versions is strong enough to support new interpretations. The question of whether Berlioz himself (who so carefully provides chains of thematic links in

27 As Dunsby observes, 'If we have just one good idea of what constitutes a unified work, it will probably conflict with the evidence to be found in Opp. 116–19 [or in *Les Nuits d'été*]: such an idea [...] simply diverts our attention from the evidence'. 'The multi-piece', 188.

other multi-movement works) was aware of these relationships is, as I hinted at the opening, not only unanswerable for lack of evidence, but of doubtful relevance: not all important artistic qualities result from authorial intention. There are few, in this case, who would dispute the aesthetic excellence of the result.

6

'Ritter Berlioz' in Germany[1]

DAVID B. LEVY

In his classic study *The Orchestra from Beethoven to Berlioz*, Adam Carse observes that the 'enduring strength' of the symphonic repertoire from the first half of the nineteenth century derived mainly from German symphonists. But to this observation he quickly adds the name of Hector Berlioz, 'whom Nature, perhaps rather capriciously, decided to make a Frenchman'.[2] In a more recent study, Brian Primmer places the question of musical nationality in a somewhat different light:

> Whereas men like Beethoven [and] Schumann were [...] salient individuals, able to work within a recognizable but continually developing tradition, those such as Berlioz [...] were forced to become solitary egotists. They stood out against the backcloth of conventions which was French artistic life and protested their difference with a vehemence which seems exaggerated from any other point of view. They acted out their Romanticism on the stage of history publicly, whereas their colleagues from across the Rhine experienced it in private.[3]

Robert Schumann, in a more famous aphorism, was more succinct: 'Tell me where you live, and I will tell you how you compose'.[4] While each of these statements has a certain validity, all oversimplify what in fact is a complex issue – the nature of, and relationship between, German and French styles in the early nineteenth century. German musicians at that time were still trying to come to terms with the impact of Beethoven, whose works cast a long shadow and provoked lively debate. Little did they expect to find that a French composer – Berlioz – was also working

1 An earlier version of this paper was given at the annual meeting of the American Musicological Society and the Society for Music Theory in Baltimore, in November 1988. I am grateful to Professors Ralph Locke, Hugh Macdonald and Peter Bloom for their helpful suggestions as the paper evolved into its present form.
2 Adam Carse, *The Orchestra from Beethoven to Berlioz* (New York, 1949) 2.
3 Brian Primmer, 'Unity and ensemble: contrasting ideals in Romantic music', *19th-Century Music*, 6 (1982) 99.　　4 Cited in Leon Plantinga, *Schumann as Critic* (New Haven, 1967) 122.

in that same shadow. How did German musicians and critics view this unexpected phenomenon?

I should like to follow this relatively little explored avenue of enquiry by taking a look at the early reception of Berlioz in Germany. Reports from Paris on Berlioz's concerts during the 1830s may be found in the *feuilletons* of the Leipzig *Allgemeine musikalische Zeitung* and Schumann's *Neue Zeitschrift für Musik*. Longer reviews of individual works were penned by Schumann and Kastner in the pages of these journals.[5] Isolated German performances of Berlioz's music also took place, often to enthusiastic receptions. One such event, a concert held on 19 March 1837 in Weimar that featured the Overture to *Les Francs-Juges*, inspired J. C. Lobe, at that time a violist in the Grand Archduke's Kapelle, to publish an invitation to Berlioz to visit Germany. Lobe's 'Sendschreiben' indicates that he (and, presumably, many other German musicians) knew how French critics, especially F.-J. Fétis, had chastised the composer. But Lobe hears in Berlioz's music 'an entirely new form for entirely new ideas', and maintains that the rules followed by this composer 'we do not yet know, [but] that [these rules] demonstrate more learning than many of the trained theorists have stuffed into their heads from dusty books'.[6] What Lobe probably did not know is that Berlioz had long intended to visit Germany, first as one of the requirements of his Prix de Rome fellowship, and later (when this obligation became moot) as a way of earning money.[7] By the time Berlioz set foot on German soil in 1842, his reputation there – or more properly, a multitude of reputations – had, to a degree, already been established.

An important and useful document concerning Berlioz's first German tour, one that has thus far escaped extended scholarly consideration, is Wolfgang Robert Griepenkerl's *Ritter Berlioz in Braunschweig*.[8] This

---

5 In addition to Schumann's famous review of the *Symphonie fantastique*, readers should note his review of the *Grande Ouverture de Waverley*, 'Concertouverturen für Orchester', *Neue Zeitschrift für Musik*, 10 (1839) 186–7. *Roméo et Juliette* was reviewed (by Georges Kastner) in the *Allgemeine musikalische Zeitung*, 42 (1840) 17–20.

6 Johann Christian Lobe, 'Sendschreiben an Herrn Hector Berlioz in Paris', *Neue Zeitschrift für Musik*, 6 (1837) 147–9.

7 In fact Berlioz's first trip to Germany may have been partly sponsored by the French government. See Peter Bloom, 'La Mission de Berlioz en Allemagne: un document inédit', *Revue de Musicologie*, 66 (1980) 70–85.

8 Wolfgang Robert Griepenkerl, *Ritter Berlioz in Braunschweig. Zur Charakteristik dieses Tondichters* (Braunschweig: Eduard Leibrock, 1843). The copy used for this paper is in the Boston Public Library (ML 410 B5 G6). (Three hundred and fifty copies of the pamphlet were reprinted in 1974 by the Literarische Vereinigung Braunschweig.)

thirty-one page pamphlet, a highly enthusiastic and at times angrily worded defence of the French composer, was written and hastily issued in 1843 in response to the negative or at best tepid notices of Berlioz's work that had appeared in the Leipzig musical press – especially in the *Neue Zeitschrift für Musik*. Dedicated to the members of the Brunswick ducal chapel (whose performances of Berlioz, as we shall see, were well executed and well received), the pamphlet was presumably intended to quiet some of the nay-sayers of the German musical press as well as to inspire some of the musicians and concert directors who might have been discouraged by negative criticism from performing Berlioz's music.

In order to understand Griepenkerl's staunch partisanship, it is necessary at least briefly to examine the basic premise of his aesthetic posture. Griepenkerl (1810–68) was the son of Friedrich Konrad Griepenkerl, a pupil of J. N. Forkel and the editor of many works by Johann Sebastian Bach. Wolfgang Robert, himself a playwright and music critic, taught at the *Kadettenanstalt* in Brunswick.[9] His most important ideas about music had been expressed in the 1838 *Novelle, Das Musikfest, oder die Beethovener*, excerpts from which were published in the *Neue Zeitschrift* itself.[10] Griepenkerl's central thesis is that humour is the key element of Beethoven's mature style; that humour is perceivable in Beethoven's 'middle' or 'heroic' period, and deepens in the later 'period of reflection'. In fact Griepenkerl is one of the first critics seriously to discuss the question of humour in music. Griepenkerl's approach derived from literature: the principal figures to whom he links Beethoven, with regard to that question, are Shakespeare and Jean Paul.

Griepenkerl's concept of humour, with its references to Jean Paul, is not dissimilar to that found in the writings of Ernst Ortlepp, one of the founders, with Robert Schumann, of the *Neue Zeitschrift*.[11] E. T. A. Hoffmann's influence may also be discerned, although Griepenkerl chose to look beyond Hoffmann's fantastic and metaphysical vision of an 'unknown realm' to embrace more tangible concepts such as 'organic', 'dramatic', 'historical' and 'humouristic'.[12] Griepenkerl claimed that

---

9 In 1856, Henry Litolff, who had settled in Brunswick in 1849, composed an overture to Griepenkerl's five-act tragedy, *Robespierre* (1851).

10 Griepenkerl, *Das Musikfest, oder die Beethovener* (Leipzig, 1838). For further information about Griepenkerl, see David B. Levy, 'Wolfgang Robert Griepenkerl and Beethoven's Ninth Symphony', *Essays on Music for Charles Warren Fox* (Rochester, 1979) 103–13.

11 Plantinga, *Schumann as Critic*, 5.

12 Indeed, the designation of Berlioz as 'Ritter' may be read as a *double entendre*, intended both to invoke memories of Hoffmann's *Ritter Gluck* and to recognise Berlioz's nomination to the Légion d'honneur in 1839.

humour derived from the juxtaposition of opposing moods, the sudden leap from the real to the sublime, the sudden shift from the objective to the subjective, the rude interruption of deep pathos by low comedy. These, of course, were precisely the characteristics of Beethoven's late style at which many critics pointed accusing fingers. And at nearly the same time, similar traits in the plays of Shakespeare were being condemned as 'barbarous', a phenomenon that hardly went unnoticed by Berlioz.[13] In fact, according to Griepenkerl, Berlioz's name was to be added to those of Shakespeare and Beethoven and thus to the pantheon to which he rightly belonged. But Germany's critical establishment, especially that of Leipzig, did not unanimously share Griepenkerl's opinion.

Any sense of vindication that Berlioz may have enjoyed in France, after the triumph of *Roméo et Juliette* in 1839, was short-lived. No new generous soul like Paganini emerged who could provide him the means by which he might concentrate on composition. The difficulties of arranging concerts proved too taxing, and the Conservatoire offered only the sinecure of assistant librarian. The already deteriorating state of his marriage to Harriet Smithson further added to his growing disillusionment. Even the initial flush of excitement and controversy surrounding the introduction of Beethoven's symphonies into Parisian musical life – works that continued to inspire him – was waning among his friends. Almost instinctively, and with encouragement from Liszt, Berlioz decided that a tour of Germany would form the next logical step in his musical career. Had he not, after all, clearly demonstrated his identification with the loftiest German ideals by his staunch partisanship of Beethoven? Had not Richard Wagner publicly hailed Berlioz as the composer in France best able to compose recitatives for Weber's *Der Freischütz*, an effort that would go far towards eradicating the earlier corruptions of Castil-Blaze's *Robin des bois*?[14] Surely the Germans who shared his hatred for the 'triviality' of Pacini, Bellini, Donizetti and much of Rossini would embrace him as one of their own. Fully aware, however, that many Germans also idolised these Italians, he set forth with missionary zeal in December of 1842, first to Brussels, then to the land of Goethe, Schiller and Beethoven.[15]

13 See Peter Bloom, 'A return to Berlioz's *Retour à la Vie*', *The Musical Quarterly*, 64 (1978) 370. Bloom notes that Berlioz's original text of 1832 includes a diatribe against Beethoven's critics.
14 Richard Wagner, 'Der Freischütz in Paris', *Prose Works*, ed. W. Ashton Ellis, VII, 92–107.
15 Bloom, in 'La Mission', reminds us that Berlioz's tour may perhaps be seen as a belated fulfilment of his official duty as a Prix de Rome laureate.

DAVID B. LEVY

Berlioz's personal accounts of his travels, preserved in open letters written to friends in Paris and printed in the *Journal des débats*, record the progress of his appearances in German cities including Berlin, Mannheim, Weimar, Leipzig, Dresden and Brunswick. Many of these open letters made their way as well into the pages of the *Neue Zeitschrift für Musik*.[16] Hugh Macdonald relates that everywhere in Germany he received 'enthusiastic welcomes';[17] and D. Kern Holoman reports that in spite of some doubters in the Parisian press, German reactions to Berlioz were 'resoundingly positive'.[18]

What in particular did some of the German critics have to say? A review in the Leipzig *Allgemeine musikalische Zeitung* of Berlioz's two concerts in Berlin, for example, indicated that both of these events (especially the second) were poorly attended. The same correspondent found the music to be 'idiosyncratic, original, but often unclear and overladen with instrumental effects'. The Overture to *Benvenuto Cellini* was 'too long and scarcely comprehensible'. The outer movements of *Harold en Italie* contained 'isolated motifs of idiosyncratic invention, but little working out, thereby [rendering] precise understanding of the ideas [...] impossible'. The critic concluded that Berlioz's compositions 'are less suitable for Germany than for the over-strained French taste'. He recognised Berlioz to be 'an important talent' who showed far more '*Esprit* than *Gemüt*' ('more animation than substance').[19] A reviewer from Weimar again identified Berlioz as original, but suggested that 'no small degree of the bizarre and the baroque occurs that could impress unfavourably'. The same writer lamented a paucity of beautiful melody and a reliance on sudden and unexpected modulations. He claimed to have heard the Overture to *Les Francs-Juges* on three occasions, caring for it less each time.[20]

The critic for the *Allgemeine musikalische Zeitung* (identified as 'S...') assigned to Berlioz's Leipzig concert of 4 February 1843 recorded that the hall of the Gewandhaus was 'less filled than expected' and that the applause was marked by a 'distinct uncertainty, and could in no way be called unanimous'. He found Berlioz's music to be of a 'very gloomy

16 German translations of these letters appeared under the title 'Bericht über Berlioz' musikalische Reise', *Neue Zeitschrift für Musik*, 19 (1843) 125–7, 130–32, 137–8, 141–2, 145–7, 149–50, 154–6, 159–60, 171–2, 185–7, 189–90.
17 Hugh Macdonald, 'Hector Berlioz', *The New Grove Early Romantic Masters 2* (New York, 1985) 111. 18 D. Kern Holoman, *Berlioz* (Cambridge, Mass., 1989) 301.
19 *Allgemeine musikalische Zeitung*, 45 (1843) 358. The words 'esprit' and 'Gemüt' defy precise translation; the writer clearly intends to differentiate French and German sensibilities.
20 *Allgemeine musikalische Zeitung*, 45 (1843) 264–5.

140

colour', and filled with the 'harshest dissonance'; he surmised that Berlioz 'does not wish to please us, he wishes to be original'. Of the *Symphonie fantastique*'s last movement, he wrote: 'compared to the Witches' Sabbath in the Fantastic Symphony, Weber's Wolf's Glen must be labelled a lullaby'.[21]

Two assessments of Berlioz's appearances in Leipzig may be found in the *Neue Zeitschrift für Musik*. The first was written by the composer-critic Hermann Hirschbach, the second by a critic identified only as 'Z', perhaps Anton von Zuccamaglio, who also wrote under the pseudonym of G. Wedel. Both articles figured prominently as targets for attack in Griepenkerl's subsequent pamphlet. Leon Plantinga has given us a concise summary of Berlioz's treatment in the *Neue Zeitschrift*, concentrating largely on Schumann's ambivalent attitude towards the Frenchman, particularly as expressed in his extraordinary 1835 review of the *Symphonie fantastique*, a review that was written in response to Fétis's condemnation of the work.[22] Schumann ultimately considered Berlioz to be an important composer, but qualified his judgement by designating him as one who 'belongs to France'.[23] If Schumann was unable to reconcile himself fully to Berlioz's music, he did at least admire the sincerity of Berlioz's motivation. Plantinga suggests that the objections Schumann had to Berlioz's style at the beginning 'loomed larger in his thinking' later on, offering this as a possible explanation for his public silence in the wake of Berlioz's Leipzig concerts. We shall see that Griepenkerl went so far as to suggest that Schumann's silence would be seen as an expression of his tacit agreement with the negative views of Berlioz's enemies. Schumann, not wishing to enter into the growing fray, partially generated by his colleagues on the *Neue Zeitschrift*, explained his critical absence:

At present, I confess, I should be harsher with much of his work [harsher, that is, than in the *Symphonie fantastique* review]. The years make one more severe, and the unlovely things I found in Berlioz's early music (and I think I pointed them out then) have become no more beautiful in the interim. But this I also said: there is a divine spark in this musician. I hoped that maturity would improve and purify it to produce a clear flame. Whether this has happened I cannot tell, for I know no mature works of Berlioz – none have been printed.[24]

---

21 *Allgemeine musikalische Zeitung*, 45 (1843) 217–21.

22 Plantinga, *Schumann as Critic*, 235 ff.

23 *Ibid.*, 248. Schumann's public voice may have been silent, but not his private one. Upon hearing the *Offertoire* from Berlioz's *Requiem* in rehearsal, Schumann was quick to voice his admiration. See, among others, Holoman, *Berlioz*, 297.

24 *Neue Zeitschrift für Musik*, 18 (1843) 177–8 (translation from Plantinga, 249).

Schumann did not make a habit of reviewing concerts, preferring to write about published music. Berlioz's 'mature' works, according to the composer's own wishes, would not appear in print until after he had tested them with German orchestras under his own direction.

Berlioz's concert in Brunswick took place on 9 March 1843. His programme was enormous, featuring the Overture to *Benvenuto Cellini*, the *Offertoire* and *Quaerens me* from the *Requiem*, *Rêverie et Caprice* for violin and orchestra, *Harold en Italie*, 'Absence' and 'La Belle Voyageuse' (sung by Marie Récio), and two movements from *Roméo et Juliette* (*La Reine Mab* and *Roméo seul, Grande Fête chez Capulet*). The performers charged with the execution of these difficult scores comprised the orchestra and chorus of Brunswick's ducal chapel. Meyerbeer had told Berlioz that he would find a 'vintage orchestra' there and this certainly proved to be the case.[25] Among its principal virtuosi were the members (all brothers) of the Müller String Quartet, whose performances of Beethoven's quartets in Paris in 1837 had been a revelation to Berlioz. Yet another Müller brother, Georg, was the Kapellmeister. In a letter addressed to Heinrich Heine, in Paris, Berlioz wrote that never had he encountered 'in France, Belgium or Germany' a more conscientious and dedicated ensemble:

An hour before I arrived each morning (I discovered later) the orchestra met to practise the most hazardous phrases and rhythms. I was more and more astonished at the rapid change I found from one day to the next and at the confidence with which they attacked difficult passages which even my Paris orchestra, the Young Guard of the Grand Army, had approached warily.[26]

The artistic effect of the concert and its enthusiastic reception by the Brunswick audience were unsurpassed elsewhere during Berlioz's first German tour. The conclusion of his report from Brunswick introduces the name of Griepenkerl:

So you see, I am much indebted to the artists and music-lovers of Brunswick. I owe a great deal too to the leading music critic, Robert Griepenkerl, who in an erudite pamphlet vehemently took issue with a Leipzig journal and gave what seems to me a very accurate idea of my music and of the force and direction of the musical impulses that drive me on.[27]

As Griepenkerl noted, two works by Berlioz had been performed in Brunswick as early as 1839 – the overtures to *Les Francs-Juges* and *Le Roi*

---

25 See Cairns, 252.   26 *Ibid.*, 254. See also Holoman, *Berlioz*, 299.

27 *Ibid.*, 257. Berlioz discovered Griepenkerl's pamphlet in Hanover, in May, and (as the letter of 6 May 1843 cited below makes clear) had it translated into French by an acquaintance in that city.

Lear. The resulting opinions of the public and professionals, he added, reflected those of people elsewhere in Germany, and could be divided into three distinct categories: (1) outright rejection, (2) unqualified praise, and (3) indirect praise. Griepenkerl held this division to be the fate of any manifestation of new and unusual art, because such art conceals in itself 'a power that would generally make this disagreement possible'. He cited as examples the figures of Meyerbeer, Spontini and, of course, Beethoven. He further observed that some critics of Beethoven had yet to come to terms with this composer's later style. With Berlioz's personal appearance in Brunswick, 'the public voice of derision has fallen silent', admirers have consolidated their position because their high expectations were surpassed, and others have modified their stance by recognising him to be a great, if isolated, musician.

Berlioz's music transcends what Griepenkerl calls casual subjectivity and builds, instead, 'universal powers of history, the true universal, that which pertains to all, the objective, moral manifestation'. When Griepenkerl read Hirschbach's categorisation of Berlioz as a Frenchman who failed to manipulate his musical materials in the 'artistic and natural' way of a German, and who lost himself in 'objective representations', he felt that the lines of battle had been drawn. For Hirschbach had not only failed to recognise the very strength of German music, but he had missed the principal quality that Berlioz's music shared with it. Berlioz's glory, according to Griepenkerl, was that he had transcended national boundaries and entered into the 'depth of the German spirit'. The truly Romantic spirit is not simply lyrical (that is, subjective), it is also epic and dramatic (that is, objective). Shakespeare and Beethoven knew this, he continues, and so does Berlioz – hence Berlioz's choice of Lear, the trials of the Vehmic courts and the life of Benvenuto Cellini as subjects for musical treatment. Griepenkerl goes on to suggest that Berlioz's next symphony will be modelled on 'our German Schiller's *Jungfrau von Orleans*'.[28]

28 Griepenkerl, *Ritter Berlioz*, 10. This is the only mention of a *Jungfrau von Orleans* Symphony that I have seen. Perhaps Berlioz implied some interest in such a Schiller project during an informal conversation with Griepenkerl. Holoman mentions that in 1829, Gérard de Nerval had approached the composer with his translations of Schiller, hoping that Berlioz would set something to music (*Berlioz*, 58). It is possible that Berlioz's interest in *Die Jungfrau von Orleans* dates from this time or from slightly later, in 1831, when, as Mendelssohn noted, Berlioz dreamed 'of nothing but Beethoven, Schiller and Goethe' (cited in David Cairns, *Berlioz* [London, 1989] 445). In any event, Griepenkerl's reference to this unrealised project perhaps deserves mention in future listings of 'Works Contemplated But Not Composed', such as that included in Holoman's *Catalogue*.

The 'objectivity' of Germany, then, is for Griepenkerl what led Berlioz to German soil. Paganini, upon hearing the première of *Harold en Italie*, had pronounced Berlioz the rightful heir to Beethoven, an assessment with which Griepenkerl agreed. He refused, however, to label Berlioz a 'second Beethoven', seeing him rather as standing in an 'organic' relationship to Beethoven, and holding a place for which no German composer can compete. Why, then, should he be rejected by the press instead of being embraced as a brother? Was he a prophet to be stoned? Griepenkerl cites a report from one journal in which the cynical reviewer noted that had Berlioz visited Germany in 1842, his appearance would only have 'increased the streak of calamities of this year!'[29] He continues by telling of reports from Leipzig that Berlioz's appearance had been greeted with derisive laughter. Griepenkerl refuses to believe – and he was correct in this regard – that Mendelssohn and Schumann were among those who mocked Berlioz. But he does lament Schumann's silence, as we have seen, in the face of the critics' intemperate assaults.

Griepenkerl writes of how Berlioz's music, upon its first appearance in Germany, created a sensation among the public (attested to by Lobe's 'Sendschreiben'). But this initial enthusiasm was broken by reflections on the part of critics who came 'hobbling after'. Griepenkerl's most pointed barbs are aimed at critics such as 'Z', critics whose chastisements of Berlioz were worded with special ferocity, but whose identities were hidden behind pseudonyms and initials. Any scholar who has attempted to ascertain the identities of anonymous nineteenth-century critics must sympathise with Griepenkerl when he asks, 'Who could all these disembodied letter-men be?!' ('Wer nur diese verkappten Buchstaben-männer alle sein mögen?!')[30]

According to Griepenkerl, Berlioz possesses the ability to express humour in musical terms. By turning to England and Germany, 'the father- and motherlands of humour', Berlioz associates himself with Shakespeare and Beethoven, and thereby relinquishes his peculiarly French identity. By so doing, he leaves himself open to the derision that all humourists, regardless of national origin, must endure. Griepenkerl joins a specific passage from the Finale of *Harold en Italie* to a passage from Shakespeare to demonstrate his point:

---

29 Griepenkerl, *Ritter Berlioz*, 12. Griepenkerl fails to mention the journal in question, and I have been unable to locate the citation.   30 *Ibid.*, 27.

[He] makes the violins laugh demonically while the trombones warn in a quite frightening manner of the day of judgement. Then it is said – how indeed it is said, it is much too mad. O how one might wish to cry: 'There are more things in Heaven and earth, Horatio, Than are dreamt of in your philosophy'.[31]

Other excerpts from the *Orgie de brigands*, though not cited specifically by Griepenkerl, surely fit into his particular humouristic world. The passages I have in mind come towards the end of the movement, at the moment when the distant strains of the Pilgrims' March threaten to jar the Byronic hero's conscience (Breitkopf edition, p. 160). I think that Griepenkerl would wish us to hear the alternation of the ferocious D's and E flats (p. 169) and of the minor-mode subdominant chords with the major tonic (p. 170) as a mockery of everything held sacred by society. If we view these passages in this context, we may discern the essence of Griepenkerl's definition of humour – the close juxtaposition of opposing moods. Even more, I believe that Griepenkerl would wish us to experience these passages as Berlioz's musical answer to those critics who dared to berate Shakespeare, Beethoven and Berlioz himself. Griepenkerl ends his pamphlet by asserting that Berlioz's music represents 'a progress in the development of instrumental music' unlike anything since the appearance of Beethoven; by citing a verse from Calderón –

> What is life? madness!
> What is life? merely froth,
> A poem, scarcely a shadow!
> Fortune can grant us but little;
> For all life is but a dream
> and the dreams themselves but a dream.[32]

– and by laying his judgements at the mercy of History, which 'rules over everything'. He suggests that others share his view of Berlioz, and feels no regret for having set them forth in writing.

Berlioz's admiration for Griepenkerl and his colleagues in Brunswick as expressed in the letter to Heine has been mentioned earlier in this study. In fact the friendship between Berlioz and Griepenkerl that began in 1843 continued by correspondence until 1855. A second personal meeting took place in 1846, when Berlioz returned to Brunswick during his second tour of Germany. They probably met on two further occasions, in October

---

31 *Ibid.*, 27. The quotation is from *Hamlet*, Act I, scene v.
32 *Ibid.*, 30. The quotation is from Calderón's *La vida es sueño*, Act II, scene xix.

1853 and April 1855. Letters from Berlioz to Griepenkerl dating from 1843 to 1846 underscore how much the composer appreciated the Brunswick critic's support:[33]

(Hanover, 6 May 1843)
[Thank you for providing me with a copy] of the knowledgeable and kind pamphlet [...] that you have written on my compositions and my musical propensities. Such a work pleases me all the more because it gives me confidence, for everyone can see from the opening lines that it emanates from an intelligence both lofty and entirely free of prejudice. [...] Your chapter on temperament is admirable, and, I believe, perfectly true. Your work has just been carefully translated for me into French.[34]

(Paris, 26 July 1844)
Let me only shake your hand and thank you from the bottom of my heart for your warm sympathy. Nothing in the world is better able to give me patience, force and courage than the parallelism between my ideas and those of such a distinguished intelligence as your own. A thousand thanks for all that you care to say and to write about me. I cannot get hold of my *Harold* Symphony at this moment, as it is now the property of Schlesinger, who will publish it soon. The *Symphonie fantastique* is engraved and will appear in one month if I have time to correct the proofs. I will try to send you soon my new overture, the *Carnaval romain*; it is a little caprice ['une jolie *folie*'] that was wildly successful this winter in Paris. [...] Please believe, my dear M. Griepenkerl, in the sincere friendship that you have inspired in me since our first meeting. I shall never forget it.

(Paris, late March or early April 1845)
It has been a long time since I've had news from you. [...] What is happening in your dear city of Brunswick? Are you still quarrelling with the *savants* of Leipzig? How appreciative I am of all the proofs of warm sympathy that you have given me!

(Prague, 1st April 1846)
I thank you for all the efforts that you are making in behalf of *our ideas* [italics original] about music. Time is the greatest of masters, and you may be certain that they will triumph, perhaps sooner than we thought, over all the north of Germany; as for the south, victory will soon be ours.

Some of these letters shed interesting light on the orchestral requirements that Berlioz deemed essential for the proper execution of his music. The last letter cited above, sent from Prague, finds Berlioz eager for Griepenkerl to become acquainted with the *Symphonie fantastique*. The composer specifies the need for two tenor trombones in B flat or bass

---

33 See CG III, 93–4, 193–4, 238–9, 332.
34 I translate Berlioz's word 'humeur' as 'temperament'; however, this letter has come down to us in only fragmentary form, and no autograph has been preserved. It is quite possible that Berlioz wrote 'humour' rather than 'humeur'.

146

trombone in E flat to play the second and third parts in the *Marche au supplice*, rather than the trombones in F normally used by German players. He points out that only the correct instruments can play the low B flat and A (at bars 78–81 in the *Marche au supplice*) that will 'produce a terrifying effect'.[35] He also reported that the lack of capable timpanists in Prague ruined the effect desired at the end of the *Scène aux champs*.

Leo Schrade, writing in the 1940s, observed that the growth of the idea that was 'Beethoven in France' was a powerful stimulus with extraordinarily diverse intellectual ramifications.[36] When that seed took root in the person of Hector Berlioz and returned to Germany, the stimulus also proved to be powerful, and hardly less complex in the response that it elicited. German critics, Griepenkerl and precious few others excepted, were loathe to see Beethoven's mantle placed on French shoulders. As I have suggested, many German critics in 1843 were still struggling to come to terms with Beethoven, especially with his late style. Berlioz hardly could be held to blame if he stepped on to German soil with an understanding of Beethoven that surpassed that of most Germans.

At the very least, the phenomenon of 'Ritter Berlioz' in Germany should cause us to reconsider our penchant for defining musical style in the nineteenth century according to nationality – a concept that at best is elusive – especially where instrumental music is concerned. Perhaps we would be better advised to contemplate kinships created by the force of individual minds and striking concepts, not the least of which is Griepenkerl's intriguing notion of humour. The blind Earl of Gloucester, in Act IV, scene vi, of Shakespeare's *King Lear*, approaches the cliffs of Dover and asks his legitimate son, Edgar, 'When shall we come to the top of that same hill?' Griepenkerl chose this line – 'Wann kommen wir zum Gipfel dieses Bergs?' – as the epigraph for *Ritter Berlioz in Braunschweig*. The thrust of the pamphlet is that only he who is the legitimate heir to humour – be he English, German or French – will gain the mountain's summit.

---

35 CG III, 331. The 'terrifying effect' still remains obscured by modern instruments. Roger Norrington's recent recording with period instruments is revelatory in light of the intentions Berlioz articulates in his letter.
36 Leo Schrade, *Beethoven in France* (New Haven, 1942).

7

The Damnation of Faust, or the perils of heroism in music

KATHERINE REEVE

I : BERLIOZ AND GOETHE, MUSIC AND WORDS:
THE POLEMICAL BACKGROUND

The idea of a Faust in music has always appeared as ludicrous to some as the idea of Faust in a ballet appeared to Berlioz, who thought it more preposterous than a history of Rome in madrigals. When in the face of such prejudice he produced a musical drama based on the first part of Goethe's *Faust,* in 1846, cries of sacrilege from German critics provoked him to defend himself in a preface. He had been accused – 'often with bitterness', he reports – of 'mutilating a monument'.[1] More even than bitterness, the word 'mutilation' betrays so visceral a response as to arouse not only scepticism about its pertinence, but curiosity about its cause. Not that language of this kind is unusual in the history of music criticism. Classical critics regularly denounced operas for emasculating the virile actions and passions of spoken drama.[2] Lately a new twist to the

---

1 The preface to *La Damnation de Faust* appeared with the publication of the score by Richault in 1854. Berlioz tells in chapter 54 of his *Mémoires* about the criticism to which his work was subjected in Germany. Otto Jahn and later Eduard Hanslick were among the more famous of those who branded the *Damnation* a 'mutilation' of Goethe. See Julien Tiersot, *La Damnation de Faust de Berlioz: Etude historique et critique* (Paris, n. d.) 79–81. Berlioz's quip about a Faust ballet comes from *A Travers chants,* 361. (Cf. his article in *Le Rénovateur,* 3/291 [18 Oct. 1834].) He had none the less himself undertaken a Faust ballet for the Paris Opéra in 1829.

    The score of the *Damnation* appears in *NBE* 8a and 8b. A separate text of the libretto may be found, along with useful articles about the work, in *L'Avant-Scène Opéra,* 22 (1979), and in the brochure with the London/Decca recording of the work (1982) LDR 73007, which includes an English translation by David Cairns. Unless otherwise attributed, translations here are mine.

2 For examples of Classical, misogynous charges against music see Saint-Evremond's letter to the Duke of Buckingham (1677), or the Preface to *Sémiramis* by Voltaire (1748), in Ulrich Weisstein, *The Essence of Opera* (New York, 1964) 32 and 78; see also James A. Winn, *Unsuspected Eloquence: A History of the Relations between Poetry and Music* (New Haven, 1981) 241–51, for some blatant examples in Dryden and other English critics. Typical reactions to the treatment of

tradition has come from another German critic, Hermann Hofer, who in an analysis of great perspicacity and goodwill towards the 'modern' Berlioz has interpreted the hero of *La Damnation de Faust* as an anti-Faust – intellectually barren, politically ineffectual and sexually impotent.[3] Extreme though it may sound, such a view pushes to its logical conclusion a standard response to Berlioz's work from the first. In effect we find Berlioz charged, in France as elsewhere, with castrating both the text and the hero of Goethe's classic.[4]

That so much should be at stake in an aesthetic argument goes far towards explaining the emotions involved. What is not so clear is the logic of the charges, which reflect opposing estimates and concern the different levels of plot and genre. The suspicion immediately arises that those levels are related. There is every reason to believe that Berlioz's early critics attacked his *Faust* in large part because they perceived its hero as an unworthy match for his literary model. The question then occurs: could music – the musical transposition itself – be responsible for sapping a hero's manly vigour?

Classical critics were convinced of it. For Boileau and Voltaire, music was the culprit that prevented opera, which as a reincarnation of ancient Greek drama ought to have been the noblest of art forms, from properly representing action, the primary object of classical tragedy.[5] By a contradiction well known to feminist thinkers, music was at once despised and feared: feared for its power over the senses, despised for its irreducibility to 'reason'. The voluptuous pleasures of melody in the aria-laden Italian operas of the eighteenth century, for instance, tempted both hero and listener to 'stay', to prolong 'the moment' – precisely what Goethe's Mephisto intends for Faust. Already Goethe calls for music, along with love, as a means to that end. Consequently the scenes by the Elbe of the *Damnation* not only set Goethe's text but represent music enacting its own powers, seductive but disabling in the tradition of the

---

literary models in librettos are discussed by Herbert Lindenberger in *Opera: the Extravagant Art* (Ithaca, NY, 1984) 41 ff.

3 'Faust einmal ganz anders: "La Damnation de Faust" von Hector Berlioz neu gelesen', *Lendemains*, 31–2 (1983) 30–42.

4 Joseph-Marc Bailbé is struck by Faust's 'docile' passivity (*L'Avant-Scène Opéra*, 11). Henry Barraud sees Berlioz as having bypassed the depths of Goethe's play and made the hero into 'un vague jouisseur [qui] perd son temps à séduire une midinette' (*ibid.*, 24), yet pronounces the *Damnation* 'one of the richest musical scores' of the century (55), thereby assigning it a value roughly equivalent to that of Goethe's play in literature.

5 Weisstein, 52–3 and 75–80. On the primacy of action for the doctrine of mimesis, see Gérard Genette, 'Genres, "types," modes', *Poétique*, 32 (1977) 393 ff.

Orpheus myth. In that tradition music and love were metonymically interchangeable as enchanting, subversive forces embodied in operatic sirens like Dido and Armide, who treacherously diverted warrior-heroes from their path to greatness.

The nineteenth century would seem to have changed all this. In the wake of a new idealist aesthetic, music came to boast the highest moral and spiritual force; instrumental music especially, in the absence of verbal clues to the contrary, was imagined to reflect a kind of Pythagorean heaven of perfect order and beauty. From the lowest rank in the Classical hierarchy, music rose to supreme favour with the Romantics, who could no more think music a danger to morals than good Christians could impute evil to the deity. Yet music's 'absolute' remove from human affairs remained questionable. Opera and song posed the most obvious challenge to the new theory, but insofar as it remained expressive, even instrumental music resisted abstraction; indeed with Haydn, Mozart and Beethoven, music achieved both a new range of expressiveness and – through the dynamics of tonality in sonata form – a powerful capacity for rendering dramatic action.[6] As a result, music embodied potentially conflicting forces to the mid-nineteenth-century consciousness: action and emotion on the one hand, the Absolute on the other. In other words, everything Faust is striving for.

From the absolutist point of view, it is easy to see which of those forces must belong to the devil. To an idealist philosophy expression in art is inherently suspect – diabolical. Whereas 'absolute' music represents the highest intimation of spirit, offering a new road to truth where intellect and language have failed, music with words counts as fundamentally inferior, even corrupt, because that is where expression – the feeling, contingent human presence – is most tangible.[7] For the Romantics it is not music but words, action and scenery that threaten the integrity of opera; for this nineteenth-century work it is the text rather than the music that at the level of both plot and genre constitutes the potentially fettering, obtrusive element. Berlioz says as much in his preface when he defends himself for sending his hero to Hungary without any precedent in Goethe:

---

6 See Charles Rosen, *The Classical Style* (New York, 1971) 177; Carl Dahlhaus, *Die Idee der absoluten Musik* (Kassel, 1978); and John Neubauer, *The Emancipation of Music from Language* (New Haven, 1986).

7 See Rose Rosengard Subotnik, *Developing Variations: Style and Ideology in Western Music* (Minneapolis, 1991) 173–5, on the ideological shift from language to music as epistemological medium.

he would have sent Faust anywhere in the world 'if he had found the slightest musical reason for doing so'.

Such an extreme assertion of musical liberty does not, at first sight, encourage attention to the libretto. It would seem to mock die-hard Classicists who defend the integrity of the text, and to condone 'Romantic' absolutists who prefer to ignore it altogether. But when Berlioz responds in a preface to charges of infidelity to Goethe, it is not to take sides in the age-old power struggle between music and words. The logic of his claim applies to music and words alike: the Faust legend is public property, he argues, and departures from Goethe prove neither disrespect for his model nor disregard for his own text.

Proof and agreement are hard to come by in such disputes, which bear the seeds of dissension in the very terms they employ. Classical theorists endlessly debated the 'supremacy' of music or words in opera, and Wagner still spoke (in reference to Berlioz, on one occasion) of music needing words to 'dominate' it, 'as woman needs man'.[8] Yet even as they adopted the polarising rhetoric of the Classics, the Romantics were dismantling its premises. Berlioz himself spoke aggressively of music as 'free and proud and sovereign and triumphant', but did not on that account reject words; what he demanded was expressive freedom for all music, regardless of their presence or absence.[9] For Berlioz as for Wagner, the dialectic of music and words resolved itself in the decision to compose his own librettos – a solution that ensured to him and his music the first and final say, while simultaneously declaring the text so crucial that the composer alone could be relied on to do it justice.

It is fitting that the Faust theme first impelled Berlioz to become his own librettist, since many of the conflicts it embodies – power and weakness, liberty and subjection, prose and poetry, masculine and feminine – belong to the history of musical drama as well. Those conflicts are already reflected in Goethe's idiosyncratic form, and it is in the choice of form and genre that Berlioz too first came to grips with them when, with the help of a writer by the name of Almire Gandonnière initially hired for the

---

8 The phrase referring to Berlioz occurs in Wagner's letter to Liszt of 8 September 1852 (*Correspondence of Wagner and Liszt*, trans. Francis Hueffer [London, 1888] I, 222); the general statement may be found in *Oper und Drama* 1/7 (*Gesammelte Schriften* XI, 105), quoted by Lindenberger, 112, who deals with the master-slave terminology in operatic history on pp. 108–12.

9 Letter of 12 August 1856, where Berlioz also applies to music the (approximate) words of Corneille's *Médée*: 'Moi! c'est assez' (CG V, 352).

versification, he began reworking his *Huit Scènes de Faust* of 1829 – settings of nine poems from Gérard de Nerval's *Faust* translation – into a full-scale drama.[10]

I have so far spoken of *La Damnation de Faust* as if it were an opera. That it is not an opera matters chiefly for what it tells us about the artist's choice of aims and audience. When Liszt composed a Faust work, he signified his loftiness of purpose by selecting the highest genre in the prevailing hierarchy – a symphony. Berlioz himself originally thought of a Faust symphony when he first conceived the *Symphonie fantastique*, whose *Ronde du sabbat* may still pass for a *Walpurgisnacht*. But the liberty with which Berlioz and Liszt approached the symphony – more a point of reference than an adequate mark of category – serves notice of a highly independent attitude towards the notion of genre itself. To the Romantics, inherited forms were no longer guides to proper artistic behaviour but shackles to be broken by genius in favour of the individual, the unique, the inimitable. By its very disregard of pre-existing genres Berlioz's 'Légende dramatique', as he ultimately called it, constituted a triumph of the new poetics – an example of what Adorno wittily dubbed the 'genre of the masterpiece'.[11] The phrase can serve to answer those who question whether Berlioz devised a hybrid form because he could not get a commission for a 'real' opera. Closed doors at the Opéra merely opened those of his deeper inclinations: 'if only I had enough to live on', he confided to a friend in 1834, 'I would write plenty of other things besides operas. Music has powerful wings that cannot fully expand in the confines of a theatre'.[12]

Romantic propaganda notwithstanding, when in the following decade Berlioz threw caution aside and spread his wings in a work that radically defied the confines of genre, the immediate result was financial disaster.

---

10 Berlioz had written the prose text of *Lélio* as early as 1832 and occasional lines of verse, but never before attempted a major verse libretto. He tells in chapter 54 of his *Mémoires* how he came to take over the versification himself, at the same time making it clear that structure and content were his from the start. The nine poems at the core of the work come from the first edition of Nerval's *Faust* translation; in later editions Nerval substantially revised his translations, turning some into prose (whence the frequent supposition that Berlioz produced the revisions). See *Les Deux Faust de Goethe*, ed. Fernand Baldensperger (Paris, 1932). Gandonnière's portion is spelled out in *NBE* 8b, Appendix I.

11 Theodor W. Adorno, *Prisms*, trans. Samuel and Shierry Weber (London, 1967) 164. On the erosion of generic norms in Romanticism, see Carl Dahlhaus, 'Uber den Gattungsbegriff der Romantik' in *Gattungen der Musik in Einzeldarstellungen*, 1st series, ed. Arlt, Lichtenhahn, Oesch (Berne and Munich, 1973) 840–95. Dahlhaus classifies the *Damnation* as a 'symphony-cantata' – 'a non-existent genre, insofar as it consists only of exceptions' (878).

12 *CG* II, 198.

Adverse circumstances played their part – bad weather for the first performance, unfashionable singers, inadequate familiarity with the Faust story on the part of the audience – but in retrospect those seem merely to have betokened the larger aesthetic difficulties. The Classical dogma of generic purity retained a strong hold in the nineteenth century, and the critics who cried 'mutilation' added 'monster' in the next breath, denouncing the work as an adulterous, incoherent fusion of opera, symphony and oratorio.[13] Theatre directors later evaded the discomforts of a 'mixed' genre by adapting the work for the stage and, for better or worse, treating it as if it were indeed an opera. French audiences especially have liked it that way, and have since generously allowed the *Damnation*, in versions staged and unstaged, a share of the enormous popularity of Gounod's *Faust*.

My point is not to condemn adaptations of the *Damnation* for the stage, one of which Berlioz himself envisioned in 1847, but merely to insist on what an operatic frame necessarily alters and flattens out in the generic tensions of the original. For it is clear that Berlioz, like Goethe, aimed to go well beyond the norms of dramatic convention. Both *Fausts* are problematic to stage, their free-wheeling use of time and space demanding imaginative leaps that a pre-cinematic *mise-en-scène* can only partially fulfil. Formally they have in common a free, 'organic' blend of music and words, prose and poetry, real and unreal, for which they sought a warrant and a model in Shakespeare. That both works began their published life as fragments and occupied their authors during much of their careers may be taken as symptomatic of their kindred aims and problems.

In the interpretation of the Faust story as well, there is to my mind more kinship than contradiction in Berlioz's version of Goethe. Not that Berlioz's 'reading' has anything to do with the common idealised view of Goethe's hero (a counterpart to idealised portraits of the 'Olympian' Goethe himself) as the personification of the Deed, who triumphantly achieves his goal of self-fulfilment through a noble course of service to others. By taking his Faust to a harrowing conclusion Berlioz follows the

---

13 Dahlhaus reviews the persistent concerns for generic purity among eighteenth- and nineteenth-century critics in 'Gattungen', 874 ff. Otto Jahn is one of those who characterised Berlioz's work as a 'monster' (Tiersot, 80); even Berlioz's admirers have frequently charged him with inconsistency and incoherence, as in *The Music Criticism of Hugo Wolf*, trans. Henry Pleasants (New York, 1978) 197. On the social and psychological issues involved in attacks of generic 'adultery' in art see Tony Tanner, *Adultery in the Novel* (Baltimore, 1979). A related metaphor occurs in Carl Zelter's verdict to Goethe on Berlioz's *Huit Scènes de Faust* – an 'abscess, a freak of nature (*Abgeburt*) born of a hideous incest' (*Briefwechsel zwischen Goethe und Zelter*, ed. Riemer [Berlin, 1834] V, 251).

darker implications of Goethe's Part I, where the hero is a long way from salvation and believes himself inexorably headed for destruction.[14] Just how much of Goethe we are expected to read into Berlioz will always remain open to question. But to say, with Hofer, that Faust rejects the revolutionary call of the Hungarian March out of disdain and inertia, and thereby condemns himself to an *ennui* from which political commitment would have rescued him, seems to me to miss the Goethean overtones of Berlioz's opening. The musical Faust expresses envy for the frolicking peasants ('ma misère est jalouse') and admiration for the soldiers, whose presence he trumpets in a rising E flat major arpeggio. When he regretfully takes his distance, leading the way to the remote A minor of the March, he recalls the hesitancies of Goethe's doctor-hero, sobered by the experience of dispensing medical treatment more fatal than the plague it was to cure (1022–55). The Faust who refuses the smug optimism of the scholar Wagner, Goethe's caricature of an Enlightenment intellectual, is as much removed as Berlioz's from shiny-eyed dreams of military glory or spontaneous merry-making with a crowd. Consequently the retreat from action of Berlioz's hero marks no retreat from Goethe; at issue in both works is rather a new scepticism about heroic action and human progress, with a resulting change in the notion of heroism altogether.

At the same time, even if Berlioz had wanted to produce a musical equivalent of Goethe's drama, his work inevitably remains – to borrow a phrase of Harold Bloom's – a 'creative misinterpretation' of its predecessor.[15] The very conditions of music presuppose a new interpretation of the Faust theme. Music thrives on texts that are brief, singable and repetitive, qualities that from a literary point of view produce banality, awkwardness, fragmentation and redundancy. Whereas in literature the words are themselves the music, so to speak, in music they are only the skeleton to be fleshed out according to their cues of 'désir', 'ennui', 'amour'. It is therefore an exercise in futility to compare the 600 lines of Berlioz's libretto with the 3,600 of Goethe's Part I. Berlioz omits Goethe's various prologues, most of the opening scene in the study, the complex wager with the devil (he reverts to an old-fashioned pact, whose signing means instant doom), and so condenses the plot that only the three central figures remain. Even compared with Gounod's opera Berlioz's 'dramatic

14 *Faust: Der Komödie erster und zweiter Teil*, ed. Erich Trunz (Hamburg, 1966), for example lines 3348–51 and 3363–5. Subsequent line references to Goethe will appear in parentheses in the text.
15 The phrase comes from *The Anxiety of Influence* (New York, 1973), but my immediate source is Hans Robert Jauss, 'Goethe and Valéry's *Faust*: on the hermeneutics of question and answer' in *Toward an Aesthetic of Reception* (Minneapolis, 1982) 135.

legend' looks sparse: there are no village girls, no Marthe, no Valentin; no jewel scene, no cathedral scene, no *Walpurgisnacht*.

This does not mean the libretto is of no consequence. It may be the music that 'counts', but the words tell *how* it counts. Whatever its failings as literature, the brief text of the *Damnation* provides both a suggestive verbal fabric and a strong framework for the drama, which in its totality – music and words – yields a new, compelling and musically conditioned version of the Faust myth. It is this version and the nature of its hero that I mean to examine here. In so doing I will proceed from the direction of the text, taking 'legend' in the Latin sense as an invitation for the work 'to be read'. This is the sense Berlioz seems actually to have intended: according to a publicity release for the first performance, undoubtedly from his own hand, the label of 'opéra-légende' in use at the time indicated 'a work designed to be read rather than staged'.[16] Further corroboration comes from the presence of stage directions in the score and the separately printed libretto. In a work not destined for the stage, to whom but the reader – performer or concert-goer – would those directions be addressed?

Our habits of approaching music rarely lead very far along the path Berlioz suggests. To attend closely to the words, as Catherine Clément observes in her recent feminist critique of opera, is to commit sacrilege, to deflate the ineffable experience of the music.[17] It also risks uncovering cultural assumptions and prejudices that we might rather leave untouched, including some that Berlioz himself can have had no thought of our finding. Nevertheless the method works to his advantage: just as Clément rejuvenates the operatic war-horses she scrutinises, so a careful look at Berlioz's text can open our ears to the music in ways the most reverent blindness never could. Reason enough to take the risk in stride and set foot on the devil's territory.

II : MEPHISTOPHELES AT WORK: A TEXTUAL ANALYSIS

A common saying in the opera world, supposedly derived from a complaint of Martin Luther's, holds that the devil always gets the best tunes. It would be logical to assume that the devil will get the 'best tunes'

---

16 From *L'Illustration*, 21 November 1846; quoted in *CG* III, 380 n. The fluctuations in title from *Opéra de concert* to *Opéra-légende* to *Légende dramatique* underscore the work's generic indeterminacy. 17 *L'Opéra, ou la défaite des femmes* (Paris, 1979) 28.

in a work whose title announces his victory from the start. Even in Goethe's *Faust* Part I, Mephistopheles so dominates the action that many readers of the work in the decades before the appearance of Part II took it for granted that Faust would be damned. One early reader of considerable influence, Germaine de Staël, not only predicted that ending but went so far as to conclude that Mephisto was the real hero.[18] No one familiar with Part II could grant him so much, but in a work based on Part I his role is predictably crucial – so much so that it will be convenient to begin our enquiry from his perspective, before returning to Faust and to the questions of the hero and the heroic with which we began.

A look at the appearances – or rather the absences – of Mephisto, in *La Damnation de Faust*, affords a quick grasp of the action. He appears neither in Part I (Faust Alone, In the Plains of Hungary) nor in the Epilogue (On Earth; In Heaven). The real action takes place in between and ends with his victory in hell. Yet Mephisto never opens that action. Parts II and III begin with Faust alone, Part IV with Marguerite, as Berlioz and Nerval (no doubt for reasons of euphony) prefer to call Gretchen. At section closings, on the other hand, Mephisto is always there. In the collective finales of Parts II and III he sings in the chorus, hovering in the background and surveying the scene. Mephistopheles typically lurks and waits, poised for the pounce: 'Et le moment approche où je vais te saisir', he warns in the Finale of Part III. His very existence hinges on the hunt, for once he captures his prey he vanishes – at which point the action stops.[19]

Part I, then, is introductory. It prepares Mephisto's arrival, and the onset of the narrative proper, by establishing an idyllic mood that it exposes at once as flawed. Faust is alone, delighting in nature at the return of spring, when groups of villagers and soldiers intrude upon his reverie and disturb not only the immediate calm, but also the larger quest for spiritual peace in nature. Hints of longing and unrest surface as early as the sixth bar through a characteristic Berliozian flattened sixth in the orchestra, while Faust sidesteps the instruments' pastoral D major and enters in the minor. As a result we quickly suspect lingering ills for which the intruders cannot be blamed. Nevertheless the first explicit clue to those

18 *De l'Allemagne* (Paris, 1968) I, 343 (Part II, chapter 23): 'the devil is the hero of this play'. Nerval reprinted this passage in the introduction to his translation of 1828.

19 In 1844, Sören Kierkegaard in *Der Begriff Angst* recalls that an otherwise trivial contemporary Faust ballet had as its one convincing feature the idea of having Mephisto enter in a jump and remain there, poised in a springing position. *Werke*, I, trans. and ed. Liselotte Richter (Rowohlt, 1967) 120.

ills comes from Faust's ambivalence towards the group. He will envy the simple joys of the peasants and admire the energy of the soldiers, as we have seen, yet he has sought out these remote plains to get away from the crowd: 'Qu'il est doux de vivre [...] loin des multitudes'. Though the difficulty might be skirted by distinguishing between the ignoble multitude (*la foule*) and the noble *peuple*, as Victor Hugo was fond of doing, the distinction remains as precarious as the attempt to live life at its fullest in a pastoral retreat.

'Life' is what the devil comes to offer in Part II. He is summoned implicitly – as in Goethe – both by Faust's state of mind and by his gesture of putting poison to his lips, during a scene that conflates Goethe's opening in the study with the second study scene after the morning walk. By an irony more pointed than in Goethe it is the Easter Hymn that directly brings on Mephisto, who cuts short Faust's momentary ecstasy and offers a material solution to his discontent: supernatural entertainment or – 'life' ('Partons donc pour connaître la vie'). Berlioz's Mephisto identifies himself, in what appears at first an astonishing contradiction to Goethe's 'spirit of negation' ('Geist, der stets verneint' 1338) as 'the life spirit' ('l'esprit de vie'). The definition actually grasps well Mephisto's place in the Goethean world order, correcting any simplistic view of him as pure evil. At the same time the life that Mephisto offers is treacherous, like the poison that is either to 'illuminate' or 'kill' Faust's 'reason';[20] the Classical equation between 'reason' and 'life' is precisely what this devil puts in question.

The word 'vie' itself, recurring at the rhyme, later takes on poisonous overtones through Mephisto's subversive echo. In the trio ending Part III, Faust claims to have learned 'tout le prix de la vie' and Marguerite ecstatically gives her 'vie' to Faust, while Mephisto translates their bliss in his own terms: 'Je puis donc à mon gré / Te traîner dans la vie'. With a further turn of the screw, Mephisto rhymes *his* 'vie' with 'folie': 'l'amour en t'enivrant doublera ta folie'. So when Marguerite uses the same verbal juxtaposition on her first appearance, alluding to her vision of Faust in a dream, it is possible to detect an early sign of Mephisto's influence ('Nous verrons-nous dans cette vie? / Folie!'), the more so as Faust is already in the room while she speaks. Such verbal subtleties

---

20 At the end of the *chant-récitatif* opening Part II. Note the persistence of the poison motif in Brander's Song of the Rat, in the 'innocent poison' that kills Marguerite's mother and in the related theme of intoxication – in the drinking scene, the 'grappes vermeilles' of the *Chœur des Sylphes* and the figurative 'ivresse' of the love scene.

reinforce what the opening tritone – the medieval *diabolus in musica* – of the following song, *Le Roi de Thulé*, conveys musically: Marguerite has already fallen under the devil's spell. David Cairns has shown how Berlioz uses the tritone to systematic structural purpose throughout the work.[21] Here the 'diabolical' *mi contra fa* underscores the sense of foreboding propelled by the drone-like bass and the rocking accompaniment figure in the viola, which comment ironically on the utopian picture of a love 'faithful unto death'. Like the nostalgic *Chanson d'Hylas* that opens the final act of *Les Troyens*, Marguerite's retrospective *Chanson gothique* ushers in her own tragedy by evoking an innocence past reclaim.

If to the coupling of 'vie' and 'folie' at the end of Part III we add the triple rhyme 'désir / saisir / mourir' of the same climactic trio, we discover another grim portent of the tragedy ahead. Marguerite alone pronounces 'mourir', here and in the libretto as a whole: her 'Tout s'efface … Je meurs' figures the moment of seduction; 'je suis morte / Si l'on te trouve ici' reacts to the neighbours' outcry; 'cercueil', 'deuil', 'consume', 'se glace', 's'exhaler' in her Romance amplify the death theme that dominates her brief part. Meanwhile Faust and Mephisto do battle in the trio over 'désir' and 'saisir'. The musical convention of shared, repeated words provides Mephisto with a simple means of deflating his companion's lofty rhetoric: Mephisto's very utterance of the word 'désir' debases it (as in his offer of 'tout ce que peut rêver / Le plus ardent désir') and finally negates it in the Finale of Part III ('Sans combler ton dévorant désir'). Despite the majestic enjambement of Faust's later Invocation to Nature ('le désir / D'un cœur trop vaste'), before Mephisto's caustic gaze 'désir' will equal 'mourir'.

From the moment he appears Mephisto controls the proceedings, manipulating the two other principals in their relation to each other and to society. Faust is naturally his chief concern. The action unfolds in a succession of scenes *à deux* between Mephisto and Faust, sometimes beginning solo or augmented with chorus. By contrast, Mephisto is never alone with Marguerite and she is only once alone with Faust, in the love scene interrupted by Mephisto. (This last condenses three scenes from Goethe: the 'evening' scene; the garden scene; the serenade scene with Valentin.) Once only, in the Finale of Part III, do we hear all three characters together. Based on soundings like these, a structuralist view of the plot would see Mephisto as primary and Marguerite as a mere pawn in his pursuit of Faust's soul. There is a sense, as we shall see, in which

---

21 Cairns, 'Le Mal de l'isolement', *L'Avant-Scène Opéra* (see note 1), 16–17.

Mephisto does have the ominous last word on Marguerite. But structure is not everything: we will also see that she holds the key – at Mephisto's expense – to the question of the hero and the heroic in the work.

Our sole glimpse of Mephisto on his own, when he invokes the will-o'-the-wisps in Part III, does little to dissipate his mystery. Mephisto remains as elusive and insubstantial as his will-o'-the-wisps, or as the fire that is their common element.[22] Fire is the image that first impresses itself on Faust under the effect of Mephisto's gaze – a 'burning', 'penetrating' look which, 'like fire, burns and devours the soul' – and that image supplies one clue to Mephisto's identity. According to Promethean tradition and metaphorical usage, fire is alive and life-giving: 'I'll snuff you all out' ('je vous éteins tous'), Mephisto threatens his will-o'-the-wisp fiddlers. The 'life' he offers Faust comprises fiery amusements – will-o'-the-wisps who dance and sing a nuptial song ('un bel epithalamium') for the lovers, a flaming punch-bowl in the drinking song, a 'grilled' rat in Brander's song – and a lightning-motion in the rides that bring about swift, imaginary changes of scene. Yet that motion – either circular and repetitive or erratic and aimless like that of Mephisto's 'esprits des flammes inconstantes' – is of questionable effect; where Faust aspires to a forward movement of progress and ascent (even the chap-book Faust wished to fly among the stars), Mephisto offers him a perpetual motion that leads only to a scorching extinction. Death from the 'life-spirit'? The mystery deepens, although the cryptic motto from Goethe's poem 'Selige Sehnsucht', 'Die and become!' ('Stirb und werde!') could attest that death no more contradicts life than the dangers of fire invalidate its benefits.

Mephisto exhibits a further Goethean ambiguity in his capacity of 'enchanteur', both as a magician and an entertainer – a 'chanteur'. (The related verbs 'enchanter' and 'charmer' pervade the text, specifically the devil scenes and the love scenes.)[23] If anything, theatre is the essence of this

---

22 In Goethe, Mephisto's connection with fire is made explicit (1377). The German connotations of 'Irrlicht' carry through well in the French 'feu follet', although 'folie' is not as morally weighted as 'irren' ('Es irrt der Mensch, solang er strebt', 317). Goethe uses the will-o'-the-wisp motif notably in the *Walpurgisnacht* and in Mephisto's advice to Faust's disciple to study logic, so that his mind 'trotte prudemment dans le chemin de la routine et n'aille pas se promener en zigzag comme un feu follet' (trans. Nerval) – whence an inference as to the positive virtues of the 'feu follet'.

23 Mephistopheles on first appearance: 'ces cloches […] ont charmé […] tes oreilles'; 'j'enchanterai tes yeux et tes oreilles'; (by the Elbe) 'Songes d'amour vont enfin te charmer'; 'Le charme opère; il est à nous'; 'bercez son sommeil enchanté'; (Evocation of the will-o'-the-wisps) 'Vos lueurs

protean being, who is actor, singer, director, critic (social critic in his *Chanson* in Scene vi), even orchestra conductor, instructing his players, Hamlet-fashion, before the *Menuet des follets*. As a singer he performs three songs: the lullaby to Faust; the serenade to both lovers, though the message aims at Marguerite; the mock-ballad to the company in Auerbach's cellar. Each represents a genre that plays out a mode of cultural integration: soothing a child, courting a woman, amusing 'the boys'. But with Mephisto the gestures remain a kind of aesthetic game that fails to make Faust any less 'der Unbehauste' (3348) – 'homeless' – in mind or society.[24]

Like the theatre, fire is known for playing tricks. Though it may 'enchant', fire is deceptive and therefore dangerous, the ultimate danger consisting of the eternal 'lake of flames' into which Faust is plunged at the end. Mephisto gets him there by a series of deceptions, figured in part by the related theme of the veil, as in the 'voile / D'or et d'azur' of the vision by the Elbe. Faust, for his part, first becomes culpable towards Marguerite when he joins Mephisto in subterfuge: to reach her he takes cover among the soldiers and students (he sings with the latter of 'Stellata velamina' – starry veils) and then in her room ('Sous ces rideaux de soie / Cache-toi').[25] Veils in art tend to serve as equivocal shields for feminine charms; here it is the intruder whose presence is equivocal. By having him remain hidden while Marguerite sings her ballad, Berlioz in effect turns Faust into a voyeur, compounding the offence of the uninvited visit – and 'visit' is a delicate way of putting it. Goethe's Faust has in mind only the very crudest of seductions, one may recall, until chastened by the sight of Gretchen's room.

Mephisto's 'fire' bears erotic connotations from the start, his phallic gaze 'penetrating', 'burning' Faust 'like a dagger' on their first meeting. Not only does the devil promote sexuality as his ordinary stock-in-trade, but he also acts as seducer in his own right: Mephisto pursues Faust as Faust does Marguerite. Both as metaphor and as character his presence therefore gives bite to the conventional imagery of the love scenes where

malfaisantes / Vont charmer une enfant'; (Faust in Marguerite's room) 'ô ma charmante'; (Love scene) 'ivresse [...] enchanteresse'; (Romance) 'Le charme de ses yeux', 'sa voix enchanteresse'.

24 See Hofer, 32–3, on the dangers of aestheticism for Faust. On the theatricality appropriate to diabolical comportment cf. Kierkegaard, 118–19.

25 Although the theme of the veil occurs in Goethe (e.g. 673) these uses are Berlioz's alone, as is the caricature of the student song, *Gaudeamus igitur*, and the idea of Faust accompanying the student procession to reach Marguerite's house and remaining in the room during her ballad. Cf. also the 'veil' of night in the scene in the study and the 'cloud' that has hidden Marguerite in the love duet.

(in her duet with Faust) Marguerite succumbs to a 'burning' ecstasy ('Je ne sais quelle ivresse / Brûlante'), and (in her Romance) she is 'consumed' by the 'burning flame of love' ('D'amour l'ardente flamme') before praying to die in her lover's 'caresses de flamme'. The 'consuming' fire relates etymologically to the 'consummation' of the love; in keeping with Nerval's free, erotic rendering of Goethe's famous spinning song, 'Meine Ruh ist hin', Berlioz dispenses with the spinning-wheel and gives us, rather than the pining of a girl on the verge of physical love, the strongly sensual unrest of a woman physically bound. There seems to me no need to deny Faust's amorous 'success', as Hofer does, even though in Goethe the union comes after rather than before the 'Wald und Höhle' scene partly corresponding to Berlioz's Invocation, and even though in Berlioz there is no infanticide to offer proof. The 'nocturnes amours' (Mephisto's phrase) promised by the urgent 'demain' of the trio may be imagined to occur, with classical French restraint, between the acts, much as the consummation of Aeneas and Dido's love, in *Les Troyens*, occurs during an orchestral interlude. An even more graphic imagination might point out that we can more easily witness erotic climaxes in music than in spoken drama, and that Faust's long diminished-chord seduction has reached its E major resolution – on the words 'je meurs' – just before Mephisto's interruption.

There are in any case disquieting implications, for Faust, in the diabolical influence on his love-making. Not by accident is the love action – from the opening of Part III to the end of Marguerite's Romance – framed by a military retreat, its rhythmic pulse and unvarying harmony indifferent to the emotional trauma it accompanies. Increasingly distant and constrained, the persistent drum-beat under a single trumpeted chord provides martial music of a very different sort from the confident, musically imaginative march to glory and liberty that ends Part I, and in retrospect it casts some doubt on those ideals. The chord of the retreat seems actually to question itself, immediately abandoning root position for the unstable second inversion, resolving on to nothing more than a tonic empty of its mediant. When the same imperturbable rhythm sounds again at the end of the Romance, followed by snatches from the earlier soldiers' and students' choruses, its desolation infects not only Marguerite, but those exuberant young men as well.

At this point the words they speak demand attention, even if choral words are among the hardest to understand in performance. These carousing students and soldiers are out hunting for girls, whom they compare with towns under siege: the students claim themselves 'fortunati Caesares' and sing 'veni, vidi, vici!' of their feminine conquests. Juxtaposed with Marguerite's suffering, the dead metaphors of victory and conquest come alarmingly to life, harmless though they may have sounded in the Finale of Part II. One of the devil's main functions is after all the recharging of worn metaphors, in the way common to the literature of the fantastic. 'Damnation!' cries Faust, when the neighbours interrupt his love-making: Mephisto will take him at his word.

Ironically, then, Faust does join in with the soldiers, though in the less glorious of their traditional spheres of action. And despite his ecstasies over the 'angel' at the foot of whose 'celestial image' he longs to worship, in the love scene his language is very much the predator's: Marguerite speaks of 'giving' (her life!), while Faust – like Mephisto – is intent on 'grasping' ('le bonheur m'apparaît [...] je vais le saisir'). The entire hushed section after Mephisto's interruption, 'Adieu donc belle nuit', brings further nuances of self-seeking. Though a love aria in miniature, this interlude differs strikingly from the ongoing love scene: musically it reverts to the key and mood of the solitary aria in Marguerite's room; verbally it retreats from her in tense and person. Faust's 'adieu' addresses not the beloved but the 'festin d'amour que je m'étais promis', in Gandonnière's stale image of woman as a 'feast' for the lover's consumption. A final farewell, again disregarding Marguerite, apostrophises the 'heure fugitive où mon âme au bonheur allait enfin s'ouvrir'. Any charge of impotence could certainly allege this solipsistic withdrawal at the 'highest moment' (the text makes a brief allusion, here, to the terms of the Goethean wager). Marguerite might logically be supposed to have left the premises, were she not needed to sing the trio.[26]

What all this tells us is that by the end of the Romance, Marguerite is not merely a forlorn, love-sick girl, but also a victim of violence. Her doom, foretold in the choruses' model of seduction as siege, battle and victory, is enacted musically by the absorption of her vocal line into the rhythm of the soldiers' march, and by the stifling of the English horn as it attempts to restate the theme. Not that she herself has objected to playing out her given role: when in the love scene Faust sings of his 'victory' over the 'cloud' that has hidden her from him, Marguerite rapturously joins in,

---

26 Susan McClary points out the autoerotic nature of such 'transcendental' moments in 'Sexual politics in classical music', in *Feminine Endings: Music, Gender, and Sexuality* (Minneapolis, 1991) 53–79. I should like to thank Professor McClary for allowing me to see an early version of her article and to acknowledge the stimulating influence of her thought on my work in general.

celebrating her own demise ('Du jaloux nuage / Qui me (te) cachait encor ton (mon) amour est vainqueur'). Faust is later more lucid ('Horreur!') when Mephisto, in turn, cries victory ('Je suis vainqueur!'). When he stands in adoration by Marguerite's 'virginal' bed, Faust speaks ominously of the 'fatal moment' at hand; the phrase recurs in Mephisto's sardonic serenade, warning 'petite Louison' to offer 'great resistance' to her lover before the 'fatal moment'. In French translation that lover specifically becomes a soldier – 'drille', which rhymes provocatively with 'fille'. By final coincidence, Faust signs away his soul in a 'fatal document' ('acte fatal'), and plummets to the abyss on a cry echoing Marguerite's sigh at the end of her opening song.

Brief as it is, Berlioz's libretto thus manages to retain many of the minor incidents in Goethe that bear on the central love plot. Although the love action does not begin until the second half of the Legend, the first half tells us what we need to know about the climate in which this action will take place. Among the details that set the stage is the grotesque parody of the *Chanson de Brander*, where love's torments are compared with the death throes of a poisoned rat. Another is the moment in the *Ronde de paysans* when a man takes advantage of his wife's absence to waylay a girl, silencing her protests: 'Paix! ma femme n'est point ici'. He does so under cover of a whirling, frenzied kind of dance in which all are 'Dancing, jumping about like mad' ('comme des fous') on lurching octave jumps that recall the overlapping, falling fifths of Berlioz's early *Ballet des ombres* and of the Queen Mab Scherzo in the *Romeo and Juliet* symphony.[27] As we know, madness is of interest to the devil, whose jeering presence can be felt in the 'ha!' that punctuates this and later choruses. (The frequent interjections disrupting Mephisto's lines of verse point to his native medium – the pagan prose used in parts of the devil scenes.) When the dancers fall down in exhaustion ('Tous tombaient à la file'), they prefigure the 'fall' of 'petite Louison', of the girls 'conquered' by the soldiers and students, of Marguerite herself. Nerval's translation accentuates these elements of Goethe's text, and by sending his Faust to hell Berlioz follows their logic through to the end.

Mephisto is easily associated with the coarse, material, violent side of love. Less readily apparent but no less important is his alliance with love's

---

27 The *Ballet des ombres* dates from 1829, the same year as the projected Faust ballet (for which it was presumably intended).

'pure' side, which supplies him with his chief bait for Faust. From his opening sarcasm, 'O pure emotion', Mephisto captures and questions Faust's aspiration to a transcendental purity, expressed in the 'souffle pur' emanating from his 'poitrine ardente' in the prologue and in the 'pure jouissance' remembered from his childhood at the sound of the Easter Hymn. Those phrases, each verging on oxymoron, prefigure the seductive 'purity' of Mephisto's display by the Elbe.

In retrospect this shimmering riverbank vision serves as the immediate psychological preparation for the love drama, after which the soldiers and students can swing into action and lead directly to Marguerite. Everything about Mephisto's magical panorama is 'young', 'cool', 'green', 'joyous' – epithets so far equally applicable to the roistering youth of the Finale. What does not apply to them is the apparent chastity ('ingénue', 'timide') of the dream-vision. In this lush, lyrical atmosphere Mephisto's fire is conspicuously absent; by what right does he conjure up his 'feminine' antithesis, water, and the figure of Marguerite herself? The answer is that if water is purity and freshness, transparence and frailty ('une larme furtive'), it is also fertility, sexuality and engulfment: the 'bitter waves' into which the bravest of the lovers cast themselves recall the treacherous domain of the water nymph fatal to the fisherman of Goethe's ballad, set by Berlioz in *Lélio*. Since woman herself is the most powerful weapon in the devil's arsenal, there is no need to single out the overt signs of Mephisto's presence in the muttering brass accompaniment of 'Voici des roses'. According to the mythology of the 'second sex' so acutely analysed by Simone de Beauvoir, he is everywhere involved in the ambiguities of feminine enchantment.

Like Berlioz's own listeners, Faust can scarcely fail to succumb to these choral and instrumental waves of veiled sensuality. Indeed his own contribution to the texture encapsulates the surface duality of body and spirit upon which the master of ceremonies stakes his game: in voicing the name of Marguerite, Faust gives it its Latin form, 'Margarita', which indicates the spiritual even as it enables the more sensuous vocal sonority. The Latin form recurs in the prayers of the women and children to 'Sancta Margarita', in the *Course à l'abîme* and in the *Apothéose*, where Marguerite herself is sanctified. We will see shortly how suspect this sanctification is – and how dangerous for women, let alone hapless scholars and fishermen. In Mephisto's pageantry, feminine sanctity, virginity and emotion function, like the veil, as duplicitous means of setting off female charms.[28] Just as Ophelia's and Desdemona's very innocence provokes male brutality, so Marguerite's unspoiled beauty primes her for sacrifice. Curiously, the myth of the devil as fallen angel is not unrelated to this sort of desecration, and the ill-fated 'star' that appears to Faust ('Au front des cieux va briller ton étoile') sounds a distant echo of the devil's heavenly origin. More concretely, the 'beloved star' ('étoile chérie') 'lit up' for the young lovers seeking 'la vie' subtly reintroduces the fire metaphor, in a spiritual guise related to the 'mille feux éclatants' of Faust's opening scene, to the 'clartés infinies' of the sun in the Easter morning scene and to the 'Mondes qui scintillez' of the Invocation.

As the 'life-spirit' Mephisto evidently has access to both realms, material and spiritual; one might say that his treachery consists in exploiting the myth whereby the two are distinct. (In Goethe's text the proverbial 'two souls' of Faust are not separate, they only yearn to separate.) To Faust he holds out the lure of a woman-spirit, a 'trop idéale amante', when her music immediately reveals her sensual, feeling humanity; he beguiles both lovers with the illusion, quickly dispelled by the neighbourhood vigilantes, of a passion beyond law, infinite and sufficient unto itself – an illusion that recalls the image of music itself, as we saw, in Romanticist thought. And his victory consists in upholding the orthodox stratification of heaven, earth and hell so closely implicated in the preceding tragedy. For all that he aids and abets rebellion, Mephisto therefore acts as an agent of order, cynically defending the laws that make transgression possible. Repeatedly he sets the example of social compliance and urges restraint ('Modère-toi'; 'contiens tes transports') where Faust would rush in, heedless of the proprieties. He offers 'moral' advice to 'petite Louison' – by implication to Marguerite – the better to catch her when she goes against it. Under the terms of the Goethean wager, he means Faust to 'stay' ('verweilen'): with means captivatingly mobile, he works for stasis – for death.

It is usually taken for granted that Berlioz's ending supplies an edifying moral, whereby Faust is punished for his mistreatment of Marguerite while she is wafted back to a realm of pure spirit that she supposedly

---

28 Though illustrated by women, to whom the 'duplicity' is therefore usually attributed, these stereotypical functions are patriarchally motivated and defined. In *The Painted Witch* (London, 1985), Edwin Mullins analyses the use of the veil by male artists for the voyeuristic pleasure of male viewers, and the insidious process through which the representation of women in art – ostensibly 'as they are' – has chained women all the more strongly to male standards.

originates from and would never have left, were it not for Faust – or the devil. The main problem with this theory is that Faust is punished at the very moment his new-found pity and terror make him worthy of salvation. Too little too late, argues Hofer. The coincidence suggests a grimmer possibility: that Faust is condemned precisely because, as a man destined to 'higher' goals, he has yielded to 'lower', unmanly emotions. Certainly there remains something deeply disturbing about the final opposition between an ethereal, predominantly feminine heaven and a turgid, impenitent stag-party in hell, leaving nothing in between but a few lone voices on earth who report blankly, like newsmen, on the horrendous cost of this return to order. What is lost, at both ends of the spectrum, is nothing less than the human – the entire realm of 'la vie' that Faust so compulsively pursues, and that Marguerite so evidently belongs to. The angelic realm to which she is 'returned' is ultimately as fictitious as the dream-world where Faust first saw her image, and consequently just as much a prison as the 'lake of flames' below. With their disciplined ecstasy the otherwordly harps and high voices mask a male form of transcendence, in which the feminine has been domesticated in the service of a shadowy 'Seigneur'.

This uncomfortable message is further reinforced by a telling contradiction in the text of the Apotheosis. Marguerite is saved, we are told, because (in the Gospel phrase) she has 'loved much': 'Elle a beaucoup aimé, Seigneur'. By that token love would logically be the supreme value, something akin to the 'Eternal-Feminine' towards which Faust is steered at the end of Goethe's Part II. Yet in the next instant love is branded as the 'error' that 'altered' her 'primitive beauty'. Only a very rarefied form of love evidently passes muster in this sphere: Marguerite can be 'saved' if she renounces her sexuality, her humanity, her very life, and becomes pure spirit. How ironic that the final word of the score, the angels' 'Viens!' should recall both Faust's urging in the seduction scene and his call to the vial of poison in his study ('Viens, noble cristal'), moments that lend disquieting, erotic undertones to this last transcendental summons. Rather than admit such an undertow, religious custom maintains a strict separation between the 'pure' beauty and goodness of heaven and the evil beneath. More precisely, it allows only one means of bridging the gap: marriage, a prosaic solution put forward by Mephisto, diabolically enough, when he preaches to 'petite Louison' about the importance of the 'conjugal ring' in the course of his 'wedding song' to the lovers. If marriage or death – even in the guise of pure spirit, held out as an eventual hope for Faust as well – are the alternatives, then Mephisto has triumphed on all counts and at all levels.[29] Or rather, once again, a restrictive social order has won out, whose 'folie' Mephisto has only to exploit.

In the remembered excitement of the *Course à l'abîme*, listeners have been known to forget the Epilogue and final Apotheosis of the *Damnation*, as they occasionally do the moralistic epilogue of *Don Giovanni*. Conventional though they are, these endings have at least the virtue of anchoring the love theme in its broader social setting. Love in the *Damnation* turns out to be not simply one of the various distractions Mephisto has to offer, but a force implicated in all the others. As the 'life spirit' Mephisto symbolises that ambiguous force, which both threatens and is threatened by the social order and which Mephisto, as a character in the drama, both fosters and imperils. Elements of oppression and inequality corrupt the love between Faust and Marguerite as well as the 'friendship' between Faust and Mephisto. ('Faust condescends to love Marguerite', commented Berlioz, whereas Romeo and Juliet are equals.)[30] Love and friendship, in turn, menace established hierarchies because they 'equalise' partners despite outward differences, while bare-faced sexuality necessitates control at any cost. But Goethe's Faust yearns for the uncontrollable, the 'Urkraft' of nature itself: it is his drive to 'equal' the great spirits of nature, in the early scene with the 'Erdgeist', that propels his discontent and his endless striving. Berlioz chooses a parallel confrontation for his work's 'philosophical' centre, the Invocation to Nature. As we shall see further on, its placement directly after the love action signals even more explicitly than in Goethe the connection between the two.[31]

The use of names and terms of address, in which vocal drama tends to be lavish, affords a brief survey of the social tensions underlying the plot. On the one hand the protracted vocatives of Faust and Marguerite reaffirm given names and roles, aspiring to a love safely integrated in society; on the other hand Faust's offer to change his name – a Romeo-

---

29 The chorus of angels exhorts Marguerite to 'keep hope' ('conserve l'espérance'); an early version of the libretto explicitly envisions Faust's eventual salvation ('L'Eternel te pardonne, et sa vaste clémence / Un jour sur Faust aussi peut-être s'étendra'). See *NBE* 8b, Appendix IV.

30 'Faust *condescend* à aimer Marguerite; il la protège. Roméo s'élève jusqu' à l'amour de Juliette, elle est son égale' (*CG* V, 222). The comparison hides a shift of perspective – condescension implies a distinction of class rather than sensibility. A true parallel would hold that Faust 'ne s'élève *pas* jusqu' à l'amour de Marguerite'.

31 Jauss demonstrates this connection in *Goethe* (127–9). It is perhaps worth recalling that when Berlioz assumed the function of librettist, the Invocation was the part he undertook first.

like gesture that rejuvenates him as effectively as any love-potion – reaches for escape from social bounds. In contrast to these nominalistic ecstasies, Mephisto's name remains unspoken until his last scene, *Pandaemonium*, an absence registered by fearful questions from the drinkers and from Marguerite. Disdainful of common superstition, Faust boldly asks the devil's name and even calls him names ('pauvre démon', 'un sot'), refusing to play along with Mephisto's diabolical blarney in greeting him as 'friend'. This speaks well for his mettle, but the match is unequal: Mephisto is inherently stronger, a part of the larger power ('Ein Teil von jener Kraft', 1335) represented by the devils' chorus he rejoins at the end. Whereas in Goethe Faust eventually gets the better of Mephisto, in Berlioz there is no such vindication of Faust, and the fundamental difference in status between the partners remains.

The very outcome of the plot pivots on the master–slave opposition implied by the pact. Up to the moment of the *Course à l'abîme*, Mephistopheles has been Faust's 'servant' ('Qu'as-tu fait pour moi / Depuis que je te sers'); by the end of the Ride he claims himself 'forever master' of 'so proud a soul'. Underlining the disparity between them is Mephisto's mock-respectful 'docteur' ('Je t'admire, docteur') and a passing 'enfant' ('Enfant du saint parvis', both on Mephisto's first appearance), the latter in harmony with the subsequent lullaby. An early version of the libretto uses this second form of address in a striking manner during the *Course à l'abîme*: where Faust shudders at a line of skeletons, Mephisto chides him with the words 'Enfant! [...] pense à sauver sa vie / [...] et ris-toi des morts'. Apparently this 'enfant', later deleted, served a metrical regularity unnecessary for the music.[32] Poetically it was appropriate, both as a sign of Faust's vulnerability and as a reminder of the couple in another fatal nighttime ride, whose popular setting by Schubert Berlioz would later orchestrate: the father and son of Goethe's 'Erlkönig'.

When Mephisto voices the names of Faust and Marguerite, even more sinister overtones emerge. It is disturbing to find that his soothing endearment in the enchantment scene ('O mon Faust bien-aimé') speaks ahead of time the exact words of Marguerite in the love scene. At his report of Marguerite's imprisonment, Faust cuts him short: 'Car tu rêves ici / Quand cette pauvre enfant / Marguerite... – Tais-toi'. The interruption bespeaks not only impatience, as Mephisto immediately takes it,

---

32 The discarded text may be found in *NBE* 8b, Appendix IV.

nor even a lingering guilt, but also a protective reflex (explicit in Goethe) to shield Marguerite's name from profanation. Mephisto at once discredits this chivalrous impulse by an ironic reminder of Faust's own role in the disaster ('Ah! je suis le coupable!'). Listeners, for their part, may recall that Faust declared possession of his 'ange adoré' in a triumphant fanfare on her name: 'Marguerite est à moi'. Faust's own demise appropriately occurs, on a sinister stroke of the gong, at the precise moment he delivers his name – his signature – to Mephisto: 'Voilà mon nom!'

At this climactic moment there is no mistaking the eroticism of Mephisto's 'fire' or the parallel between his pursuit of Faust and Faust's pursuit of Marguerite. Cast in dialogue, the sequence of Recitative and Ride to the Abyss matches the love scene in structural and dramatic importance. And the analogy goes further: Berlioz's Ride resembles the scenario of Bürger's famous *Lenore*, where a ghostly suitor comes on horseback to fetch his betrothed and lures her past terrifying visions to a graveyard-wedding bed.[33] Given the ambiguities of 'possession' (by a devil, by a lover), of the horseback ride itself, of the very idea of fulfilment pursued by Faust, the entire scene reveals itself as a kind of rape – a grotesque parody of Faust's love-suit. Mephisto consummates here the seduction he aimed at from the first, the headlong descent fulfilling in reverse the ascent promised in the Easter Hymn. Add to this the allusion to the hunt in Mephisto's disconcerting response to Faust, who starts at the news of Marguerite's plight ('Quoi! – J'entends des chasseurs qui parcourent les bois'), and we have Mephisto associated with that most masculine of sports and Faust, by implication, with the hunted. An intervening horn call explains the verbal *non sequitur*, but Mephisto's alertness to the foreign sound betrays a preoccupation with his own 'hunt' reminiscent of Phèdre's notorious irrelevance about 'l'ombre des forêts' – the forest where Hippolyte goes hunting.[34] As an object of pursuit Faust becomes one with the women and children trampled by the devil's horses and with the girls 'hunted' by the students and soldiers

33 That Bürger's 'Lenore' was the probable inspiration for Berlioz's *Course à l'abîme* is demonstrated by John B. Ahouse, 'The *Course à l'abîme*: a possible source', *The Berlioz Society Bulletin*, 83 (April 1974) 13–17 and 84 (July 1974) 19–23. Bürger's 'Der wilde Jäger', summarised just after *Lenore* in *De l'Allemagne*, may well have suggested the riders' heedless dispersal of the women and children.

34 Racine, *Phèdre*, I, iii: 'Dieux! que ne suis-je assise à l'ombre des forêts! [...]' Phèdre's confidante, Oenone, responds in surprise: 'Quoi, madame?' Each term of the inner rhyme 'Quoi / bois' in Berlioz's alexandrine thus picks up – no doubt unconsciously – one element of the famous passage in Racine.

earlier in the action. While Faust identifies himself with Marguerite, the feminine sufferer, and experiences fears that recall hers of earlier on, Mephisto is at his most commanding, ruthless, impassive. Well may we ask, at this point, who the real hero is, and in what heroism is supposed to consist.

III : FAUST AS HERO AND THE QUESTION OF THE HEROIC IN MUSIC

If action, domination and power, those badges of male supremacy, were sufficient to designate a hero, Mephisto would unquestionably fit the part. On the surface it might appear that Berlioz was merely following out the implications of his scenario when, in 1847, he briefly envisioned turning his *Légende dramatique* into an opera called *Méphistophélès*. Yet what we know of the project argues just the reverse. A major impetus for the transformation came from the prospect of a Mephisto sung by the great baritone Pischek, for whose sake the immediate task was to supplement the role with at least one aria.[35] Far from garnering the 'best tunes', in the *Damnation*, Mephisto does not even get a full-fledged aria: the brief *Air de Méphistophélès* ('Voici des roses') serves to lull Faust to sleep rather than to attach our sympathies with intimate revelations about the singer. A simple count of the major solo numbers – Faust has four to Mephisto's three and Marguerite's two – leaves Mephisto outnumbered in the running for centre attraction.

Even for Faust, to be sure, arias prove an unstable criterion for first place. Only the *Air de Faust* from Part III, 'Merci, doux crepuscule', is actually so designated; arguably, Marguerite's Romance comes outwardly closer than any of Faust's music to a conventional aria, with its soaring lyricism, syncopated 'heartbeats' and *agitato* ending. But in the end, convention is what discredits the Romance by comparison with Faust's unpredictable, through-composed ariosos. Where Mephisto and Marguerite fall short of the aria, Faust repeatedly goes beyond, rupturing and evading even the noblest traditions of operatic monologue. In keeping with the composer's generic strategy for the work as a whole, his main character holds aloof from the strophic forms typical of the other two, as well as from most of the choruses. Even in the more elaborate choral textures where Faust does take part, his voice generally maintains its own

---

35 See *CG* III, 473–4 and 484–5; the correspondent is Eugène Scribe.

stamp. Consequently the very signs that mark him as an outsider affirm his status within the work: musically, Faust is where the action is.

The paradox is that the 'action' defining Faust as the hero of the *Damnation* amounts in dramatic terms to virtual passivity – the antithesis of the physical valour and moral purpose that drive the hero of a Classical epic, a Corneille tragedy or a Hollywood western. At one level the paradox resolves itself easily enough by the neutral modern meaning of the word 'hero', which since the seventeenth century has been used to designate the principal character of a work of fiction, apart from any presuppositions of grandeur.[36] But heroes have never fully escaped the epic standard, a standard that falls especially hard on a medium where lyric prevails over drama, 'feminine' emotion over 'masculine' action. Indeed throughout operatic history heroines rather than heroes have often taken centre stage, and in the *Damnation* the real challenge to our involvement with Faust comes not from Mephisto but from Marguerite. Despite the brevity of her part, she is the one who holds her own emotionally against Faust. Like so many doomed heroines of nineteenth-century opera, she has the privilege of tugging at our heartstrings before she dies, and Faust's Invocation to Nature, the high point of his role, is hard put to match the seductive impact of her Romance.

For all his fireworks, Mephisto cannot offer such entrancement. Devoid of the emotions he manipulates in others, he can only parody the humans he mocks. Parody is in fact his literary element. He begins by imitating the Faustian cascade of noun-adjective phrases during the *Chant de la Fête de Pâques* (Faust: 'âme tremblante / foi chancelante / jours pieux', etc.; Mephisto: 'pure émotion / pieuses volées', etc.). Later he apes Faust as a lover: where the latter raves of 'céleste image' and 'ange adoré', his companion glibly alludes to 'ce divin trésor' and 'cet ange', in a doubly hypocritical use of religious metaphor. In Berlioz's code of ethics, such misuse of the powers of expression amounted to an artistic immorality of the sort he tirelessly attacked in his criticism. Ironically, Mephisto himself acts the critic with the Amen fugue when he calls attention to the 'bestialité' – his word, borrowed from a physical context in Goethe – of the sacrilege whereby the holy word of prayer is rendered by a boisterous, pedestrian setting.[37] His own sacrilege takes the form of a rhetoric

36 Edith Kern gives a useful history of the word 'hero' in 'The modern hero: phoenix or ashes?' in *The Hero in Literature*, ed. Victor Brombert (New York, 1969) 266–78.
37 Whether the audience 'gets' the intended irony obviously depends a good deal on the manner of execution, yet the frequency with which audiences have applauded the piece as 'serious' music – apparently even at performances Berlioz himself conducted – suggests widespread reverence for

without emotion – 'rhetoric' in the pejorative sense. Like parody itself, that most parasitic of genres, Mephisto remains dependent: he cannot be first on stage because the 'spirit of negation' needs something outside itself to negate.

To these impediments Berlioz's clever solution in his opera project was to have Mephisto suffer from his inability to suffer. The plans called for an aria based on the threefold cry: 'Si je pouvais aimer! si je pouvais souffrir! si je pouvais mourir!' What gives pause here again is that the three verbs offered as a model of 'action' for a male hero sum up Marguerite's role even better than Faust's. When the woman's part – *aimer-souffrir-mourir* – becomes the model for a hero, the male image is clearly in jeopardy.

Even before music enters the picture, the meditative scholar of Goethe's Part I, ancestor to the modern intellectual hero, seems at first glance little apt to perform heroic deeds. But in the literary drama he does at least command the Word: where the Goethean Faust can prove himself Mephisto's equal or better in wisdom, wit and good-old-boy vulgarity, Berlioz's Faust retains barely a trace of his Goethean wit and none of the crudeness that allowed him to speak of his 'appetite' for Gretchen (2653). And when Goethe's Faust rejects mere 'words' in favour of 'the Deed', as he translates the biblical *logos*, he is doubly validated from the Classical perspective, which prizes the word for its power to represent action in narrative and in general to articulate rational thought as the basis of action. Music, by contrast, counts as passive, inarticulate, 'feminine' – qualities that condemn a musical Faust before he ever sets foot on stage.

That such reasoning should even now continue to prevail in judgements of musical *Fausts*, as we have seen, has a special irony in that the Faust story, from its inception in the Renaissance, tended already to put that reasoning in question. Even in its chap-book form the legend told the failure of rational language as a tool in the drive for power and knowledge, and the consequent recourse to alternative, ill-reputed avenues of approach. Hans Robert Jauss has shown how the Gretchen episode in Goethe, far from representing a frivolous diversion from the deeper epistemological quest, brings Faust the revelation of the secrets of the macrocosm and the Earth Spirit that had remained closed to his earlier

the fugue as a particulary 'pure' form of music. In *Les Grotesques de la musique*, 49–50, Berlioz perceptively compares this confusion to the enthusiasm of Molière's contemporaries for Oronte's sonnet in *Le Misanthrope*.

rationalist assaults.[38] To judge a musical *Faust* inferior by definition because it centres on love rather than loftier issues of metaphysics, or simply because it is musical rather than verbal, is therefore to overlook an implicit message of the Faustian myth itself.

Classical critics who blamed music for the undoing of heroes in opera forgot not only that language has its own thoroughly 'irrational' uses, most notably in poetry, but that unheroic heroes are equally typical of the literary genre that arose alongside opera during the seventeenth century – the novel. Both newcomers fell prey to similar attacks for their parade of love stories, lover-heroes and improbable adventures, on the one hand, and their 'vulgar' choice of styles on the other: prose rather than verse for the novel, solo-voiced virtuosity rather than equal-voiced polyphony for the opera. Boileau incriminated the two at once when (like Berlioz mocking Faust ballets) he satirised the novels of his day for transforming the military heroes of antiquity into singers of love-songs.[39] Since then the novel has come to fare better with critics, especially insofar as it has distanced itself from its romance origins as a story about love.[40] But opera remains subject to ridicule, even though music – independent, instrumental, 'absolute' music – has long since acquired its titles of nobility for addressing the male spirit. In response, musical reform movements have periodically attempted to bolster an endangered manliness by reinforcing dramatic truth. Just as Plato thought to ensure the musical morality of his Republic by excluding the 'weaker' modes popular in his day, so the founders of the French Republic (following close upon Gluck's reform of Italian opera) took pains to encourage the kind of music that would 'support and bestir, by its accents, the energy of the defenders of equality' and eradicate the kind that 'softens the soul of the French with effeminate sounds'.[41]

To hold music capable of so energetic a task severely hampers any generalisation about the art as 'feminine'. What is more: within the conventions of opera, before the footlights, so-called 'feminine' emotion becomes heroic in its own right. A recent book speaks plausibly of opera's

---

38 Jauss (see note 15), 127–9.
39 In his satire 'Les Héros de roman', *Œuvres*, ed. G. Mongrédien (Paris, 1961) 294: 'Hé! [...] vous qui étiez autrefois si déterminé soldat [...] qui est le fou ou la folle qui vous ont appris à chanter?'
40 On the critical reception of the novel in France, see Georges May, *Le Dilemme du roman au XVIIIe siècle* (New Haven, 1963). Stendhal assumes the kinship of novel and opera when he remarks that the Italians have no novels (*romans*) to express their notion of love, but they have opera (*Vie de Rossini* [Paris, 1824] chapter 5).
41 Gossec in 1793, quoted by Jacques Attali, *Noise: the Political Economy of Music,* trans. Brian Massumi (Minneapolis, 1985) 55.

'traditional epic commitment to heroic characters and heroic actions', and George Bernard Shaw calls Verdi's *Trovatore* a 'heroic work' whose effect depends on its being 'heroically performed', specifying that there is 'nothing unheroic to fall back on [...], no relief to the painful flood of feeling surging up repeatedly to the most furious intensity of passion; nothing but love'.[42] To equate heroism with 'the painful flood of feeling' and 'the most furious intensity of passion' ('nothing but love') flies in the face of a longstanding reluctance in Classical and modern thought to admit love and its attendant emotions to the heroic sphere. But devotees of opera know and have always known exactly what Shaw is talking about. From the time when Monteverdi invented the warlike *concitato* style, dramatic music has had the capacity to render heroic action, which capacity it extends quite impartially to the private domain. Such is the persuasive power of operatic illusion for heroic purposes that for two centuries it could even naturalise the use of artificially high voices for male heroes – *hautes-contres* in France, counter-tenors in England, castrati and even female voices in Italy.

Between the castrato operas and Verdi a profound shift of sensibility occurred, its extent measurable by the shock Berlioz expressed at encountering a female Romeo in an opera performance of 1831 in Italy.[43] Whereas the high-voiced hero apparently posed no threat to an *ancien régime* secure in its structures of authority, the crumbling of those structures unsettled the prevailing norms of 'masculine' and 'feminine' and toppled the reigning castrato in favour of the more 'natural' tenor. By the time Berlioz wrote his *Faust* that voice-change was complete, while another was in the process of displacing the lyric tenor by what came to be known as the *Heldentenor*, able to produce – in Edward J. Dent's unflattering terms – 'the trumpeting noise of the forced-up baritone considered appropriate to the expression of exaggerated virility'.[44] More kindly, one might relate the *Heldentenor* to other examples of post-

---

42 Lindenberger, 263; review of 4 June 1890 in *Shaw's Music*, ed. Dan H. Lawrence (New York, 1981) II, 78, quoted in Lindenberger, 146.

43 See *Mémoires*, chapter 35. An especially good example of shifting conventions may be found in the sexual vicissitudes of Gluck's Orpheus, whose role Berlioz rearranged – contrary to what his earlier position on female Romeos might have led one to expect – for Pauline Viardot's contralto, thereby producing a version examined by Joël-Marie Fauquet elsewhere in this volume. David Rissin, in *L'Avant-Scène Opéra*, 23 (September–October 1979) 21, observes that a male falsetto (*voix de tête*) gives today an even greater impression of 'hermaphroditism' than a female contralto. Berlioz was apparently affected the same way.

44 *The Rise of Romantic Opera*, ed. Winton Dean (Cambridge, 1976) 179. My thanks to Ralph Locke for calling this passage to my attention.

revolutionary excess such as the titanic endings of Beethoven's *Eroica*, the extravagantly protracted opening of Wagner's *Rheingold*, or the volubly rationalised world of Balzac's *Comédie humaine*, each of which suggests a desperate effort to re-create a lost universal order through individual force of will.

Berlioz was by no means indifferent to the new breed of tenor, which made its appearance over a decade before the *Damnation* in the person of Gilbert Duprez, first to sing his high C's 'from the chest'. But when Duprez performed the *Sanctus* of Berlioz's *Requiem* and the lead role of *Benvenuto Cellini*, in the 1830s, he had little occasion – as the tenor Richard Gandy has put it – to 'belt out his top notes as if he were storming Valhalla'.[45] Faust's high C sharps in the love duet of the *Damnation* are to be sung passionately but softly, 'a mezzo voce ed appassionato assai', and it seems fitting that Berlioz's most explicit praise of a performer in the part cites a Viennese tenor's ability, in 1866, to sustain the soft high notes of 'Que j'aime ce silence'.[46] Whereas the 'forced-up baritone' betrays an attempt to infuse the 'Romantic' tenor with some of the masculinity and power traditionally ascribed to the deeper male voices – or was it to recapture some of the fabled *éclat* of the castrati? – the tenor role in Berlioz generally retains a wider measure of humanity. Not that all his tenors are of a kind: in the *Huit Scènes de Faust*, where Faust does not appear, Mephisto is a tenor in his Serenade, as befits the genre and the seducer aspect of his role. But no less a seducer than Don Giovanni is a baritone, and Mephisto ends up sharing with him the commanding resonance that – as Kierkegaard noted – serves so well in Mozart's opera, through the ideally ambiguous association of the deeper voice with the villain of Romantic opera, on the one hand, and the comic bass of *opera buffo*, on the other.

Of Berliozian tenors, the most useful for comparison with Faust is the epic hero of *Les Troyens*. Berlioz's Aeneas is the grandest of heroic tenors – a 'dynamo' of 'sheer energy' and 'purpose', writes Paul Robinson, next to whom 'all other operatic heroes are apt to seem slightly limp'.[47] Preceded by the aura of Trojan glory, Aeneas enters the love action with a rescue and exits on a betrayal, moving on to further glory in the name of a 'greater' cause. Under very different circumstances Goethe's Faust

---

45 'The tenor roles in Berlioz', *Berlioz Society Bulletin*, 84 (July 1974) 5–15, here 10.
46 For his praise of Walter, the tenor in question, see Berlioz's letter to Ernest Reyer of 17 December 1866 (*Correspondance inédite*, ed. D. Bernard [Paris, 1879] 335).
47 *Opera and Ideas* (New York, 1985) 132–3.

also manages to surmount the 'diversion' of the Gretchen tragedy and proceed to the adventures of the 'big world' in Part II. As a good Second Empire role model, Aeneas submits to fate and so reaffirms the social order, specifically the Classical priority of duty over love. Berlioz's Faust on the contrary defies fate, casting away his soul in a grand and poignant gesture for which he is destroyed ('Eh! que me fait *demain* quand je souffre à cette heure?'). Goethe's Faust too disdains the threat of the hereafter, but when at the end of Part II he finally gives in (conditionally) to 'the moment', it is not under the pressure of human suffering, nor does the admission cost him his soul. Faust's death and damnation, in Berlioz, give an entirely new weight to the attempted rescue of Marguerite. They mark a return to the resolve shown in the suicide scene, transforming his once futile gesture into a selfless act of courage.

Since Faust reaps neither success nor glory from his sacrifice, the result stops considerably short of the clear-cut triumph of bravery and will that Classical norms theoretically demand of a hero. It is therefore hardly surprising that he does not suit the traditional operatic categories. On the one hand he is too mature for a role of young lover – a Tamino; despite his acquired wisdom, on the other hand, he lacks the authority of a Sarastro. Nor is he a villain, tainted though he is by his association with Mephisto and punished by the fate generally assigned to villains. The helpful parallel is again Don Giovanni who, as Dent remarks, fits the model of the operatic villain better than that of the tender-voiced lover-hero. Dent even goes so far as to contend that Don Giovanni 'is not technically the hero of the opera' for the simple reason that 'he suffers defeat at the end, not triumph'.[48] Without stopping to question whether tragic heroes do not regularly suffer defeat, one must ask any logic so rash as to deny the title of hero to the generator of all the energy and interest (in favour, perhaps, of the unimpeachably qualified but vapid Don Ottavio?) to reconsider its assumptions.

There is to be sure one familiar role that Don Giovanni and Faust both fulfil perfectly: that of Romantic hero. But the coupling of two such different characters shows why it was so easy for Dent to miss the obvious. The 'Romantic hero' is far more complex and elusive than any of his Classical forebears, so much so that it is customary to sort the breed into at least two types: the ultrasensitive Wertherian soul-searcher who shrinks from action; the Byronic villain-hero, who on the contrary acts

48 Dent, 180.

and lives to excess.[49] Romantic critics tended to present those types not as mutually exclusive so much as complementary – two aspects of one pervasive state of mind. Thus Berlioz's own Lélio, a forerunner of his Faust, successively assumes the role of brash pirate drinking out of skulls and that of gentle bard and lover, imagining his own death. For Schiller, Chateaubriand and Staël, the new hero – northern, Christian and 'sentimental' – is broadly opposed in his depth and complexity to the Classical hero, southern, pagan and 'naive'.[50] Far from a godlike incarnation of his people, like the eponymous hero of *The Aeneid*, the Romantic hero stands as a vulnerable exception in society, at odds with its standards of good and evil while torn by those standards from within.

The new image of the hero necessitated a reshuffling of values, and the oppositions that articulate the new values betray a certain nostalgia for older, simpler times when Men were Men. One appeal of the villain figure for the Romantics was undoubtedly the relief it provided from the tortured, 'feminine' sensibility of a Werther or a René. If Staël goes so far as to pronounce Mephisto the hero of Goethe's drama, it is presumably because his whirlwind, outward action corresponds better than Faust's inner turmoil to her inbred assumptions about the heroic mould. For all her intellectual awareness of the new model's legitimacy, she cannot help censuring Faust as a 'changeable, restless creature whose feelings are more ephemeral than the short life he complains about', a sum of 'all the human weaknesses', a limp figure of 'more ambition than strength'.[51] Such a view coincides remarkably with Hofer's view of an 'impotent' Faust in Berlioz. In both cases the character falls short of a standard that measures heroes by their pursuit of direct, unequivocal, 'higher' goals. By that standard Faust, like all *mal-du-siècle* heroes, is plainly unsatisfactory, not to say exasperating: not only is he 'restless' and 'changeable', but his 'striving' amounts by its excess to a mockery of the Enlightenment ideal of a well-defined social purpose straightforwardly pursued. How re-freshing, by contrast, Mephisto's single-minded tenacity in the chase! Here again we need to remember that with Berlioz, as with Staël writing in 1810, Goethe's Part I alone is at issue. In Part II Goethe rescues Faust from his wayward path by supplying him with all the traditional attributes

---

49 Wolfgang Dömling, in chapter 4 of *Hector Berlioz und seine Zeit* (Regensburg, 1986), ably summarises these two strains in the Romantic image of the hero.

50 'Über das naive und sentimentalische in der Dichtung' is the title of a classic essay by Schiller; Chateaubriand's *Génie du christianisme* takes up a similar opposition in the famous discussion of *le vague des passions*; Staël likewise in *De l'Allemagne* (I, 212–13 [Part II, chapter 11]).

51 *De l'Allemagne* I, 345 (Part II, chapter 23).

of heroic glory – rank, political power, wealth, social action, the love of a beautiful and illustrious woman – and by rewarding him for 'ever striving' in much the way a boss approves faithful exertions in the workplace. Heine and Wagner were among those for whom this conciliatory close amounted to a travesty of Goethe's own premises.[52]

Staël's harsh judgement of the unregenerate hero of Goethe's Part I shows again that music cannot be held responsible for deflecting Berlioz's Faust from the well-defined path she implicitly favours in a hero. Music offers, on the contrary, a strong parallel to her values. Tonal music is all about goals, while harmonic theory furnishes orderly rules for achieving them, or rather it, in the singular, since Classical tonality, like monotheism, admits only one goal – the tonic. In the Damnation, tonality provides Mephisto with one of his most potent means of thwarting the divine, or tonal, purpose. (His other chief means is rhythm, as in his Serenade's radical dislocation of the metrical order.) His first entry in B major jars symbolically with Faust's ecstatic cadence in F, while his exit plays out this tritonal antagonism in reverse: Pandaemonium begins in Mephisto's original B major but ends in F, musically enacting the Goethean precept that compels Mephisto to achieve good while intending evil. Faust, for his part, does not so much defy the deity as pursue transcendence to excess and on his own terms, his strivings less indecisive than divergent and immoderate in their goals. To that effect, his Invocation to Nature comes as close to tonal chaos as the Berliozian idiom permits. The harmonic vocabulary itself is not extreme, as Julian Rushton points out; what frustrates and disconcerts is not the diction but the syntax, whose persistent avoidance of the tonal goal goes so far as to 'negate' the tonal system altogether by ending with a modal cadence.[53] Things need not go this extreme to convey the sense, everywhere present in the Damnation, that in Romantic music as in Romantic heroes the well-focused Classical process has come unhinged: the musical elements once kept in line by the tonal frame now strike out freely in directions resistant to order, proportion and closure.

---

52 In a letter serving as preface to his own Faust ballet (Tanzpoem), Heine writes that Goethe's Faust 'ends like a frivolous farce – I was tempted to say like a ballet'. Sämtliche Schriften, VI (Munich, 1975) 374. Disdain for ballet obviously did not prevent Heine any more than Berlioz from undertaking a Faust in that medium. On Wagner's conception of Tristan as a corrective to the 'wasted opportunity' of Goethe's Part II, see Arthur Groos, 'Appropriation in Wagner's Tristan libretto' in Reading Opera, ed. Groos and Roger Parker (Princeton, 1988) 25–9.

53 Rushton, The Musical Language of Berlioz (Cambridge, 1983) 243. As Rose Subotnik observes in Developing Variations, 121, effects of modality in Romantic music 'are not merely subversive in effect, like chromaticism, but openly irreconcilable with tonal relationships'.

In the aftermath of his *Faust* Symphony of 1854, dedicated to Berlioz as the *Damnation* is dedicated to him, Liszt wrote a long article on 'Berlioz and his "Harold" Symphony' in which he raised the issue of music's capacity to portray the Classical and modern types of hero. Instrumental music, he argues – programme music in particular – is better suited than either opera or oratorio to render 'those modern poems which, for want of a better name, we shall call *philosophical epopoeias*; among [which] Goethe's *Faust* is the colossus'. This is because the modern poem does not 'aim to recount the exploits of the principal figure; it deals with affections active within his very soul'. Since not all men share these 'affections', however, they do not speak to 'the majority of mankind', in the way of the ancient epos. Such feelings, 'in their height and depth, are inaccessible to the majority who make up the bulk of the dramatic audience'. The implied preference is for the elite world of the instrumental concert – that of the inner 'soul' and the happy few.[54]

Besides justifying Liszt's own choice of medium and consequent return to the *Harold* Symphony rather than the *Damnation* as a model, this statement summarises the 'Romantic' value system that once conditioned and often still conditions the judgement of literary adaptations in music. Opera is suspect, by this system, for its capacity to do precisely what Classical critics thought it never could – to portray action and thereby speak to 'the majority of mankind'. The stress on the inner man has now become so imperative that it blinds such critics to what considerable action and drama do remain in the so-called 'modern epopoeiea', as it tended to blind the Romantics to anything in *Hamlet* but the soliloquies. At all costs, the aim is to protect the modern hero's manhood and nobility – now located in his 'inner' qualities – from the trivialising banalities of operatic convention.

A singing Faust runs a grave danger from this perspective, even in an unstaged version like Berlioz's Legend. Certainly the most 'operatic' or 'popular' sections of the work must bear much of the blame for putting its Faustian qualities in doubt. Thus Julian Rushton finds that the love duet and trio, in which (he says) the hero is 'externalized and made not a little ridiculous', are 'more Marguerite's domain than Faust's'.[55] It is easy to see what he means: this overtly operatic part sounds almost antithetical to what has gone before by way of establishing Faust's character. But it

---

54 Part of the essay is translated in Oliver Strunk, *Source Readings in Music History* (New York, 1950), 847–73, here 865–6. The *Faust* symphony dates from 1854, the essay from 1855.
55 Rushton, 229.

remains open to question whether, on the one hand, the world-thirsty Goethean Faust cannot encompass such an antithesis, and on the other hand whether music is not better equipped to convey his range when it does not renounce any of its means, however indecorous or 'popular' they may be. Writing in the 1850s in Weimar, Liszt is plainly on the defensive against the autonomist current that, in 1854, had just produced Hanslick's treatise *On the Beautiful in Music*, whereas Berlioz in the 1840s – and to the end of his life – remains faithful to more broadly grounded ideals of the 'complete' artwork, inclusively expressive in the spirit of Hugo's Preface to *Cromwell*. How those ideals apply to his Faust and how music is capable of enacting them may be further deduced by examining some of the musical conventions through which his 'Romantic hero' is constructed.

As in *Harold en Italie*, we are first introduced to the protagonist by means of a fugato. Although for Berlioz the 'good' fugue is expressive, and although the fugatos that accompany Faust in Parts I and II are both suffused with emotion, the fugue – even in its freer guise of fugato – remains symbolically contrary to the operatic world of outward passion and drama. Within the operatic tradition itself fugues could serve dramatic but limited ends, rendering the mysteries of secret sects and exotic rites, for example, or as Grétry succinctly advised, 'choruses of priests, conspiracies, and all that pertains to magic'.[56] This association by convention is as close as we come in Berlioz to Faust's necromancy; what we are to hear in the fugato of 'Sans regrets' is more evidently the dusty, arcane world of the scholar, confined in a stifling world order from which he longs to escape. In this way Faust's part moves between the two extremes of 'fugue' and 'opera', from the diurnal and nocturnal fugatos of the first two parts to the extroverted world of the operatic ensemble at the end of Part III.

Well before the latter stage, however, the 'scholar's music' has been left behind. It is worth considering exactly how this occurs by looking at the fate of the fugato in 'Sans regrets', the one piece where Faust is fully on home ground. The contrapuntal windings come to a halt at the cry 'Oh je souffre, je souffre', which summons a clutch of expressive devices from the dramatic repertory – a searing minor second; descending phrases, one in whole-tones ending in a hushed Neapolitan chord; a syncopated, pulsating bass pedal. Afterwards the counterpoint resumes, continuing

56 In *Mémoires ou Essais sur la musique* (Paris, 1812), cited in Weisstein, 156.

until Faust's next outburst but increasingly at odds with the declamatory character of the voice. By the third phrase ('Par le monde, où trouver ce qui manque à ma vie?') we have taken leave of the fugato and crossed over entirely into recitative. In this medium Faust works himself up to the resolve to drink poison, climaxing in a blaze of C major set to four masculine rhymes in quick succession ('poison/raison'; 'illuminer/tuer'). The effect is of an eruption of drama out of lyric, as if to illustrate the Classical equation of the lyric with 'feminine' passivity, the word-bound recitative with 'masculine' action. But that action is emotional – not to say orgasmic – through and through. We are in the domains of 'souffrir' and 'mourir' of operatic heroism, with 'aimer' close at hand. The rhymes 'vie', 'envie' and 'ravie' pre-empt those of the love music, itself foreshadowed by the cadential flourish on 'à mes désirs ravie'.

This extraordinary *chant-récitatif* takes us beyond the opposition of aria and recitative in opera to confront opera and non-opera, so to speak, as though re-creating a Monteverdian disruption of the older communal, contrapuntal order by an emancipated solo voice. The music dramatises the struggle between the repressed world of a scholarly Melancolia and the voice of emotion, self-assertion and freedom. But the erotic or bodily component of the Faustian rebellion has not yet reached the level of consciousness. The final word of the recitative is a triumphant 'raison', as in a Cartesian *tabula rasa* of the stifling weight of philosophical tradition. Even so, the music belies this verbal stoicism, and Faust's passionate assertion of 'reason' leaves him open to the seductions of the Easter Hymn and of Mephisto. It may be observed that the *Chant de la Fête de Pâques* moves through a similar emotional course, from the sighing plaints of the forlorn disciples abandoned 'below' to a joyous identification with the arisen Saviour. Musically, Berlioz's strategy in this piece follows the eighteenth-century practice of using dissonance to show the disharmonious 'passions' of the soul, which consonance then resolves into a superior spiritual harmony. As Faust himself joins tentatively, then ardently in these transcendental ecstasies, resurrected scenes from his childhood stir the fires of his unconscious; Mephisto will need only conjure up the profane counterpart of these 'heavenly' scenes to bring him – literally – to his senses.

Well before Marguerite's appearance, then, and even before Mephisto's, the Faustian music reveals a pronounced erotic drift. But it is when he becomes a lover, beginning with his aria in Part III, that Faust openly enters the dangerous waters of the operatic – what Rushton calls

Marguerite's domain. Even then the piece is ostensibly (as in Goethe) a prayer, a moment of communion. But not with Marguerite. Faust begins by hailing the sunset in a poetic personification ('Merci, doux crépuscule') and ends by addressing a conventional 'Seigneur'. Only for a moment in between, when the music breaks into euphoric triplets on the words 'O ma jeune fille, ô ma charmante, ma trop idéale amante', does he directly acknowledge his distant feminine vision. Those triplets function here as a sign of the erotic and the operatic both. They have already insinuated themselves earlier in two unusually expressive moments: the first during an extreme modulation to a key a tritone away from the tonic, under the evocation of a 'morning's fresh kiss' ('le frais baiser d'un matin qui se lève'), after which the return to the tonic on Faust's tentative recognition of love – 'c'est de l'amour, j'espère' – seems a perfunctory response to the cautious qualifier; the second on the word 'silence' ('Que j'aime ce silence') in a passage insistently marked *pianissimo, sostenuto, perdendo, rallentando*.[57] Outside the love duet and trio, this aria's central passage in triplets constitutes the one time Faust succumbs to an operatic voluptuousness akin to that of Marguerite's Romance. Significantly, this happens in her absence: we have already seen that erotic fulfilment, for Faust, depends on distance – on a 'ferne Geliebte'.

The *Air de Faust* ends with a long, discursive instrumental coda in which, according to directions in the score, Faust walks slowly around, examining Marguerite's room 'with passionate curiosity'. Derived from decorative orchestral material in the aria, this music nevertheless differs considerably in character from the foregoing, as if moving from the operatic to the non-operatic in a reversal of the 'Sans regrets' dynamics. Although the music is paced appropriately to the theme, the mind's eye need not take this 'walk' literally: it belongs to a poetic tradition of lovers' solitary wanderings that goes back at least to Petrarch. These thirty-four bars return us to the brooding, introspective, questing and obsessive Faust of the earlier fugatos.

This being our last encounter with Faust before he plunges into the love duet, it is no wonder the latter disconcerts. But to call the Finale of Part III 'Marguerite's domain' is to discount both the strong libidinal currents in Faust's 'meditative' music (underlined by the 'curiosité passionnée' of the previous example) and his dominant part in the Finale itself. To foist sexuality on to the female is convenient, perhaps, but

---

57 See Rushton, 234–42, for an account of this 'air', and some articulate puzzling over the 'really strange event' of the modulation after the words 'frais baiser'.

misguided: the real difference between the sexes lies rather in the way each is conditioned to respond to this shared given of human nature. Marguerite both yields to passion and holds on to its pain and intensity. Her Romance, sung after the love episode has in effect ended, provides the most openly sensual, 'operatic' music of the score, all the more so that 'operatic', here, does not mean exhibitionistic: Marguerite is a sultry, poignantly lingering mezzo rather than a stereotypically sweet or agile-voiced soprano. Joined to the Romance by a single-note bridge suspended over a long rest, Faust's Invocation to Nature forms its logical pendant. Yet nothing in the music or the words directly alludes to the immediate past. Marguerite and human love have been forgotten – rejected. The music performs that rejection by extreme contrast: where Marguerite's exorbitantly wide-ranging vocal line gives in to its pain, melodically and rhythmically crying out its loss of control, everything here aims at order, strength, power; the broad $\frac{9}{8}$ augments and ennobles but by the same token suppresses the Romance's ingratiating $\frac{3}{4}$. Both pieces are marked Andante, but Faust's is 'maestoso', to be sung 'très large et très sombre'. His short phrases proceed with deliberation, at first, step-wise or in diatonic, decisive arpeggios, all sternly masculine in character; dotted rhythms and rushing upbeat scales in the bass, giving a semblance of motion to the static orchestral texture, inject elements reminiscent of the French overture, that quintessential expression of 'majesty'.[58]

Meanwhile the words address a 'proud', 'immense' nature, in which the hero finds new strength – 'je retrouve ma force et je crois vivre enfin'. 'Retrouver' implies a previous loss. Given the immediately preceding turmoil of the Romance, it is not quite enough to take this with a nod to the Faustian distress, or to a nebulous 'vague des passions'; there is nothing 'vague', in any case, about the way Chateaubriand ascribes that male malady to an excessive commerce with women.[59] From that perspective, Faust has just experienced the ultimate danger to male control in his encounter with female sexuality. Marguerite, the victim, has become the culprit – a dangerous quarry from which the wilderness affords the hunter unlikely protection. But that is only one of the ironies

58 Leon Plantinga traces these elements to 'the accompanied or obligato recitative used for scenes of special gravity or supernatural import by composers of serious opera since the seventeenth century' (*Romantic Music* [New York and London, 1984] 218).
59 Addressing the male reader in the preface to *René*, Chateaubriand writes that women render 'our' manliness ('notre caractère d'homme') less decisive: 'nos passions, amollies par le mélange des leurs, prennent à la fois quelque chose d'incertain et de tendre' (*Atala, René*, ed. F. Letessier [Paris, 1962] 171).

of the Invocation's 'rescue'. Despite the defiant energy of the vocal line, the music is anything but secure. Though the pace remains steady, the harmony continually pulls the ground out from under it, cadencing then instantly darting away, shifting to far-flung tonalities, finally breaking into anxious tremolos in a reflection not of inner peace ('trêve à mon ennui') but of the surrounding chaos depicted and welcomed by the words ('Croulez, rochers! Torrents, précipitez vos ondes!'). Even the vocal line does not stay under control for long but climbs steadily to a high G on the word 'désir', a G sharp ('vaste'), an A ('âme') – all to be sung *forte*, evidently 'from the chest' – in a final grasp for the elusive contentment. Again, an instrumental coda completes the picture, this one in hollow octaves and deliberate quavers. The contrast with the lilting triplets at the parallel moment of Marguerite's Romance brings out the full grimness of this ending, a bleak image of power alienated from humanity.

Once more the words take the irony considerably further. Fleeing the sensual and emotional upheaval of Marguerite's passion, Faust has turned to the 'breast' of an 'impenetrable', destructive, equally agitated but wholly indifferent female, Nature, though her pleasures proved elusive even in her earlier, friendlier guise in the prologue. He none the less prefers the distant, 'impenetrable' and thus ever-pure object to Marguerite, the flesh-and-blood village girl. One is reminded of Berlioz's own adolescent passion for an unattainable Estelle, whose Christian name he always took at face value (he called her his *Stella montis*), while ignoring her glaringly down-to-earth family name of Dubœuf.

With Estelle we have slipped into the domain of Berlioz's private mythology, and come up against some of the contradictions in the worship of nature and art that Berlioz and Goethe practised in common. The nature that Faust 'adores', in the Invocation, is a feminine deity as opposed to Goethe's Earth Spirit ('Erdgeist'), but one that evidently encompasses the masculine, much as the Christian God claims to encompass the feminine. Music too appears most often in the feminine in Berlioz's imagination. When he pictures 'his' art as a beautiful woman, the possessive is not entirely innocent: 'she' is a naked Andromeda, divine but vulnerable, to whom the composer aspires as a resolute but respectful Perseus, setting her free at the cost of seeing her escape him; a Juliet for whom he gladly braves the danger of Capulet daggers; an imaginary mistress to whom the artist in *Lélio* makes a passionate appeal: 'Oh, music, pure and faithful mistress, as much respected as adored – your friend, your lover calls for your aid! Come to me, unfold all your charms, intoxicate me, surround me with your splendour – come, come, I abandon myself to you!'[60] In this last passage it is the male lover who wishes to be captivated and 'possessed', in an ambivalent posture that recalls Faust's in the *Damnation*. But the purity of his ideal mistress is a fiction, as Mephisto is there to prove. Threats to 'purity' lie both on the outside, in the monster threatening Andromeda or the composer who might 'rape' her, and in music itself which, manifold and material as it is, cannot be confined to the pretty, the soothing, the ineffable. Like the sublime wilderness of the Invocation, destructive and altogether earthly despite its haughty magnificence, music is no more fundamentally pure and transcendent than woman ('das Ewig-Weibliche'), or than love itself.[61]

Berlioz recognises as much elsewhere, with characteristic about-faces in the middle of his most heady flights of idealistic fancy. At the very end of his *Memoirs*, for example, after an idyllic recapitulation of the opening chapters through the return of the Estelle theme, he writes loftily of music and love as the two wings of the soul. Such a conclusion might have served nicely, matching the Apotheosis at the end of the *Damnation*. Instead a Mephistophelian voice breaks the spell with a grotesque reminder of the way love is understood by the common run of mortals. Mephisto appears in this light not simply as an external force battling against Faust's good angel, Marguerite, but as an inherent part of Faust's own psyche. Berlioz leaves no doubt that he identified with both characters, as he did with the different facets of his Lélio. In his *Memoirs*, describing the fits of 'spleen' he experienced as a youth, he characterises the mood that overcame him as either 'ironique, railleur, emporté, violent, haineux' – distinctly Mephistophelian – or as 'taciturne et sombre', like Faust. He tells, in Faustian rhetoric, of longing for wings, for 'de l'amour, de l'enthousiasme, des étreintes enflammées [...], *la grande vie*'; whereupon a familiar voice calls him back to reality: 'quel amour?... quelle gloire?... quel cœur... où est mon étoile... la *Stella montis*?...'[62]

---

60 'O musique! maîtresse fidèle et pure, respectée autant qu'adorée, ton ami, ton amant t'appelle à son secours; viens, viens, déploie tous tes charmes, enivre-moi, environne-moi de tous tes prestiges, viens, viens, je m'abandonne à toi!' (from the monologue preceding the *Fantaisie sur La Tempête*). For the Andromeda parable, see *CG* IV, 404–5; the analogy with Juliet is spoken by the fictional composer-hero of Berlioz's short story 'Le Premier opéra', in *Les Soirées de l'orchestre*, 28.

61 On the fallacies of art as religion, see Jacques Barzun, *The Use and Abuse of Art* (Princeton, 1974) 73–96.

62 *Mémoires*, 223. For a summary of the 'double' theme in the Faust tradition see Rosemary Jackson, *Fantasy: the Literature of Subversion* (London and New York, 1981) 54–7.

At the desolate close of the Invocation to Nature, prey to what the *Memoirs* call 'the disease of isolation', Faust may seem ripe for a Pandaemonium. The withdrawal from human passion is a gesture in the direction of the underworld, where the passions have no place: 'ghosts, oracles, all supernatural forces must be monotonous', declares Staël, summing up the traditions of the operatic underworld in *De l'Allemagne*.[63] Not that Berlioz's *Pandaemonium* is monotonous. With its busy tonal shifts and orchestral commotion it is more like an orgy than a wake; the projected opera included plans for a contrasting scene in hell towards the beginning, as sombre and static as this one is turbulent. Yet the orchestral agitation amounts to no more than a kind of motionless movement, in which the princes of darkness strut about in a self-satisfied parody of Faust's earlier efforts at mastery and control. As in the Invocation and the following Apotheosis, the marking here is 'Maestoso', but the majesty remains pure show – the trappings of power covering up the void beneath.

At the same time, Faust's failure at his own misogynist 'show' indicates that he does not belong in hell after all. From the combined experience of love and nature he has somehow emerged more whole, more human. Whether the plaintive oboe of the *Course à l'abîme* 'represents' Faust or Marguerite is immaterial; what counts is that, combined with the wailing feminine endings expressing Faust's pity and despair ('O douleur insensée'; 'O pauvre abandonnée'; 'Dans mon cœur retentit sa voix désespérée'), and with his concern for the women and children praying, the sound conveys a newfound humanity, capable of suffering and of identifying with the suffering of others. Mircea Eliade writes in an essay on 'Méphistophélès et l'Androgyne' about a common rite of passage in primitive societies whereby young men are subjected to experiences of chaos, including rites of sexual transference ('androgynisation').[64] Closer to home, in pre-Romantic and Romantic thought, the economy of the sublime presupposes a similar process: man must feel his impotence in the face of an overwhelming nature before he can be empowered to assume his own humanity.[65] After the musical and emotional 'chaos' of the Invocation to Nature, Berlioz's Faust gains not the integration into the patriarchy that Tamino does at the end of *The Magic Flute*, but a kind of androgyny, or assimilation of the feminine, that makes him more fully human. The upshot is a fund of renewed energy such as Lélio exhibits

63 I, 241 (Part II, chapter 13).   64 (Paris, 1962) 111–79, here 160–64.
65 See René Wellek, 'Kant's aesthetics and criticism' in *Discriminations* (New Haven, 1970) 132.

when he turns to 'action' in art after the temptations of suicide. If those energies are doomed to failure, it is not because Faust is any less 'heroic' than Tamino or Aeneas, but because success in human terms is ultimately bound up with social and transcendental sanctions he refuses.

There is no question that by epic or romance standards Faust dies an unheroic death. Knights in shining armour who go to rescue damsels in distress are not supposed to be foiled in the attempt; I suspect that if the German critics who first attacked Berlioz's work were upset, among other things, that Mephistopheles is made to deceive Faust, it was out of concern not so much for Mephisto as for Faust, who is thereby cast as the butt of the jokes in farce.[66] And Berlioz's music, far from being the effeminate art of classicist libel, plays the joke on him, cutting him off brutally as it does Marguerite at the end of her Romance: where her final 'Hélas!' disappears into the soldiers' marching rhythm, Faust's terrified 'Ah!' sinks enharmonically into the triumphant 'Has!' of the forces of evil.

The final close is deceptively benign, as we have seen, resting as it does on a justice that uses diabolical force as its agent, and that punishes Faust at his best by acting like an abstraction of him at his worst. Despite the musical seductions of the *Apothéose*, I therefore persist in sympathising with Faust, as with Otello, Falstaff or Rigoletto, those mocked and fallen heroes of Verdi, all of whom fail to fulfil the epic ideal of heroism and who end up, like operatic heroines, 'feminine' victims of the patriarchal order.[67] Everything we know about Berlioz assures us that he too shared in such sympathies. Yet like all dramatists he is in some manner implicated in the fate he assigns his characters, just as we the audience are implicated in the aesthetic pleasure we take in their suffering. We are given to share in the Faustian revolt *and* its suppression. Like the composer we become, in Baudelaire's phrase, 'Et la victime et le bourreau', both victim and executioner.

Marguerite's fate leaves behind even more troubling questions, as I have suggested earlier. Though we may pity her, we may also (especially if 'we' is male) gain through her a surreptitious revenge on all the distant Estelles of the world. From the reviled and caricatured *idée fixe* of the *Ronde du sabbat* ('No, the revenge is not excessive', Berlioz commented in a letter) to the abandoned Dido of *Les Troyens*, there is in Berlioz' œuvre a gallery of female victims who remind us that Romanticist efforts

66 CG IV, 528 (27 April 1854).
67 See Clément, chapter 6 ('Les Fous, les nègres, les bouffons ou les héros de la déception').

at incorporating the 'feminine' in the heroic ideal usually operated at the expense of women.[68] Marguerite is to be sure something of an exception among Berliozian heroines in playing the victim so meekly. Beginning with the warrior Herminie who in an early cantata incarnated what later became the *idée fixe* of the *Fantastique*, Berlioz had a predilection for energetic heroines, and it could easily be argued that *Les Troyens*, written with the steady encouragement of Liszt's strong-minded companion, Carolyne von Sayn-Wittgenstein, hands over the supreme acts of courage to the women. If heroism consists of inner suffering, as the Romantic model implies, then suicide forms its highest expression; by that standard Cassandra and Dido, dying by their own hand, easily hold their own against the onward-marching Aeneas. What renders the compensation precarious is the Classical model of heroism that keeps intruding – that gives Aeneas the last word on Dido's tragedy, and absorbs her death (even by her own dying prophecy) into the proud rebirth of the Trojan nation. The more valiant the woman, under those conditions, the more certain her demise. At best it could be said that men and women are all victims in the end, subject to the inexorable workings of musical convention and the culture it reflects. There is no resisting triumphal marches and heavenly harps and the demands of tonic closure. Unless the musical order itself is called into question – and we have seen the process already at work in Berlioz – heroes and heroines alike must submit to its demands, or be destroyed by it: such are the perils of heroism in music.

68 This is the burden of Margaret Waller's cogent analysis, 'Cherchez la Femme: male malady and narrative politics in the French Romantic novel', *Publications of the Modern Language Association*, 104/2 (March 1989) 141–51.

I am grateful to Jacques Barzun, David Cairns, Jay Caplan, Jocelyne Kolb and Hugh Macdonald for their advice and encouragement during various stages of this article's gestation. Special thanks to Peter Bloom for painstaking editorial assistance well beyond the call of duty.

8

Berlioz's version of Gluck's *Orphée*

JOËL-MARIE FAUQUET

In chapter 5 of the *Mémoires* Berlioz tells us that it was Gluck who inspired him to become a musician, and that prior even to studying Gluck's music, he felt for the composer of *Orphée* a kind of 'instinctive passion'.[1] Before Gluck, Virgil had been the catalyst of Berlioz's extraordinary sensitivities. We might therefore say that the future composer's creativity was conditioned by two 'poetic shocks' which in a way revealed (to himself) his own inner predilections. It would not be long before Berlioz became aware of the Virgilian sources of the Orpheus myth, sources called to his attention by lines from Book IV of the *Georgics* cited in both early French and Italian editions of *Orphée*.[2] Virgil and Gluck, for Berlioz, would forever remain the most original of geniuses; he would eventually glorify the former by making use of the 'tragédie lyrique' as modernised by the latter. Indeed, it should be emphasised that Berlioz was to revive Gluck's *Orphée* in 1859 just as he was completing *Les Troyens*, and that one particular contralto voice was to act as an inextricable link between these two works – namely the voice of Pauline Viardot.[3] Such a constellation raises several questions: What were the

For having made available to me her unique copy of the score of *Orphée*, I should like to express my sincere appreciation to Miss Marilyn Horne. Professor Philip Gossett very graciously acted as my intermediary with Miss Horne, and offered encouragement during the preparation of this article for which I am deeply grateful. I should also like to thank Professor Hugh Macdonald and Mlle Thérèse Husson for having provided access to letters of Berlioz concerning *Orphée*, some of which are as yet unpublished.

1 *Mémoires*, 59. [Translator's note: The original French texts from readily available sources – the *Mémoires*, the *Correspondance générale*, *A Travers chants* – are usually not given here in the notes.]
2 'Te dulcis conjux, te solo in littore secum / Te veniente die; te decedente canebat.' Berlioz cites these lines from Virgil (*Georgics*, IV, 465–6) in his review of the revival of *Orphée* in the *Journal des débats* of 22 November 1859. On the origins of the Orpheus myth see Lionel de La Laurencie, *Orphée de Gluck* (Paris [*ca.* 1925]) 157 et seq.
3 Pauline Garcia (1821–1910), singer, but also pianist and composer, married Louis Viardot, director of the Théâtre Italien, in 1840.

respective roles played by Berlioz and the celebrated diva in the resurrection of Gluck's score? What influence did Viardot exercise on Berlioz's work? What did the public make of the transposition of the role of Orpheus to fit the female contralto voice? The import of these questions is heightened by one of the many paradoxical aspects of Berlioz's personality: hardly enthusiastic about the music of the eighteenth century, Berlioz remained none the less intransigent towards interpreters of the music of Gluck. He even went so far as to claim knowledge of historically appropriate traditions of stage action – a claim which, from the mouth of anyone else, would have met with Berlioz's own utter scepticism.[4]

Berlioz read Gluck before hearing him: the outlines of his 'ideal' conception of the work were forged early on, when he discovered fragments of *Orphée* in his father's library.[5] Shortly after arriving in Paris, at the beginning of November 1821, he attended a performance of *Iphigénie en Tauride* at the Opéra, on the 26th.[6] And he went regularly to the library of the Conservatoire, there to devour the scores of his idol.[7] But it was only later, on 14 May 1824, on the occasion of the Opéra's eleventh revival of *Orphée* since the Parisian première on 2 August 1774, that Gluck's *chef-d'œuvre* was fully revealed to Berlioz – though in a version with an altered text. On 10 June 1824, from his home in La Côte St André, he asked Humbert Ferrand if he had seen *Orphée*;[8] and on 22 June he wrote more prophetically to Edouard Rocher: '*Alceste*, *Armide* [...] – what operas! They have another advantage over *Orphée*, for the snarling dilettantes won't like them; but of *Orphée*, to its disadvantage, they will approve'.[9]

As a candidate for the Prix de Rome in 1827 Berlioz wrote a cantata, *La Mort d'Orphée*, which was soon, as he told his sister Nanci, judged 'unplayable'[10] – curious fate for an essay by a composer who would never cease trying to bring to life, on the stage, Gluck's celebrated opera.

---

4 Berlioz mentions 'les vrais mouvements dont je connais les traditions' in a letter to Emile Perrin of 10 January 1855; see CG IV, 695.

5 *Mémoires*, 58.	6 CG I, 56.	7 *Mémoires*, 59.
8 CG I, 56.	9 CG I, 58.	10 CG I, 157.

I : THE HISTORICAL BACKGROUND

Orphée as tenor prior to 1859

The revival of *Orphée* at the Opéra took place in February 1824; the principal role, rewritten by Gluck for the *haute-contre* voice of Joseph Legros, was readjusted and slightly modified for that of Adolphe Nourrit;[11] the *mise-en-scène* was deplorable. Some ten years later, recalling those performances (which were dominated by a tenor whom he admired), Berlioz would again cry profanation; the seeds of desire to resurrect *Orphée* seem already to have been planted in his imagination:

> What would be needed, if one were to revive the work in the theatre, is a performance by the chorus rather more careful than we have had up to now, and a representation of the Elysian Fields rather less absurd, more elaborate, more worthy of such a subject, and more worthy of the music, the public, and the theatre itself.[12]

The work reappeared on 25 March 1829, and twice again in 1830 and 1831. In 1833 there was a partial performance. Thereafter, until the revival on 28 July 1848 (with the now-forgotten tenor Poultier), only fragments of the work were to be heard in the French capital.[13]

It was in the *Scène des enfers* that Gilbert Duprez replaced Adolphe Nourrit at the Opéra, in March 1838, during a benefit performance for Mlle Noblet. Berlioz was favourably impressed by this music that was 'neither young nor old' but 'eternal', for it was 'vraie, naturelle, grande, sublime'. Duprez's dramatic voice produced 'a profound impression on the entire auditorium':

> He added not one note, not one accent; he reproduced this admirable music in all its severe and majestic beauty, music which he feels and understands not only as a singer, but as a great artist.[14]

---

11 The manuscript in the Bibliothèque de l'Opéra, A 230 b, shows that certain passages were transposed for Nourrit down by a third. In addition, for the aria 'Amour, viens rendre à mon âme' that closes the first act, Nourrit substituted the aria 'O combats, ô désordre extrême' from *Echo et Narcisse* – a substitution of which Berlioz approved. See *A Travers chants*, 154.

12 See Berlioz, 'Du répertoire de Gluck à l'Académie royale de Musique', *Le Monde dramatique* (18 July 1835) 182. Berlioz returned to this subject in the *Journal des débats* of 17 March 1839.

13 See the Journal de l'Opéra, in the Bibliothèque de l'Opéra. Cf. La Laurencie, 124. Without counting the revival of 1848, *Orphée* had attained 229 performances at the Opéra since its première in 1774. See Henri de Curzon, 'La Manie des remaniements', *Le Guide Musical* (18 and 25 July 1909) 510.

14 See Berlioz's review in the *Revue et Gazette musicale* (1 April 1838) 141.

Berlioz expresses his appreciation of textual fidelity here at the same time that he affirms the primacy of dramatic truth. And he lets it be known that Duprez, who had become a 'tenore di forza' in Italy, still knew how to be a 'tenore di grazia' when he took the role of Orphée in France.

Berlioz was soon offered another occasion to write about *Orphée*, this time at greater length, when, at a concert on 3 February 1839 sponsored by the *Revue et Gazette musicale* and held in the salons of the piano-maker Pape, Pauline Garcia sang Eurydice opposite Duprez's Orphée in the duet from Act III. This was the first time Berlioz had heard Mlle Garcia (who was soon to marry Louis Viardot), and he found her performance deeply disappointing. 'It was hardly worth it to make so much fuss over this supposed artist', he wrote to Victor Schœlcher the next day; 'she is a diva manquée'; for Gluck, he said, one needs singers who have a real voice, 'soul' and 'genius'.[15] Measuring the distance between his uncompromisingly ideal interpretation and Pauline Garcia's actual one, Berlioz notes that she had 'overcome enormous difficulties' in singing Gluck, since she had been schooled in an Italian tradition which was in Berlioz's view contrary to the higher aims of art. But she none the less fell far short of the goal she had set for herself, because 'in this music, whose sublime simplicity makes such extraordinary demands on the singer, every bar of aria or of recitative is an obstacle for anyone whose ear and whose heart have not been trained from the beginning to appreciate the true accents of passion'. And if she was lacking in emotion, she was also lacking in fidelity, for at the end of her recitative she made 'a brief incursion to the lower register of her voice in order to make its sonority known to us; but she did so at the expense of fidelity to the musical text and fidelity to the character she had undertaken to portray'. As for Duprez, had his voice not been extremely fatigued, 'he would have been perfect'.[16] These comments are of considerable importance: they tell us that Pauline Garcia's voice was evolving towards a lower tessitura, and they tell us that at a time when standard pitch was rising, the range of the role of Orphée posed especial problems to even the hardiest of tenors. In

15 CG II, 530.
16 Berlioz, '2e concert de la Gazette musicale', *Journal des débats* (17 March 1839) 1; repeated in the *Revue et Gazette musicale* on 24 March (90–93). The original quotation from the *Journal des débats* reads: 'Dans cette musique, dont la simplicité sublime est si exigeante, chaque mesure, soit de chant, soit de récitatif, est un obstacle pour quiconque n'a pas de bonne heure accoutumé son oreille et son cœur à l'accent vrai de la passion. [... Mlle Garcia s'est permis] à la fin de son récitatif une petite incursion dans les registres inférieurs de sa voix dont elle nous a fait connaître la sonorité dans le grave, mais aux dépens de la fidélité qu'elle devait au texte musical et aux dépens de la vérité du caractère qu'elle s'était chargée de reproduire'.

his article Berlioz contrasts the Vienna version in Italian and the Paris version in French, and in so doing demonstrates his profound knowledge of both scores. In evoking the scene in the Elysian Fields, he draws what he finds to be a natural comparison between Gluck and Virgil: 'If it were not for the anachronism, one might think that Gluck wanted to portray the still-suffering spectre of the Queen of Carthage, Dido, whom we find in Virgil *indignata sub umbras* and who, on seeing the Trojan warrior – the source of all her grief – flees into the shaded woods, there to hide her wounds and her grief'.[17]

Orphée would remain on the boards in Paris only with the *Scène des enfers* of Act II. In 1843, François Delsarte did the scene in concert with the Société de Musique vocale religieuse et classique, founded by the Prince de la Moskowa.[18] Berlioz himself conducted the scene at his first concert at the Cirque Olympique, on 19 January 1845,[19] when Orphée, along with Atys (from Lully's opera), was sung by Auguste Ponchard. And on 8 March 1846, for the Société des Concerts du Conservatoire, Gustave Roger took a turn at interpreting the scene. The critic Maurice Bourges praised the 'smoothness of his head voice [and] the power of his chest voice'. Emphasising the extreme difficulty of a role written for the uppermost register, Bourges added that Roger followed the advice that Gluck had given to Legros by using his head voice as much as possible (except at the phrase 'Ah! la flamme qui me dévore') – a technique that allowed the singer 'to give the melody a veiled and heart-rending quality' and 'to shed real tears with [his] voice'.[20]

It should be noted here that in 1838 Duprez created the role of Benvenuto Cellini; Roger, who created the role of Faust when *La Damnation* was premièred in 1846 and who also sang the *Sanctus* of the *Requiem*, became one of Berlioz's good friends. Less closely associated with the composer, Delsarte would compete with him in the exegetical 'purification' of Gluck's scores. Both Duprez and Delsarte had been trained by Alexandre Choron, a passionate defender of the Classical tradition. And Ponchard had been a student of Pierre-Jean Garat, himself one of the great interpreters of Gluck. All four – Duprez, Roger, Delsarte and Ponchard – were still able to sing the role of Orphée because all four

---

17 *Ibid.* 'S'il n'y avait anachronisme, on pourrait croire que Gluck a voulu peindre l'ombre toujours souffrante de la reine de Carthage, de cette Didon que Virgile nous fait trouver *indignata sub umbras* et qui, à l'aspect du guerrier troyen, cause de tous ses maux, s'enfuit au fond des bocages sombres pour y cacher sa blessure et sa plainte'.   18 See below, p. 216.
19 CG III, 223.   20 *Revue et Gazette musicale* (15 March 1846) 81.

had abandoned the mixed-voice technique for which Berlioz, let us not forget, actually conceived all of his own tenor roles (with the exception of that of Aeneas in *Les Troyens*). But of course not one of these four ever sang the role of Orphée in its entirety. Because it was largely forgotten at the time, the Vienna version could not be used to counterbalance the French version that had now become too high; likewise the intermediate version (with the title role adapted to the high castrato voice of Giuseppe Millico), which Gluck made for the third part of the *Feste d'Apollo* given in Parma in 1769.

Orphée as contralto prior to 1859

It seems to have been that 'diva manquée', Pauline Viardot, who was responsible for the revival of the version of *Orphée* written by Gluck for the castrato contralto Gaetano Guadagni and first performed in Vienna on 5 October 1762. On 3 February 1842, at the royal court, Viardot sang the 'Scène des enfers' accompanied by the Musique de la Chambre du Roi under the direction of D. -F. -E. Auber. (Louis-Philippe apparently liked to hear the lyrical works which had charmed him in his younger years.) Then, on 20 February, at the Société des Concerts, the same singer performed the 'grande scène' from Act III of *Orphée* in what Berlioz tells us, in his review, was the Italian version: 'Despite a cadenza added at the end of the third verse', he writes, 'Mme Viardot reproduced those noble and touching melodies with scrupulous fidelity'.[21]

What we really discover here are two opposing notions of correct interpretation: one, Berlioz's, based, as we have seen, on a kind of literal fidelity to the text; the other, Viardot's, marked by an interest in the problems of ornamentation.[22] If Berlioz qualified Pauline Viardot as a 'great musician' capable of overcoming the imperceptible but none the less very real difficulties presented by the pure style of 'la grande école dramatique', he also suggested that she might have demonstrated, in her entreaties, 'just a little more warmth, just a little more anguish and emotion'. At the time of the musical festivities in Bonn, in August 1845, Viardot again sang the *Scène des enfers* 'with her exquisite method and her poetic expression, both of which', notes Berlioz, 'seem to have been technically enriched during her sojourn in Russia'.[23] Berlioz later tells us

---

21 *Revue et Gazette musicale* (27 February 1842) 81.
22 At the end of the third verse Viardot seems to have used a cadenza written for this moment by an earlier castrato. See below, p. 211.   23 See *Les Soirées de l'orchestre*, 431, 432 and 625.

that a few months before creating the role of Orphée at the Théâtre Lyrique in November 1859, Pauline Viardot did not yet own the score of the Paris version, even though she had been singing a fragment of the role of Eurydice, in French, since 1839.[24]

The example that Viardot had set by taking the role of Orphée was closely followed at the Conservatoire. On four different occasions (29 December 1844, 11 March 1849, 11 May 1851, 29 April 1856) the public in attendance at the students' 'Exercices publics' would hear the role as interpreted by contraltos – namely Emma Courtot, Justine Montigny, Palmyre Wertheimber and Anne de La Pommeraye.[25] Viardot herself would sing fragments of *Orphée* in both Paris and in London. *Orphée* reappears in Berlioz's correspondence only in 1855, when the title role is associated with the name of Rosine Stoltz, also a student of Choron's (and one of Viardot's chief rivals). Like Viardot, Stoltz had the temperament of a tragic actress as well as a wide-ranging mezzo-soprano voice, very sonorous at the bottom, very rich and agile at the top. On 10 January 1855 Berlioz let it be known to the then director of the Opéra-Comique, Emile Perrin, that

Madame Stoltz has wanted for a long time to take the role of Orphée, which was originally written by Gluck for a contralto. She has asked me to show her the transpositions that would have to be made in the French version of the score in order to fit the role to her voice. I really doubt that the Opéra will decide to revive the work as a whole, but I think Madame Stolz would be delighted to sing excerpts from the first act and the *Scène des enfers* at our concert.[26]

The cultural significance of Orphée

Nothing was to come of this project. But we have proof here that from at least 1855 Berlioz hoped to revive the Vienna version of the opera and have the title role sung by a female contralto *en travesti*.

The conditions surrounding the birth or disappearance of a certain kind of voice-type considered as a symbolic cultural expression of its society have so far been little studied. The process by which Pauline Viardot became identified with Orphée provides an excellent case in point, for her

24 See Berlioz's letter to Viardot of 13 September 1859 (to appear in CG VI – in preparation as of this writing. Many of the letters to appear in this volume, of which I have been able to consult the early proofs, have been dated by the editor, Hugh Macdonald. In this article I refer to such letters by date only).

25 See Constant Pierre, *Le Conservatoire national de musique et de déclamation* (Paris, 1900) 502, 504; L. de La Laurencie, 125. 26 CG IV, 695.

career, neither long nor steady, would clearly have been less memorable had it not been for the mythic dimension lent to it by her association with that opera and that character. Berlioz before all others noted that music lovers were by no means the only ones responsible for the justly merited success she enjoyed, for painters and sculptors, pencil in hand, had captured the various attitudes of this lyric tragedienne,[27] and had given to the Viardot-Orphée constellation a meaning well beyond that of music alone. The cultural resonance of what might be called the 'Orpheus effect' was as durable as it was reassuring. To give but a single example: in March 1872, Pasdeloup engaged Pauline Viardot (then in decline) to sing excerpts from Gluck's score as a precautionary measure – in order to lessen the shock of the new work on the programme, the piano concerto by Alexis de Castillon. As it happens, however, the measure was ineffective, for the concerto caused a scandal none the less.

In fact, the cultural context of 1859 would almost guarantee the successful restoration of *Orphée*: the interest in antiquity fostered by the imperial regime, and manifest by numerous archaeological explorations and by the institution of educational policies that affirmed the value of ancient civilisations and of teaching dead languages, was in accord with the interest in the effect on the sensibilities of the contralto voice – something already celebrated by Théophile Gautier in 1849.[28] And let us not forget that the hermaphroditic sonority of the 'intermediate' contralto voice has been frequently associated, in twentieth-century opera, with societally marginal characters, or with characters situated on the borderline between the real and the supernatural world. Orphée, himself a magician both human and divine, has become the archetype of the 'desexualised' artist such as those vaunted by the Parnassian poets. Who could be more suited than he, then, to the contralto voice (replacing the voice of the castrato)? Who, even today, could be more suited than he to 'incarnate' the contralto voice in the theatre? The prevailing idea of classicism during the Second Empire, of course, was a rather idealised one; it was in perfect agreement with what was known of the music of

27 'Painters and sculptors admired her no less than writers and musicians. During one recent soirée [...] one could see artists tracing the poses and sculptural attitudes of the actress.' This passage appeared in Berlioz's *feuilleton* in the *Journal des débats* of 9 December 1859; see *A Travers chants*, 461.

28 Gautier's poem 'Contralto' appeared in the *Revue des deux mondes* of 15 December 1849. René Jasinsky argues, in *Poésies complètes de Théophile Gautier* (Paris, 1970) I, ci, that the poem was inspired by Ernesta Grisi. But this hypothesis seems to me less convincing than that which would have the poem inspired by the creation of Meyerbeer's *Le Prophète* at the Opéra, on 16 April 1849, with Pauline Viardot in the role of Fidès.

Gluck – which, for most listeners, was only the dramatic *Scène des enfers*, the scene that had become a speciality of that veritable 'musical museum',[29] the Société des Concerts du Conservatoire. Offenbach and his librettists thus had the right idea when they named their brilliant parody *Orphée aux enfers*, which was created at the Bouffes-Parisiens on 21 October 1858 – just one year before the restoration of the 'model' of the parody undertaken by Berlioz and Pauline Viardot. It should be emphasised that the satirical effect of *Orphée aux enfers* is all the more striking in that what is derided is not the version by Gluck and Moline but rather the version by Gluck and the 'reformer' Calzabigi. Calzabigi had had the dramatic 'brainstorm' of returning to the original myth and having the test of Orpheus' and Eurydice's fidelity trigger the 'azione teatrale' – a test retained by neither Ovid nor Virgil. *Orphée aux enfers* thus not only ridicules the couple's fidelity (that fidelity so dear to bourgeois morality), it also violently attacks autocracy and dictatorship in a way that could be considered subversive, for it takes aim at the very foundations of the imperial regime.[30] One revealing detail: the auditorium of the Bouffes-Parisiens would be filled to capacity only after Jules Janin cried blasphemy in the *Journal des débats*. Berlioz, his friend and colleague, was first to follow suit: the devastating triumph of Offenbach's parody 'which I am not permitted to name', he wrote, demands an exemplary act of reparation.[31]

II : ORPHÉE'S RESURRECTION

Contracts and preliminary work

It was after hearing her sing during a benefit concert for his wife, Caroline Miolan-Carvalho, on 24 May 1859, that Léon Carvalho, director of the Théâtre Lyrique, decided to engage Pauline Viardot for the role of Orphée.[32] For many artistic and sentimental reasons, Berlioz would favour such a project: first, his desire to take revenge, on Gluck's behalf, for Offenbach's parody; second, his affectionate admiration for Pauline Viardot; and last but by no means least, his hope for a performance of *Les*

29 This revealing expression, 'musée de l'art musical', was commonly used at the time, and recurs in A. Dandelot, *La Société des concerts du Conservatoire* (Paris, 1898).
30 See Siegfried Kracauer, *Jacques Offenbach ou le secret du second Empire* (Paris, 1937) 192 et seq.
31 See *A Travers chants*, 147.
32 See Camille Saint-Saëns, *Portraits et souvenirs* (Paris, 1909) 205; and T. J. Walsh, *Second Empire Opera* (London, 1981) 111.

Troyens, which he may have seen as strategically linked to Carvalho's initiative. This comes out clearly in two letters he wrote only a few days after the première of *Orphée*: 'Madame Viardot, who sings the role of Orphée, is admirable in it [...] Here is my Dido all ready and full of ardour and devotion', he wrote to Camille Pal on 21 November 1859;[33] and to Marc Suat, on 25 November, he wrote: 'You can understand how much pleasure I take from this revolution (for it really is a revolution), and from this return to the subject of antiquity [...]. Carvalho [...] is more than ever inclined to put on *Les Troyens*'.[34]

According to Saint-Saëns, Pauline Viardot began studying the works of Gluck, which he says were 'entirely new to her', probably at Berlioz's instigation'.[35] Henri de Curzon reports that Viardot began by refusing totally to consider the role of Orphée, claiming that she found Gluck's operas 'deadly dull', and that a fusion of the two versions of *Orphée* would be a 'compromise and a monstrous hybrid'. It seems that it was her husband, Louis Viardot, who persuaded her to accept the engagement, even though she thoroughly disliked the idea of singing *en travesti* and expressing the emotions of a man. She confided to Curzon: 'It was only with the orchestra, and only on the evening of the dress-rehearsal, that I began to find [the opera] beautiful, and to put my heart into it'.[36]

Her decision to take on the role became firm in August 1859, at the time of Berlioz's return from Baden, where she had sung the duet from *Les Troyens*. The echoes of this concert began to mix with the rumours aroused by the announcement of the revival of *Orphée*.[37] 'The chorus and orchestra have been augmented to proportions which respond fully to the grandiose character of the work. Finally, the *mise-en-scène*, conceived in accordance with historically accurate and precise traditions, will, we are told, be equivalent to that of the most impressive performances that have ever been given at the Théâtre Lyrique.'

In a letter written to Pauline Viardot on 8 September 1859 Berlioz speaks for the first time explicitly of the nature of his collaboration with the singer:

33 See *CG* VI (in preparation).   34 *CG* VI.
35 Camille Saint-Saëns, 'Orphée', *Revue de Paris* (1 July 1896) 222.
36 Henri de Curzon, 'La Manie des remaniements', 510.
37 See the *Revue et Gazette musicale* (4 September 1859) 297; (11 September 1859) 305; (16 October 1859) 346; (13 November 1859) 382; *La France musicale* (13 November 1859). The quotation in the text is from the last-mentioned newspaper; the same text appeared with minor variants in that day's issue of the *Revue et Gazette musicale*: its style and precision suggest that the author was Berlioz himself.

Everything you say about the first act of *Orphée* is already marked in pencil in my scores and works very well. The other revisions in the second and third acts are also quite feasible, and will be done, don't you worry. As for the grotesque love aria, Carvalho will do with that what he will; I wish not to be involved with any cuts, and even less with the addition of the chorus from *Armide* (which I find ridiculous).[38]

Berlioz was thus prepared to submit the first act 'mis au net' – polished and ready. On 13 September 1859 he noted the further progress of what he called his 'mosaic-making': the first act and a part of the second were ready for the copyist (Rocquemont), and Carvalho had given up the idea of making a potpourri from the Overture to *Iphigénie* and a chorus from *Armide*. Carvalho was going to engage fourteen women from the Théâtre Italien to round out his vocal forces; and he was going to hire two mimes, 'which I told him were needed', wrote Berlioz (for the grand demon and the ghost in the ballet of the Elysian Fields); he had found a 'Eurydice named Sasse', and 'Mlle Marimon will take the role of l'Amour'.[39]

On 23 September Berlioz wrote to his son that with Rocquemont's help he had finished his work on the first act of *Orphée* just in time for the rehearsals that were about to begin at the Théâtre Lyrique; at the same time he was in the midst of correcting the score of *Les Troyens*: Mme Viardot, says Berlioz, rather than singing Orphée, would prefer to sing Cassandra right away.[40] On 25 September Berlioz told the Princess Sayn-Wittgenstein that he had been charged with arranging both the Italian and the French versions of the score.[41] On the same day he informed Viardot that the question of the ballets was to be discussed,[42] and on 20 October the question of the famous aria 'Amour, viens rendre à mon âme' was put on the table: Viardot had asked Berlioz to reorchestrate it; he had refused, pointing out how often he had 'exterminated those who took such liberties' with a score.[43] (In the end Camille Saint-Saëns was given the task.)[44] On 14 November Berlioz wrote out for Viardot part of the cadenza to be sung at the end of the aria;[45] on the 18th he invited Wagner to attend the first performance,[46] which was to take place that very evening under the perfectly satisfactory direction of Adolphe Deloffre.[47]

---

38 See *CG* VI.   39 *Ibid*. On Marimon and Sasse, see *A Travers chants*, 393–4.
40 *CG* VI.   41 *Ibid*.   42 *Ibid*.   43 *Ibid*.
44 Cf. *Orphée et Eurydice*, publié par Mlle Fanny Pelletan, C. Saint-Saëns et Julien Tiersot (Paris: Durand, *ca*. 1915) 282.   45 *CG* VI.   46 *CG* VI.
47 The cast is given in Berlioz's letter to Viardot of 13 September. Adolphe Deloffre (1817–76), violinist and composer, was frequently the conductor at the Théâtre Lyrique during Carvalho's directorship, and was at the helm for the première of *Les Troyens* in 1863. In 1860 he published 'Laissez-vous toucher par mes pleurs!, scène d'*Orphée* de Gluck transcrite pour violon ou violoncelle, piano ou orgue ad lib.' (Paris: Au Ménestrel).

Orphée, which followed Weber's *Abu Hassan* and Mozart's *Enlèvement au sérail*, was an immediate and triumphant success. By 1863 it had had no fewer than 138 performances.[48] At the time of the revival on 4 November 1860, Marie Sasse was replaced by Mlle Oprawil in the role of Eurydice; the role of l'Amour was taken by Caroline Girard.[49] Hugh Macdonald has posed the question of whether Viardot herself sang at all of these performances, and the answer is not clear. We do know that Berlioz alluded to her poor health in December 1859,[50] and that she was not well for the performances of November 1860, when the *Revue et Gazette musicale* attributed 'certain exaggerated aspects of her acting and singing' to illness.[51]

In addition to her performances in Paris, Pauline Viardot would on one occasion sing *Orphée* in London, in July 1860, and she would sing excerpts from the work in concert, notably at the musical festivities in Metz on 2 and 3 June 1860, and in Baden, at Berlioz's concert of 27 August of that year. We know that it was at her own instigation that she took on the role of Alceste at the Opéra, in 1861, but this had not required Berlioz's persuasive efforts. Indeed, the relations between the two artists seem to have become strained during the summer of 1860, for their correspondence at the time trickles to nearly nothing.

The success of the opera

In general, the reviews of *Orphée* were enthusiastic.[52] Pauline Viardot was admired for her vocal mastery, her sense of style, her energy, and for the graceful and natural aspects of her acting. The other principals were little mentioned. Still, the critic Paul Scudo (who had also been educated at Choron's school) probably knew what he was talking about when in an otherwise positive review he noted (as did others) that Viardot's voice 'had long ago lost some of its charm and sonority'.[53]

---

48 Twenty performances in 1859, seventy-six in 1860, twenty-eight in 1861, twelve in 1862, and two in 1863. See A. Soubies, *Histoire du Théâtre-Lyrique* (Paris, 1899) 26. These figures may be verified in the registers of the Société des Auteurs et Compositeurs dramatiques (where Berlioz's name is nowhere to be found).

49 See the *Revue et Gazette musicale* of 11 November 1860.   50 See *CG* VI.

51 *Revue et Gazette musicale* (11 November 1860).

52 L. de La Laurencie gives a synthesis of the principal reviews of the revival, in *Orphée de Gluck*, 131 et seq.

53 *Revue des deux mondes* (1 December 1859) 719 et seq. In the issue of 1 January 1860 he wrote that Viardot was pleasing 'even to those who wished she had a younger voice and a more musical timbre'.

Berlioz, who had participated in the preparation of the *mise-en-scène* as well as of the score, also participated in the critical response, devoting two of his *feuilletons* in the *Journal des débats* (22 November and 9 December 1859) to the revival of *Orphée*. If he sang in unison with his colleagues in admiration of the remarkable oneness of Viardot's singing and acting, he none the less sounded a note of disapproval in criticising the changes she made at the end of 'J'ai perdu mon Eurydice' and elsewhere in the text, and he deplored the fact that she had introduced several roulades into a recitative, where they were totally out of place.[54] Even in the heady atmosphere of the successful opening performances, Berlioz – uncompromising when it came to problems of diction – continued to offer advice. On 12 December 1859 he wrote:

Dear Orphée,
The other evening I neglected to tell you two things: first, the phrase 'La mort est tout ce qui me reste!' is now fine; the timbre of the adopted notes is excellent; change nothing.
    Then, in the name of the god of day, your father, who is also the god of poetry, please don't say: 'Ah! je te suis tendre – hobjet de la foi!' If you absolutely must breathe before the word 'objet', say 'cher-objet' and thus avoid making a horrible line of eleven feet with an abominable hiatus; there will still be one h too many in 'objet'…But nobody's perfect.[55]

On 11 January 1860 Berlioz admitted that the singer was 'increasingly sublime' in the role,[56] on 29 January he said that her handling of the role was 'of an ideal beauty'.[57]

From these quotations one sees that Berlioz attributed equal importance to the musical text and to accurate textual declamation. On several occasions during the composition of *Les Troyens* he insisted upon the priority of the poem over the music and the priority of declamation over singing.[58] This preoccupation was again manifest on 12 January 1861 when, at a meeting of the Académie des Beaux-Arts, Berlioz complained of the errors in declamation found in the work of the Rome-Prize competitors: citing examples of poor declamation taken from works already performed, he expressed the wish that 'composition students be

54 See *A Travers chants*, 145.
55 CG VI. [*Translator's note*: Berlioz's penultimate phrase reads 'il ne restera qu'un h de plus à objet', which I have translated loosely. I am grateful to Katherine Reeve for suggesting, no doubt rightly, that Berlioz is here guilty of 'une négligence de style'; what he means is that even the one 'h' required of the singer to sound the first syllable of 'objet' is, for him, one 'h' too many.]
56 CG VI.   57 *Ibid.*
58 See Joël-Marie Fauquet, 'Vienne une Cassandre, vienne une Didon', *L'Avant-Scène Opéra* (February-March 1990) 137 et seq.

given declamation lessons and be admitted to declamation classes at the Conservatoire'. In reply, it was suggested, with unsubtle allusion to the deciding role Berlioz had had in the current Gluck renaissance, that Gluck himself 'had not had a declamation teacher, yet his recitatives and his arias were models; indeed, they were lessons in profound expression'.[59]

III : THE SOURCES

The two editions annotated by Berlioz

Berlioz began his 'restorations' by making annotations in two printed copies of the score, one, the Vienna version of *Orfeo*, the other, the Paris version of *Orphée*. Originally in the library of the Menus-Plaisirs, they are currently in the music division of the Bibliothèque Nationale.[60] The annotations were summarily described in 1906 by Julien Tiersot, who justly suggested that the value of these early editions of Gluck was heartily enhanced by their having also become autograph manuscripts of Berlioz.[61]

There are relatively few annotations to be found in the Vienna edition. On page 53, Berlioz noted 'Allez à B': he thus cut the reprise of the prelude to Act II and went directly to the aria 'Deh placatevi'. He also wrote 'Allez à B dans la partition française', but he crossed this out when he decided to keep the Italian version at this point (and avoid the transposition that Gluck made in the French version). But at the end of Orphée's moving dialogue with the infernal voices, Berlioz wrote 'Copier ici en transposant les 6 mesures de la partition française page 62' – the six bars being the amplification that Gluck made at the end of Orphée's supplication, 'Soyez sensible à mes malheurs', the transposition being to the original key of B flat major. He then corrected the faulty pagination of pages 57 to 60 and marked the first three bars of the aria 'Che faro', on page 129, with crescendo marks and *sforzandi*.

There are far more annotations to be found in the Paris edition. Tiersot by no means described all of them, but in fact they mark the first stage of the 'mosaic-making' in which Berlioz said that he was engaged. (Tiersot

59 Archives of the Académie des Beaux-Arts, Registre des procès-verbaux (2 E 13) 112.
60 *Orfeo ed Euridice* / Azione teatrale per Musica del Sign' Cav. Cristofano Gluck [...] gravé par Chambon [...] Parigi [...] Duchesne, M.DCC.LXIV [Bibliothèque Nationale, Musique, D. 4702 (1)]; *Orphée et Eurydice* / Tragédie Opéra en trois actes / Mises en musique par Gluck / Les parolles sont de Moline [...] A Paris chez Des Lauriers [...]. [B.N., Mus., D. 4582]. It should be noted that Berlioz did not make use of the original edition, which was published in Paris by Le Marchand.   61 Tiersot, 'Berlioziana', *Le Ménestrel* (11 February 1906) 43.

did accurately note that some annotations here, such as the date 'le 15 juin 1818' at the beginning of the score, are not in Berlioz's hand.) Berlioz's notations, variously in ink and in pencil (black, red or blue), may be classified as follows:

(1) Corrections of errors due to Gluck's carelessness (pages 32, 34, 35, 50, 56, 62, 67, 148). Here Berlioz corrects the errors he mentions in his *feuilleton* of 22 November 1859.[62]

(2) Transposition. On page 17, above the aria 'Objet de mon amour', Berlioz writes 'partition italienne', thus indicating his intention to retranspose this piece to its original key of F major. From page 50 to page 54, he mentions the transposition to C minor for the chorus 'Quel est l'audacieux' (no. 21). On page 57 he writes 'en mi b', then writes in pencil 'fa ♯-la ♮-mi-do ♯' and gives the figures for the diminished seventh at no. 22, the chorus with solo 'Laissez-vous toucher par mes pleurs'. He writes a bass part, different from Gluck's, under the harp part, in order to support Orphée's phrase 'Laissez-nous toucher', etc. (see Example 1). On page 62, above the chorus 'Qui t'amène en ces lieux', he writes 'mi b', and on page 65, 'en fa mineur' above 'Ah la flamme'. On page 69, at the chorus 'Quels chants doux', he notes 'dans le ton'.

Example 1

62 See *A Travers chants*, 136–7.

(3) Shifting or removal of complete numbers. Tiersot said nothing of these modifications, but they are in fact of considerable significance. On pages 18, 19 and 21, Berlioz notes the reference marks that show how the recitatives are to be interpolated into the aria 'Objet de mon amour'.[63] On page 23, after the recitative 'Eurydice de ce doux nom', he writes 'J'ai perdu p. 147'. On page 150, at the end of the aria 'J'ai perdu', he notes a return to the recitative of Act I, 'Divinités de l'Achéron'. He would later abandon the idea of shifting these two numbers – an idea that would have seriously affected the dramatic structure of the work as a whole. On page 155, after the recitative 'Arrête, Orphée', he draws a *fine* sign and writes 'Dieu de Paphos', the chorus from *Echo et Narcisse* which, from the 1790s, had traditionally served as the opera's Finale.

(4) Nuances. In the aria 'Si les doux accords' from Act I, on page 29, Berlioz inserts hairpins at 'tu la ramèneras'. And on page 72, he inserts a *forte* marking at 'Tout cède à la douceur'. (This would become *poco f* in the edition of 1859.)

The 'Berlioz-Viardot' manuscript

In the Fonds du Conservatoire at the Bibliothèque Nationale there is a bundle of sixteen manuscript pages, in ink, with pencil annotations,

63 See below, pp. 212–13.

relating to the transposition of the role of Orphée.[64] A note in the hand of the former librarian, Julien Tiersot, dated 2 June 1911, indicates that these pages had been classified among Berlioz's autograph manuscripts (where they had been found), but that this classification was in error. 'I had observed', notes Tiersot, 'that this arrangement of Gluck's *Orphée* was not in Berlioz's hand'. But in fact, a close examination of these pages reveals that among the three different hands that can be distinguished, Berlioz's does seem to appear on pages 4 and 5. Indeed, Berlioz seems hastily to have written the words, if not the vocal lines, at 'Laissez-vous toucher par mes pleurs' and at 'Ah la flamme qui me dévore' (from Act II, scene i).

If, according to Tiersot, this arrangement 'differs notably from the edition made for the performances at the Théâtre Lyrique', there is none the less evidence that it constitutes a step preparatory to that edition. Tiersot speaks of the manuscript's 'transcription of the role of Orphée for a woman's voice', avoiding mention of a specific female register. He seems to have thought that since the role is written in the C first-line (soprano) clef, it was probably for a soprano, not for a contralto. But he forgot that Fidès, the celebrated role in *Le Prophète* created by Pauline Viardot, is also notated in the soprano clef in Meyerbeer's score. In the case of *Orphée*, the choice of the soprano clef was clearly justified by Viardot's remarkably wide range (in both the Vienna and Paris scores, the solo role is cast in the alto clef). Finally, Tiersot seems surprisingly to have failed to notice the obvious links between Berlioz's annotations in the two earlier printed scores and the annotations found in these important manuscript pages.

The contents of the manuscript (which was not assembled in any logical fashion) may be charted as follows:[65]

p. 1:   Act I, scene i (no. 2): 'Récit après le 1er chœur' 'Vos plaintes, vos regrets', etc. (see Example 2). Here the vocal line and the accompaniment are modified in ways that correspond neither to Gluck's versions nor to that published by Berlioz in 1859.

p. 1:   Act I, scene i (no. 5): 'Après le 2^{d} chœur' 'Eloignez-vous ce lieu convient à mes malheurs' (see Example 3). Again, the modifications correspond to versions by neither Gluck nor Berlioz.

p. 1:   Act I, scene ii (no. 11): 'L'onde murmure…' (see Example 4). A cadenza is found here, in pencil.

64 Bibliothèque Nationale, Musique, ms. 1522.
65 From this point I use the numbering of the score of *Orphée* edited, with Berlioz's assistance (see below), by Alfred Dörffel. The score published by Peters, which uses the same numbering, is still readily available.

Example 2

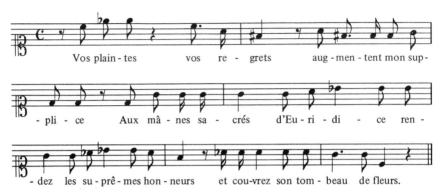

Vos plain - tes vos re - grets aug -men - tent mon sup-

- pli - ce Aux mâ - nes sa - crés d'Eu - ri - di - ce ren -

- dez les su - prê - mes hon - neurs et cou-vrez son tom - beau de fleurs.

Example 3

E - loi -gnez vous ce lieu con -vient à mes mal-

- heurs Et je veux sans té - moins y ré - pan - dre des pleurs.

Example 4

l'on - de mur - mu - re l'on - - - - - - -

- de l'on - de mur - mu - - - re

p. 2:   Act I, scene ii (no. 7): 'Objet de mon amour', etc. This passage
conforms to Berlioz's edition, with added nuances and ornaments
in pencil, including a cadenza at 't'appelle encore'.

p. 2:   Act I, scene ii (no. 10): from 'Eurydice Eurydice' to 'une main
tremblante'. This passage conforms to Berlioz's edition of 1859.

p. 3:   Act II, scene i (no. 22): from 'Laissez-vous toucher par mes pleurs' to 'de mes malheurs'. This passage conforms to Berlioz's edition of 1859.

p. 4:   Continuation and incomplete reprise. The voice line may be in Berlioz's hand; the passage has been transposed to the key of the edition of 1859.

p. 4:   Act II, scene i (no. 24): 'Ah la flamme qui me dévore', etc. The voice line may be in Berlioz's hand; the passage has been transposed to the key of the edition of 1859 (C minor) but with the key-signature of F minor.

p. 5:   Continuation to 'ce que je ressens'; Act II, scene i (no. 25): 'la tendresse qui me presse' to 'votre rigueur'. The voice line may be in Berlioz's hand; the ornamentation added in pencil is in another hand. There are four different versions, in pencil, of the cadenza at 'votre rigueur' (see Example 5).

Example 5

p. 6:   (Blank)

p. 7:   Act I, scene iv (no. 16): 'Impitoyables dieux'. The recitative has been transposed down by a fifth. (This is altered in Berlioz's edition of 1859.)

p. 7:   Act I, scene iii (no. 14): 'Dieux! je la reverrais!'. The recitative appears in a transposition different from all published editions.

p. 7: *Ibid.*: from 'Ah! qui pourrait me retenir?' to 'préparée'. This passage conforms to Berlioz's edition of 1859.

p. 8: *Ibid.*: 'Eh bien, j'obéirai', etc. This passage has been crossed out.

p. 9: Act I, scene iv (no. 16): 'Impitoyables dieux'. The recitative has been transposed down by a fifth and rewritten with an orchestral accompaniment that does not appear in Berlioz's edition of 1859.

p. 10: There is the note 'Allez au second acte scène des enfers p. 50'.

p. 11: Act I, scene ii (no. 12): from 'tyrans' to 'toutes vos fureurs'. The recitative with orchestral accompaniment has been transposed down by a fifth, a step lower than that of Berlioz's edition of 1859. This page also contains the beginning of Amour's recitative (scene iii) with the note 'Comme à la partition française'.

p. 12: There is the note 'Après l'air J'ai perdu mon… de L'Italien de suite le récit suivant'. Also on this page: Act I, scene ii (no. 12): 'Divinités de l'Achéron', etc. The recitative with orchestra has been transposed down by a fifth, a step lower than that of Berlioz's edition of 1859.

p. 13: There is the note 'B après la romance en fa'. Also on this page: Act I, scene ii (no. 10): 'Eurydice Eurydice,' etc. (see Example 6). The recitative has been orchestrated in a manner different from that of all printed editions.

Example 6

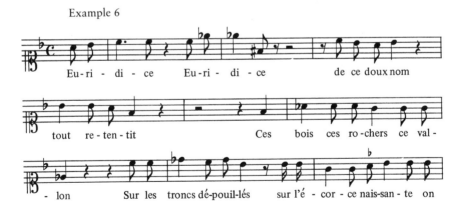

p. 14: There is the note 'Air j'ai perdu mon Eurydice en ut comme dans la partition italienne' crossed out in pencil, with the note 'p. 147' – the page-number of this aria in the editions published by Des

Lauriers and Le Marchand. There is a cadenza here, in pencil, at 'déchire mon cœur' (see Example 7).

Example 7

dé - - chi - - - re mon cœur.

p. 15: Act I, scene ii (no. 10): 'Eurydice n'est plus', etc. The recitative, for voice and piano, is different from all printed editions. After the double bar there is the note 'J'ai perdu mon Eurydice' in pencil. Also on this page: Act I, scene ii (no. 11): 'Plein de trouble et d'effroi'. The passage, crossed out in pencil, is in the key of Berlioz's edition of 1859.

p. 16: *Ibid.*: from 'Divinités de l'Achéron' to the beginning of Amour's recitative in scene iii. The passage appears a step higher than it does in Berlioz's edition.

The most conclusive proof that this manuscript is linked to the first phase of Berlioz's projected revision of the score is that it requires the removal of the aria 'J'ai perdu mon Eurydice' from Act III and its placement at the end of Act I: this is noted, as we have seen, on the early French score, and it is noted here, in pencil (not in Berlioz's hand, and later crossed out) at the same spot. Thus, perhaps at Pauline Viardot's instigation, Berlioz first envisaged a remodelling of the opera, but then decided to maintain the purist position that we know so well from his correspondence. This would explain the textual differences that exist between the manuscript in question and the voice-and-piano edition that Berlioz prepared to conform to the performances at the Théâtre Lyrique.

It is indeed possible that this manuscript was prepared by Pauline Viardot and her entourage, and that it is to it that Berlioz alludes in his letter to her of 8 September 1859.[66] Much later, to Reynaldo Hahn, Viardot would admit having 'revised and restored' *Orphée*, though she claimed to have done nothing without the approval of Berlioz and Saint-Saëns.[67]

66 Further proof may be had from the postscript of Berlioz's letter to Viardot of 13 September 1859 (see CG VI): 'It was unnecessary for M. Viardot to translate the first recitative that precedes the romance', etc.
67 See Reynaldo Hahn, *Notes / Journal d'un musicien* (Paris, 1933) 7.

The majority of the 'arrangements' in this manuscript concern the first act, which, in the version performed at the Théâtre Lyrique, is the act that was by far the most reworked. Furthermore, two elements support the hypothesis that what we have here are the fragments of preparatory sketches exchanged by Berlioz and Viardot: one, the presence of cadenzas, for which Berlioz would chastise the singer; and two, the identical nature of the passage from the aria with chorus 'Laissez-vous toucher par mes pleurs' (no. 22) as found both in the copy of the score that Viardot herself annotated[68] and in this manuscript (on page 3).

The conductor's manuscript

Another important manuscript source has also been heretofore neglected, namely the seventy-six page part marked 'Violon conducteur / Orphée et Eurydice / Musique de Gluck' – an undated and apparently unused part that was given to the Bibliothèque du Conservatoire by an unknown donor in the later nineteenth century.[69] The role of Orphée is transposed for contralto (using the soprano clef) and some of the modifications of the vocal line, in the recitatives, are identical to those that appear in the 'Berlioz-Viardot' manuscript described above. The role of Amour is copied here without text. Act I concludes with the recitative 'J'obtiens des dieux la plus grande faveur'; Act II omits the pantomime of the furies. At 'malheurs' there is an added cadenza – identical to the one added at this point in the 'Berlioz-Viardot' manuscript and in the edition annotated by Viardot. The orchestral coda of the chorus 'Près du tendre objet' (no. 37) is omitted. The aria 'Cet asile aimable' (no. 32) provides an intermezzo, with Act III beginning with the recitative 'Viens, viens Eurydice' (no. 38). (This number comes at the beginning of Act IV in the version of 1859.) As in the early French version annotated by Berlioz, the score concludes with the recitative on the words 'jouissez des plaisirs de l'amour' (no. 44) followed by the mention 'chœur final'.

Several pencil annotations are superimposed here on the copyist's manuscript. The most important are the cadenza at the end of the aria 'Objet de mon amour' (no. 7) (see Example 8) and the cadenza at the end of the aria 'La tendresse qui me presse' (no. 26) (see Example 9).

68 See below, p. 229.
69 Bibliothèque Nationale, Musique, L. 16380. A programme attached to the part suggests that it was prepared prior to 1866.

Example 8

t'ap - pelle en - co-re t'ap-pel - - - - - - le t'ap - - pelle en- co - - re

Example 9

- gueur___ flé - chi - ront vo - - - - - - tre ri - gueur

'Ornamental' sources

For Berlioz, the sobriety of Gluck's vocal lines, inflected with the dramatic accents of the literary text, was diametrically opposed to 'bel canto' – that is, to the ornate style of singing so adored by the dilettante public; for Berlioz, 'bel canto' was inexpressive and antimusical. But for Pauline Viardot it was not: she was attached to the tradition of 'bel canto' and attempted to reconcile the two styles by adding ornaments and by embellishing fermatas with cadenzas. Convinced (mistakenly) that the aria 'L'espoir renaît dans mon âme' was by Ferdinando Bertoni and not by Gluck, Berlioz did not hesitate to suggest to the singer that she write a cadenza for the fermata at the end. And in his own works, Berlioz did not always refrain from adding such embellishments (which led to much applause): in Act I of *Benvenuto Cellini*, for example, Teresa sings an aria with stretti and roulades; and Hero's aria in *Béatrice et Bénédict* – perhaps on the basis of the composer's experience with *Orphée* – also ends with a vocalise 'di bravura'.[70]

Shortly after having undertaken the revision of *Orphée*, on 13 September 1859, Berlioz wrote to Viardot:

I forgot to tell you that in your 'air à roulades' that concludes the first act, it is absolutely essential to sing an astounding cadenza at the last fermata. Gluck calls for it. So compose a lively mixture of vocalises for this moment and you will bring down the house as you leave the stage.[71]

70 Hero's aria is no. 3 in the Brandus edition of the piano-vocal score (see *NBE* 3, 91–2). Berlioz completed the score on 25 February 1862.
71 See *CG* VI.

The next day he returned to the composition of this cadenza, suggesting that 'one might perfectly well reuse a previously heard theme, just as instrumental virtuosos do in their concertos', namely, the theme of the aria 'Objet de mon amour', which Berlioz notates as in Example 10.

Example 10

We will say, if we have to, that *this is the cadenza sung by Legros* [...]. The Parisians will surely swallow it whole. I think that you could leave the stage with a triple salvo of applause and thus enable us to avoid finishing on that stupid word 'appas'.[72]

This ingenious idea was to be retained – the text was changed but the rhyme was saved: in place of 'Je vais revoir ses appas', Pauline Viardot sang 'Je vais braver le trépas'. Later the singer would confide to Reynaldo Hahn that this celebrated cadenza,

for which I have had the honour of being criticised [...] was manufactured by *all three of us*! [...] The first part (by Berlioz) is good; the second (by Saint-Saëns) is a bit odd; the several lines written by the singer are too 'singerish'; and the last part, by Berlioz, might also have been written by the concierge.[73]

None the less there is no doubt that this little bit of prestidigitation had a good deal to do with the enthusiasm of the response to the Théâtre

---

72 CG VI.

73 '[La cadence] qu'on m'a fait l'honneur de me reprocher [...] a été décidée par *nous trois!* [...] La première partie (de Berlioz) est bien; la seconde (de Saint-Saëns) est un peu toc; le petit trait écrit par la chanteuse est trop "chanteur"; et la dernière partie, de Berlioz, pourrait être aussi bien du concierge.' See Hahn, 8. Like Berlioz, Saint-Saëns too was persuaded that the aria was by Bertoni. He later wrote: 'We took up the task [of writing the cadenza] with even greater enthusiasm as we were convinced we were fooling about with a piece whose composer merited no fidelity'. (*Portraits et souvenirs*, 211.)

Example 11

'Cadence faite par Mme Viardot au dernier point d'orgue de l'air précédent'

Lyrique's revival of *Orphée*. In his *feuilleton* of 22 November 1859, Berlioz attributes the cadenza entirely to Viardot, and writes that its effect was 'as thrilling as it was unexpected'; it 'would have by itself ensured the success of the act'.[74] On 9 December 1859, speaking of the piano-vocal score that had just appeared, Berlioz again mentioned the 'famous cadenza added by Mme Viardot [...] which caused frenzy and excitement and cries of joy from both connoisseurs and the amateurs alike'.[75]

This virtuoso show-piece was published in the piano-vocal score as an appendix to the aria (see Example 11).[76] In fact, as we shall see, Pauline

---

74 See *A Travers chants*, 459. Berlioz removed this passage from the final text of *A Travers chants* and in so doing removed a falsehood fabricated 'for the cause'.

75 *Ibid.*, 462. 76 See p. 42 of the score.

Viardot added further important ornaments to the aria which adroitly added to its effect; she was convinced that 'Gluck was undoubtedly in favour of such "agréments", not only in vocal music, but everywhere'.[77] As proof she played for Reynaldo Hahn 'a horribly ornamented rococo' version of 'J'ai perdu mon Eurydice' which her brother had found in an eighteenth-century manuscript copy that once belonged to a famous singer at the Sistine Chapel.[78]

Lost and hypothetical sources

A close reading of Berlioz's correspondence provides us with a further list of lost and hypothetical sources for the performances at the Théâtre Lyrique in 1859 and for the revised version of the score. These may be enumerated as follows:

(1) A manuscript (by Berlioz?) of Act I 'mis au net'[79] and Act II, submitted to Viardot but prepared for the copyist, Rocquemont, in mid-September 1859;

(2) A copy of the score of Act I prepared by Rocquemont and corrected by Berlioz;[80]

(3) Copies of the full score and parts prepared by Rocquemont for the Théâtre Lyrique(?);

(4) A copy of the full score prepared for the publisher, Heugel;[81]

(5) A manuscript of the reduction for voice and piano prepared under Berlioz's supervision by Théodore Ritter;[82]

(6) Proofs of the reduction for voice and piano corrected by Berlioz;[83]

(7) A copy of the full score printed by Gustav Heinze, corrected by Berlioz and sent to that publisher in June 1866;[84]

(8) Proofs of the full orchestral score published by Heinze and corrected by Berlioz.[85]

---

77 See Hahn, *Notes*, 8.

78 See *Notes*, 8, and Hahn, *L'Oreille au guet* (Paris, 1937) 136. Viardot had apparently known this cadenza for some time; she sang it as early as 1842 (see above, p. 194).

79 See CG VI.   80 See CG VI.

81 See Berlioz's letter to Carvalho of 1 November 1859; CG VI.

82 *Ibid.*

83 See Berlioz's letter to the Princess Sayn-Wittgenstein of 2 December 1859; CG VI.

84 See the letter from Heinze to Berlioz (dated 21 June 1866), now in the collections of the Musée Berlioz at La Côte St André. A copy of this letter was graciously made available to me by Mlle Thérèse Husson.

85 See Berlioz's letter to Heinze of 24 September 1866, in Jacques Barzun, *New Letters of Berlioz* (New York, 1954) 254.

IV : NINETEENTH-CENTURY FRENCH EDITIONS OF ORPHÉE TO 1859

Editions for voice and piano

Répertoire des Opéras français / Orphée / opéra en Trois actes / avec accompagnement de / Piano-Forte / Musique de Gluck / Edition Nicolo (Paris: Veuve Nicolo, *ca.* 1824).

Ibid., 2ᵉ édition (with neither plate number nor date).

Orphée / grand opéra en trois actes / paroles françaises / musique / de / Gluck / Paris, Vve Launer (plate no. L. 3287; 1842). This score was later reprinted by E. Girod.

Edition for piano solo

Orphée / Opéra en trois actes / musique de / Gluck / Partition / pour Piano solo / 42ᵉ livraison / L'arrangement de Piano est la propriété des Editeurs / Paris, / chez Mme Vve Ch. Marquerie, 1859.

The Nicolo edition includes the changes adopted at the time of the 1824 revival, with Adolphe Nourrit, and some may date from even earlier. In Act I, aside from the excision of the orchestral ritornello (no. 6) and the second couplet ('Accablé de regrets') from the aria 'Objet de mon amour' (no. 9), the principal modification is the substitution of the aria 'O combats, ô désordre extrême' (from *Echo et Narcisse*) for the aria 'Amour, viens rendre à mon âme'. The latter is printed at the end of the act, among the 'morceaux supplémentaires', which also include two numbers removed from Act II – the 'Danse des furies' (no. 28) and the aria 'Quel nouveau ciel' (no. 33). Act III ends with the recitative 'Arrête Orphée' (no. 44). The conclusion consists of the chorus 'Le dieu de Paphos et de Gnide' (borrowed from *Echo et Narcisse*) followed by the shortened finale, 'L'Amour triomphe'. The final ballet was cut in its entirety. Later editions reproduce this abridged version.

Editions of separate numbers

'Scène et chœur d'Orphée / Musique de Gluk [*sic*] / chantée par Monsieur Delsarte / Aux concerts de la Société, n° 32' in the *Recueil des morceaux de musique ancienne, exécutés aux Concerts de la Société de musique vocale et religieuse* [...] (Paris: Pacini, 1843). (This is the *Scène des enfers* in the version for tenor.)

Idem, in the *Archives du chant* / recueillies et publiées par / François Delsarte / XXIIIe livraison, IIe vol., n° 7.

Idem, in the *Répertoire des morceaux d'ensemble* exécutés par la Société des concerts du Conservatoire arrangés très soigneusement / pour piano seul, 20e livraison (Paris: Schonenberger, 1850).

The revival of *Orphée* at the Théâtre Lyrique in 1859 turned out to be a godsend for publishers. As Berlioz noted in his *feuilleton* of 9 December 1859, 'spread out on the shelves of all the music stores we now see the scores of the tenor version of *Orphée* with mediocre piano accompaniments made who knows when by who knows whom'.[86]

V: EDITIONS OF ORPHÉE RESULTING FROM THE 1859 REVIVAL AT THE THÉÂTRE LYRIQUE

On 1 November 1859, Berlioz informed Carvalho that two Parisian publishers, Heugel and Escudier, both wished to publish the score of *Orphée*; and he suggested that Carvalho 'reconcile the two competitors'.[87] Escudier seems to have been the first to make his wishes known, and it was thus for him that Théodore Ritter, under Berlioz's close supervision, began the task of preparing a reduction for voice and piano.[88] One month later, on 1 December, Berlioz finished correcting the proofs, and on 9 December he announced that 'the only edition of Gluck's masterpiece conforming to the performance at the Théâtre Lyrique, with a new reduction for piano by Théodore Ritter, has just been published by Escudier'.[89] Heugel, for his part, had a copy of the full score at his disposal, and would publish numbers from *Orphée* in ten fascicles.

86 See *A Travers chants*, 461.　　　　87 See above, note 81.
88 Théodore Ritter (1838–86), a pianist and composer whom Berlioz greatly admired, had already prepared the reduction for voice and piano of a section of *L'Enfance du Christ* and of the love scene of *Roméo et Juliette*.　　　89 See note 86.

The Escudier reduction for voice and piano

The title page of the Escudier piano-vocal score was printed as follows:

> Seule édition / conforme à la Représentation / Orphée / Opéra en quatre Actes / Musique de Gluck / Représenté au Théâtre Lyrique / Réduction au Piano / par / Théodore Ritter / prix 10 F net / Paris, / Propriété de Léon Escudier rue Choiseul, 21 (plate no. L.E. 1845).

It appears as though there were two consecutive printings of this first edition. Copies of the first printing, which are extremely rare,[90] include, after the title page, a dedication – 'Edition / dédiée à / Mme Pauline Viardot Garcia' – and a preface by Berlioz. The latter offers no hint of Berlioz's role in preparing the score, but rather gives an account of the two versions of the opera, of the circumstances in which the principal role was rewritten, at Carvalho's behest, for the contralto voice of Pauline Viardot, and of the improvements and additions Gluck made to the Vienna version when preparing the score for Paris. Berlioz singles out the reinsertion of 'one of the most beautiful recitatives' of the Italian version at the end of Act I, attributes the removal of the final *divertissement* to the insufficient choreographic resources of the Théâtre Lyrique, and mentions the substitution of the chorus from *Echo et Narcisse* for the aria 'L'Amour triomphe'. He concludes by rendering gracious homage to Théodore Ritter for the intelligence and fidelity of his transcription. Because this preface is little known even among specialists (we have summarised its full contents), we give Berlioz's original text here:

Gluck composa en premier lieu son opéra d'*Orphée* sur un texte italien. Le rôle principal, destiné au castrat Guadagni, fut écrit pour la voix de contralto. Plus tard, le maître allemand remania cet ouvrage, afin de l'approprier aux ressources de la scène française. Le rôle d'Orphée fut alors transposé pour la voix de ténor du chanteur Legros, mais aussi modifié en maint endroit de la façon la plus heureuse, et l'ouvrage s'enrichit d'un certain nombre de morceaux nouveaux d'une valeur au moins égale à celle des morceaux contenus dans la partition italienne. Désireux de donner carrière, dans ce chef-d'œuvre, au merveilleux talent musical et dramatique de Mme Pauline Viardot, le directeur du Théâtre-Lyrique, M. Carvalho, a fait rendre à la voix de contralto le rôle d'Orphée, en ajoutant à la version de l'opéra italien les perfectionnements que Gluck lui avait apportés, et les airs qu'il composa lors de la mise en scène de cet ouvrage à l'Académie royale de Musique de Paris. Telle est, dans son ensemble, la partition

90 The copy used for this paper is in my own collection.

de piano et chant qu'on offre aujourd'hui au public. Un des plus beaux récitatifs (au 1er acte) appartient seul, en propre, à la partition italienne, et ne fut pas admis dans l'opéra français. Tout le reste est conforme à l'*Orphée* que l'on entendit pour la première fois, à Paris, le 2 août 1774. Le divertissement final, que les ressources chorégraphiques du Théâtre-Lyrique n'ont pas permis d'exécuter, ne s'y trouve point, et l'on s'est permis de substituer à l'air : 'L'Amour triomphe,' le délicieux chœur d'un autre opéra de Gluck (*Echo et Narcisse*), dont le dénoûment, amené par l'intervention de l'Amour, est semblable à celui d'*Orphée*.

Ajoutons que la réduction pour le piano de l'orchestre de Gluck, souvent si difficile à traduire malgré sa simplicité, a été faite, par M. Théodore Ritter, avec l'intelligence des ressources de l'instrument que possède nécessairement un tel virtuose, et la fidélité scrupuleuse qu'on doit toujours apporter dans l'interprétation des œuvres de génie.

H. BERLIOZ[91]

The second printing includes neither the dedication nor the preface, yet it is this second printing that seems to have been put into circulation.[92]

The separate numbers published by Heugel

Carvalho seems to have succeeded in 'reconciling the two competitors', for Escudier did indeed publish the score, while at the same time Heugel published 'morceaux détachés' in ten fascicles, with a lithographed frontispiece by de Crauzat. The Heugel edition gives neither the date of the Théâtre-Lyrique performance nor the name of the transcriber, but at the head of each separate number it does give the name of the appropriate soloist. The keys, too, are those of the edition that Berlioz had overseen.

Act I: (1) Romance d'Orphée 'Objet de mon amour'; (2) 1er air de l'Amour 'Si les doux accords de la lyre'; (3) 2e air de l'Amour 'Soumis au silence'; (4) Grand air 'Amour! viens rendre à mon âme'.

Act II: (5) Air d'Orphée avec chœur 'Laissez-vous toucher par mes pleurs'; (6) Air de l'Ombre heureuse 'Cet asile aimable et tranquille'; (7) Air d'Orphée 'Quel nouveau ciel pare ces lieux'.

Act III: (8) Duo d'Orphée et d'Eurydice 'Viens, suis un époux qui t'adore!'; (9) Air d'Eurydice 'Fortune ennemie'; (10) Air final d'Orphée 'J'ai perdu mon Eurydice'.

---

91 See note 90.

92 The Bibliothèque Nationale and the Bibliothèque de l'Opéra possess copies of only the second printing, one of which was used for the *dépôt légal*. It should be noted that in his review of the first performance of *Orphée* (*La France musicale* [20 November 1859] 462), only two days after the première, Escudier mentions and quotes Berlioz's preface. Thus, as was often the case, even before the first performance, the publisher must have ordered a very limited first printing, for the singers, the press, etc.; he then ordered a second printing which – given the immediate success of the opera – no longer needed Berlioz's 'justification'.

Tous les airs de l'Amour sont aussi gravés transposés pour contralto, le n° 10 pour ténor ou soprano.

(Plate no. H. 2533 [nos. 1–10])

It can be seen that Heugel decided to divide the opera in three acts. Later, in 1872, having purchased the complete voice-and-piano reduction from Escudier, he would make use of the original plates to reissue that first reduction.[93] The orchestral score used for the Théâtre-Lyrique performances was actually prepared by Alfred Dörffel, corrected by Berlioz and published in Leipzig by Gustav Heinze.[94]

Further separate numbers

Orphée musique de Gluck / 'J'ai perdu mon Eurydice' / Air chanté par M. Viardot-Garcia [*sic*] / Paris, Lemoine aîné, Harand successeur [...] (1860; plate no. H. 1218).

The aria is transposed to D major.

Idem, in *Ecole classique du chant* / Collection de morceaux choisis / dans les chefs-d'œuvre des plus grands maîtres classiques italiens allemands et français / avec le style, l'accentuation, le phrasé et les nuances propres à l'interprétation traditionnelle de ces œuvres / par Mme Pauline Viardot-Garcia [...] (Paris: Gérard, 1861).

The aria is in C major, with a number of markings to be compared below with the score annotated by Pauline Viardot.[95] The next-to-last bar of this version includes 'a variant sung at the performance by Mme Pauline Viardot' that is reproduced in no other source (see Example 12).

The revival at the Théâtre Lyrique also occasioned a series of transcriptions of separate numbers for solo piano.[96]

Example 12

à__ ma__ dou - leur!

93 The plate no. is H. 5336.   94 See below, p. 233 et seq.   95 See p. 237 et seq.
96 At the beginning of 1860 Escudier published Wilhelm Krüger's 'transcriptions brillantes' for piano, Op. 92–3 (the 'Scène des enfers' and the 'Romance d'Orphée'); Heugel published Charles Neustedt's Op. 22–3 – transcriptions of 'J'ai perdu mon Eurydice' and 'Les doux accords de ta lyre'; Emile Prudent also published an arrangement of 'J'ai perdu mon Eurydice', and Camille Stamaty, an arrangement of 'L'Ombre heureuse et les champs élysées'.

Berlioz's role in preparing the version of 1859

What, precisely, was Berlioz's role in the revival of *Orphée*? He would call himself the 'metteur en ordre' of the French and Italian versions as well, three days after the première, as the 'metteur en scène'.[97] In truth, at rehearsals, by indicating tempos and directing the singers and dancers, he acted as though he were himself the composer of the opera.[98] But he would make light of the fact that the press paid him personal tribute and would say that the success belonged solely to the 'chef d'œuvre, which I simply protected from the imbeciles and the slaves to routine'.[99] On what Berlioz was paid for his labours we unfortunately have no information whatsoever.

We have already cited the two *feuilletons* that Berlioz devoted to the revival of *Orphée* and that he reprinted (with some important omissions) in *A Travers chants*.[100] These give us more than a glimpse of the operations Berlioz performed on Gluck's score. Very discreet about his own role, Berlioz never once mentions his collaboration with Pauline Viardot and Camille Saint-Saëns. In the first *feuilleton*, which makes use of earlier writings,[101] the critic gives a reasonably accurate history of the Vienna and Paris versions and a description of Gluck's alterations; he lingers over Gluck's careless mistakes (in particular his scoring for violas above violins) and notes the printer's errors in the French edition which are all the more deplorable as they have become accepted in practice. In addition to rendering for contralto the recitatives and arias added by Gluck, he had to take out the trombone parts added by an unknown author, to replace the cornetto part with a part for the modern brass instrument ('no one in Paris plays the wooden cornetto'), and to correct those parts of the libretto that featured verses by Moline – verses 'so nonsensical as to be unacceptable and even dangerous'.[102]

---

97 See above, note 33. By 'metteur en scène' Berlioz meant not the producer or director (the official 'metteur en scène' was Arsène Michot, known simply as Arsène) but the inspiring force behind the revival. It is none the less true that Berlioz gave advice and counsel concerning the sets, the costumes, the use of mimes, etc.

98 See *CG* VI (letter of 17 December 1859).　　　　　99 *Ibid.*

100 See *A Travers chants*, 133 and 147. (The second *feuilleton* is primarily devoted to a supposed plagiarism, committed by Philidor, of the aria 'Objet de mon amour'.) The notes in this edition, by Léon Guichard, have been a priceless resource for the preparation of this paper; among other things they give texts from Berlioz's original articles that were omitted in the book publication.

101 See *A Travers chants*, 399.

102 *A Travers chants*, 137.

Berlioz's modifications of the libretto[103]

The following table records Berlioz's modifications of the libretto.

Table 1

no. 5	
Eloignez-vous ce lieu convient à mes malheurs.	Eloignez-vous ce lieu convient à ma douleur.
no. 8	
Eurydice, Eurydice, Ombre chère Ah dans quel lieu es-tu? Ton époux gémissant, interdit, éperdu, Te demande sans cesse à la nature entière les vents hélas emportent sa prière.	Eurydice, Eurydice! ombre chère, Entends-moi. D'un tendre époux entends la plainte amère. Il invoque les dieux, dans son cruel émoi, mais l'écho sans pitié répond à sa prière.
no. 12	
...pour braver toutes vos faveurs. L'Amour: dans les Enfers tu peux descendre...	...pour braver toutes vos fureurs. L'Amour: dans les enfers tu peux te rendre...
no. 16	
Impitoyables Dieux qu'exigez-vous de moi? comment puis-je obéir à votre injuste loi. Quoi j'entendrai sa voix touchante je presserai sa main tremblante sans que d'un seul regard ô ciel quelle rigueur eh bien j'obéirai je saurai me contraindre et devrais-je encore me plaindre lorsque j'obtiens des Dieux la plus grande faveur.	Qu'entends-je qu'a-t-il dit? Eurydice vivra! mon Eurydice! Un dieu clément, un dieu propice me la rendra! Mais quoi! je ne pourrai, revenant à la vie, La presser sur mon sein? ô mon amie, quelle faveur. Et quel ordre inhumain. Je prévois ma terreur. Et la seule pensée D'une épreuve insensée D'effroi glace mon cœur. Oui, je pourrai! Je le veux! Je le jure! Amour, j'espère en toi Dans les maux que j'endure; Douter de ton bienfait serait te faire injure. C'en est fait, dieux puissants, J'accepte votre loi.
no. 17	
L'expoir renaît dans mon âme pour l'objet qui m'enflamme. L'Amour accroît ma flamme je vais revoir ses appas. L'enfer, etc.	Amour, viens rendre à mon âme Ta plus ardente flamme Pour celle qui m'enflamme. Je vais braver le trépas. L'enfer, etc.
no. 33	
...Chère épouse, objet de ma flamme toi seule, etc.	...O toi doux objet de ma flamme toi seule, etc.
no. 36	
...hâtez-vous de la rendre à mes empressements Ah! si vous ressentiez le feu qui me dévore je jouirais déjà de ses	...hâtez-vous de la rendre à mes embrassements. Ah! si vous ressentiez le feu qui me dévore, Si vous étiez aussi de

---

103 A version of this table and the table in the following section, by David Rissin, appeared earlier in *L'Avant-Scène Opera* (September-October 1979) 15–16; I have added corrections and additions based on my own findings.

Table 1 (*cont.*)

embrassements offrez à mes regards la beauté que j'adore Hâtez-vous, etc. **no. 38** Viens, viens Eurydice suis-moi du plus constant Amour objet unique et tendre. C'est toi, etc. …je vis encor, etc. …Eurydice suis-moi hâtons-nous de jouir de la faveur céleste sortons de ce séjour funeste non, etc. …Nous pourrons resserrer les noeuds d'Amour et d'Himénée, etc. **no. 39** …je suivrai toujours tes pas – Parle contente mon envie – Dût-il m'en coûter la vie, etc. **no. 44** …je touche encor aux portes des Enfers, etc.	fidèles amants, J'aurais déjà revu la beauté, etc. Viens, viens, Eurydice, suis-moi, Unique et doux objet de l'amour le plus tendre. C'est toi, etc. …j'ai voulu vivre encor Eurydice, suis-moi, Profitons sans retard de la faveur céleste; Sortons, fuyons ce lieu funeste. Non, etc. …Nous pourrons resserrer d'Amour la chaîne fortunée? etc. …Ah! viens je t'implore suis mes pas – Parle, réponds je t'en supplie; Réponds, je t'en supplie. Dût-il m'en coûter la vie, etc. …je touche encor aux portes des enfers, etc.

Berlioz's modifications of the structure and musical text
Formal modifications (refer to Table 2)

The most obvious of Berlioz's formal modifications is the new, four-act structure, with the *Scène des enfers* and the *Scène des Champs-Elysées* forming two separate acts. This modification was presumably made to balance a score from whose second act he had amputated the *Danse des furies* and from whose third act he had removed the chorus and *Airs de ballet*.[104] In the preface to the Escudier edition of the piano-vocal score Berlioz attributes these cuts to the limited forces available at the Théâtre Lyrique. But as early as 1839 he had commented on the 'undeniable nullity' of the overture and the airs de danse, including the chaconne.[105] The shortening of the score is all the more surprising in that even in its original guises the opera was not long. Thus the grand 'air de bravoure' at the end of Act I, with its final cadenza, simply had to be maintained, as we learn from Saint-Saëns (who would have preferred to use the Vienna version of the conclusion): 'We had to make the piece, which is short, last as long as possible'.[106] As Table 2 suggests, Berlioz attempted to arrange the score in such a way as to put forth a series of dramatic episodes.

104 These numbers were reinstated in the Dörffel edition, with Berlioz's approval.
105 *Journal des débats* (17 March 1839).   106 *Revue de Paris* (1 July 1896) 222.

Table 2

Table 2 charts the similarities and differences among the Vienna version, the Paris version, the Berlioz version of 1859 and the Dörffel version supervised by Berlioz.

Vienna 1762 (in Italian)	Paris 1774 (in French)	Berlioz 1859 (in French) (with the numbers from the Dörffel edition of 1866 in parentheses)
Overtura	Ouverture (unchanged)	Ouverture (unchanged)
Atto primo	Act Ier	Ier acte
Scene 1: Orfeo ed il coro	**Scène 1ère**: Orphée et le chœur	
(a) 'Ah, se intorno'.	'Ah! dans ce bois tranquille'. The trombones are partially removed; the cornetto is replaced by a clarinet; Orphée's vocal line is modified.	N° 1. Chœur. The original Vienna version is re-established; the cornetto is replaced by the modern cornet à pistons (no. 1).
(b) Recitativo (Orfeo) 'Basta, basta'.	Récitatif (completely recomposed) 'Vos plaintes, vos regrets'.	The Paris version is used (no. 2).
(c) Ballo	Pantomime	N° 2. Pantomime et chœur
(d) Coro 'Ah, se intorno'.	Choeur 'Ah! dans ce bois'.	The Vienna version is used (nos. 3 and 4).
	Récitatif 'Eloignez-vous', with orchestral ritornello.	The Paris version is used, with some octave doubling and modification of the melodic line (nos. 5 and 6). There is a link to part (b) of the following aria (no. 8).
	Scène 2: Orphée seul	
(a) Aria (Orfeo) 'Chiamo il ben cosi' and recitativo.	The scene is transposed from F to C major; the chalumeau and English horn are replaced by the clarinet; the recitatives are modified. (a) Air, 1er couplet: 'Objet de mon amour'. (b) Réc.: 'Eurydice, ombre chère'. (c) Air, 2e couplet: 'Accablé de regrets'. (d) Réc.: 'Eurydice, de ce doux nom'. (e) Air, 3e couplet: 'Plein de trouble et d'effroi'.	N° 3. Romance et récitatif. The Paris version is used. The passage is transposed to F major and the order is modified to (a) (d) (c); (e) is removed. (Dörffel re-established (e) and the order of the Paris version.) (nos. 7–11.)

223

Table 2 (*cont.*)

Vienna 1762 (in Italian)	Paris 1774 (in French)	Berlioz 1859 (in French) (with the numbers from the Dörffel edition of 1866 in parentheses)
(b) Recitativo (Orfeo) 'Numi, barbari numi'.	Récitatif 'Divinités de l'Achéron'.	The Paris version is used: the passage is transposed down a fourth; there is a link to (c) (no. 12).
Scena 2: Amore e detto	Scène 3: Orphée, l'Amour	
(a) Amore: 'T'assiste Amore!'.	The recitative is shortened; the aria 'Si les doux accords' is added along with a new recitative for Orphée, 'Dieux! je la reverrais!'	Amour's recitative is linked to the preceding section; the aria is retained. N° 4. Ariette. The tessitura of Orphée's recitative is modified and there are added octave doublings (nos. 13 and 14).
(b) Aria (Amore) 'Gli sguardi trattieni'.	Air (Amour) 'Soumis au silence'. A repeat is removed.	The Paris version is used. N° 5. Air (no. 15).
Recitativo (Orfeo) 'Che disse?' (with an orchestral conclusion).	Récitatif 'Impitoyables dieux' (completely modified). The orchestral conclusion is removed and the piece is linked to the following aria.	N° 6. Récitatif et air. For the recitative 'Qu'entends-je?' new words are adapted to the Vienna version (no. 16). Berlioz removed the orchestral conclusion; Dörffel included it *ad libitum*.
	Ariette (Orphée) 'L'espoir renaît dans mon âme' (in B flat major).	Air 'Amour, viens rendre à mon âme' (transposed to G major, orchestrated by Camille Saint-Saëns, with a cadenza by Pauline Viardot, Berlioz and Saint-Saëns) (no. 17, without the cadenza).
Atto secondo Scena 1	Acte IIe	2e acte
(a) Sinfonia	The conclusion of the orchestral introduction is altered in order to lead to D minor rather than C minor; the horn is replaced by the trumpet.	N° 7. Scène, chœur et air. The Vienna version is used but with the orchestration of the Paris version (no. 18).

224

Table 2 (*cont.*)

Vienna 1762 (in Italian)	Paris 1774 (in French)	Berlioz 1859 (in French) (with the numbers from the Dörffel edition of 1866 in parentheses)
(b) Coro 'Chi mai dell'Erebo'; Ballo. There is a repeat of the chorus, then a repeat of the sinfonia (oboe, bassoons, horns, in C minor).	Chœur 'Quel est l'audacieux'; 'Air de furie'. The chorus is repeated but not the orchestral introduction (clarinets and trombones, in D minor).	The trombones are removed; the 'Pantomime des furies' is in C minor (nos. 19–21).
(c) Arioso (Orfeo) 'Deh placatevi con me', in E flat major.	Orphée 'Laissez-vous toucher par mes pleurs', with added vocalises (and trombones), transposed to B flat major.	The Paris modifications are used, but the passage is transposed back to E flat major (no. 22).
(d) Coro 'Misero giovane', in E flat minor.	Chœur 'Qui t'amène en ces lieux'. The melodic line is modified, trombones are added, and the piece is transposed to B flat minor.	The E flat minor Vienna version is used (no. 23).
(e) Arioso (Orfeo) 'Mille pene', in F minor.	Orphée 'Ah la flamme qui me dévore'. The piece is transposed to C minor and the ending is modified.	The Paris version is used, but is transposed back to F minor (no. 24).
(f) Coro 'Ah, quale incognito', in F minor.	Chœur 'Par quels puissants accords'. The cornetto is replaced by the clarinet, trombones are added, and the piece is transposed to G minor.	The key and orchestration of the Vienna version are used (no. 25).
(g) Arioso (Orfeo) 'Men tiranne', in F minor.	Orphée 'La tendresse qui me presse', transposed to C minor.	The piece is transposed back to F minor (no. 26).
(h) Coro, reprise of (f) developed.	Chœur lent 'Quels chants doux et touchants' (in the original key of F minor). The reprise is removed, clarinets and trombones are added.	The orchestration of the Vienna version is re-established; the reprise of the chorus (by the orchestra alone) serves as conclusion (no. 27).
	Air de Furie.	Removed (restored by Dörffel) (no. 28).

Table 2 (*cont.*)

Vienna 1762 (in Italian)	Paris 1774 (in French)	Berlioz 1859 (in French) (with the numbers from the Dörffel edition of 1866 in parentheses)
Scena 2: Orfeo, e indi, Coro di Eroi ed Eroine, poi Euridice	**Scène 2**	**3ᵉ acte**
(a) Ballo, in F major.	Air lent très doux (in F major).	Nº 8. Pantomime. The Paris version is used (no. 29).
	Flute solo (in F major); the Air is repeated.	*Idem* (no. 30).
	Air (in C major/minor).	*Idem*, air de danse (no. 31).
	Air (Eurydice) et chœur 'Cet asile aimable et tranquille' (in F major).	*Idem*, Nº 9. Air et chœur (for 'une Ombre heureuse') (no. 32).
	Scène 3	
Arioso (Orfeo) 'Che puro ciel'.	Récitatif (Orphée) 'Quel nouveau ciel'. The vocal line is modified to permit the tenor to sing in the original key of C major; the orchestration is lightened by the use of winds and solo cellos.	Nº 10. Récit et chœur. The vocal line is further modified; the orchestration is that of the Paris version (no. 33).
(c) Coro 'Vieni a' regni del riposo'.	Chœur 'Viens dans ce séjour paisible' (unchanged).	*Idem* (no. 34).
(d) Ballo (in B flat minor).	Air (unchanged).	*Idem*, Pantomime (no. 35).
(e) Recitativo (Orfeo) 'Anime avventurose'.	Récitatif (Orphée). The passage is completely rewritten; the conclusion is with chorus.	The rhythmic and harmonic properties of the Paris version are used, but the melodic line is much modified (no. 36).
	Scène 4	
(f) Reprise of the chorus (c) with the words 'Torna, o bella'.	Reprise of the previous chorus with the words 'Près du tendre objet qu'on aime', with two bars added to avoid an unsymmetrical phrase.	*Idem* (no. 37).
Atto terzo Scena 1: Orfeo ed Euridice	**Acte IIIᵉ** Scene 1ʳᵉ	**4ᵉ acte** Nº 11. Scène et récit.
(a) Recitativo (Orfeo) 'Vieni, segui i miei passi'.	Récitatif (Orphée) 'Viens, Eurydice suis-moi'. The	The Paris version is used. The opening is adapted to

Table 2 (*cont.*)

Vienna 1762 (in Italian)	Paris 1774 (in French)	Berlioz 1859 (in French) (with the numbers from the Dörffel edition of 1866 in parentheses)
	passage is completely rewritten.	the modified text and to the contralto tessitura (no. 38).
(b) Duetto 'Vieni, appaga il tuo consorte' (in G major).	Duo (Orphée and Eurydice) 'Viens, suis un époux qui t'adore'. The melodic lines are modified, the oboe is replaced by the clarinet, the piece is transposed to F major.	Nº 12. Duo et air. The Paris version is used, but is transposed back to G major (no. 39).
(c) Recitativo (Euridice) 'Qual vita è questa mai'.	Récitatif (Eurydice) 'Mais d'où vient qu'il persiste?'. The structure is the same but the melodic lines are considerably modified; the passage is transposed down a fifth.	The Paris version is used (no. 40).
(d) Aria (Euridice) 'Che fiero momento'.	Air (Eurydice) 'Fortune ennemie'. Interventions by Orphée are added, making the central section of the aria a duet.	Nº 13. Air. The Paris version is used in its entirety (no. 41). Nº 14. *Idem*, 'Je goûtais les charmes'.
(e) Recitativo (Orfeo) 'Ecco un nuovo tormento'.	Récitatif (Orphée) 'Quelle épreuve cruelle'. Some melodic lines are altered, some passages are transposed.	Some passages are retransposed to the levels of the Vienna version (no. 42).
(f) Aria (Orfeo) 'Che faro senza Euridice' (in C major).	Air (Orphée) 'J'ai perdu mon Eurydice'. Two melodic passages are modified; the piece is transposed to F major.	Nº 15. Air. The Paris version is used, but is transposed back to C major (no. 43).
(g) Recitativo (Orfeo) 'Ah finisca una volta'.	Récitatif (Orphée) 'Ah! puisse ma douleur'.	The Paris version is used, but is transposed back to the original key.
Scena 2: Amore e detti	**Scène 2**	
Recitativo (Amor) 'Orfeo, che fai?'	Récitatif (Amour) 'Arrête Orphée'.	The passage is linked to the previous recitative (no. 44). Nº 16. Chœur final 'Le dieu de Paphos et de Gnide' (taken from *Echo et Narcisse*).

227

Table 2 (*cont.*)

Vienna 1762 (in Italian)	Paris 1774 (in French)	Berlioz 1859 (in French) (with the numbers from the Dörffel edition of 1866 in parentheses)
Scena 3 e ultima		
Introduzione	Chœur avec soli 'L'amour triomphe'. The passage is partly transposed.	The passage is removed in Berlioz's version (no. 45).
1. Ballo, grazioso (A major).	'Dolce' (A major).	Removed (no. 46).
2. Allegro (A minor).	Gavotte (A minor).	Removed (no. 47).
3. Andante (D major).	Air vif (C major).	Removed (no. 48).
4. Allegro (D major).	Menuet (C major).	Removed (no. 49).
Coro (with Orfeo, Amor and Euridice) 'Trionfi Amore' (in D major).	Trio 'Tendre amour' (from *Paride ed Elena*; in E minor).	Removed (no. 50).
	Orchestral introduction (from the Vienna version; in A major).	Removed (no. 51).
	Air de ballet ('très lentement'; in D major).	Removed (no. 52).
	Chaconne (D major).	Removed (no. 53).

Roles and voices

In Act II, scene ii, Berlioz substituted 'une ombre heureuse' for the role of Eurydice.[107] Saint-Saëns was not at all pleased by this alteration, recognising as he did that in the Elysian Fields, having forgotten Orpheus and her own terrestrial existence, Eurydice was perfectly happy. 'But neither M. Carvalho nor Mme Viardot nor Berlioz himself wanted to admit that Eurydice could be happy without Orpheus', he wrote; so they made a ghost of her – 'something Gluck never even dreamed of'.[108]

Let it also be noted that Carvalho was obliged to add some twenty voices to the chorus – which normally included twenty-two men and

---

107 The piano-vocal score (p. 69) calls for 'Eurydice ou une Ombre heureuse'; the Dörffel edition also offers this choice.   108 See note 106.

eleven women – in order to add power, Berlioz tells us, to 'la masse chorale'.[109]

Musical modifications

Although Berlioz would have preferred to make no changes in the score whatsoever, motivated as he sometimes was by an almost puritanical zeal, he none the less found it necessary to make a number of changes in Orphée's vocal line, and not only those required by the use of the contralto voice. Most of these changes occur in the recitatives. See Examples 13 and 14. For nuances of phrasing and articulation Berlioz followed the earlier Paris edition.

Example 13

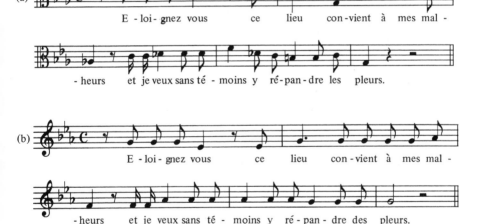

109 See *A Travers chants*, 459; and Archives Nationales, F²¹ 1123. In his letter to Viardot of 13 September 1859 (cited above), Berlioz mentions the addition of fourteen women from the chorus of the Théâtre Italien.

Example 14

(a) O vous om - bre que j'im - plo - re   hâ - tez vous de la ren - dre à mes em - pres - se - ments   Ah! si vous res - sen - tiez   le feu qui me dé - vo - re   je jou - i - rais dé - jà   de ses em - bras - se - ments   o - ffrez   à mes re - gards   la beau - té   que j'a - do - re   hâ tez-vous de me rendre heu- reux.

(b) O vous, om-bres que j'im - plo - re,   Hâ - tez - vous de la ren - dre à mes em - bras - se - ments   Ah! si vous re - sen - tiez   le feu qui me dé - vo - re,   Si vous é - tiez aus - si   de fi - dè - les a - mants,   J'au - rais dé - jà re - vu   la beau - té que j'a - do - re,   Hâ - tez-vous de me rendre heu- reux.

230

Instrumentation

Berlioz claims to have retouched the instrumentation 'solely in order to render it precisely as it was composed by Gluck'. Of course he regretted that Gluck had called for a wooden cornetto, and replaced this antiquated instrument with a modern brass cornet. On the other hand, sensitive as he was to instrumental colour, he probably would have liked to use the original chalumeau for the echo-effects that are found in Act I. He removed some ill-considered trombone parts (added after Gluck's time) and returned to the original parts, notably in the *Scène des enfers*. Finally, he points out that the string section of the orchestra at the Théâtre Lyrique – which normally consisted of seven first violins, seven second violins, six violas, six cellos and five double basses – had to be reinforced by a certain number of supplementary players.[110]

The Pauline Viardot copy

One copy has been preserved of the piano-vocal score (prepared by Théodore Ritter under Berlioz's supervision) with annotations by Pauline Viardot. Engraved on the title page of this copy is the name not of Escudier, but rather 'Au Ménestrel [...] Heugel et Fils'.[111] Contrary to what some have thought, therefore, this score did not serve as Viardot's working copy during the opening performances, since Heugel's reprint (using Escudier's plates) did not appear until the end of 1872.[112] On the interior page that contains the catalogue of numbers, 'Sarita Craig Hale / Paris 1884' is written in pencil; but this pencil marking does not permit us to assert that the annotations made here in ink by Pauline Viardot date from roughly 1884.

The Viardot copy is obviously a capital source of information regarding the singer's conception of the role of Orphée; were it to be reproduced in its entirety (we include two important excerpts in the Appendix here), collation with other sources would be possible and would surely prove fruitful.[113] The indications found here reveal the singer's profound

110 See *A Travers chants*, 459; and Archives Nationales, F²¹ 1123.
111 This copy is in the collection of Miss Marilyn Horne.
112 I should like to thank Mme Mansuy for having granted me permission to consult the plate-number record-books of the Maison Heugel and for having placed at my disposal a number of original editions. (It is to be noted that the 1859 Escudier edition has 'Euridice' while the 1872 Heugel reprint has 'Eurydice'.)
113 Particularly with the annotated aria published by Viardot in *L'Ecole classique du chant*. See above, p. 219.

concern for dramatic expression. If we compare them to those of the role of Fidès in *Le Prophète*, which Meyerbeer wrote expressly for Pauline Viardot, we find essentially two tendencies. The first is towards the intensification of the declamation and the shaping, by accentuation, of the 'geste vocal'. This explains the influence of Viardot exercised on the role of Orphée; it explains the perfect equation that was realised, by the magic power of her singing, between the voice and the operatic character – a perfection that was remarked upon by painters and sculptors as it was by writers and musicians.[114] The second concerns the ornamentation of the vocal line in both aria and recitative. Viardot's ornamentation gave free reign to her vocal prowess and thus thrilled those whom Berlioz had always called 'les chiens de dilettanti'.[115]

For example, in the Viardot copy, in the aria 'Amour, viens rendre à mon âme' (n° 17), the 'mirobolant' effect of the famous cadenza, printed on page 42, is prepared by two lesser cadenzas (in manuscript) on the word 'sépare'. Thus Viardot sang even more cadenzas than those found in the sources that were available to Berlioz, though all may not be written out fully in the copy she annotated. In 'Eurydice, Eurydice, ombre chère' (n° 8) there are four; in 'Eurydice, Eurydice!' De ce doux nom' (n° 10), five; in 'Qu'entends-je? qu'a-t-il dit?' (n° 16), four; in 'Amour, viens rendre à mon âme' (n° 17), four; in 'Ah! la flamme qui me dévore' (n° 24), one; in 'La tendresse qui me presse' (n° 26), one; in 'O vous, ombres que j'implore' (n° 36), one; and in 'J'ai perdu' (n° 43), four.

Sometimes Viardot would modify the vocal line, as in 'Quels sons harmonieux' (n° 33); sometimes she would shift accent by shifting tempo, as in 'Aux manes sacrés d'Eurydice' (n° 2), where the marking 'lento' is added; sometimes she would alter the tessitura, as at 'Viens, viens, Eurydice' (n° 38), which is transposed down a fifth. (The low G that she added at 'fleurs' at the end of the recitative [n° 2], where Berlioz has D, does occur in the Paris score of 1774, and is not of her own invention.) Particularly noteworthy is the singer's inclination to have the accent of the prosody fall on the strong beat of the bar, such as at 'Divinités de l'Achéron' (n° 12).

Given what Berlioz said to Viardot in his letter of 12 December 1859,[116] it is not surprising to find certain nuances marked at the words 'le désespoir, la mort est tout ce qui me reste' (n° 42); 'tendre objet' (n° 44) is cautiously marked *p* with a long crescendo: the singer could thus

114 See *A Travers chants*, 461.   115 See above, p. 190 and note 9.
116 See above, p. 201 and note 55.

control her breathing carefully and avoid the hiatus that Berlioz found objectionable. The numerous dynamic indications and breath marks found throughout suggest in a general way the singer's strong determination to make each melodic inflection as expressive as possible. The word 'expression' is of course central to Romantic interpretation: Viardot, desirous of remaining faithful to Gluck, thus linked expressivity to ornamentation, the latter – for listeners, in 1859 – indicative of an authentic return to the 'classic' style.

The Dörffel edition

The piano-vocal score of *Orphée* published by Escudier in 1859 includes no mention of the instrumentation required, and neither Escudier nor Heugel proposed to publish Berlioz's version of the full orchestral score. This initiative was taken by the Leipzig publisher Gustav Heinze, with whom, in early February 1866, Berlioz was negotiating the publication of a German translation of his *Mémoires* (through the intermediacy of Frédéric Szarvády).[117] Berlioz had obviously been asked to supervise the publication of *Orphée*, for on 21 June 1866 Heinze asked him to send along 'the score of *Orphée* that you have corrected'[118] – 'the score' being an initial printing of which Heinze had already sold some twelve copies. Berlioz found so many errors in this printing that Heinze nearly decided to abandon the effort and to 'break up all the plates'; but he soon determined to persevere and to have a number of the plates re-engraved. Thus, in the same letter which speaks of the publication of the *Mémoires*, Heinze also asks Berlioz to correct the preface of the forthcoming edition of *Orphée* – a preface printed over Heinze's signature but no doubt written, at least in part, by Berlioz himself; a preface that explains the synthesis that had to be made of the two 'original' (Vienna and Paris) editions without mentioning, of course, the more recent piano-vocal score published in 1859 by Escudier.

Nous fîmes donc à M. Hector Berlioz la proposition de se mettre pour nous au même travail que pour le Théâtre-Lyrique.

Malheureusement M. Berlioz fort souffrant ne put alors accepter notre proposition. A sa place M. Alfred Dörffel, bien connu comme musicien et historien, Directeur de la partie musicale de la grande bibliothèque de Leipzig, se chargea de ce travail difficile pour l'édition de notre partition, d'après les représentations modèles du Théâtre-Lyrique.

117 Szarvády, a publicity agent, was the husband of the pianist Wilhelmine Clauss; Berlioz 'presided' over her Parisian début in 1851.   118 See note 84.

Avant tout nous avons [...] pris à tâche de reproduire la première partition de
Gluck, et d'y ajouter tout ce que le compositeur lui-même avait ajouté à la
deuxième ; de manière que l'élément primitif s'y trouve correct et complet au plus
haut degré.[119]

[We therefore proposed to M. Hector Berlioz that he do for us what he had
done for the Théâtre Lyrique.

Unfortunately M. Berlioz was very ill and was thus unable to accept our
proposition. In his stead, M. Alfred Dörffel, the director of the music section of
the Bibliothèque de Leipzig, well known as musician and historian, took on the
difficult task of editing our score in accordance with the examplary performances
that took place at the Théâtre Lyrique.

We have above all attempted to reproduce the first version of Gluck's score,
and to add to it what the composer himself added to the second version, such that
the original contents might appear here as fully and as accurately as possible.]

On 7 July 1866 Heinze told Berlioz that he hoped Dörffel would adopt all
of Berlioz's corrections, and on 24 September of that year Berlioz returned
the corrected preface to Heinze with the following remarks :

[The score] is now more or less acceptable. Please remove the remaining errors
very carefully [...] I cannot understand why M. Dörffel thinks that Orfeo's aside
during Eurydice's aria is somehow destructive of his original character – this is
simply not true. Orphée *speaks* during the first duet, he speaks to her during the
recitatives, and he has no reason not to pronounce those several asides which
make a duet at the end of this aria.

I am sure you have also corrected the error in Latin on the title page by putting
'decedente' and not 'decendete'. This error does not occur in our library's
score, which proves that you have a copy of a faulty first printing. Congratulate
M. Dörffel for me for the great care and cautious wisdom he has lavished upon
this edition [...]

We are now producing *Alceste* at the Opéra and this takes much of my time,
since the director asked me to conduct the practice sessions and rehearsals. The
work is of a sublimity that surpasses everything else that is known in *truly*
dramatic music. Gluck is simply a colossus; he's a demigod.[120]

To the very end Berlioz revered Gluck as the epitome of the dramatic
musician. He did as much to preserve the works of his idol as he did to put
forth *Les Troyens*, as we can see from one of the last letters he addressed
to Pauline Viardot, in June 1861, in which he speaks of his (provisional)
refusal to touch the score of *Alceste*:

119 *Orpheus und Eurydice*, /oper/ in drei Acten. [...] Neue Ausgabe von Alfred Dörffel (Leipzig:
    Gustav Heinze, 1866) xi. In the preface to the second edition of *Orpheus* published by Peters in
    1873, A. Dörffel makes use of Heinze's preface, but in the preface to the third edition, Berlioz's
    name is nowhere to be found.
120 See note 85. It should be noted that Berlioz participated in two revivals of *Alceste* at the Opéra,
    that of 21 October 1861 and that of 12 October 1866.

J'aime mieux *la* musique que *ma* musique, et tous les outrages que l'on fait subir
à d'illustres hommes de génie me blessent mille fois plus que ceux que l'on
pourrait m'infliger à moi-même.[121]

[I prefer *high* art music to *my* art music, and all scurrilous attacks made against
illustrious men of genius are a thousand times more hurtful than those that could
be inflicted upon me.]

Berlioz, the initiator of the Gluck revival, would invoke the eighteenth-
century composer throughout his life. But his efforts in this regard, it
would seem, did not quite live up to his expectations. This at least is what
one is led to believe from the Postface of the *Mémoires* written in 1864:

There is much that I could say about the two Gluck operas, *Orphée* and *Alceste*,
which I was invited to put on, the one at the Théâtre Lyrique, the other at the
Opéra. I have, however, discussed them at some length in my book *A Travers
chants*, and although there are things that I could certainly add to that account...I
prefer not to do so.[122]

As we have seen, Berlioz had so closely incorporated Gluck into his
compositional universe as to forget the delicate boundary between piety
and zeal. In his quest for the ideal model, he ferreted out the nearly
forgotten Vienna version of *Orfeo* and fused it with the Paris *Orphée*. He
reworked the score, divided it into dramatic sequences arrayed in four
acts, and rewrote some of the recitatives. Claiming that the resources of
the Théâtre Lyrique were insufficient, he cut as much as possible of the
material he took to be outdated, notably the final *divertissement* – that is,
the Baroque vestige that remained attached to the 'azione teatrale'
transformed into 'tragédie lyrique'. The piano-vocal score, the only
edition 'conforme à la représentation', gives us the version of *Orphée*
performed at the Théâtre Lyrique in 1859: this is the version sanctioned
by Berlioz, the version he wished to pit as much against Offenbach's
degrading parody as against Wagner's 'music of the future', which he
found odious and revolting.[123]

But, one will object, Berlioz did stand behind the thorough 'reconstruction' of the full score undertaken by Heinze and Dörffel in 1866
– a reconstruction based on Berlioz's own version of 1859. In fact, if he
approved of the German edition, it must have been with a certain
reticence, for Berlioz did not undertake the reconstruction himself, even

121 Bibliothèque Nationale, N. Acq. fr. ms. 16272. A copy of this letter was kindly communicated
   to me by Hugh Macdonald.
122 *Mémoires*, 565–6; Cairns, 415 [slightly modified by the present translator].
123 See Berlioz's letter of 29 January 1860 to Adolphe Samuel.

though his earlier serious research would have enabled him to do so with relative ease. Still, it is this German edition (with the text in French), edited by Dörffel, published by Heinze and subsequently by Peters, retranslated into Italian, that became known and remains known to this day as 'Berlioz's version' of Gluck's opera; it is this version that is used when the leading role is taken by a female contralto. One might even go so far as to say that Gluck's *Orphée* and Berlioz's *Orphée* have, by assimilation, become one. It is after all rather surprising that Berlioz's version of 1859, so indicative of his creative processes, figures nowhere in D. Kern Holoman's magnificent catalogue of the complete works of the French composer.

Berlioz, always innovative as a composer, was equally innovative in treating the question of the revival of earlier music. His answer, rather debatable in view of today's more 'scientific' criteria, seems artistically justified if only because it clarifies the composer's own aesthetic stance – a stance that is in vivid contrast to that of Franz Liszt, for example. In Weimar in 1853 and 1854, rather than attempting a reconstruction, Liszt enclosed Gluck's *Orphée* in 'Romantic parentheses', as it were, with a prelude (Liszt's own symphonic poem *Orpheus*) and a postlude. Berlioz may thus be seen to have accepted a kind of compromise with History that Liszt refused to make.

'Gluck is the first of the Romantics', wrote Berlioz, applauding enthusiastically the revival of *Orphée*.[124] Is it not also apt to say, paradoxically, that Berlioz is the last of the Classics?

Translated by Peter Bloom

124 See Berlioz's letter to Varnier of 25 January 1860.

APPENDIX

The excerpts printed below will permit the reader to compare two versions of parts of *Orphée* that were crucial to the success of the opera in 1859. On the left: the vocal line of the title role as revised by Berlioz and printed in the piano-vocal score, *Seule Edition conforme à la représentation*, published by Escudier in 1859. On the right: the vocal line as annotated and modified by Pauline Viardot in a copy of the score published by Heugel in 1872 (using the plates of the earlier Escudier edition). Among the many subtle changes to be noted is the spelling of 'Eurydice'; in the 1859 publication she was 'Euridice'.

Escudier edition (1859)

[Nº 16]
ORPHÉE

All.º moderato

Qu'en - tends-je   qu'a-t'il   dit?

Eu - ri - di - ce vi - vra!   mon Eu - ri - di - ce!   Un dieu clé-ment, un

dieu pro-pi - ce   me la ren - dra! Mais quoi! je ne pour - rai,   re-ve-nant à la

Andante

vi - e, La pres-ser   sur mon sein?   ô_____ mon   a - mi - e,

quel-le fa-veur,   Et quel ordre in-hu-main! Je pré - vois   ses soup-çons, je pré-

- vois ma ter-reur,   Et la seu-le pen-sé - e   D'une é-preuve in-sen-

Allegro

- sé - e   D'eff - roi   gla - ce mon cœur.

Oui, je pour-rai!   je le veux, je le ju - re!   A -mour, a-

- mour, j'es - pè-re en toi   Dans les   maux   que j'en - du - re.   Dou-

- ter   de ton bien-fait   se - rait   te faire in - ju - re.

C'en est fait, dieux puis - sants, J'ac -cep-te vo-tre   loi.

Heugel edition (1872) annotated by Viardot

[Nº 16]
ORPHÉE

(Escudier)

[Nᵒ 17]

All.ᵒ maestoso

A - mour, viens ren - - dre à mon â - me

Ta plus ar - den - te flam - me Pour cel - le qui m'en -

- flam-me Je vais bra - ver ___ le tré - pas A -

- mour, viens rendre à mon â - me Ta plus ar-den - te

flam - me; Pour cel - le qui m'en flam - - - - -

- - - - - - - - - - -

- - - - - - - me je vais bra-

- ver ___ bra - - ver ___ le tré - pas l'en -

- fer en vain nous sé - pa - re, en vain nous sé -

- pa - re Les mons - tres du tar -

240

(Viardot)

(Escudier)

(Viardot)

-la - re Ne m'épouvant - tent pas, Je sens croi - tre ma

flam - - - - - - - - - - - - -

cresc.

- - - - - - - me Je vais bra - ver le tré - pas

A - mour viens ren - dre à mon âme Ta plus ar -

-den - te fla - me; Pour cel - le qui m'en flam - me; Je

bra - ve le tré - pas je bra - - - - - -

cresc.

- - - - - - - - ve Je bra - ve le tré - -

- pas L'a - mour vient rendre à mon â - me

Ta plus ar -den - te flam - me, L'a - mour ac - croit ma

flam - - - - - - - - - -

(Escudier)

- - - - me je vais bra - ver_____ le tré - pas L'en -

- fer en vain nous sé - pa - re, en vain nous sé -

pa - re Les mons - tres du tar -

- ta - re ne m'é - pou - van - tent pas

Je sens croi - tre ma flam - - - - - - - - -

- - - - - me je vais bra - ver le tré - pas

Allez au renvoi pour le point d'orgue [Example 11]

Je vais bra - ver le tré - pas.

(Viardot)

- - - - - me je vais bra - ver___ le tré - pas L'en -

- fer en vain nous sé - pa - re, en vain nous sé -

pa - - - re Les mons - tres du tar -

- ta - re ne m'é - pou - van - tent pas

Je sens croi - tre ma flam - - - - - - - - - -

- - - - - - - - - - -me Je bra - - - - - - -

- - - - - ve je vais bra - ver le tré - pas

℔ Allez au renvoi pour le point d'orgue [Example 11]

Je vais bra - ver le tré - pas.

245

(Escudier)

[N° 42]

(Viardot)

[N° 42]

(Escudier)

[N° 43]
ORPHÉE

J'ai per - du mon Eu - ri - di - ce, Rien n'é - ga - le mon mal - heur; sort cru - el!__ quel - le ri - gueur!__ rien__ n'é - - ga - le mon mal - heur, Je suc - combe à ma dou - leur. Eu - ri - di - ce, Eu - ri - di - ce, ré - ponds.__ Quel sup - pli - ce! ré - ponds _____ moi C'est ton é - poux, ton é - poux fi - dè - le; en - tends ma voix qui t'ap - pel - le, ma voix qui t'ap - pel - le. J'ai per - du mon Eu - ri - di - ce, Rien n'é - ga - le mon mal - heur, sort cru - el!__ quel - le ri - gueur!__ rien n'é - ga - le mon mal - heur, je suc - combe à ma dou - leur. Eu - ri - di - ce, Eu - ri - di - ce!

248

(Viardot)

[N° 43]
ORPHÉE

Andante

J'ai per - du mon Eu - ry - di - ce, Rien n'é -
- ga - le mon mal - heur; sort cru - el!__ quel - le ri -
- gueur!__ rien__ n'é - - ga - le mon mal - heur, Je suc -
- combe à ma dou - leur. Eu -ry - di - ce, Eu -ry -
- di - ce, ré - ponds.__ Quel sup - pli - ce! ré -

p

Adagio
p

- ponds _____ moi C'est ton é - poux, ton é - poux fi -

f *f*

- dè - le; en - tends ma voix qui t'ap - pel - le, ma voix qui t'ap-

I° Tempo

- pel - le. *pp* J'ai per - du mon Eu - ry - di - ce, Rien n'é -

p

- ga - le mon mal - heur, sort cru - el!__ quel - le ri -
- gueur!__ rien n'é - ga - le mon mal - heur, je suc -

p ten.   Moderato   *f*

- combe à ma dou - leur. Eu -ry - di - ce, Eu -ry - di - ce!

249

(Escudier)

250

(Viardot)

Adagio

Mor-tel si - len - ce! Vaine es-pé - ran - ce! Quel - le souf-

- fran - ce! Quel tour - ment___ dé - chi - re mon

I⁰ Tempo animato

coeur! J'ai per - du mon Eu - ry - di - ce, rien n'é -

- ga - le mon mal - heur sort cru - el!___ quel - le rig-

- gueur!___ rien n'é - ga - le mon mal - heur, sort cru -

Animato

- el!___ quel - le ri - gueur!___ je___ suc - combe à ma dou -

a tempo

- leur, à ma dou - leur,_____ à ma dou - leur.

[N⁰ 44]

Ah! puis-se ma dou-

- leur fi - nir a-vec ma vi - e! Je ne sur-vi-vrai point à ce der-nier re-

- vers Je touche en-cor aux por-tes des en - fers, J'au-rai bien-tôt re-

Adagio

- joint mon é-pou - se ché - ri - e. Oui, je te

251

(Escudier)

suis, ___ tendre ob - jet de ma foi, je te suis, at -
- tends-moi, at - tends - moi. Tu ne me se - ras plus ra -

il tire son epée pour se tuer; l'amour le retient

- vi - e, Et la mort pour ja - mais va m'un-ir av- ec toi.

(Viardot)

suis,— tendre ob - jet de ma foi, je te suis, at -

- tends-moi, at - tends - moi. Tu ne me se - ras plus ra -

f presto

ff

il tire son epée pour se tuer; l'amour le retient

- vi - e, Et la mort pour ja - mais va m'un-ir av- ec toi.

9

Overheard at Glimmerglass ('Famous last words')

JACQUES BARZUN

In the garden next to the theatre on this June evening three figures walk slowly towards the area set up for picnickers. They are: Daniel Ergo, a banker and art collector, now retired; Barry Van Dusen, a composer just short of middle age; and J. B. Stead, a music critic whose white hair and lined face betray an eternity of concert-going. Something in their gait suggests that they are old friends.

STEAD: Let's take that corner table. The night is still pleasant, but I feel a breeze that might turn cold. The trellis there will shield us.

VAN DUSEN: Wasn't it exquisitely done? – aside from a few accidents, as always, but they didn't matter.

ERGO: Somarone was all wrong. I can't stand buffoons who are conscious of their buffoonery.

VAN DUSEN: You shouldn't look at the actors so much and should listen to the music more.

ERGO: Why shouldn't I look? Beatrice is a lovely creature and Benedict very handsome; he has the calves nature reserves for operatic starts. But that doesn't make up for others' bad acting.

VAN DUSEN: Enjoy the good, forget the bad. Opera is so complicated, none is ever done entirely right.

STEAD: You can say that about all music; it's a vulnerable art.

ERGO: That's why I collect pictures. They stay put. Music's a fine thing, but it's powerful and fragile at the same time, so it always leads to arguments. I bet we none of us agree about this thing tonight. You, Barry, like the exquisite. For me Berlioz is best when he bangs away at

---

Glimmerglass is a charming opera house in upper New York State, at Cooperstown. The eavesdropping reporter, Jacques Barzun, is the author of a book on Berlioz and the Romantic century (1950). *Ed.*

some great subject – the Day of Judgement, marching to the scaffold and the like. I get restless – I was tonight – when he tunes his orchestra to sing the moonlight.

VAN DUSEN: How wrong a clever man can be! I grant you Berlioz has grandeur whenever he wants, but other composers have it too. What I go to Berlioz for is just the opposite, something which he alone can do. After all, that's what we want different creators for – the unique.

STEAD: And what is this opposite he alone can do?

VAN DUSEN: Intimate revelation where you least expect it, a colouring, not added but infused, which makes the emotion more complex, more distinct from every other. The names we use – joy, love, fear – fool us into thinking each is one thing. Each is a hundred different things, with no names to tell them apart. That's where music comes in: it distinguishes – and we respond. Take sadness, for example: in the *Romeo and Juliet* Symphony the Capulets as they go home after the big party sing the dance tune we've heard in the festivities, but in altered metre. Somehow that gives their jollity an undertone of melancholy that is heart-rending. The same thing, yet different, occurs in *Benvenuto Cellini*, in the song 'How happy the sailors at sea' – so happy you want to cry; and again in the *Damnation of Faust*, the students' and soldiers' roistering: it ends with the brass sounding utterly forlorn – three types of sadness. I could mention other gems of nuance. There are more Berliozes than your ordinary critic has ever suspected.

STEAD: You needn't look at me. I agree with you. Berlioz's variety has worked against him. But now there's no longer any need to argue: the first volume of David Cairns's biography is out. That marks the closing of the frontier on lawless opinion. What's left to do is to look for the sort of thing you've mentioned – the makings of a new set of clichés. Then anybody will be able to talk about 'the Berlioz mind'.

ERGO: But haven't I read in some biography before Cairns – two big fat volumes I have somewhere – that in his music Berlioz is always the dramatist? All his works are built on real dramas or some he made up: Virgil, the Mass for the dead, Benvenuto's memoirs. Now a dramatist expresses what *others* think and feel, not his own mind. It's the Shakespeare question over again. We'll never know what he was like himself.

VAN DUSEN: True enough in general. We can take it that Berlioz did not view Carthage like Aeneas's soldiers in Act IV and didn't prophesy like the whirling dervishes at Herod's court. But no artist can keep himself

255

out of his work; his nature and that of his characters intersect somewhere, and we can spot the where from the traits that keep cropping up. The very subjects treated express affinity. We know from his own hand that Berlioz hated plots involving torture, massacre, fanaticism. He could not have composed *Les Huguenots* or *Tosca*. But give him the *Dies irae* and he gives you back the Last Trump.

ERGO: That's what I said. He objectifies whatever he touches, and you want to make him out subjective, an Impressionist. The evidence is on my side: in the *Fantastique* we get the Ball, the March, the Witches' revels. The Roman carnival in *Benvenuto* is a regular vaudeville show. I could go on: the Pilgrims file past you – and he wrote *fourteen* other marches. Listen in the *Lacrymosa* to the way the voices of hope get beaten down by the relentless repetition of the main figure – reminds me of the London blitz – one crashing bomb after another.

STEAD: You certainly like to visualise your music, Dan – always programming. What a computer wizard you would make! Of course, what you point out is there, but perhaps not quite as you see it. You must remember, the Romantics believed that the dramatic and the lyrical belong together, in any work – Shakespeare once more. The dramatic is objective in your sense, but it merges without a break into the lyrical, so we always get the Berlioz mind in two aspects.

VAN DUSEN: You have it the wrong way round. All art begins lyrical – the single voice saying, shouting, singing something deeply felt. But it turns into the dramatic when it encounters some other voice, contradicting, modifying the first. That's the way Greek tragedy developed. It happened again in music for the church service and all the way to Verdi –

ERGO: – and Monteverdi. So the French are right, not perverse as they usually are, when they call opera 'lyric theatre'?

STEAD: Yes, and Wagner was wrong in the *Ring* to cut out the chorus almost altogether and give us a series of lyric monologues interlarded with objective events – fire, water, blacksmiths and the like. He disproves one of your points, Barry, that the lyrical soon turns dramatic.

ERGO: It all depends what you mean by soon. Wagner takes his time.

VAN DUSEN: Anyhow in Berlioz there's no lyricism that doesn't *very soon* bring dramatic contrast by some change in that first voice. His songs are little playlets, most of them. But I want to go back to his marches. J.B. is right in thinking they're not wholly 'out there' and that they reveal the mind at work. Think of the way he ends the cortege for

Hamlet's funeral: after a seemingly conclusive *fff* he gives you twenty bars of the most desolate music you've ever heard – muted, introspective, nothing to 'see'. Then the main theme returns once and, as bidden in the play, the soldiers shoot. That's the sort of hair-raising thing to notice in Berlioz: not only how he does things, but the things he thinks of doing.

ERGO: I don't know the *Hamlet* March; only that it exists, so your gem is hidden indeed.

VAN DUSEN: If you won't weep for Hamlet, weep for Juliet. At the end of *her* funeral dirge, there's a repeated note for flute and violin over tremolo strings – seventeen bars that distil the quintessence of grief. It isn't conventional punctuation to say 'Here endeth'; on the contrary, it also leads musically into the passionate scene that follows. As I said, the intimacy, the imagination, doesn't reside simply in the audible effect but in the musical conception. Take the three marches in the *Trojans* for the sailors, farmers and builders. How suggestively they differ – and what an idea to celebrate a queen!

ERGO: Surely, that's in Virgil to begin with.

STEAD: No, it isn't. I looked it up once. There's nothing, unless you consider four words that occur before the Trojans ever see the queen. She is going to worship at the temple and passes through the crowd of her subjects *instans operi regnisque futuris*; that is, 'urging them to their labours for the future of the state'. That's a slim hint, if indeed it served at all.

VAN DUSEN: Hints are butterflies: you need a practised net. That's Berlioz – and me too. I look for them. Listen to the Trojan March: it is not all triumphant; the very theme has in it the exiles' woe. You have only to compare it with the jubilant religious march in Troy before the town was sacked.

ERGO: What price programmes now? You're both bent on reading character traits into things you'll find in any opera – music that goes more or less well with physical ac –

STEAD: You don't see –

VAN DUSEN: You misunderstand –

ERGO: Let me finish, you two. My point is plain. Everybody can see it and would agree with it. Yours is a matter of individual intuition – bad criticism.

VAN DUSEN: Nonsense! Good criticism is based on fine intuitions. I repeat that if you want to catch the man's mind red-handed, so to speak, you must go to his lyrical inspirations.

ERGO: You mean the love scenes and such.

VAN DUSEN: There of course, but not exclusively: they often serve drama as well. I mean rather passages like the soliloquies in the *Damnation*, particularly 'Sans regret, j'ai quité ces riantes campagnes'. That kind of recitative-melody is unique in form and character, and so expressively moulded to his temperament as we know it from other sources that many people find it eludes them altogether. Think back to Beatrice's aria tonight. 'Il m'en souvient'. The audience was disconcerted and gave the girl a hand mainly for effort. She sang beautifully what is to me more enthralling even than the moonlight duet. If you're looking for the soul of Berlioz, it's in those moments.

STEAD: If what you say is in fact a special thing – and I'm inclined to agree – it must be possible to define it and give it a name. You can't let Dan think criticism is helpless.

VAN DUSEN: That's *your* pigeon. But there's enough material to work with – the angelic host, *Tibi omnes*, in the *Te Deum* – 'dull', people will tell you; the Quintet in *Les Troyens*, overshadowed for most listeners by the wonderful septet that follows, but 'more unique' – if I may borrow a solecism from the press – and then the middle movement in the *Funeral and Triumphal* Symphony, the *Oraison*.

STEAD: I must say, that was a stroke of genius – to put there a discourse for solo trombone – chamber music, really, deeply moving, and not outward- but inward-bound.

ERGO: Discourse? Inward-bound? I refrain from comment.

STEAD: Discourse here isn't entirely a metaphor. The trombone readily plays portamento, which is what the human voice does in speaking. So a parallel effect –

ERGO: Maybe so, but how can you be so sure it all adds up to a portrait of Berlioz, his psyche?

VAN DUSEN: Oh, please, no psyche: mind, soul, spirit, temperament, intellect, anything you like, but nothing in p-s-y.

ERGO: No need to get upset over a little Greek. But I ask again, How can you prove that your clues mean what you say?

VAN DUSEN: Of course I can't prove it! In art, in life, nobody ever proves anything. All you can do is think and feel, then try to organise your thoughts and feelings coherently.

STEAD: But make sure first that your perceptions don't *dis*prove your conclusion.

VAN DUSEN: Right. That's as far as one can go, and few who scribble and jabber about art get as far as that.

ERGO: How rude you artists are! If what you say is true, criticism and theory are at an end. But I want them; I want reasons that can't be refuted, demonstrations.

VAN DUSEN: That's because your name is Ergo. It made you give up music after college and go into banking, where the numbers always match. The bottom line is now your figured bass.

STEAD: We mustn't be too clever. Dan has a serious question. Is it a fact that we can never be sure about an artist or his work?

VAN DUSEN: That's not the way to put it. Everybody is sure – for himself.

STEAD: Then the question is, Can we convince anybody else? And do we have to?

VAN DUSEN: I say the answer to both is No. There is no agreement anywhere about anything really important. So forget the childish hope of unanimity. It doesn't exist even in science.

STEAD: But remember that disproof *is* possible – and necessary to clear the air. It's hard work, as I can testify. Over the last fifty years, I've written what feels like a million Notes for concert-goers to read after they sit down and reviews for when they get up the next day.

VAN DUSEN: What a life! I don't know what 'picking oakum' is that convicts are supposed to do, but it sounds more humane.

STEAD: More selective, anyhow. A reviewer can't pick what he has to write about.

ERGO: Writing can't be the hard part. I've seen you turn out a column like writing a letter home. It must be the listening. I read the other day an interview with our American composer Charles Wuorinen. He said that under present conditions, a Beethoven symphony had come to be 'a blob of toothpaste'. It can't be fun listening to that. He meant that now 'orchestras are bored and audiences indifferent'. The Beethoven Fifth, for example, which he called 'a rather fierce, unpleasant work', gets done so often and so absent-mindedly it doesn't upset anybody.

VAN DUSEN: True, we drug ourselves, the dose is too big. It was so already in Berlioz's day, which is why he argued strenuously for his idea of 'festivals' a year or more apart, at which one or at most two great works would be performed – carefully prepared, as they aren't now.

The audience would come with high anticipation and leave with plenty of time ahead to reflect and remember.

STEAD: It wouldn't suit the players, who have to live, or the modern audience, trained to be consumers. Buy, use and throw away so as to buy again. As for Berlioz, he must be happy. His great works are kept fresh by a respectful infrequency of performance.

ERGO: In France and the U.S., at any rate.

VAN DUSEN: Thank God for that. I'm afraid that in England they're overdoing their zeal for all twelve of his blockbusters. The French have a Berlioz Festival at Lyons every other year, with much enthusiasm among his admirers, but poor preparation, and no influence on the old guard of his detractors.

STEAD: Richard Strauss used to say that the French can't appreciate real genius, and he would instance Berlioz.

ERGO: I don't like what you said about consumers. I can't see why good things shouldn't be available on the market. I'm a collector, you know.

VAN DUSEN: That means a squirrel who stores up for later enjoyment. But it never comes, because there's more to collect and *that* becomes the enjoyment.

ERGO: Not always. But J.B. is right. The Berlioz idea would strike people as pompous, it would smack of religion, not art.

VAN DUSEN: Just so. Art started as the handmaiden of religion, now it's the pimp of tourism. Art was the religion of the great creators of the nineteenth century, and no artist was more religious than Berlioz.

ERGO: What! He was a declared atheist!

VAN DUSEN: I know, but –

STEAD: Barry will tell you that three of his big works and some little ones are on religious themes and played in church.

VAN DUSEN: That by itself wouldn't mean much; they're dramas first. What's relevant is that his attitude to life, art, nature, human beings was spiritual, not sensual or materialistic.

STEAD: You might add highly moral. Compared with most other artists of his calibre, he stands out as a man of uncommon rectitude.

ERGO: What does that matter? The work of art s the thing –

VAN DUSEN: If a work's big enough, it gives away the maker's moral tone. And I say Berlioz 'had religion'. His atheism was directed at the storybook creed he was brought up in, which science was then discrediting. He was a reading and a thinking man. But study his life, read his criticism, and you find the core of all elevated religions –

reverence and transcendence. It's not only in *L'Enfance du Christ*, as some people think, that these attitudes inform the music; it's in the Easter Chorus of the *Damnation*, especially the marvellous entrance of Faust's voice there, and again in Gretchen's Apotheosis; in the *Te Deum* the tortuous and pathetic *Te ergo* –

ERGO: Don't get personal!

VAN DUSEN: – the *Quid sum miser* of the *Requiem* and even the jubilant *Hosanna* – I could go on...

STEAD: But you're overlooking the glaring fact that he was a nature worshipper. I could start making a list too. He was a pantheist. Is that transcendence or is it heathenish idolatry?

ERGO: Perhaps a ploy borrowed from Goethe, just for *Faust*.

VAN DUSEN: No indeed. Read the *Memoirs*: as a child, alone in the fields, he was overcome by the power of Nature. You can hardly avoid it in those majestic French Alps; they're in the third movement of the *Fantastique*, which owes nothing to Goethe.

STEAD: Rather to Virgil, another man in love with nature. Berlioz does him proud in *Les Troyens* with Iopas, who sings of the fields, and the scene by the shore, the pastoral start and finish of the Royal Hunt, and the nostalgic Hylas up in the rigging of his ship. But it's nothing to do with religion.

ERGO: Yes, and what of the words in his *Invocation à la nature*: 'je vous adore'? That's addressed to the rocks and trees. You're fluent in French, J.B., is it good verse? Does it sound sincere?

STEAD: Better than good, it's a poem, short and irregular, but true poetry, like a good many passages in the half dozen 'books' he wrote for his own dramas. But Barry hasn't answered my question: does a nature worshipper feel transcendence?

VAN DUSEN: Obviously neither Goethe nor Berlioz worshipped the rocks and trees as such; they weren't voodooists. Nature was to them the manifestation of the creative spirit, as it was for Rousseau –

ERGO: – you can add Spinoza, the 'God-intoxicated man' I believe the German Romantics called him when he too was thought an atheist. You see: my college education wasn't wasted.

VAN DUSEN: Yes. That whole poetic crew – Wordsworth, Shelley, Byron, Emerson, Goethe, Hugo, Musset – and Berlioz with them – all in different ways sing spirit-in-nature.

ERGO: But not spirit beyond, the Creator?

VAN DUSEN: Necessarily spirit beyond. If orthodox religion says the divine is in Man, then when thinkers come to feel the unity of man and nature, spirit envelops the cosmos. That was the great discovery of the Romantics after the mechanistic ideas of the Age of Reason. Nature is alive, not dead – even coal and oil were once alive. Spirit circulates.

ERGO: I'm going to worship at the next gas station.

VAN DUSEN: You know, it strikes me suddenly: this whole argument is an exact parallel to the debate about meaning in music.

ERGO: I didn't know there was one.

STEAD: One what, meaning or debate?

ERGO: Well, both. How can anybody seriously maintain that a piece of music means something? You have only to read the stuff you and your colleagues write – the jumble of wild adjectives, all contradictory. The morbid and tortured Bruckner, says one; no, vital and soulful, says the other. I'm quoting.

STEAD: I seem to remember your finding the London blitz in the *Lacrymosa*.

ERGO: I don't deny it. Our words tonight prove I'm right: all our 'meanings' differ and cancel each other out. If a piece really had *a meaning*, it would emerge and be acknowledged.

STEAD: You're right on one point: everybody rejects the other fellow's analogy, despises it, in fact, and at once produces his own. That gives the impression that they're all valueless.

VAN DUSEN: True, and in that mood critics forget the sins by which they make their living and gang up on Berlioz, pretending he was the first-and-only to find significance in sounds. That's the issue in the debate and the one about pantheism is a parallel.

ERGO: I still don't see.

STEAD: A bit far fetched, I think.

VAN DUSEN: It's this way. Assume that nature worship in modern times implies a belief in spirit at large, *überhaupt*, all-encompassing – put it any way you like. Therefore it resides not just in 'heaven' and privileged humanity but also in the objects of sense, animal, vegetal and mineral.

ERGO: Like Twenty Questions, a most spiritual game!

VAN DUSEN: Similarly, Meaning, which is not a physical but a mental fact, resides in things, actions, faces. There's nothing you can name that a human imagination can't find meaning in.

ERGO: Have you tried modern poetry? The Abstract Expressionists? The silences of John Cage?

STEAD: Hush. This is interesting.

VAN DUSEN: Your sarcasm makes my point. Even the worst gibberish that a would-be poet publishes must elicit a meaning-finder, or it wouldn't get published. Now music is not just an object, it's one made on purpose, and purpose gives a presumption of meaning. Shakespeare, you recall, in this very play we saw tonight, wonders how music can 'hale men's souls out of their bodies'. It couldn't happen if music were meaningless. The meaning is *in* the music. The wrangle is with those who want it again in words; they're told they can't have it that way. What they're told is correct – and so is the opposite. Nobody denies that words fail to *reproduce* musical meanings. Yet a listener will report his visceral and spiritual impressions on hearing a piece. Those impressions are facts – experiences – and all experience can be talked about *in the same inadequate way*. I defy you to reproduce your joy or sorrow in words. And who can deliver the meaning of the Sistine ceiling or *King Lear*? As in music, the meaning is in the experience. But it also lives beyond it – in the memory to begin with, and in the words that it prompted, because words will revive the impression and can convey it to someone else. I ask you, has the incompleteness, the imperfection of such verbalising ever stopped anybody from talking about his joys and sorrows, about plays and concerts? People may talk nonsense, like some critics –

STEAD: and composers –

VAN DUSEN: – and composers, but they may also talk wisely, like our philosophers and *great* critics. Their words then enable us to see deeper into our experience.

ERGO: Now I see what you mean. What you say applies to painting as well. People used to think the subject of a painting was its meaning. That annoyed the 'pure art' boys; they started preaching meaninglessness, and now the cliché is that painting is just line and colour. Bunk! What goes on inside you after looking at a picture again and again becomes more and more meaning-full – or you wouldn't buy one rather than another.

STEAD: So your thesis, Barry, is: the meaning of anything is what it evokes in a conscious being –

ERGO: – preferably rational –

VAN DUSEN: If you insist, but not required: meaning overflows statement. What I'm saying is: any experience is at once inexpressible and communicable. And when I say meaning, it should be meanings – in the plural, because meaning differs with each observer.

ERGO: What about Form, then? That's something clearcut. It's intrinsic, permanent, provable, same for everybody. People with deep minds tell me that's what they go to art for – the thrill of beholding eternal forms.

VAN DUSEN: I have no use for Platonists. I compose with hard matter, like all other artists; what I produce is concrete and particular and, God knows, not eternal. I let J. B. here play around with form. It helps fill up his column.

STEAD: And why? Because nothing is more debatable than form, once you get beyond the gross features common to works of the same genre. You'll find disputes about key, rhythm, harmony, proportion – anything significant.

ERGO: Art makes people feel so strongly they want to fight.

VAN DUSEN: They enjoy it. But back to meaning in music for a moment. There was greater tolerance in Berlioz's day. Critics had more sense than to think descriptive words were to be taken literally like the label on a jar of pickles.

STEAD: And believe me, that load of sense and nonsense helped. Beethoven's uncouth, formless works were gradually made lovely and couth by the spate of poetic programmes that E. T. A. Hoffmann and dozens of my predecessors printed in defence. The musical public had been brought up on opera and oratorio; they couldn't follow the new instrumental music without a crutch.

VAN DUSEN: Beethoven himself put descriptive words in his notebooks and some of his scores. Berlioz's analogies served to point the imagination in the right direction. And technical notes about 'form' are no different, though people think they are. But now that the public has been taught by J. B.'s ten million programme notes and is supersaturated with music under directive titles à la Debussy, Strauss, Elgar, Copland, we've forgotten how long this education took.

ERGO: Slow pupils, the public. But what about it from the other side? How do you, Barry, start composing something that isn't a song or an opera which gives you a canvas, so to speak?

VAN DUSEN: I start from anything that comes of its own accord – a melody that pops into my head; or the memory of a poem or play – or place, or some feelings inside – for example, the sensation that I'm seeing myself from a great distance, from the hereafter. Or it may be an instrumental combination I haven't tried. There's no limit to what can start notes tingling in my head.

STEAD: It's clear enough in Berlioz: something musicable triggered the *melos* and it poured out. As he said, it's a mysterious business.

VAN DUSEN: Hence my interest in the hidden places where his unpremeditated self is disclosed – his tenderness, gaiety, melancholy, sense of grandeur and of humour, and above all, his erotic outlook.

ERGO: Erotic!

STEAD: You don't mean that!

VAN DUSEN: Yes I do. I didn't say sexual. I mean Eros, love. I told you before: his music isn't sensual, it's sensuous. Read Milton for the difference; or think of Shelley and Keats, both men of passion, but the one distilling it through his mind, the other through his senses. Berlioz lived in the erotic century par excellence. The Romantics loved everything in human experience – nature, art, science, the people, ideals, themselves, tradition, the nation-state, history, far away places, the Middle Ages, death, tragedy, Greece, liberty –

ERGO: All right, all right; we get the idea.

VAN DUSEN: Possibly. But what you don't get, like the rest of us discontented, sentimental cynics of the twentieth century, is that all this loving accounts for the great burst of artistic creation between 1790 and 1870. With it, of course, went what we are pleased to laugh at – their enthusiasm and faith, introspection, melancholy, lyricism and drama, their belief in the greatness and wretchedness of Man.

STEAD: Don't complain too much; it's become a cliché that a playwright – or a novelist, for that matter – must love his characters if he wants to make them live. There's a fine subject for a Ph.D.: 'Eros as the Tenth Muse'.

VAN DUSEN: Laugh if you like, but how else can one present a diversity of creatures unless one loves them? The ordinary man is loveless (in my sense) and therefore a partisan – he favours Falstaff and can't stand the Prince, so if he writes a play, the Prince comes out a stick. Drama and diversity are synonyms. Just think how Berlioz differentiates his lovers: Romeo, Faust, Aeneas, Gretchen, Cassandra, Dido, Beatrice – you can't do it by sitting down with 'ideas'; you must have each creature in your system like a lover.

STEAD: Not like a man *with* a system.

ERGO: I don't like that remark. You're thinking of a great genius who *had* a system and whom I admire immensely.

STEAD: Admire away; this is a free country.

VAN DUSEN: Not in the arts, it isn't. No country is ever free on that score. Fashion and dogma rule everywhere. There's a secret list you're supposed to know: what isn't in it is out. And you've got to revise it on short notice – and as you go from nation to nation.

STEAD: True. I misspoke. We swallow dissent in politics, rather admire it in fact. In the arts, you can dissent only within limits or you ruin your standing. Doubt about Mahler is worse than doubt about God. Vested interests favour *him*, not Him – how could conductors show their stamina without Mahler's podium-eroding works?

ERGO: Enough! I love his lengthy confessions the way you love Berlioz's brief ones, and though he's often sentimental, he's never vulgar the way Berlioz often is.

VAN DUSEN: Ah, vulgarity! Where do you find it?

ERGO: Well, the whole Finale of the *Roméo* Symphony, the last movement of the *Funeral and Triumphal*, and some other places.

STEAD: That's a matter of taste. If –

VAN DUSEN: Not at all, of aesthetics. Have you ever heard the *Roméo* Finale well played?

ERGO: I don't know. I don't read score well enough.

VAN DUSEN: You don't have to. The test is, Does it hang together? I've never heard it properly done, live or on disc. But I know how it should go and why it is as it is – why it shouldn't sound as you'd like it. Think: here are two gangs of bigoted fools – Montagues and Capulets; they've killed each other for generations and all they want is to keep on. They trade insults and challenges. Only the news that their children have married and are dead shuts them up – for a moment. Friar Laurence – he should sing, by the way, not bawl – takes the opportunity to read them a lesson, and slowly, little by little, they soften and forgive. It's the strong man with a simple idea quelling a mob. Now all the feelings in this drama are vulgar – the crowd's obviously – and the priest's are commonplace. No subtlety or loftiness anywhere. But this triumph of Sunday-school morality is none the less gripping. That's what Berlioz with his sure dramatic instinct has rendered in music. I realise that many would prefer Gounod's sugar plums.

STEAD: Berlioz probably thought of Beethoven's Ninth, last movement, where the glorious and elevated strains descend to the vulgar tune by

which the *Millionen* are summoned to seek peace. You spoke, Dan, of
the last movement of the *Triumphal*, coming after the delicate solo we
spoke of. It's again the people singing, as in the French Revolution.
Berlioz was steeped in its atmosphere by being born when he was. And
after all, 'vulgus' means nothing worse than 'crowd', a strange and –
er – vulgar force. If we left our intellectual boudoirs and joined a
protest in the street, we'd find ourselves on no higher emotional level.

VAN DUSEN: You said it. Look at our scholars during campus unrest.
But let me guess what other vulgarities in Berlioz offend your anti-
aristocratic taste. I bet –

ERGO: Another compliment! You mean anti-populist. Why am I anti-
aristocratic?

VAN DUSEN: Because like a good bourgeois you love only nice things.
Aristocrats are closer to the pee-pul. I was going to say, I bet you dislike
the *Corsair* Overture.

ERGO: I do. That big tune at the end to me is no better than military
music.

STEAD: And what would be the matter with military music?

VAN DUSEN: Too full-blooded for Dan. He doesn't believe that music
has charms to Sousa's savage breast.

ERGO: Oh please, no bad puns!

VAN DUSEN: I thought it was a good one. Anyhow, Sousa is a composer
of genius in his own line and that tune in the *Corsair* is just the thing for
the crew of a pirate ship. If you prefer the Q.E.2, you can sail on the
lovely Adagio that precedes the big bad tune. Your trouble is, Dan, you
talk drama, but you don't really like it. Drama calls for unflinching
fitness, but like the poet in Molière, you'd much rather be given 'all of
Roman history in madrigals'. You enjoy drama, mobs, vulgar emotion
only when it's varnished over, as in most operas – luscious brown sauce
on everything.

ERGO: Them's harsh words. The most popular operas are full of true
drama: *Norma, Lucia, Traviata, Tosca, Rosenkavalier*.

STEAD: Dan is right. The greater ones, by Handel, Gluck, Mozart,
Musorgsky don't use means any different to express passion.

VAN DUSEN: I didn't make myself clear. In what I've called the popular
pieces I can hear the contrasts and menaces and climaxes too, but
they're wrapped up in make-believe, like the speeches of the characters.
Do you know that it takes only forty words of Italian to understand the

whole repertory in that language? Now Berlioz is in another realm altogether, that of *Orfeo* and *Don Giovanni*, which –

ERGO: Do you approve of every note Berlioz ever set down? You remind me of Victor Hugo about Shakespeare – he said: 'I admire like a brute'. He swallowed everything.

VAN DUSEN: Nothing of the kind. But first of all, it's not for me to 'approve' of what Berlioz wrote. Let's have a little humility. I can't forget the centuries that thought Shakespeare no artist and Ben Jonson a great one. As for liking, I certainly feel very differently about the *Requiem*, which I adore, and the *Te Deum*, which I merely respect. It doesn't move me as it should, as *I* should.

STEAD: Don't you love that Prelude in the *Te Deum* which is usually omitted in performance? It's the first piece of minimalist music: in less than three minutes, it gives one the impression of having lived an age – an æon of 'far off things and battles long ago'. His other prelude, to *Carthage*, is as brief and evocative; but the one is dark and the other luminous.

ERGO: I don't see how all that's possible, but I will say this, Berlioz is compact; he not only expresses but compresses. There are times when I choke over it; he moves on to a whole other world before I'm at home in the first. I like a more measured pace, with – how shall I put it? – more musicality in the music, pleasure for the ear, luxury instead of the bare necessities.

VAN DUSEN: Wallow, wallow, wey! You're quite right. His orchestra isn't upholstered; the ear must relish the beautiful sound as it passes, you can't stretch out on it.

STEAD: Wait a minute! You have those opening chords in the *Te Deum*, in the *Roméo* love scene, and also many lingering closes, for instance in the Pilgrims' March or the Royal Hunt.

VAN DUSEN: Not quite what Dan means, I think. I think he wants continuous, palpable 'beauty' in the softer, melting sense.

ERGO: Right you are. I –

VAN DUSEN: – and what he gets instead is a nervous, sinewy texture that takes getting used to: remember your first olive. Each line rings out distinct, unblended. This is even more marked when Roger Norrington plays Berlioz with the original instruments. It makes you appreciate how novel the orchestration is and how the piece is constructed. Rhythm, melody, timbre and harmony have independent life – counterpoint plus – and/again, drama through diversity.

268

ERGO: But not throughout. You forget the thundering *fortissimos* in the tutti. It's what I like and expect from those hundred and ten machines of wood and metal. For instance, after the brooding introduction of *Harold in Italy*, he heralds the solo viola majestically, through a sort of towering archway.

VAN DUSEN: That's another movement I *don't* relish. Up to your archway, and under it, it's fine, but the rest leaves me cold. I perk up again at the March and I grow ecstatic when the innocent-looking serenade reaches its poignant contrapuntal close – the part that astonished old Franz Liszt when he was young.

STEAD: And I love the first three and not the final orgy. Critics need more than that randan to make them lose their cool.

VAN DUSEN: But they're bandits all the same. And like it or not, the fact remains that in those first two symphonies Berlioz assailed the human ear with new sounds and rhythms, harshly expressive, of a kind that did not enter the musical vocabulary till nearly a hundred years later.

STEAD: No doubt. I was saying, that fourth movement is well put together, with the reminiscences of earlier movements cleverly worked in, but it doesn't rouse the beast in me as the Witches do in the *Fantastique*. I can't account for it.

VAN DUSEN: But you have accounted for it. You critics always think that the response to a work of art is all explained when you've trotted out the four horsemen – Technique, Judgement, Emotion and Æsthetic. But there's one more –

ERGO: You mean taste.

VAN DUSEN: I mean sensibility. Taste implies a judgement of some kind. Sensibility doesn't judge, it receives. Or it fails to. Sensibility equals the number and fineness of your nerve ends. It's the obverse of one's limitations.

ERGO: I knew I had limitations. Their obverse is a new one to me.

STEAD: It's only Barry's way of calling people obtuse.

VAN DUSEN: I was in fact thinking of *my* obtuseness. The word means blunted. We're all blunted when faced with some particular thing that requires sharpness. This defect shows up as resistance, refusal, denial. Take Brahms: I enjoy only his songs, *plus* the last movement of the Fourth – it's my superb sensibility at work with all its pores clogged.

STEAD: Too many metaphors here. I believe this closed door has a simple explanation: it's bodily – a mismatch between the composer's visceral rhythms and yours.

ERGO: My word!

STEAD: German music after Mozart and Beethoven is rhythmically uniform, unexciting, and that –

ERGO: – that makes for a relaxing quality which lets the marvellous harmony have full effect. I hadn't thought of it before, but the opposite in Berlioz is what often makes me feel as if I were perpetually shifting gears. His metrical gymnastics make me dizzy.

VAN DUSEN: Ah, yes. You have to listen to everything separately and they don't all tend the same way all the time. If you want the orchestral purée that has become standard, you have to go elsewhere. It's that handling of the components that makes some conductors unable to foresee how a Berlioz piece will sound, and ought to sound. Some try to put it through a blender, but the good ones bring out details you've never heard before.

ERGO: In other words, he's a *sui generis* – as bad as Blake. It took me a long time to latch on to that. You have to change all your habits of listening.

STEAD: Not all, just two: the one developed by hearing orchestras; the other by playing and listening to the piano.

ERGO: That doesn't leave much, does it? The guitar, perhaps.

VAN DUSEN: Yes, a very good introduction to Berlioz, the guitar, but still better, the human voice. He's a lyricist and writes melodies for instruments to sing. Once you really hear them, the rest comes along, easy-like. Development, for example, is not by thematic accretion, it's by –

ERGO: One ought to study with a tutor like you, I suppose.

VAN DUSEN: God forbid! Only listen hard. We've gone crazy, turning everything into studies. It's not that we're stupid; we've simply lost our innocence, ruined our sensibility; we distrust it and ask for a theory, a system, critical essays, panel discussions, a handbook with bibliography, and a society with a newsletter. Each artist theorises and then gets defenders in serried ranks. A reviewer recently wrote: 'The Villa Lobos Society periodically reminds us of music that slips our mind.' The slippery mind is ubiquitous –

STEAD: – and no wonder. We suffer from a surfeit of art, too much music since Palestrina. And as Wuorinen said, we overdo its diffusion. The machine does it whether we like it or not.

ERGO: The museum at least can put things in the basement.

STEAD: The orchestra is a museum too, and its basement is what it won't play because the public stays away from what it doesn't know – unless there's a soloist attached, one with a name.

ERGO: Yes, 'personalising art'. Museums also have their soloists: Van Gogh, King Tut – Barnum's Greatest Show on Earth. My little collection is all I need, or can stand.

STEAD: Chilling thought!

VAN DUSEN: It certainly cools one's urge to compose. Everything's been done before and the people gorge on the over-digested. Give me the nameless soloist.

STEAD: But there's always been a lion in the path. Think of Berlioz keeping going in the teeth of every difficulty you can name, including oversupply, yet rousing Europe by conducting his works everywhere while earning his living as a reviewer. You don't know what it's like. There have been times when I thought I'd hang myself rather than write another Sunday piece – and I hadn't any music of my own bubbling up inside me as he had.

But speaking of chilling thoughts, I begin to feel that cold wind even in this corner. I think we should adjourn.

ERGO: And with nothing resolved!

STEAD: Oh no! I'm sure each of us resolved something for himself, and that's a great deal.

VAN DUSEN: True, even if you don't know quite what. One shouldn't say 'reach a conclusion'. Conclusions ripen – while others rot.

ERGO: Maybe. I'm a bit disappointed, though, that we didn't settle anything about Berlioz – or for that matter, anything that came up alongside.

VAN DUSEN: Oh, my dear Dan! We've been having a civilised conversation; it's not meant to end with a vote on a motion.

STEAD: But I *have* proposed a motion – a motion out of this frigid garden, where the night has ceased to be *sereine*, and the damsels' voices in thirds are no longer here to charm us.

Index

273

Index